Debating World Literature

Debating World Literature

Edited by
CHRISTOPHER PRENDERGAST

with contributions by

Benedict Anderson, Emily Apter, Stanley Corngold,
Nicholas Dew, Simon Goldhill, Stephen Heath,
Stefan Hoesel-Uhlig, Peter Madsen, Franco Moretti,
Francesca Orsini, Christopher Prendergast,
Timothy J. Reiss, Bruce Clunies Ross, John Sturrock,
Elisa Sampson Vera Tudela

V
VERSO
London • New York

First published by Verso 2004
© in the collection Verso 2004
© in individual contributions the contributors 2004
All rights reserved

1 3 5 7 9 10 8 6 4 2

Verso
UK: 6 Meard Street, London W1F 0EG
USA: 180 Varick Street, New York, NY 10014–4606
www.versobooks.com

Verso is the imprint of New Left Books

ISBN 1–85984–592–4
ISBN 1–85984–458–8 (pbk)

British Library Cataloguing in Publication Data
Debating world literature
    1. Literature – History and criticism 2. Criticism
    I. Prendergast, Christopher
    809

ISBN 1859845924 – HB
        1859844588 – PB

Library of Congress Cataloging-in-Publication Data
Debating world literature / edited by Christopher Prendergast with
contributions by Benedict Anderson . . . [et al.].—1st ed.
     p. cm.
Includes index.
    ISBN 1-85984-592-4 (alk. paper) — ISBN 1-85984-458-8 (pbk. : alk. paper)
    1. Literature—History and criticism.   I. Prendergast, Christopher.
    II. Anderson, Benedict R. O'G. (Benedict Richard O'Gorman), 1936–

    PN501.D43 2004
    809—dc22

                                                             2003017639

Typeset in 10/12.5pt Baskerville by SetSystems Ltd, Saffron Walden, Essex
Printed in the UK by William Clowes

Contents

Introduction

Christopher Prendergast

In recent years, Goethe's idea of *Weltliteratur* has received a fair amount of attention in two (often overlapping) areas of inquiry, comparative literature and postcolonial studies, most notably (and especially in the United States) in connection with the theme of globalization. More generally, however, contemporary globalization theory (since it now has a theoretical department all of its own) has had relatively little to say about literature. For example, Arjun Appadurai's remarkable work (in *Modernity at Large*) on the formation of 'diasporic public spheres' concentrates – for obvious reasons – on the visual and electronic media in tracing the forces of contemporary cultural border-crossing; the written word, especially in book form, is conspicuous by its absence as the new public spheres are 'increasingly dominated by electronic media (and thus delinked from the capacity to read and write)'.[1] A recent publication, however (Pascale Casanova's *La République mondiale des lettres*[2]), has put the question of literature back in the spotlight, in terms, moreover, that take the question outside the narrow precincts of professional academic expertise (she is herself a journalist). Casanova's intervention is the point of departure for the present venture. Yet quite what *Weltliteratur* meant (to Goethe and his age) and what it means (or might mean) to us are still

---

1. Arjun Appadurai, *Modernity at Large: Cultural Dimensions of Globalization*, Minnesota, 2000, p. 22.
2. Pascale Casanova, *La République mondiale des lettres*, Paris, 1999.

very live issues, if only for the reason that 'globalization', if it exists at all, is not a state but a process, something still in the making. Goethe's idea was itself cast in the form of a thought-experiment, a groping reach for a barely glimpsed future. Instructively, his best-known formulation of the idea is cast in the grammar of the subjunctive mood and the impersonal pronoun.[3] The idea is thus not, strictly speaking, 'Goethe's' at all; it belongs to no-one in particular by virtue of the fact that its determinate shape and content are as yet far from clear. By the same token, what we make of it today is necessarily open to indefinitely extended reflection and debate.

The following collection of essays is offered as an addition to this continuing discussion. It does so in a variety of ways, from the general to the particular, and in a manner that is not beholden to any one ideological parti pris. Some of the essays take the form of a theoretical overview, others more that of case-studies centred on diverse times and places, the common thread consisting in a reach for complexity against the grain of some of the polemically simplifying tendencies at work in cognate areas of inquiry. The volume begins with an account of Casanova's book and the problems thrown up by its argument (in particular its construal of literary 'internationalism' as based fundamentally, even entirely, on relations of inter-national competition). This is followed by a return to the true *fons et origo* of the whole topic, with Stefan Hoesel-Uhlig's exegesis of the terms and contexts of Goethe's fragmentary sketches of the contours of a concept, as well as the (often influential) misunderstandings to which it has given rise.

Peter Madsen in turn considers the afterlife of Goethe's idea in the work of two of his greatest disciples in the field of literary scholarship, Georg Brandes and Erich Auerbach. Both insisted that, however we are to understand world literature, it is not simply as a library or collection of books, but as intimately bound up with world-historical processes (what we now call modernization and globalization). Brandes was a committed synthesizer of a classically nineteenth-century type, marrying Goethe and Hegel in the view that thinking literature as world literature helped in

---

3. Cf. John Pizer, 'Goethe's "World Literature": Paradigm and Contemporary Cultural Globalization', *Comparative Literature*, vol. 52, no. 3, 2000, p. 215.

generating grand 'world thoughts' (pre-eminently the idea of freedom). Conversely, Auerbach, out of the less propitious conditions of his experience of Nazism, entertained, in his famous essay 'Philologie der Weltliteratur' the melancholy, even apocalyptic, possibility that the future of an integrated world was difference-obliterating standardization. The task of a philology of world literature was to preserve, for future generations, a memory of a world literary system characterized as a play of similarities and differences. Auerbach, of course, found himself in Istanbul in exile from Nazi Germany, and this is where Emily Apter takes us, with reference to the work of that other Istanbul exile, Leo Spitzer. The philological school created by Sptizer in collaboration with a number of Turkish scholars was the centre of a thriving form of comparative literary study, combining Turkish-language politics and European philological humanism. Many of the issues associated with the heuristic challenges posed by the paradigms and problems of *Weltliteratur* – global translation, linguistic imperialism, transnational humanism, nationalism and modernity – are seen to be strikingly anticipated by Spitzer's pedagogical vision and philological practice.

Some of the theoretical and analytical problems associated with an attempted mapping of internationalist scenarios of literary contact and cultural exchange are the concern of the next three chapters. Timothy Reiss's essay (originally published a decade ago) is republished here, not just for the sweep and lucidity of its critical review of the false starts and dead-ends that beset the discussion almost from the word go (in particular his ruthless dissection of what was wrong with the 'self/other' polarity of western metropolitan discourse), but also because of its status as a timely intervention at the very moment some of the new doxas were being formed. Franco Moretti's essay on the world travels of the genre of the novel and Stephen Heath's essay on the cultural politics of the category of 'genre' itself also belong here, but with an additional feature: their attention to the specifics of literary kinds. It is fair to say that, even in the field of literary studies, it is really only the first term in the expression 'world literature' that has elicited serious interest. 'Literature' has for the most part been confined to quarrels about the syllabus (the relative places of canonical 'great' works and 'marginal' works, literary and non-literary texts, and so forth, usually in connection with arguments about representation and identity politics). But without an account of the actual structures and modes of functioning of literary genres, the story of their differential 'world' locations and global journeys will make only limited sense.

This must also include inspecting the meaning and reference of the term 'literature' itself. If the migratory (and thus the interconnected) is one of the principal themes of this volume, so too is the comparative (and thus the divergent). As several contributors here stress, the reference to *Weltliteratur* has been one of the constants of reflection on the origins, aims and development of the discipline of comparative literature. Initially, the latter shared the migratory interests of the former, if only in the somewhat dispiriting form of a positivist study of 'influences' across national boundaries (although even in this narrow form it was animated by the admirable desire to break the grip of the national). With the anthropological turn, however, 'comparative' has also come to signify alertness to differences and relativities. Nowhere is this more pressing than in relation to the historical and cultural variables of the term 'literature'. This explains in part the inclusion of Simon Goldhill's essay on the idea of literature in classical antiquity, and in particular his emphasis on the extent to which understandings of writing and reading were heavily inflected by the oral, and in particular conceptions of citizenship and education as based on speech. On the standard definitions, orality falls outside the scope of the 'literary'. But, then, this perforce excludes not only what has been but what continues to be the most widespread form of verbal art in the world. In the fetching analogy of one of the most distinguished experts on 'orature' in a global context (James Foley), if we think of history on the model of a calendar, writing emerges only on the last stroke of midnight, 31 December.[4]

The status of the oral is of particular importance when an indigenous oral culture comes into contact, on the back of colonial conquest, with an imported written one. The innovative transactions which ensue are the subject matter of the two essays by Benedict Anderson and Elisa Sampson on nineteenth-century imperial legacies (of the Spanish variety) in the Philippines and

---

4. James Foley, 'Oral Literature Today', in Mary Ann Caws and Christopher Prendergast, eds, *World Reader*, New York, 1984, vol. 2, p. 2591.

Latin America, respectively on the Filipino and Peruvian writers Isabelo de Los Reyos and Ricardo Palma. In both cases (though in very different political circumstances), there is an encounter between traditional 'folklore' and the resources of colonial literacy. Folklore and orality were typically mobilized in the nineteenth century to support developing nationalist ideologies (what Casanova names the 'Herder-effect' of nineteenth-century literary nationalisms). The grafting of 'voice' and 'letter' in the writings of Isabelo and Palma, however, is shown as opening sites of mediation that are not reducible to the terms of a populist nativism, but are, rather, historically resonant examples of what we now – sometimes all too easily – call the 'hybrid'. From the point of view of the forging of a 'world' literary system, there is little that could be more 'world-historical' than the conjunction of the unwritten and the written.

Complexity of transaction (beyond the settled binarisms of more orthodox views) is also the brief of the two essays on versions of Orientalism, Nicholas Dew's on d'Herbelot's *Bibliothèque orientale* in the late seventeenth century and John Sturrock's on the paradoxes of the twentieth-century European *exote* as represented by the remarkable figure of Victor Segalen and his writings on Tahiti and China. As a fulcrum for the 'meeting' of cultures, the scene of Orientalism is doubtless open to endless revision in the footsteps of the canonical works on the subject by Raymond Schwab and Edward Said. Against the tendency to see Orientalist texts as fixed items in a discursive paradigm, Dew takes us inside the actual *making* of d'Herbelot's book (the forms and contexts of its material production) with a view to showing how it too is in fact an early instance of the 'hybrid', born of the 'complex and fortuitous mediations' that link two scholarly worlds (European and Arabic). Its modality, so to speak, is Borgesian rather than Benthamite. For Sturrock, Segalen is exemplary by virtue of his double insistence on the imperative necessity of 'listening' to other cultures and, at the same time, the radical difficulties of simply tuning in to difference (no tourism, slumming or going-native here). According to Segalen, we are never 'closer' to another culture (and hence liberated from the traps of ethnocentrism) than when we fail to understand it, when confronted with points of blockage to interpretive mastery. He is also alert to the 'two-way play' between Here and There, where 'difference' is entirely dependent on the contingencies of a particular location at a particular time. This echoes one of Appadurai's themes: that, for the traveller or migrant, the 'Other' can come to be the forsaken homeland.

The last three chapters also constitute a related group, around the oppositions big/small, centre and periphery, in a constellation joining issues of nation, ethnicity, empire and literature. Stanley Corngold's essay on Kafka takes up the question of his positioning as a Prague Jew writing in German, in terms of what Kafka himself called 'small literature'. Gilles Deleuze and Félix Guattari translated 'small' into 'minority', thus at a stroke recruiting Kafka to the grand narratives of culture and imperialism, as a hero in the imperial/provincial struggles of centre and periphery (traces of this view also remain in Casanova's account). Corngold argues that this is to misconstrue not only Kafka himself but also the form and meaning of his strange meditation on the concept of small literatures. Conversely, Bruce Clunies Ross addresses a 'big' literature or, more accurately, a big language, English as a 'world' language, but once again with a view to rectifying some of the misconceptions he sees as having taken hold in postcolonial studies. He does so by turning his attention – analytical as well as historical – to the particular genre of verse poetry, a generic focus relatively, and symptomatically, neglected in postcolonial literary studies. Poetry, Clunies Ross maintains, exists 'in language, not in nation', and the diasporic character of contemporary English means that 'from the point of view of poetry, the English-speaking world is polycentric', thus confounding the model of centre and periphery that is central to the structure of the relevant grand narrative (and also going some way to alleviate the dark prophetic concerns of Auerbach). Finally, Francesca Orsini reviews critically some of the recent modellings of *Weltliteratur* (in particular Moretti's and Casanova's) in relation to the multiple languages and literary traditions of the Indian subcontinent, arguing that much of the latter is obscured in the standard metropolitan celebration of the exiled 'multicultural' author writing in English ('Rushdie' is its shorthand). The principal claim here is, again, that the model of centre and periphery, the latter pulled inexorably into the orbit of the former, simply fails to do justice to the complex facts on the ground.

But beyond all differences of view and emphasis, the essays

gathered here share one thing in common. Franco Moretti claims that a branch of study concerned with 'world literature' cannot just be a matter of reading 'more', but that it calls for a change in our ways of thinking; 'world literature' is not an object but a 'problem', whose elucidation demands a shift of categories. Stephen Heath makes of this an occasion for affirming as a possible definition of world literature 'the newness *its study makes*'. This is the underlying commitment of the present volume.

The World Republic of Letters

Christopher Prendergast

1

In today's conditions, what, if anything, might it substantively mean to speak of the 'world republic of letters'? Rhetorically, the phrase of course signals entry into the game nowadays routinely known as going global, where, in a set of major disciplinary and perspectival displacements, time is mapped onto space, history onto geography. Time inflected by space, moreover, yields a geography that is fluid rather than fixed. As borders blur, nation-states implode and the 'world' both speeds up and contracts, 'migration' has become the new buzzword. Rewriting the map of literary history against this turbulent background perforce calls for special ways of thinking and seeing, whose own borders are themselves necessarily blurred, not least because, whatever the world-wide view might productively be, it cannot – other than in the paradoxical form of the deeply ethnocentric – be the view from nowhere. A literary geography underpinned by that kind of complacent transcendentalism merely forgets (or 'ends') history, typically issuing in the tacky Third Way clichés of a dominant strand of globalization theory; while actual immigrants remain locked up in detention centres, the more fortunate can go in for fantasy-migration at will, trying on 'identities' in a manner akin to trying on hats. Even that analytically and ideologically more robust engagement with the world-wide view, postcolonial studies, has not proven entirely immune to these temptations, as reflected, for instance, in the spectacularly successful marketing of its more high-profile practitioners as the academic equivalent of super-commodities.

A recent arrival into this intellectually messy space has come from France: the book by Pascale Casanova bearing the bold, if controversial, title, *La République mondiale des lettres* (1999). Its terms and arguments, even when (as here) contested, are the catalyst for the enterprise represented by the following collection of essays. One reason for this is that one of Casanova's starting points is historical: namely, the play of forces which produced that extraordinary moment of nineteenth-century literary thought, the idea (and the ideal) of *Weltliteratur*, famously sketched by Goethe as the dream of 'a common world literature transcending national limits'. 'We hear and read everywhere', wrote Goethe, 'of the progress of the human race, of the wider prospects in world relationships between men. How far this is the case is not within my province to examine or to determine: for my part I seek only to point out to my friends my conviction that a universal world literature is in process of formation'. As Stefan Hoesel-Uhlig shows in his contribution, quite what Goethe had in mind is to a large extent a matter of speculative inference, since the record of his thinking on the subject of *Weltliteratur* consists mainly of fragmentary jottings and remarks experimentally addressed less to an actuality than to an emergent tendency. What, however, appears to be imagined in and for this half-glimpsed future is a form of what Hoesel-Uhlig calls 'cultural traffic', a kind of grand cosmopolitan gathering of (some of) the literatures of the world to engage in what an earlier and influential commentator on Goethe termed 'an international conversation'.[1]

Goethe's idea, however generously conceived, is of its time, and hence circumscribed and constrained by the presuppositions and preoccupations of an age that is no longer ours. In the first place, although Goethe's aspiration is towards a transcendence of the 'national' ('national literature has not much meaning now-

---

1. Fritz Stich, *Goethe and World Literature*, Port Washington, NY, 1972. For a review of the bibliography and terms of the various attempts, past and present, to link *Weltliteratur* and globalization, cf. John Pizer's, 'Goethe's "World Literature": Paradigm and Contemporary Cultural Globalization', *Comparative Literature*, vol. 52, no. 3, 2000.

adays'), the parties to the imagined conversation are essentially national literatures (world literature concerns 'the relationship of nation to nation'). Secondly, there are the limiting implications of the central, even privileged, place assigned by Goethe to Europe in his account. While it would absurd to accuse Goethe of a kind of blind Eurocentrism (given the extraordinary sensitivity with which he entered into the spirit of Persian and Chinese literatures), in several of the fragments there is what appears to be a virtual identification of world literature with European literature ('a European, in fact a universal world literature', 'European, in other words, World Literature'). But, for all its limits, Goethe's example matters a great deal. If we start here, it is at once to acknowledge those limits and then to take from him what is useful for our own times.

A later definition (by one of the founders of the discipline of comparative literature, Richard G. Moulton) describes world literature as 'the autobiography of civilization'. The definition is at once curious and attractive, but also problematic, principally because the analogy with autobiography not only reads back through time from what is essentially a very modern notion, but also implies a view of the history and structure of world literature as a single, coherent story told by a single subject. In today's conditions, we are more likely to want to break up and diversify this story and its subjects according to the plurality of human cultures. Perhaps then we might start to redefine the idea of world literature in terms of an observation by Carlos Fuentes, to the effect that 'reading, writing, teaching, learning, are all activities aimed at introducing civilizations to each other' (there is here a resemblance with the characterization of Goethe's idea as 'an international conversation'). This version of the idea is likely to speak to us more powerfully and directly. But it too is problematic as well as attractive. In the first place, such 'introductions' do not necessarily constitute a polite get-together. The terms on which civilizations 'meet', both in and out of books, are not necessarily, or even generally, those of equal parties to the encounter. Moreover, the effects of such meetings can range widely across a spectrum from exhilaration to anxiety and vertigo, as questions are raised, problems explored and identities challenged.

Furthermore, in so far as Fuentes's view is a version of what we

now call 'multiculturalism', there is the quite fundamental issue
as to who actually gets invited to the meeting in the first place; as
the Japanese-American poet David Mura has argued, for many
literatures multiculturalism is a matter of sheer 'survival', of
whether or not there will be any representation at all at the
international rendezvous. This is a two-way consideration involving both terms of the expression 'world literature': it concerns
not only who is included in the 'world', but also what belongs to
'literature'. Indeed arguably the most basic – or at least the first –
question has to do with what counts as 'literature'. What in the
West is normally understood by it (imaginative writing, plays,
poems, novels, etc.) is of relatively recent invention (a point to
which I shall return). The history of the idea of 'literature' in fact
reveals a process of increasing specialization of meanings,
whereby 'literature' is originally equated with all kinds of writing,
then subsequently, in the post-Gutenberg era of printing, with
printed works, and only much later restricted to the notion of
works of the imagination. Above all, we need to sever the idea of
literature or, more generally, verbal art from a fixed attachment
to *writing*. Henry Louis Gates has shown how the European
Enlightenment established a link between 'reason', 'civilization'
and writing, thus confining oral culture to a position of inferiority,
often attaching the pejorative valuation 'barbaric' or 'savage'. The
argument that a culture attains to civilization only when it is
capable of 'inscribing' itself not only devalues the oral tradition
in the name of a specious fable of 'development', but also
overlooks the very real ambiguity of the acquisition of writing: at
once an immense cultural gain, but also helping to institute
structures of power and domination, within which those who have
the skills of writing and reading enjoy advantages over those who
do not. Finally it also overlooks the simple fact that, both historically and geographically, the oral vastly exceeds the written; the
former is and even today remains the most fundamental mode of
humankind's self-expression.

How, then, does one enter, delimit and define the object of
study known as world literature? To some extent, help has been
to hand from the now well-established 'world-systems' theory
developed in that paradoxically specialized branch of historiography known as world history, and whose most distinguished practitioners include Fernand Braudel, Immanuel Wallerstein,

William McNeill and Janet Abu-Llughod. McNeill divides human history into three constitutive phases: first, from around 3500 BC (early Mesopotamia) to 500 BC; secondly, from 500 BC to AD 1500; and thirdly, from AD 1500 to the present. The first phase witnesses the emergence of four major civilizations: the Middle East (Egypt, Mesopotamia and Asia Minor); India; China; and Greece (defined, in conjunction with the later emergence of the Roman Empire, as the starting point of a 'European' civilization). The second phase (500 BC to AD 1500) is at once a period of the consolidation and extension of the above, along with the birth of Christianity, the rise of Islam in the seventh century AD, the creation of the Ottoman Empire and the installation of feudalism (notably in Europe and Japan). The third period, from around AD 1500 onwards, is broadly the period of the creation of the 'modern' world, crucially linked to the so-called 'rise of the West', fuelled by economic take-off in Europe, the expansion of the world trading system and the related colonial adventures of 'discovery' and conquest (initially of the Americas and then later vast portions of the globe), and issuing finally in a form of modernity that McNeill calls 'global cosmopolitanism'.

Wallerstein charts in great detail the place of Europe in these developments, in a comprehensive survey of the principal factors in the formation of the 'modern world-system': techniques of modern capitalism and technologies of modern science, especially of transport and communications (and warfare); division of labour, both occupational and geographical; constant expansion of the system (imperialism) but with a 'skewed distribution of its rewards'; a multiplicity of cultures and fluid boundaries but with power residing in the metropolitan centres and nation-states of the West. On the other hand, Janet Abu-Lughod (in a book significantly titled *Before European Hegemony*) takes the formation of the world-system back into the thirteenth and fourteenth centuries, arguing that in period before the West became dominant, regions of the so-called Old World had already established a complicated network of contacts through a trading economy and a system of exchange stretching from North West Europe to China across the Middle East and India. This system consisted of eight sub-systems or 'loops' grouped into three larger circuits of trade. The Middle East was a 'geographic fulcrum', while Europe was more at the 'periphery'. India also was a fulcrum, with land routes to Russia in the north and China in the east, as well as having links to the Muslim world. The whole network depended on the strategic role of a number of 'world cities' (especially Baghdad and Cairo) and the geographically variable use of a multiplicity of languages, principally Arabic, Greek, vernaculars of Latin and Mandarin Chinese.

Quite how one might adapt the long temporal and spatial reach of world history to the idea of world literature is not straightforwardly obvious. For one thing the parameters of inquiry are not identical. In the perspectives of world history, one might be tempted to classify the 'literatures' of the world into three broad kinds: folk literatures (that is, orally transmitted unwritten literatures), traditional literatures and modern cosmopolitan literatures. The study of 'world literature' does not typically seek to incorporate all of these, and it is difficult to conceive of a methodology which could cope with such a vaulting ambition (for one thing, it would be impossible to avoid the inbuilt ethnocentrism of literary-historical periodizations, what Appadurai calls 'Eurochronology'[2]). Rather it has in practice concerned itself with printed literatures that, by some mechanism or other, have entered into 'relations' with others, whose historical point of departure is usually the European Renaissance and the development of national literary traditions, and whose terminus (so far) is the literary world 'marketplace' of the late twentieth and early twenty-first centuries. 'World' here (including the term *mondiale* in Casanova's title) thus does not mean 'global' (in the sense of all the literatures of the world) but rather 'international' structures that arise and transactions that occur across national borders.

In this context, Franco Moretti has taken from Wallerstein's world-systems theory the formula 'one but unequal' as a basis for re-thinking the idea of world literature. Although – amazingly – there is no reference to either in Casanova's book, this notion underlies her entire project (if there is no mention of Wallerstein, she does cite Braudel's formula of 'unequal structures'). Goethe, however, does enter the picture, namely his stress on world literature as a meeting of national literatures, but less as some

---

2. Arjun Appadurai, *Modernity at Large: Cultural Dimensions of Globalization*, 2000, p. 30.

ecumenical gathering (Goethe, in anticipation of his notion of world literature, once referred to literature as a 'common world-council') than as a competitive market. Echoing Antoine Berman's association of *Weltliteratur* with *Weltmarkt* and quoting Goethe himself (in a letter to Carlyle) on the formation of a 'general intellectual commerce' and a 'market where all nations offer their goods', Casanova proceeds to the construction of a fully fledged theory of the international literary system based on relations of competition. In respect of its Goethean provenance, one should perhaps not press too hard on what is basically an analogy (her claim that Goethe's idea of a 'market' is 'nullement métaphorique' is strictly for the birds). There is of course a literal sense in which one can speak of trade here: for instance, Moretti's reflections (in *Atlas of the European Novel*) on the functioning of 'narrative markets' in the nineteenth century, an import/export trade carried out largely on the back of translations. Casanova glances at this sort of thing, especially in connection with the international book trade in the late twentieth century. But how far the analogy of *Weltmarkt* helps us make sense of Goethe's thinking remains moot. Goethe does not appear to have construed the circulation and exchange of works of literature across national borders as competitive, and it is unclear how he could have done so, since this would presuppose the existence of an international or common market in which literary 'value' was comparatively and competitively assessed. For Goethe, the economic conditions permitting greater circulation pointed more towards an internationalization of reading publics, a new cosmopolitanism of reading.

Rivalry and competition, however, are the foregrounded concepts of Casanova's account, buttressed by the theoretical underpinning of Bourdieu's work on the constitution of the literary 'field' (although mercifully she stays away from the most luridly pathological form of the theory of literature as agonistic war-zones, Harold Bloom's). The main contenders in this arena are nations, where there are winners and losers. The international is thus the result or expression not of some free-wheeling global cosmopolitanism but of, precisely, the inter-national, a cultural conflict between nations and national literatures to control the rhythms and outcomes of what Casanova terms 'literary time'. Literary time is related but not reducible to the time of political history (here we catch an implicit genuflection to the model of history as 'series'). The great prize is what Casanova also fetchingly calls the Greenwich Mean Time of literary history. The winners determine Greenwich Mean Time by instituting a regime of centre and periphery, the 'developed' (who stipulate and defend the norms of the 'literary') and the 'backward' (who strive to catch up). Rivalry creates a 'space' at once riven (by the contest for domination) and ultimately unified (by the cross-border movements the competition unleashes).

Historically, the argument is centred on three moments. It begins in the sixteenth century, with Du Bellay's *Deffence et Illustration de la langue françoyse.* It matters very much that Casanova starts here, by virtue of the fact that Du Bellay's text is a proto-nationalist document in which the assertion of the virtues of French against the dominion of Latin (and Antiquity generally) coincides with the formation of the nation-state (the obvious earlier candidate for starting point, Dante's *De vulgari eloquentia,* is dismissed because Dante's model of a vernacular literary language, based on a composite of Tuscan dialects, does not have the backing of a unified Italian kingdom; the Dante/Boccacio/Petrarch axis is something of a false dawn). It also matters for another reason: Du Bellay's tract sets in motion a process whereby historically France, and more particularly Paris, emerges as the dominant force in the shaping of the Republic of Letters. Paris, as the capital of the nation, also becomes the centre par excellence of the international literary order, reigning supreme right up until the late twentieth century (Casanova rebuts the anticipated charge of Gallocentrism by claiming, in some measure persuasively, that this has nothing to do with tricolour-waving patriotism and everything to do with the historical facts[3]). It does

---

3. It should be noted, however, that the persuasiveness of placing Paris centre-stage is largely of an empirical sort, based for the most part (above all where the nineteenth and twentieth centuries are concerned) on a proliferating list of the non-French writers who fantasized, eulogized or visited Paris from different parts of the world. At a deeper level the argument would require a more theoretically robust explanation than that implied by purely anecdotal accumulation. Certainly the notion that Du Bellay's intervention somehow single-handedly set the whole process in motion strains plausibility. Moreover, Casanova's Paris-centred story stops somewhere in the 1960s. It is by no means clear that Paris has remained the magnet since then, and it would not be mere Anglophone prejudice to assert that London and New York have 'overtaken' Paris as the key metropolitan loci in the West. A further consideration arises here, to do with the scope of Casanova's study

so by projecting itself and being perceived as a de-nationalized locus of the Universal, home to the Classic, guardian of Taste, resolver of Quarrels, arbiter of the New, host to the Avant-Garde – in short, all the cultural appurtenances with which a geographical capital accumulates, hoards and dispenses, in the somewhat unfortunate economic metaphor Casanova also takes from Bourdieu, literary capital (while it is perfectly legitimate to think of literary works as 'commodities', sold by authors to publishers and from there to readers, it is arguably illicit to extend the relevant thought to the notion of 'capital').

Orbiting around the Sun City, like so many provincial satellites or menacing predators (England), is more or less everybody else, in a historical trajectory running until our own time. The second moment highlighted in this relatively *longue durée* is the late eighteenth and the nineteenth centuries as the period of what Casanova calls the 'Herder-effect', with the development of various resistances to French literary rule, largely in the form of a turn to folk traditions and the corresponding ideologies of tribal

---

as a whole. Her remit is very wide-ranging geographically and quantitatively (the index of authors clocks in at around seven hundred entries), while her own overt sympathies are with the non-European (more accurately non-Western European), historically 'under-represented' literatures of the world, suggesting indeed that, rather like Edward Said's *Orientalism*, with which it has spiritually much in common, the book itself will travel widely. On the other hand, her theoretical frame of reference creates the impression of an inescapably Euro-centric purview. Wherever she goes, Europe and Paris in particular seem not to be far behind. Latin America gets a good billing but most especially in terms of those writers who at one point or other end up in Europe (even the Brazilian writers who took a principled stand against European influence are defined largely in terms of this Europe-referring stance). North America is chiefly represented by Faulkner but again largely the Faulkner as read in Europe (although also Algeria, with half a page on Faulkner in Latin America). Russia enters the picture by way of another émigré, Nabokov; otherwise silence. The Arab world scarcely figures beyond North Africa in its relations with France, although sub-Saharan Africa gets more coverage (Chinua Achebe, Ngũgĩ wa Thiong'o, Daniel Olorunfemi Fagunwa's collection of Yoruba tales). Japan gets a brief entry on the poet Sakutaro Hagiwara, with even a quotation from one of his poems (instructively the one that, in French translation, begins with the line: 'Ah! Je voudrais aller en France'), but is otherwise mentioned only in terms of its colonial relations with Korea (another 'small literature'). China is pretty well off the map. For the Indian sub-continent, Casanova rounds up the usual suspects (Tagore, Rushdie). The choices of course make sense in terms of her working hypotheses, and, as I have already suggested, whatever the study of 'world literature' can be taken to mean it can't mean *all* the literatures of the world. But it would not be unreasonable to maintain that the hypotheses themselves skew the picture, such that the inclusions and omissions, 'as well as the distribution of emphasis in the discussions, constantly return us in one way or another to the shores of the *Vieux Continent*.

nationalism (she does not herself use the term 'tribal'; acquaintance with Martin Thom's *Republics, Nations and Tribes* might well have tempered her admiration for this sort of stuff and modified the narrative of poor relations struggling for admission to the Pantheon). The third moment concerns the effects of empire and, later in the twentieth century, of decolonization, characterized by the flow across national boundaries and a strong pull to the metropolitan centres of the West, still crucially Paris, whose authority as centre of a dominant national culture is at once confirmed and yet contested (or dissolved) by the arrival of outsider figures from all parts of the globe, those whom she terms the 'ex-centrics'. This supplies the essential form of the modern international literary system, multiple, heterogeneous but also stratified and hierarchical. In connection with the 'ex-centrics', Casanova sketches three typologies: the 'rebels', who stay at home to cultivate their local cultural patch – a (post)colonial extension of the Herder-effect – or who, after wandering, return home (for example, the Kenyan writer Ngũgĩ wa Thiong'o quitting English for his native Gikuyu); the 'assimilated', who are absorbed into the system on its own terrain (Naipaul); the 'revolutionaries', whose basic position vis-à-vis the Greenwich Mean Time is neither avoidance nor assimilation but subversion (Beckett and others too numerous to mention). The revolutionaries are the real heroes of the tale, producing a new measure of literary time, a *patrimoine litteraire mondial,* a truly international form of literary capital in the capital (for the most part, again Paris). What makes them heroes is that, in besieging the citadels of the literary imperium, they succeed in conquering not only for themselves but for also the institution of literature a certain 'freedom' and 'autonomy'; literature not only becomes fully international (as distinct from inter-national), it also becomes 'literature', a practice finally freed from its subjection to national imperatives. There are thus two kinds of literary 'autonomy', a false or mystified kind, which arises when a major literary power has accumulated sufficiently large amounts of literary 'capital' as to allow the writer to go about his or her business relatively unmolested (in this reminiscent of Gramsci's 'traditional intellectual'); and a true autonomy, hard-won in the struggles of the 'ex-centric' to enter the force field of the literary system.

2

If we stand back and ask what are the key questions subtending Casanova's account, they would seem to be twofold and inter-related: the nature and significance of relations between national literatures; the status of the competitive model of literary history. These are without doubt genuinely interesting questions.[4] The devil, as ever, is in the detail. It is not that the national-competitive model is irrelevant; on the contrary, it can be made to do much useful work. In particular it should be stressed that, unlike many of her precursors who deploy the competitive view, Casanova sees that, if the latter has any grip at all, it is at the level of the national, given that nation-state relations really do unfold histori-cally as a field of rivalry. It is simply that in her hands it is made to do *all* the work, accorded such grand explanatory powers that it is effectively posited as capable of accounting for everything. But for this claim to stand up it would have to be subjected, Popper-style, to a range of counter-considerations, none of which get a look in.

---

4. We can instantly jettison Casanova's use of the term 'republic' as an intellec-tual non-starter. This has become something of a (bad) habit in French literary scholarship and is often little more than a jingle empty of any kind of determinate meaning. The modern sense of the Republic of Letters is an invention of the late seventeenth and the eighteenth centuries. In the first place, its members were scholars not imaginative writers. In the second place, they did not think of themselves as representatives of 'national' traditions and still less as caught up in relations of rivalry and competition. They saw themselves (perhaps a delusion) as participants in a cooperative community of knowledge. Finally the modus operandi of the republic of letters was that of the private communication, thus quite distinct from the more commercially based conditions that permit the international flows Goethe has in mind when, in the early nineteenth century, he formulates the idea of *Weltliteratur*; in these terms, we might indeed wish to see the latter as *replacing* rather than complementing the older Latinate republic of letters. Cf. Anne Goldgar, *Impolite Learning. Conduct and Community in the Republic of Letters 1680–1750*, New Haven, 1995. There is a further terminological point arising from Casanova's use of the word *mondiale* in her title. The standard French term for English 'globalization' is *mondialisation*. The term *globalisation* has, however, recently acquired a certain currency. Generally speaking, *mondialisation* and *global-isation* behave more or less synonomously. On the other hand, there have been some efforts, notably by the French philosopher Étienne Tassin, to distinguish them: *globalisation* refers to the world-wide export of the neo-liberal version of the market economy, whereas *mondialisation* refers to the idea of a unified 'world' actively threatened by the divisive energies of the global market; in Tassin's tell-ing pun, 'Loin d'être une mondialisation, la globalisation est, littéralement, «immonde»'.

The most predictable objection to the model is that there are variables other than nation and relations other than competition. Take two examples (one mentioned by Casanova, the other not) from the canon of one of the more powerful players in the alleged rivalry game, English literature. Both Wordsworth and Shakespeare have been adduced as major figures in the unfolding of the 'national genius', the making of the 'Englishness' of English literature, with particular reference to an alleged rivalry with French hegemony. There are unquestionably 'competitive' impulses animating Wordsworth's appeal to the language (specifically the diction) of the 'common man' in the Preface to the *Lyrical Ballads* as the basis for a new kind of poetry attuned to the textures of the ordinary and the everyday. It might just be possible to hear in this a very distant echo of a nationalist hostility (based on an assumed English common-sense empiricism of 'experience') to the formality and artificiality of French literary culture. But whereas in the roughly contemporary case of the German turn to 'folk' material we hear this not as an echo but as a roar, Wordsworth's competitive agenda seems to involve very different variables, such as class, gender and region, all of which are *internal* to pressures and debates within England itself. The appeal to the language of the *common* man is a class-based move directed at the polite discourse of eighteenth-century English poetry; the appeal to the common *man* an attempt to restore masculine virtues in the face of the 'feminizing' influence of the late eighteenth-century poetesses; and the location of these possibilities in the world of the Lake District as the opening of a regional divide between North and South, rural and urban. Relative to these concerns, nation seems to come way down the list. Wordsworth's case tells us not only that inter-national competition is not necessarily the primary motor of absolutely pivotal literary developments but also that a monolithic image of 'nation' can mask all manner of divisions and constituencies.

Secondly, take the deployment of Shakespeare from the eighteenth century onwards in the formation of a 'national' literary identity in England. Casanova has it that the use of Shakespeare in the constitution of the 'Englishness' of English literature is to be understood principally in terms of national rivalry with France and French neoclassical drama (in this she takes her cue from Linda Colley's *Britons*). Competition with France is certainly part of this story, especially in the potential kinship of Shakespeare's formal freedoms with English natural-law theories of liberty as against the rule-bound character of French drama associated more with a political culture dominated by a centralized monarchical state. But it would be just as plausible to see the Shakespeare/Racine opposition more as a debate about the poetics of dramatic art than as totemic items in an *agon* of nations (that is, as a debate concerned with what makes for successful drama rather than for a distinctively national one). For 'Shakespeare' was not a uniquely English affair. The national-rivalry scenario might, once again, make sense of the appropriation of Shakespeare in Germany, as part of the struggle against the hegemony of French 'taste' which Frederick the Great had sought to impose. But what of the appropriation inside France itself? In turning away from Racine towards Shakespeare (Stendhal's *Shakespeare et Racine* is its energetic polemical statement), the French Romantics were hardly enlisting in the cause of English literary nationalism against the French variety (on the argument that England was now poised to seize the high ground in the rivalry of nations).[5] If anything, the French Romantics were themselves fervent literary nationalists, deeply preoccupied with liberating the spirit of French drama from the dead weight of normative 'rules' but who, in pursuit of that goal, were unafraid to cross the Channel for inspiration and legitimation. They were unafraid to do so because their prime concern was less with defending a national legacy than with refashioning French understanding of what it meant, under certain conditions, to write a good play. This suggests not just a dilution of the 'national' criterion but, equally importantly, a major adjustment of the red-in-tooth-and-claw competitive model. It might make more sense to speak here of literary 'negotiations', itself of course a diplomatico-commercial term, but with the implication of at least a modicum of cooperative rather

---

5. In connection with Stendhal's *Racine et Shakespeare*, Henri Lefebvre makes precisely this point: 'Stendhal's position was certainly audacious; the "national tragedies of deep and lasting interest" he expected could only have taken their inspiration from models with the most tenuous of links with French national feelings (Shakespeare, Schiller, Goethe). . . . What did Stendhal want? A national crucible in which to achieve the high-temperature fusion of elements borrowed from foreign cultures (which had been victorious in 1815) with elements taken from the history and traditions of France' (*Introduction to Modernity*, London, 1995, p. 248).

than competitive transaction. This would not necessarily mean that the negotiations constitute a cosily eirenic exchange; they may well be fraught with tension and ambivalence.[6]

The implications of this particular case take us well into what is problematic about Casanova's terms and assumptions. It is not just that, even on its own terms, the account fails to address the full range of relevant facts. The real problem is with the terms themselves, above all 'nation' and 'literature', which behave in her text like two twins, mirror images of each other, locking the argument into a self-confirming circle. While they yield interesting questions, their effective hypostasis produces answers that are at best incomplete, at worst badly skewed. Nation in fact functions here as a kind of a priori. At one point Casanova maintains that 'le patrimoine littéraire et linguistique national est une sorte de définition première, *a priori* et presque inévitable de l'écrivain' ['national and linguistic capital is a form of primary definition, a priori and almost inevitable for the writer'], an assumption whereby conclusions are already contained in premises, thus guaranteeing in advance the outcomes the argument seeks to secure. In respect of what can go wrong with an exclusive reliance on the category of 'nation', perhaps we can do no better than pause briefly over a concept that recurs often in Casanova's text, the concept of 'small literatures'. This is famously associated with

---

6. 'Negotiation' would carry the minimalist presupposition of some common language in and over which to negotiate, although without in any way papering over the many cognitive misfits and value clashes that might and do arise in the conduct of negotiations. It would simply mean that what, for a given culture, might be experienced as 'alien conceptions' should not translate as 'the conceptions of aliens' (as Bernard Williams has wittily put it). The importance of this thought for Casanova's argument is that it meets head on one of the more fashionable and extreme types of rivalry theory, namely the so-called 'incommensurability hypothesis', according to which different cultural systems are mutually unintelligible to one another and thus non-translatable. The most influential contemporary version of this hypothesis has been Jean-François Lyotard's view (in *La Condition postmoderne* and *Le Différend*) that Western *grands récits* have not merely dominated but effectively annihilated alternative narratives by the simple gesture of refusing to recognize their terms; in Lyotard's *agon* there can be no common ground for discussion, transaction and adjudication, there is simply war between winners and losers. Casanova does not go this far, although there is a certain implicit drift in this direction. But it is not at all clear that a scenario of this type will help us make much sense of *Weltliteratur*. If, as is the case, the latter involves 'unequal' access to cultural resources, this notion is coherent only if we presume the existence of something in common, equal access to which can be imagined as in principle possible or desirable.

an essay by Kafka, which in Casanova's book is cited dozens of times and which, moreover, gets a section all to itself (although to call it an 'essay' is already to beg questions; it is more a prose poem, a kind of playful caprice, a generic consideration that has some bearing on the substantive issues it throws up).[7]

Small literatures correspond more or less to what, in Casanova's terms, are the excluded or marginalized members of the national/international literary system (in Kafka's case, Czech and Yiddish). Gilles Deleuze and Félix Guattari made Kafka's essay an early version of the script in which the Empire-writes-back, by the simple expedient of converting the concept of 'small literature' into that of 'minority literature', which is then attributed explosive 'revolutionary' potential. Happily, Casanova junks the Deleuzian assimilation of small to minority as a category-mistake, producing an image of Kafka as a prophetic revolutionary quite at odds with his real preoccupations. On the other hand, she defines these preoccupations entirely in terms of nation and nationalism. Kafka's interest in Czech and Yiddish literature has to do with the ways in which 'small' nations form a national literary identity. She even goes so far as to claim that 'pour Kafka et dans ses catégories, le nationalisme est l'une des grandes convictions politiques'. Kafka does indeed speak of the role of small literatures in forging national 'solidarity' and the like early in his essay, but – this is why its generic form as a kind of poetic arabesque is so important – the terms of small-nation ethnic nationalism are, towards the close of his enigmatic text, despatched into another space altogether, dominated by a playful tone of gaiety and wit, as if 'nationalism' were now a kind of burlesque 'topic' rather than the ground of an ardent political commitment.

The form is that of a literary *performance*, a high-spirited dance around the edges of the serious and the non-serious, in which it is difficult to tell what is being advocated, if indeed anything at all, bearing in mind what happens to the notion of 'advocacy' and the discourse of 'rights' in Kafka's own fictions (Casanova occasionally speaks the language of rights, the 'right' of small literatures to exist, as if literary history could be imagined as a kind of international court at The Hague). Small literatures do

---

7. For a full discussion, cf. Stanley Corngold's essay below.

not 'compete' with large ones, in the form of affirming ethnic 'difference' against a potentially obliterating Other. Its writers may compete with each other, in a spirit of 'liveliness', since one of their defining features for Kafka is that they lack grand canonical figures whose authority might silence dissenting voices. But this lack also confines them to a backwater, inhabited by 'petty themes' and 'small enthusiasms'. What comes out of this matters to Kafka, but not in the way that Casanova appears to think. One can respect small literatures for their popular-democratic 'liveliness' and 'intimacy' (freed from the strains and anxieties of either high-canonical or extra-territorial competition) but also want to escape them as stiflingly narrow. They are certainly not deployed by Kafka to set forth an agenda or to furnish a 'model', not least for Kafka's own literary enterprise.

This is crucial. In relation to the Czech context, Deleuze also makes a further move, which is to read Kafka's own fictional writing as itself an instance of minority literature, specifically as an instantiation of a 'dialect' called literary Prague German. This is a complete nonsense. Whatever written Prague German looked like (Deleuze doesn't tell us), Kafka didn't write it. What he wrote was an oddly focused, because simultaneously de- and re-metaphoricized, form of High German. Casanova wanders into this minefield, but with a displacement of attention from Prague German to Yiddish. The result is catastrophic: one can describe 'toute l'entreprise littéraire de Kafka comme un monument élevé à la gloire du Yiddish . . . et comme une œuvre fondée sur une pratique désespéreé de la langue allemande . . . En ce sens on pourrait considérer son œuvre comme tout entière "traduite" d'une langue qu'il ne pouvait pas écrire, le yiddish' ['Kafka's entire literary enterprise as a monument to the glory of Yiddish . . . and as an œuvre founded on a desperate practice of the German language. . . . In this sense one could consider his work as "translated" in its entirety from a language he was not able to write – Yiddish'].

This, somewhat uncharitably, suggests that, whatever the language in which Casanova has read Kafka, it does not appear to have been the original.[8] She, moreover, fails to understand that

---

8. Iris Bruce informs me that there exists a Yiddish translation of *The Trial* by Melech Ravitch. Her comment: 'The translation was very good, very literal and

what Kafka is good at is not succumbing to despair but making jokes (albeit poignant ones). An exceptionally good one is the following extract from a letter to Max Brod, on the 'impossible' relation of German-Jewish writers to German (and thus by implication to Yiddish or rather – not at all the same thing – Yiddish German; 'mauscheln', as Kafka put it): 'They existed among three impossibilities, which I just happen to call linguistic impossibilities. . . . These are: the impossibility of not writing, the impossibility of writing German, the impossibility of writing differently. One might also add a fourth impossibility, the impossibility of writing. . . .' This doubled double-bind just about covers all the angles, exhausted with the ghoulish glee of the logical permutations of a Beckett novel. As it happens, Casanova stakes all on this well-known passage, with quite a large bet on the fourth option, thus confusing Kafka's sense of humour with the statement of a literary programme. It doesn't tell us much about the prose of *The Castle*.

The scenario of underdog nations battling for a place in a literary sun blocked by the shadow of tyrant languages and literatures is also Casanova's way with another strategic example. Ireland (especially of the Irish Literary Revival centred on the Abbey Theatre and the Gaelic League) is offered as a paradigm case of the rebellion of a small nation against the colonizing dominion of a big one, 'paradigmatic' (Casanova's term) in that it offers, in every detail, a model of 'subversion' of the 'literary order' (not just the literary order of England but the literary order *tout court*). There is of course a very important national-liberationist dimension to the Irish case but it is neither adequately grasped nor adequately contextualized if it is seen as the only dimension. Irish literature is not and never was positioned historically and culturally in the same way as, say, Polish-Yiddish literature. In the first place, the potentially upbeat narrative of the Revival works only if you leave out (as does Casanova) what was also darkly regressive about it (the association of Yeats's Celtic twilight with his enthusiasm for the Irish Blue Shirts). Secondly, the exclusive insistence on the emancipatory struggles of a small nation hugely distorts the actual facts of Irish

---

faithful to the original: precisely because he Yiddishized Kafka, he made me see the *difference*' (my italics).

(including Anglo-Irish) literary history from the eighteenth century onwards. In connection with the Irish 'paradigm', Casanova cites Kafka's idea of 'small literature', as if the former were an exemplary illustration of the latter. But it will be recalled that for Kafka one of the defining features of a small literature is that it has no great canonical figures. This could scarcely be maintained in respect of Irish writing. In this regard perhaps I could cite the somewhat indirect testimony of an extremely well-read Irishman.

I have on my mantelpiece a framed document issued in 1969 by the Inner London Quarter Sessions. It is a notice confirming a sentence of conditional discharge in respect of a charge of 'threatening to murder'. The person whom my father threatened to murder was Georges Bidault of OAS fame, in the form of a letter written while under the influence on the day the London evening newspapers headlined General de Gaulle's pardon. Addressed and despatched to Mr Georges Bidault, Paris, France, the letter ran as follows: 'Dear Mr Bidault, if you were in Dublin, three of us would drive up into the Wicklow Mountains and only two of us would come back down. Yours, James Prendergast.' Two days later – the letter having been intercepted by Interpol – my father was arrested by two Special Branch officers and charged with threatening to assassinate a figure in French public life. At the trial prosecuting counsel took various tacks, one of them – rather oddly in the circumstances – being to suggest that as a pig-ignorant Irishman perhaps my father did not have a very secure grip on the finer points of English. His reply, directed to the bench, was memorable: 'Your Honour, like Dean Swift, Oliver Goldsmith, Edmund Burke, Oscar Wilde, William Butler Yeats, George Bernard Shaw, John Millington Synge, Sean O'Casey, James Joyce, Samuel Beckett, I occasionally have difficulties with the English language.' The beak found this rather droll; case – conditionally – dismissed.

The point of this mildly self-indulgent autobiographical detour of course is that, however it stands to canonical literary production in England during the period in question, this roll-call hardly reflects what Casanova (or, more pertinently, Kafka) understands by 'small' literature. Making sense of this roll-call is a complex business, and no single narrative will do justice to it. Casanova's mono-track narrative edits out these complexities and, when it reaches the cases of Joyce and Beckett, starts to creak alarmingly.

Joyce (including, indeed pre-eminently including, the Joyce of *Finnegans Wake*) is represented as an anti-English revolutionary. Joyce certainly re-located out of Ireland and the English-speaking world to become a European equivalent of the Wandering Jew, and at one point certainly asserted that he did not 'write in English'. But to claim that, in *Finnegans Wake* of all texts, Joyce strove to give back to Ireland 'une langue qui lui soit propre' will be news to Irish writers and readers and is simply to mis-identify Irish with what Anthony Burgess, characterizing the language of *Finnegans Wake*, aptly called a form of 'Eurish'.

Matters deteriorate further when Casanova turns her attention to Beckett. We still need a satisfactory account of Beckett's relations to Ireland, Irishness and Irishry (though Anthony Cronin had a shot at it in his biography). Casanova seems to believe that this is best understood by seeing Beckett's work as representing 'une sorte d'achèvement de la constitution de l'espace littéraire irlandais et de son processus d'émancipation' ['a sort of completion of the constituting of Irish literary space and of its process of emancipation']. To this end she is compelled to maintain that Beckett switched to French in order to escape the colonizing grip of English on Irish letters (where 'Irish', linguistically speaking, would now have to mean Gaelic). This does not stand up in the face of what little we know about the matter. Indeed such a motive would have made little coherent ideological sense, since it was a switch to what was itself, from the point of view of, say, North Africa, an 'imperial' language. In so far as we can have any clear view of his motives, it would seem that Beckett took up French not to escape Anglo-Irish but to escape the word-spinning seductions of James Joyce. Beckett's emancipation is not about the emancipation of 'Irish literary space'; it is about the emancipation of Samuel Beckett.[9]

---

9. I concede, however, that this is perhaps over-dogmatic, and certainly would not wish it to be taken as implying an individualist model of literary history (a more amiable version of Bloom's anxiety of influence). It may well be that it was only in his French-speaking fictional world that Beckett could manage to absorb 'Ireland'. Furthermore, if I have concentrated on these two examples, it is partly because they loom very large in Casanova's book, and partly because they are cases with which I have some familiarity. What 'small literatures' look like once one quits the Prague–Dublin axis would be for others to say (for example, the Japan/Korea relation, which Casanova briefly mentions but does not discuss at great length).

The examples of Joyce and Beckett also raise another set of questions, which returns us to the category of the 'ex-centric' in the experience of decolonization. This, we have already seen, is cast as a heroic story. It is also, curiously, sometimes cast as a teleological one, whereby what has happened *had* to happen, as a sort of progress-fable in high Enlightenment mode. Those of us of more sceptical dispositions might want at this point to recall Raymond Williams's acid remarks in *The Politics of Modernism* about the 'ratified' version of modernism and the avant-garde as a selective version marketed at the expense of other tendencies. We do not have to share Williams's scarcely veiled hostility to the City of Exiles and Emigrés (he is thinking of New York rather than Paris) and his preference for more 'settled', local cultures. There is here a whiff of Zhdanovite prejudice against 'deracinated' cosmopolitans, but there is also a corrective to the thickly upholstered jet-setting comfort in which metropolitan postcolonial discourse has recently tended to get about. More importantly, this de-heroicizing view of the footloose avant-garde may encourage a strictly analytical distinction of some note and implication. What Casanova invests in the idea of Paris as historic centre of the international literary order is indissociable from positing it as a capital city; this is vital by virtue of the link tying capital to nation. But perhaps we might want to think of the Paris of the twentieth-century avant-garde and then later the postcolonial diaspora more as a metropolis, in terms of the formal distinctions sketched by Anne Querrien in 'The Metropolis and the Capital': the capital is a political and cultural 'centre', with the power and the authority to dominate a wider 'territory', to keep in place a 'social hierarchy' and to 'subjugate a population . . . to a common heritage'. A metropolis on the other hand 'is not a centre and has no centre', it 'has no identity to preserve', it 'begins with the slightest desire to exchange', is 'made up of networks', puts 'an incongruous mix of beings into circulation' and is 'the place where migrants find their socially predetermined destination'.[10]

Twentieth-century Paris is of course neither exclusively one nor the other, but is perhaps best seen as straddling both, as political capital tied to the nation, as cultural metropolis relatively detached from the nation, an abstract space of exchange-relations

---

10. Anne Querrien, 'The Metropolis and the Capital', *Zone*, 1/2, 1986.

in which national identities (both from home and abroad) dissolve in the operations of the literary marketplace. While this has involved immensely painful struggles for some (though by no means all) individual writers, as a social reality this is not a heroic phenomenon. Moreover, it unravels the tightly knotted nation/ market interdependency that plays such a large part in Casanova's whole argument, by suggesting that, under these conditions, nation and market start to tug in different directions (it is true that in one chapter of her book, she distinguishes between literary internationalization and commercial globalization, but even here still insists on referring to Paris as a 'capital').

3

The lock on the argument engineered by the a priori category of the nation is further tightened by what goes unexamined in the other key term of Casanova's text: the meaning and reference of the word 'literature'. I have already pointed out that the idea of world literature cannot practically be taken to refer to all the verbal arts around the globe (amongst other things, it typically excludes cultures whose only or main form of self-expression is oral recitation unless and until they become transmissible through transcription). 'Literature' in this context is tied to print-based literacy and, as Benedict Anderson has shown (a source much-quoted by Casanova) is indeed directly linked to the creation of nation-states. But even within this more limited framework it does not follow that 'literature' has always signified what Casanova effectively takes it to mean. In *La République mondiale des lettres* it is relentlessly absorbed into the equation with imaginative writing but – remarkably in a book that stresses the historicity of literature – without any apparent awareness that, on a world-historical view, the equation is itself a very recent invention (a chapter headed 'L'invention de la littérature' is about many things but one thing it is not about is the invention of 'literature' in the sense that matters here).

That the restricted meaning in fact became the dominant one, largely through a process of specialization within European literary history, would of course fit neatly into one dimension of Casanova's self-imposed brief, but only if explicitly clarified as an historical phenomenon in its own right in place of the approach which merely takes for granted the sense of 'literature' as denoting essentially poems, plays and novels. One way it might have done so would be through a contrast with the term of her title, not *littérature* but *lettres*, whose semantic history, while not identical to that of its equivalent English term 'letters', overlaps with the early and much broader humanist meaning of 'literature' as forms of writing and reading that make for polite learning. There is also an anthropological as well as historical dimension to this issue. For instance, what in the West is called 'literature', in India is called *kavya* and in China *wen*; though cognate terms in some respects, they clearly are not identical. Thus, the suggestion that twentieth-century decolonization is the moment of liberation for 'tous les pays exclus jusque-là de l'idée même de littérature propre (en Afrique, en Inde, en Asie)' ['all the countries hitherto excluded from the very idea of literature proper (in Africa, in India, in Asia'] presumes a view of what is 'proper' to literature that works only if it excludes vast swathes of Indian and Chinese writing that sit quite comfortably within the systems of *kavya* and *wen*. Casanova rails here and there against ethnocentrism, but her description of the international literary system depends on a system of categories that is itself ethnocentric.

A second difficulty stems from the fact that Casanova randomly shuffles between using the term 'literature' both with and without quotation marks, in the latter case as if she were talking of the actual article, as distinct from particular ideological constructions of it. Indeed she insists that as a practice literature possesses a certain specificity, even an autonomy, although, in refusing to sever literary practice from the pressures of a wider history, she quite rightly repudiates that mystified version of 'autonomy' that hives literature off into the specialized category of the 'aesthetic'. The problem, however, is that, from her end of the autonomist position, she supplies no guidance whatsoever as to what this specificity is supposed to look like; there is no literary *analysis*. What we are given are historically situated perceptions of authors, traditions and texts (those produced by literary histories, polemical essays, publicity machines) but no sense of what makes a literary text a text. Perceptions are hugely variable. There are many perceptions, and corresponding uses, of, say, Shakespeare other than those congenial to readers of nationalist persuasions.

What we need is an account of how Shakespeare's actual practice of writing meshes with the image of Shakespeare directly relevant to Casanova's argument (the Shakespeare of the eighteenth century); that is, we need Shakespeare as well as 'Shakespeare' (on the grounds so beautifully outlined by Graham Bradshaw in his book *Misrepresentations. Shakespeare and the Materialists*). Perceptions are a perfectly legitimate object of inquiry, but without some scrutiny of the texts onto which they are projected, there can be no justification for also taking the term 'literature' out of quotation marks.

This is not a demand that the project of world-literary history make room for the techniques of close reading (although one can happily fantasize that potentially fertile if unwieldy marriage; it might yield some acquaintance with, for example, the textures of Kafka's prose). The lack of any literary-analytical perspective, however, does have major adverse knock-on effects for the validity of Casanova's more general arguments. One such is that the relatively frozen, homogenized category 'literature' entails a radical neglect of important generic discriminations, which, once restored to their rightful place, threaten to drive a coach and horses through her decisive and unbreakable anchorage of literature to nation and inter-nation rivalry. The genre that gives the best results from her point of view is the novel, as at once the most buoyantly migratory and yet the source of acutely contentious cultural politics. Franco Moretti has adapted world-systems theory to an account of the 'world' travels of the novel genre, arguing that tensions often arise from the attempt to graft the abstract formal schemes of the Western novel onto the particularity of indigenous social experience, although in terms that reveal a high degree of variability: in some cases the tensions are easily managed, in others they remain severe (an extreme case, that might well take Moretti's fancy, is the novel *Giambatista Viko* by the Zaïrean writer M. aM. Ngal, in which the narrator is put on trial by the village elders for having forsaken the oral story-telling culture in favour of the written forms of Western narrative). Moretti's conclusion is very like Casonava's competitive model: the novel is the generic site of a 'struggle for symbolic hegemony' (although elsewhere in Moretti's work relations of competition are posed in neo-Darwinian rather than Bourdieuesque terms).

But if the novel can be seen as heavily freighted with the

political, this is not patently the case with other literary genres. Drama seems to travel less anxiously. Wole Soyinka's *Bacchae* is in many ways a re-write of Euripides, but less as a combative take on ancient Greek tragedy (in respect of his other play, *Death and the Horseman*, he has explicitly repudiated the fashionable postcolonial view that it is about the 'clash of cultures') than as a successfully negotiated adaptation to indigenous material, perhaps because, by virtue of its formal conventions, drama lends itself more readily to the resources of orality and ritual.[11] How might the national-competitive construct work with lyric poetry (the concern here of Bruce Clunies Ross)?[12] Or what of that older genre within the institution of European letters, namely letters (in the epistolary sense)? The map of centre and periphery would apply in terms of the division between literate and illiterate, but there is no evidence whatsoever that it involved rivalries between cultures and nations; within the practice of the genre itself, it seems not to have occurred to anyone that there was a distinctively 'Dutch' or 'French' or 'English' way of composing a letter. One of the greatest letter-writers of them all, Mme de Sevigné, could at a stretch be made to serve the designs of French literary-imperial ambitions, but her most intelligent admirer, Marcel Proust (whose spirit Walter Benjamin described as 'intransigently French'), never saw it this way at all.

And so and so on. The devil, I said, was in the detail. This, however, should not be confused with a nominalist position that

---

11. Discussing the *Bacchae*, Soyinka has spoken of 'the capability of the drama (or ritual) of the gods to travel as aesthetically and passionately as the gods themselves', (*Myth, Literature and the African World*, Cambridge, 1978, p. 7). He also makes the devastating point that the capability of literary forms to travel cross-culturally is not always matched by corresponding recognitions of that fact. His book originally consisted of a series of lectures given at Cambridge University, of which he writes: 'The lectures were duly given, but they took place entirely in the Department of Social Anthropology. Casual probing after it was all over indicated that the Department of English (or perhaps some key individual) did not believe in any such mythical beast as "African Literature"'. If we put these two moments from Soyinka's text together, we have a prime case of what literary 'negotiations' can look like on the ground.

12. Clunies Ross argues that the polycentric energies of poetry in the English-speaking world undermine the model of centre and periphery. In this respect his argument reflects the more general proposition of Appadurai: 'The new global cultural economy has to be seen as a complex, overlapping, disjunctive order that cannot any longer be understood in terms of existing center–periphery models (even those that might account for multiple centers and peripheries)' (*Modernity at Large*, p. 32).

dissolves all grand perspectives into the messy play of particulars. It is rather that a single generalizing description misses too much and is destined to do so if the partial description is offered as *the* description. What is needed is a proliferation of competing (*sic*) but also mutually nuancing predicates, description that is thick rather than thin, though of course this is all too easily said; just how thickly it can be spun by any mortal must remain almost beyond the powers of our imagining, let alone our executive capacities. But it is certainly here that we must begin.

2

Changing Fields:
The Directions of Goethe's *Weltliteratur*

Stefan Hoesel-Uhlig

In *The Birth of Tragedy*, Nietzsche describes late nineteenth-century culture as a rationalist, or in his terms Socratic, order that has entered a state of crisis. Recent developments in philosophy and decisively in music had disturbed the seemingly unshakeable modern faith in science and codified morality. Wagner's music-dramas promised to reintegrate society with art, and Nietzsche explores how the tragic and fundamentally aesthetic orientation of archaic Greece could be renewed for the contemporary world. Meanwhile most aesthetic production is bound to fail its formative calling, and art falsely consoles theoretical culture for its enervation and discontent. In this 'general crisis', what we call world literature becomes a telling issue. At the same time as artists strain to 'imitate all the great productive periods and natures', the avid consumer of aesthetic objects finds himself 'placed amongst all the artistic styles and artists of all times'. Yet 'in vain', the reader learns, 'is the whole of "world literature" piled up around modern man for his solace'. These efforts all collude with a compensatory role for art, and its comforts prove deeply ineffectual. 'Despite all this', Nietzsche insists, the cosmopolitan student necessarily 'remains eternally hungry, a "critic" without desire or energy, Alexandrian man who is basically a librarian and proof-reader, sacrificing his sight miserably to book-dust and errors'.[1]

---

1. Friedrich Nietzsche, 'The Birth of Tragedy' (1872), in *The Birth of Tragedy and Other Writings*, ed. Raymond Geuss and Ronald Speirs, Cambridge, 1999, p. 88.

At a critical juncture, when readers look to the most compelling range of works, 'world literature' presents no more than an extensive archive of dead letters. For the purposes of this essay, this ostensibly reductive usage suggests a range of questions. Nietzsche pointedly cites the term 'world literature', as much as he employs it, yet what are we to make of his quotation marks? Do they highlight the compromised jargon of a culture in crisis, or do they hark back to a more constructive sense? In a text where Goethe has considerable presence, does the term invoke his original statements on 'world literature', or have more influential factors since recast its role? If the category simply trivializes art, *The Birth of Tragedy* perhaps anticipates its obsolescence. Yet if a modern debate has decisively misread Goethe's interests, Nietzsche's quotation marks may invite us to revise the concept. At a distance from the global archive, a more effective sense of 'world literature' might serve to redirect his readers.[2]

For comparative literary studies, Goethe's 'world literature' has never been far from the discipline's blueprints and retrospectives. For nineteenth-century comparatists, the term authorized a range of projects, and the poet's prediction of an unprecedented phenomenon has continued to legitimate cross-cultural work. Histories of the field have always recruited this new rubric as a point of origin, and 'world literature' still helps the subject to present and re-examine its distinctive object. In 1877, a new journal for this 'slowly emerging discipline of the future' looked both to the 'art of translation' and to 'Goethean *Weltliteratur*' to define its 'present tasks'.[3] Soon after, the first book-length treatise on *Comparative Literature* naturally devoted much of its space to 'world' as opposed to 'national literature'.[4] A more recent anthology of such programmatic statements warns that Goethe's term 'has been frequently misunderstood', but it nonetheless heads its selection with excerpts from Goethe's conversations, notes, essays

---

2. Before invoking 'world literature', Nietzsche frequently cites both Goethe's writings and his conversations with Eckermann, which first popularized the term and in Nietzsche's view form 'the best German book there is' (*Human, All Too Human*, trans. R. J. Hollingdale, intro. Richard Schacht, Cambridge, 1996, p. 336).

3. Hugo Meltzl de Lomnitz, 'Present Tasks of Comparative Literature' (1877), in Hans-Joachim Schulz and Phillip H. Rhein, eds, *Comparative Literature: The Early Years. An Anthology of Essays*, Chapel Hill, NC, 1973, p. 56.

4. See Hutcheson Macaulay Posnett, *Comparative Literature*, New York, 1886, pp. 235–390.

and letters.[5] It is rare to find such a clear expression of the view that 'with his notion of *Weltliteratur*', Goethe 'in essence invented comparative literature',[6] but as another commentator has recently argued, 'almost all studies of comparative literature's history' still 'recognize Goethe's *Weltliteratur* paradigm as seminal to the discipline's development', and its influence extends well into current debate. Now as before, much of the most challenging debate about the objects of comparison remains tied to Goethe's precedent.[7]

In a well-known piece, René Wellek complained that because of its lexical ambiguity, any coherent comparative project would find 'world literature' an unreliable guide. Wellek reports that in its established use, this paradoxical term either aims at an impossibly capacious object of inquiry, or selects an unhelpfully narrow one. 'Today', he notes, 'world literature may mean simply all literature', or it may equally invoke 'a canon of excellent works from many languages, as when one says that this or that book or author belongs to world literature'. This polarity has been widely noted, but Wellek insists that its central conflict between a purely cumulative and a hyper-canonical sense cannot but reflect on the discipline as a whole.[8] 'Just as the exact use of "world literature" is still debatable,' he suggests, 'the use of "comparative literature" has given rise to disputes as to its exact scope and methods, which are not yet resolved.'[9]

Earlier in the twentieth century, Fritz Strich came to analogous results, and he provides an even sharper account of how this traditionally flawed focus may affect the wider subject. As an

5. See Schulz and Rhein, eds, *Comparative Literature*, p. 3.

6. Gail Finney, 'Of Walls and Windows: What German Studies and Comparative Literature Can Offer Each Other', *Comparative Literature*, vol. 49, no. 3, 1997, p. 261.

7. John Pizer, 'Goethe's "World Literature": Paradigm and Contemporary Cultural Globalization', *Comparative Literature*, vol. 52, no. 3, 2000, p. 214.

8. For analogous accounts of the divided function of 'world literature', compare Johannes Erben, 'Weltliteratur', in Jacob and Wilhelm Grimm, eds, *Deutsches Wörterbuch*, vol. XIV, Leipzig, 1955, cols 1646–7; Árpád Berczik, 'Goethe, die Weltliteratur und die Anfänge der vergleichenden Literaturwissenschaft', *Wissenschaftliche Zeitschrift der Ernst-Moritz-Arndt-Universität Greifswald*, vol. 16, no. 2, 1967, pp. 162–3; and Erwin Koppen, 'Weltliteratur', in Werner Kohlschmidt and Wolfgang Mohr, eds, *Reallexikon der deutschen Literaturgeschichte*, 2nd edn, vol. IV, Berlin, 1984, p. 816.

9. René Wellek, 'The Name and Nature of Comparative Literature', in *Discriminations: Further Concepts of Criticism*, New Haven, 1970, p. 15.

expression of intellectual interests, the concept seems 'strangely iridescent and indefinite', and Strich insists that there is accordingly 'no scholarly study from this field which does not suffer from such confusion'. As an originary reference, the term thrives because it claims to found comparative studies on a distinctive range of texts. Yet while Strich accepts that the questions and procedures of inquiry are best derived from certain objects, the workings of 'world literature' can hardly recommend that view. For comparative literature, the term selects a canon which seems either too much or too exclusive for the subject, and such confusion 'ultimately' only shows 'that this science, which concerns itself with world literature, is unclear about its object, and therefore also about the questions that should be asked of it'.[10]

In this way, comparative literature has long used 'world literature' to find its bearings, yet Goethe's term has by turns also proved too indeterminate, uncomfortably restrictive and extravagantly ambitious to define workable objects.[11] In recent years, postcolonial and multicultural critiques of traditionally Eurocentric curricula have prompted renewed concerns that, as the object of comparative studies, conventional 'world literature' just cannot hold. If comparatists are to live up to a global claim they have rarely addressed before, there are pressing questions about the linguistic and conceptual competence needed to sustain a coherent project across the world's cultures. Returning to Goethe's remarks, Hendrik Birus finds that this current debate revives a familiar tension in comparative literature's first

---

10. Fritz Strich, 'Weltliteratur und vergleichende Literaturgeschichte', in Emil Ermatinger, ed., *Philosophie der Literaturwissenschaft*, Berlin, 1930, p. 423. Unless indicated otherwise, all translations in this text are mine.

11. Accordingly, comparatists have variously blamed their difficulties with this central term on both pedagogical constraints and commercial pressure from publishers. In 1965, the Levin Report for the American Society of Comparative Literature suggested that a distinction be drawn between 'World Literature or Great Books at the undergraduate level and Comparative Literature as a graduate discipline', and the 1975 Greene Report confirmed that at some institutions 'World Literature' means a 'large lecture course teaching literature in translation' (quoted from Charles Bernheimer, ed., *Comparative Literature in the Age of Multiculturalism*, Baltimore, 1996, pp. 23, 30). In a statement for the Modern Language Association, Robert J. Clements protests that Levin's distinction only gives 'sanction to a misnomer invented largely by the textbooks publishers', and upholds the ambition of a 'supreme discipline' of genuine 'World Literature' against such abuses (*Comparative Literature as Academic Discipline: A Statement of Principles, Praxis, Standards*, New York, 1978, p. 28).

perspective on its object. 'There is', he reports, 'currently little agreement about the systematic localization or methodology of comparative literature.' But there is a shared sense that serious work on 'world literature' has too long been confined to the European languages, and persistent calls for the representation of non-Western works and writing by ethnic minorities make Goethe's coinage all the more central. 'What is far less controversial', Birus confirms, 'is the description of the field of comparative literature as world literature.' 'But', as this emphatic reference calls to attention, 'what is world literature?' As a question about texts, he warns, such uncertainty simply renews a familiar contrast between equally unworkable objects. More than ever, inquiry in a truly global field seems either blocked by materials 'too vast to be grasped by anyone', or confined to a selective 'superliterature' that is widely considered unproductive and ideologically fraught.[12]

As if to confirm this line of argument, commentators on the 1993 Report on Standards for the American Comparative Literature Association agree that a radical extension or a restriction of focus is precisely what comparative work needs in future. To judge from the responses gathered in Charles Bernheimer's *Comparative Literature in the Age of Multiculturalism*, the discipline will either have to confront ever more extensive tasks in a multitude of languages and media, or return to a relatively restrictive base in literary and aesthetic interests.[13] The 1993 Report strongly argues for expansion, and as its co-author, Charles Bernheimer, explains, the report's intention was 'to suggest not literature's diminished role in an evolution toward cultural studies but rather literature's expanded horizon in a multicultural, multimedia world'. Goethe's 'world literature' has long been used to support such expansive claims, but in search of concrete support the case for globalization seems to jeopardize its very object. 'Just how to foreground literature in the new contextualized modes of com-

12. Hendrik Birus, 'The Goethean Concept of World Literature and Comparative Literature', *CLCWeb: Comparative Literature and Culture: A WWWeb Journal*, vol. 2, no. 4, 2000, http://clcwebjournal.lib.purdue.edu/clcweb00–4/birus00.html.

13. The contrast between the contributions by Mary Louise Pratt and Emily Apter, on the one hand, and Peter Brooks and Michael Rifaterre, on the other, exemplifies this polarity (see Bernheimer, ed., *Comparative Literature in the Age of Multiculturalism*).

parison is, of course, not evident,' Bernheimer concedes, and the injunction to broaden 'literature' only magnifies an already troubled focus. In their best efforts to heed Goethe's call, comparatists confront a sense that 'the very identity of literature as an object of study is no longer clear', and a truly global 'world literature' has come to seem all the more divisive.[14]

In the following I contend that in its unstable contribution, 'world literature' merely amplifies an incongruity which has informed the modern concept *literature* from its introduction in the early nineteenth century.[15] To suggest a different emphasis for current debate, this argument both supplies an historical profile of *literature*, and suggests that as a guide for our studies, the established use of 'world literature' has misread Goethe's interests all along. Even where comparatists have most acutely questioned the subject's other components, Goethe's ostensibly prophetic coinage still looms large. Yet this central role makes it all the more puzzling to find that his original thoughts are incompatible with key aspects of modern debate. Above all, Goethe's predictions about 'world literature' do not address any of the range of objects which have justified comparative work since its beginnings. To define a new field, to write its history or indeed to change it, Goethe's successors have as much as his contemporaries used the term to grasp what writings might best support their plans. And in this pursuit of a global *literature*, it has been the burden of 'world literature' either to prescribe too much too read, or to be contentiously selective.

For Goethe, by contrast, 'world literature' never identifies a set of texts in the first place. Instead, his proposals diagnose a dramatic increase and diversification of intellectual interest across cultures, but their abstract focus consistently ignores what concrete goods may be involved in this exchange. Conceptually, Goethe develops 'world literature' both to grasp his sense of an acute expansion in cultural mediation, and further to encourage this historic advance. But as a structural sketch, his perspective on study and information leaves their particular sources entirely untouched. Both to explain this discrepancy and to pursue Goe-

---

14. Bernheimer, ed., *Comparative Literature*, pp. 15, 2.
15. Throughout this text, I use italics to refer to concepts and inverted commas to designate or draw attention to particular terms.

the's priorities for the present, the following sets the original account of 'world literature' alongside the conflicting profile of *literature* itself. Others have noted an idiosyncrasy in Goethe's remarks, yet without reference to the dominant concept it has been hard to see why his interests were always ignored.[16] Set on a more detailed map, Goethe's global focus presents its own directions.

Launched in the late 1820s, Goethe's experiment began just as, after a protracted period of formation, the modern concept *literature* secured its field. Despite Goethe's separate interests, this central perspective promptly absorbed his new and striking term, and 'world literature' came simply to enlarge *literature* in its dominant form. As a contradictory reference for comparative work, the resulting usage frustrates the very arguments that appeal to 'world literature'. But where comparatists contend with its indiscriminate inclusions alongside equally unpersuasive restrictions, this conventional sense of 'world literature' simply magnifies the divided formation of *literature* on which it draws. Historically, this distinctly modern concept itself combines inclusiveness and institutional resilience with an intellectually undetermined focus, and the failings of 'world literature' directly amplify the general flaws of *literature* in literary studies.

Since its inception, the modern function of *literature* has been driven by two formative discussions. In the first instance, the genre of literary history presents 'literature' as the inclusive archive of written culture. As historical objects, these given bodies of writing suggest a lasting relevance that will outlive debates about method or exegesis. Beyond this enduring yet vague hermeneutic promise, moreover, modern *literature* also projects a more distinctive claim, and in this second aspect, 'literature' suggests aesthetic interest. When it was first formed, however, this investment soon proved abortive, and as an analytic tool the concept has since been critically inarticulate. For comparative

16. For more or less detailed comments on the abstract character of Goethe's term, and its incompatibility with the modern sense of 'literature', see Ernst Elster, 'Weltlitteratur und Litteraturvergleichung', *Archiv für das Studium der neueren Sprachen und Litteraturen*, vol. 107, 1901, pp. 35–6; A. R. Hohlfeld, 'Goethe's Conception of World Literature', in *Fifty Years with Goethe 1901–1951*, Madison, 1953, pp. 344–6; Schulz and Rhein, eds, *Comparative Literature*, p. 3; and Manfred Naumann, 'Zwischen Realität und Utopie: Goethes Konzept einer Weltliteratur', *Poetica. Zeitschrift für Sprach- und Literaturwissenschaft*, vol. 17, no. 3–4, 1985, p. 220.

studies, 'world literature' has served to enlarge this divided role, so that the term's archival endorsement invites an ever wider range of readings, while its weak aesthetic impulse suggests more selection. As the shape of these discussions shows, however, the underlying concept does not itself support much argument. From its broadest to its ostensibly most analytic use, *literature* perpetuates as much as it aids disputes about the textual inheritance of literary studies.

For the priorities of contemporary debate, the lost directions of Goethe's experiment hold a memorable lesson. In their engagement with a changing field, the poet's remarks are not aimed at any one discipline, but his encyclopaedic interests perceive new general structures for poetic and intellectual work. As a deliberately conceptual innovation, Goethe's response suggests a revisionary route that is rarely taken in literary studies. In the dominant line, modern *literature* and its relations suggest that distinctively literary inquiry relies first and foremost on specific kinds of writing. Whatever the secondary or procedural conflicts, the subject will still draw confidence from its legacy of primary objects, and even the most advanced proposals often expect particular sources to define their questions. In the face of a perceived transformation of cultural space, by contrast, Goethe originally attended to the emergent conditions for future interest and exchange. Unlike curatorial debates that concentrate on more or less inclusive canons, his remarks on 'world literature' therefore begin with the operative category itself. For literary studies, such conceptual critique would help to ask what specific inquiries seek to know, and expect distinctive questions to illuminate objects.

Goethe on World Literature

In January 1827, Goethe began to remark that his poetic and scholarly work was confronting an increasingly challenging cultural atlas. Towards the end of a uniquely accomplished intellectual career, the poet's interests extended far across national boundaries and on this global horizon, he now detected a crucial transformation. As for much of his life, Goethe remained a voraciously cosmopolitan reader, but his sense of impending change was most immediately provoked by the fact that his own works were increasingly discussed abroad.[17] When he first dictated 'concerning French and world literature', for instance, his reading included French responses to his recently translated *Torquato Tasso*.[18] As Goethe explained to his publisher, his personal case shows that German writers are at last acknowledged by their European neighbours. 'Since they begin to concern themselves with us', he writes, it is 'especially now' that Germans face a reciprocal obligation to 'draw attention to foreign literature'. To account for these new developments may not turn out to be easy, and 'how I think about the subject cannot be said in a few words'. Goethe also insists that 'I rather wish to publicize them effectively', and thereby hints that certain basic assumptions may have to change.[19]

The next day, Goethe summarily declared that 'a world literature is forming, that all nations are inclined towards it and therefore take favourable steps'.[20] In conversation with Eckermann, he stressed the challenge which this must involve: 'I therefore like to have a look round in other nations and advise everyone to do the same for his part. National literature does not count for much now, it is time for the epoch of world literature and everyone must help to advance this epoch.'[21] From all who work within it, this historic constellation would demand both reflection and active engagement. A few months later, Goethe's journal *Kunst und Altertum* further explored the subject in a review of the French reactions to *Tasso*.

In contemporary thought, he pointed out, arguments for a progressive logic of history had become commonplace. Whatever

---

17. On the life-long breadth of Goethe's comparative reading, see Fritz Strich, *Goethe and World Literature*, London, 1949, pp. 83–156.

18. Diary for 15 January 1827, in *Werke. Herausgegeben im Auftrage der Großherzogin Sophie von Sachsen*, section III, vol. XI, Weimar, 1900, p. 8. This edition is hereafter cited as WA. Compare Diary for 21 January 1827, in WA, section III, vol. XI, 1900, p. 10. Siegfried Unseld points out that compared to their German reception, parts of *Faust II* met with considerably more enthusiasm in Russia, France and Scotland (*Goethe und seine Verleger*, Frankfurt on Main, 1991, pp. 654–5).

19. Letter to Johann Friedrich Cotta, 26 January 1827, in *Briefe. Hamburger Ausgabe*, ed. Karl Robert Mandelkow, vol. IV, Hamburg, 1967, p. 214. This edition is hereafter cited as BHA.

20. Letter to Adolph Friedrich Carl Streckfuß, 27 January 1827, in BHA, vol. IV, 1967, p. 215.

21. Conversation with Eckermann, 31 January 1827, in *Sämtliche Werke nach Epochen seines Schaffens. Münchner Ausgabe*, ed. Karl Richter et al., vol. XIX, Munich, 1986, p. 207. This edition is hereafter cited as MA.

their general merit, he insisted that the phenomenon of 'world literature' might at any rate warrant such claims. For Reinhart Koselleck, it is precisely Goethe's detachment from the politically motivated philosophies and ideologies of history in the period which defines his 'untimely' historical role.[22] When it came to intellectual work, however, Goethe was keen to anticipate such long-term structural change. Across Europe, critical journals began to exchange their views, and even the shortest notices could support his thesis: 'It is not as if the communications I offer from French periodicals are simply meant to recall me and my works; I have a higher intention that I would briefly like to point to. Everywhere we hear and read of the progress of humanity, of the further prospects for worldly and human conditions.' And where different cultures interacted, a new intensity of attention and exchange seemed to encourage such aspirations. 'Whatever the general substance of such arguments', Goethe concentrated on his bold prediction:

> I, for my part, would like to draw the attention of my friends to the fact that I am convinced of the formation of a general world literature, in which an honourable role is reserved for us Germans. All nations look round for us, they praise, censure, adopt and dismiss, imitate and disfigure, understand or misunderstand us, open or close their hearts: we must receive all of this with equanimity, since the whole is of great value to us.[23]

At 77, Goethe had long enjoyed national fame and his works had appeared in a string of collected editions.[24] Now that they had

---

22. See Reinhart Koselleck's essay, *Goethes unzeitgemässe Geschichte*, Heidelberg, 1997. Koselleck's account of Goethe's autobiographical writings could equally describe the occasion for the poet's late interest in 'world literature'. 'With advancing age', Koselleck argues, Goethe increasingly 'conceived of himself historically' (p. 16), and his biographical recollections both identify 'external influences which have historically or currently enabled his works', and consider 'through many processes of mediation, the impact of his works' (pp. 16–17).

23. *Ueber Kunst und Alterthum*, vol. 6, no. 1, Stuttgart, 1827, repr. Bern, 1970, pp. 131–2. Between May and July 1827, Goethe sent copies of this issue to Thomas Carlyle and a number of acquaintances (see Robert Steiger and Angelika Reimann, *Goethes Leben von Tag zu Tag: Eine dokumentarische Chronik*, vol. VII, Zurich, 1995, pp. 740, 745, 750, 760).

24. In the years before his death in 1832, Goethe continued to work on *Faust II* and the final volume of *Poetry and Truth*, but the bulk of his œuvre was already available in *Schriften*, 8 vols, Leipzig, 1787–90; *Neue Schriften*, 7 vols, Berlin, 1792–1800; *Werke*, 13 vols, Tübingen, 1806–10; *Werke*, 20 vols, Stuttgart and Tübingen, 1815–19; and *Werke*, 26 vols, Vienna, 1816–22. In 1831, Goethe received

succeeded abroad, he suggested that this new interest at last heralded some wider European appreciation of German intellectual life.[25] Across national boundaries, Goethe found new and enhanced intellectual pathways, and his studies saw different cultures struggling to interpret, appropriate and judge each other's forms. To grasp these beginnings of an epoch, he insisted from 1827, a decisive new concept had to reframe these cultural dynamics. Rather than add to existing views, this period would demand a central shift of focus.

When Goethe begins to discuss 'world literature', he seems to promise a more substantial argument than his remarks eventually develop. Having coined the term in passing, Goethe quickly insists that for 'world literature' to become fully effective, the category will need sustained engagement and debate. Yet while he often returns to the first 'few words' of his proposal, these subsequent references are largely casual. Their central aim remains hard to make out and rather than define a workable concept, Goethe ties 'world literature' to a circumstantial series of causes and effects. His observations either cite influences that must favour the phenomenon, or announce the first effects of its ever-expanding process of acculturation. Translations, the success of foreign reviews as well as a growing international book trade attest to the new quality and volume of exchange. Within these loosely related interests and associations, however, 'world literature' never quite coheres as a concept. This persistent vagueness notwithstanding, Goethe continually returns to the subject, and accepts the cognitive challenge of a transforming field.

Writing to Thomas Carlyle in July 1827, Goethe likens various forms of cultural translation to an exchange of different currencies. 'The peculiarities of a nation', he argues, 'are like its language and its different coins, they make interaction easier,

---

the first forty volumes of the definitive *Werke. Vollständige Ausgabe letzter Hand*, 60 vols, Stuttgart and Tübingen, 1827–42.

25. August Wilhelm Schlegel remarked as late as 1825 that 'although Germany lies not only geographically, but also intellectually at the heart of Europe, it still is even for its closest neighbours a *terra incognita*' ('Abriß von den europäischen Verhältnissen der deutschen Litteratur' [1825], in *Sämtliche Werke*, ed. Eduard Böcking, vol. VIII, Leipzig, 1846, p. 209). On variously patriotic and cosmopolitan attitudes to such belatedness in Germany, see Conrad Wiedemann, 'Deutsche Klassik und nationale Identität. Eine Revision der Sonderwegs-Frage', in Wilhelm Vosskamp, ed., *Klassik im Vergleich: DFG Symposium 1990*, Stuttgart and Weimar, 1993, pp. 541–69.

indeed only they make it fully possible.' Cultural diversity is what sustains this trade, and 'every translator' accordingly 'strives as a mediator of this general intellectual trade, and makes it his business to advance mutual exchange'.[26] As Goethe later advised the translator of his *Wilhelm Meister*, the resulting 'connections between original and translation' will, by analogy, 'most clearly express those between one nation and another'.[27] 'To promote the prevailing and obtaining general world literature', he explains to Carlyle, such relations and connections are from now on what we 'must principally know and assess'.[28]

Across Europe, periodicals like *Le Globe*, the *Edinburgh Review* or the Italian *L'Eco* make their own efforts to advance this cause. Late in 1827, *Le Globe* discusses Goethe's public announcement 'qu'il entrevoit l'aurore d'une *littérature occidental ou européenne*', and this discussion in turn appears in *Kunst und Altertum*.[29] 'Our western neighbours', Goethe observed, 'have favourably received my hopeful declaration that given this present most turbulent period as well as genuinely easier communication we can very soon hope for a world literature.'[30] As reviews like *Le Globe* 'gradually gain a wider audience', their efforts should 'contribute most effectively to a hoped for, general world literature'.[31] Even by 1830, the formation of 'such a world literature' still seemed the 'inevitable' result of 'international exchange' and its 'ever-increasing rapidity'.[32]

Where 'world literature' seems itself a causal agent, its epochal force alters purely national views. In July 1827, Goethe engaged Eckermann in a debate about the different degrees of intellectual achievement in various fields and nations, and here, 'the great benefit that results from a world literature, and that will show itself more and more' is that its wider frame of reference makes up for local deficits. 'Given this close exchange between the

---

26. Letter to Thomas Carlyle, 20 July 1827, in BHA, vol. IV, 1967, pp. 236–7
27. Carlyle's *Wilhelm Meister's Apprenticeship* appeared in 1824, and *Wilhelm Meister's Travels* formed part of his selections for *German Romance*, 4 vols, Edinburgh, 1827. Carlyle also produced a life of Schiller for the *London Magazine*, 1823–24, and frequently wrote magazine reviews of German authors.
28. Letter to Carlyle, 1 January 1828, in WA, section IV, vol. XLIII, 1908, p. 221.
29. *Le Globe. Recueil philosophique et littéraire*, vol. 4, no. 91, 1827, p. 481.
30. 'Bezüge nach Außen', *Kunst und Alterthum*, vol. 6, no. 2, 1828, p. 267.
31. Ibid., p. 396.
32. 'Studien zur Weltliteratur', in WA, vol. XLII.2, 1907, p. 503.

French, the English and the Germans', for instance, 'we are now put in a position to correct one another'.[33] A few months later, this argument was simply reversed, and again 'what I call world literature will principally arise' as an historic effect rather than a cause. It will principally develop, that is, once 'the differences that obtain in one nation are balanced by the views and judgements of the others'.[34] Here as elsewhere, the connections made between this formation and its cultural and economic context are deeply circular. Goethe's unstable account detects a range of contextual changes, but these observations do little to define his central term.

Faced with new maps for his work, Goethe begins a conceptual experiment that he fails to complete. Years after his first pronouncements on 'world literature', he still 'won't say more' about its full implications, and warily describes the subject as 'a chapter' yet to 'be extensively developed'.[35] In 1830, he continues to wonder from which conditions 'general world literature can ultimately spring', but his public position now appears more detached.[36] To introduce Carlyle's *Life of Schiller*, he reviews recent cultural and political history, and portrays his original statements as merely another version of a broad and conventional consensus on international relations. Stripped of its historic urgency, 'world literature' blends in with all other forms of political and economic contact:

> There has for some time been talk about a general world literature, and not without reason: for all those nations, shaken about in the most terrible wars, then again separately led back to themselves, had to notice that they had become aware of much that was foreign, had taken it in, had here and there felt intellectual needs that were previously unknown. This produced a sense of neighbourly relations, and in place of having locked itself up, the intellect gradually acquired the desire to be equally admitted to relatively free intellectual trade relations.[37]

---

33. Conversation with Eckermann, 15 July 1827, in MA, vol. XIX 1986, p. 237.

34. Letter to Sulpiz Boisserée, 12 October 1827, in WA, section IV, vol. XLIII, 1908, p. 106.

35. Letter to Boisserée, 24 April 1831, in WA, section IV, vol. XLVIII, 1909, p. 190.

36. Manuscript note, 5 April 1830, in 'Studien zur Weltliteratur', p. 505.

37. 'Thomas Carlyle, Leben Schillers. Aus dem Englischen. Eingeleitet durch Goethe' (1830), in WA, vol. XLII.1, 1904, pp. 186–7.

More flexible fields of learning may be as profitable as open markets, but in this instance Goethe makes no separate case for their historic transformation: 'It is true that this movement has only lasted for a short while, but certainly long enough to start making certain observations about it and, just as you must in the commodity trade, to gain advantage and enjoyment from it.'[38] Throughout his last years, Goethe reflects on instances of such increased movement in the practices of translation, reviewing or the book trade, but he never quite defines his original rubric. Rather than explicate 'world literature', his remarks use the term to maintain their open boundaries, and the original records for his coinage are accordingly circumstantial.

To judge from its habitual predicates, 'world literature' shadows developing forms of attention. Wherever familiar practices cross into adjacent cultures, the term predicts an epoch of new learning, and its associated activities involve perceptiveness and acknowledgement as much as judgement, opinion and curiosity. What most confounds the modern reader is that 'world literature' cannot itself be read. Across established terrains, cultural traffic and diffusion transform Goethe's already capacious field of interest, but he shows no interest in selecting a new canon, or indeed any particular line of study. Ignoring the status of concrete works, his coinage recalls an abstract, neo-classical sense of 'letters' that relates strictly to learning and intellectual accomplishment. From Roman times until well into the eighteenth century, the knowledge called 'literature' depended on an essentially textual and discursive notion of discovery, but its encyclopaedic standards could reflect no particular disciplines or genres. By the late 1820s this claim to universal erudition is severely dated, but in response to new channels of learning that seem to supersede existing limits, Goethe reconceives abstract 'literature' for a future term. In this role, 'world literature' helps observe a diversifying field and, at its most ambitious, envisions transnational circuits of intellectual advance.

In 1828, Alexander von Humboldt convened the Society of Natural Philosophers in Berlin, and Goethe drafted an address that reflected on scientific collaboration. While it conflicts with most of his other statements, this note on 'world literature' clearly

---

38. Ibid., p. 187.

maps the distance between Goethe's own interests, on the one hand, and a modern concern with distinctive archives, on the other.[39] For this scientific audience, Goethe casts his enthusiasm for intellectual exchange in a different form:

> If we have dared to proclaim a European, indeed a general world literature, then this is not to say that the different nations take notice of each other and their productions, for in this sense such a literature has long existed, continues and more or less renews itself. No! What is at stake here is rather that the living and striving literators come to know each other and feel moved, by inclination and a sense of community, to work together.[40]

Compared with his arguments for the importance of translation or foreign reviews, this personalized account clearly weakens Goethe's case for a separate category. As a conceptual reflection, however, 'world literature' retains its cognitive aim. Apart from specific disciplines or their preferred objects, Goethe's varied proposals seek to conceptualize an international and more widely mediated flow of scholarly interest. In his own terms, this epochal transformation affects all inquiry, and a full grasp of 'world literature' would reshape the distinctive questions in any number of subjects. Without more substantial arguments to support them, Goethe's predictions were perhaps bound to remain inconclusive. But in response to a changing field, his recourse to conceptual critique presents an exemplary challenge.

If 'world literature' thus begins as a cognitive stance, how could comparative literature both appropriate Goethe's coinage as a point of origin, and employ the term to select its objects? In its original records, 'world literature' is as blind to historically inclusive canons as its interests are to aesthetic selection. In line with the present argument, Franco Moretti has indeed recalled this divergence, and used it to argue for distinctive projects of literary research in place of a prior selection of definitive works.[41] If Goethe's reflective example is nonetheless widely forgotten, this

---

39. Goethe did not attend the meeting in Berlin, but received several delegates in Weimar (see Eckermann's accounts of these visits in MA, vol. XIX, 1986, pp. 252–3, 257).

40. 'Acta Die Zusammenkunft der Naturforscher in Berlin. 1828', in WA, section II, vol. XIII, 1904, p. 449.

41. See Franco Moretti's 'Conjectures on World Literature' in the present volume.

is because the conceptual tradition of modern *literature* has consistently misread his 'world literature' from the start. Even for early commentators, the dominant archival sense of 'literature' soon usurped Goethe's abstract bearings. Without much sense of its conceptual history, moreover, *literature*'s dominant counsel has been all the more pervasive. Next to the modern concept's formative profile, Goethe's alternative directions stand out more clearly.

The Formation of Modern *Literature*

For the last two hundred years, literary studies have organized themselves around a focus which, compared with the traditional categories of rhetoric and poetics, brings a distinctively modern perspective to their field. As students of earlier periods know all too well, 'literature' often fails to match the genres and practices it now groups together, and before 1800 the term played an altogether different role. Since Raymond Williams dated its aesthetic or imaginative use to the Romantic period, his examples in *Keywords* have been often cited.[42] But without much further work on how 'literature' first acquired this sense, its conceptual profile has remained out of view. Goethe's own conjectures develop their stance firmly within this context and, historically, the question of 'world literature' involves the modern construction of *literature* itself.

If this development has long been hard to make out, the delay reflects on some of its basic traits. Between the 1750s and the 1820s, the European formation of current *literature* is not only slow but also intellectually divided, and further motivated from outside the field it eventually circumscribes. Without tightly defined or even unified origins, this protracted convergence draws on the two discussions which shape the concept: on the one hand an ultimately abortive episode in philosophical aesthetics; and, on the other the enormous success of literary history. For modern literary studies, moreover, this formation is literally strange in that its motivations – that is, the reasons why its new

42. See Raymond Williams, *Keywords: A Vocabulary of Culture and Society*, London, 1976, pp. 150–4.

perspective could come to succeed classical *poetry* – are not themselves literary in the modern sense. What enables this drawn-out process are not poetic or rhetorical issues, but instead a general debate about the learning or knowledge long called 'letters'. As late as Goethe's final years, the options for 'literature' begin with our knowledge of words and things, and how we acquire or extend it.

Well into the seventeenth century, the terms 'literature' and 'letters' retain their classical role as general headings for 'learning', for a cultural literacy that extends from the ability to read and write, and from a knowledge of Greek and Latin to more or less substantial levels of book-learning as such. In 1694, the dictionary of the Académie Française still defines 'letters' as 'any kind of science or doctrine', and 'literature' simply as 'erudition, doctrine'.[43] But as Anthony Grafton sums up: 'between 1550 and 1650 Western thinkers ceased to believe that they could find all important truths in ancient books', and the rising competition of alternative, more empirical modes of discovery – say through exploration or the new sciences – undermined the universal, self-evident relevance 'letters' traditionally always had.[44] When Francis Bacon proposes in the *Great Instauration* 'to try the whole thing anew upon a better plan, and to commence a total reconstruction of sciences, arts, and all human knowledge', this project must precisely be 'unincumbered with literature and book-learning'.[45] And René Descartes famously describes how he had always

> been nourished upon letters, and because I was persuaded that by their means one could acquire a clear and certain knowledge of all that is useful in life, I was extremely eager to learn them. But as soon as I had completed the course of study at the end of which one is normally admitted to the ranks of the learned, I completely changed my opinion. For I found myself beset by so many doubts and errors that I came to think I had gained nothing from my attempts to become educated but increasing recognition of my ignorance.[46]

43. *Le Dictionnaire de l'Académie Françoise*, vol. I, Paris, 1694, pp. 639–40.

44. Anthony Grafton, with April Shelford and Nancy Siraisi, *New Worlds, Ancient Texts: The Power of Tradition and the Shock of Discovery*, Cambridge, MA, 1992, p. 1.

45. Francis Bacon, 'The Great Instauration' (1620), in *The Works of Francis Bacon*, ed. James Spedding, Robert Leslie Ellis and Douglas Denon Heath, vol. IV, London, 1858, pp. 8, 12.

46. René Descartes, 'Discourse on the Method' (1637), in *The Philosophical*

And therefore: 'as soon as I was old enough to emerge from the control of my teachers, I entirely abandoned the study of letters', in future 'resolving to seek no knowledge other than that which could be found in myself or else in the great book of the world'.[47] Once learning is no longer obviously drawn from books, that is, it becomes an open question what kind of learning we might in future identify with 'letters' or 'literature', and their rubric is open to conceptual reinvestment. In the seventeenth and eighteenth centuries, there are various attempts to find a future role for text-based erudition and to revive its traditional categories. To defend the standing of 'good' or worthwhile letters, 'belles lettres', 'polite literature' and 'schöne Wissenschaften' become prominent terms. As a form of scholarship, however, 'belles lettres' do not survive, and the only discussion to retain its influence links letters specifically to the beautiful. This is one of two separate debates that will redefine 'literature'.

Around 1750, modern *literature* enters its first formative stage in philosophical aesthetics. A year after his much better known *Les Beaux Arts réduits à un même principe* of 1746, Charles Batteux's *Cours de belles lettres* – translated as *A Course of the Belles Lettres: or the Principles of literature* – complements his new canon of the 'fine arts' with a separate curriculum of poetry, oratory and history, which he defines as 'belles lettres' or the discursive 'fine sciences'.[48] Batteux's aesthetic model for a basic education tries to engage students by exercising their personal taste before they move on to more abstract subjects. The mind itself, Batteux writes, 'seizes first what is more perceptible by the senses, & then uses that to reach what is not'. In the same way, his aesthetic 'belles lettres' eventually guide the student from beauty and goodness to truth. Unlike conventional works of rhetoric, Batteux explains,

> our aim is not to teach how to speak, but to teach how to read and to judge. Now, to learn how to judge, in matters of literature, we first need to practise on works where the beauties and faults, being more

Writings of Descartes, trans. John Cottingham, Robert Stoothoff and Dugald Murdoch, vol. I, Cambridge, 1985, pp. 112–13.

47. Ibid., p. 115.

48. See Charles Batteux, *Les Beaux Arts reduits à un même principe*, Paris, 1746, repr. Paris, 1989; *Cours de belles lettres distribué par exercices*, 3 vols, Paris, 1747–48; *Cours de belles-lettres, ou principes de la littérature*, 4 vols, Paris, 1753; and *A Course of the Belles Lettres: or the Principles of Literature*, 4 vols, London, 1761.

sensible, also offer more of a hold to taste and wit, where art shows itself without any mystery; & once this art has been fully recognized for what it is, and we are sure to have grasped its true principles, we will try to recognize it even in works where it usually hides itself.[49]

In Germany, Alexander Gottlieb Baumgarten and Georg Friedrich Meier first use the familiar phrase 'schöne Wissenschaften' or 'fine sciences' to recommend their new project of 'Ästhetik'. Beyond this introductory function, moreover, their use of 'schöne Wissenschaften' helps integrate the 'beautiful learning' of poetic and rhetorical practice with Baumgarten's and Meier's ultimate ambition to create a 'science' or 'Wissenschaft' of sensate and beautiful cognition.[50] At a level below logic, and the clear and distinct ideas that form established knowledge, their rationalist aesthetics pursues clear but confused ideas. As part of this effort, the discursive 'fine sciences' serve to mediate between sensate, concrete perceptions of beauty, on the one hand, and philosophical analysis, on the other. Aesthetics, as Meier writes, is a 'metaphysics of poetry and rhetoric'.[51]

For some time, these French and German accounts of aesthetic 'belles lettres' were widely discussed and developed by Diderot, the *Encyclopédie*, Johann Christoph Gottsched and Moses Mendelssohn as much as in Adam Smith's and Hugh Blair's Scottish lectures on 'rhetoric and belles lettres'. Within eighteenth-century aesthetics, this specific association with the beautiful created a productive perspective for an interest in 'literature'. In the long term, however, this original investment developed the analytic promise of the modern concept only to frustrate it with lasting

---

49. Batteux, *Cours de belles-lettres, ou principes de la littérature*, quoted from *Cours de belles-lettres, ou principes de la littérature*. *Nouvelle édition*, vol. IV, Frankfurt on Main, 1755, p. 3.

50. See Alexander Gottlieb Baumgarten, *Meditationes philosophicae de nonnullis ad poema pertinentibus*, Halle, 1735; translated in *Reflections on Poetry. Alexander Gottlieb Baumgarten's 'Meditationes philosophicae de nonnulis ad poema pertinentibus'*, ed. and trans. Karl Aschenbrenner and William B. Holther, Berkeley, 1954; *Aesthetica*, 2 vols, Frankfurt on Oder, 1750–58, repr. Hildesheim, 1986; *Theoretische Ästhetik. Die grundlegenden Abschnitte aus der 'Aesthetica' (1750/58)*, ed. and trans. Hans Rudolf Schweizer, 2nd edn, Hamburg, 1988; and Bernhard Poppe, *Alexander Gottlieb Baumgarten. Seine Bedeutung und Stellung in der Leibniz-Wolffschen Philosophie und seine Beziehungen zu Kant. Nebst Veröffentlichung einer bisher unbekannten Handschrift der Ästhetik Baumgartens*, Leipzig, 1907.

51. Georg Friedrich Meier, *Anfangsgründe aller schönen Wissenschaften*, 3 vols, Halle, 1748–50; quoted from *Anfangsgründe aller schönen Wissenschaften*, vol. I, Halle, 1754, repr. Hildesheim, 1976, p. 5.

effect. Near the end of the century, Kant's *Critique of Judgement* at once secured aesthetics as a separate branch of philosophy, and firmly excluded the perspective of 'literature' from future debate about aesthetics.

In his attack on existing proposals for 'beautiful letters' or 'fine science', Kant effectively trivializes an entire line of inquiry with his strict separation between determined conceptual cognition, on the one hand, and aesthetic judgements of the beautiful or the sublime, on the other. Irrespective of any determinate concepts, learning or knowledge, aesthetic pleasure for Kant attests to the basic capacities that enable understanding in the first place. 'An aesthetic judgement', in his paradigmatic terms, is

> of a unique kind, and affords absolutely no cognition (not even a confused one) of the object, which happens only in a logical judgment; while the former, by contrast, relates the presentation by which an object is given solely to the subject, and does not bring to our attention any property of the object, but only the purposive form in the determination of the powers of representation that are occupied with it. The judgment is also called aesthetic precisely because its determining ground is not a concept but the feeling (or inner sense) of that unison in the play of the powers of the mind.[52]

In our engagement with such experience, Kant insists, categories of learning or inquiry can have no place. Our critical responses must forgo the certainties of science, and for the artist's perspective, only the category of 'art' is sufficiently practical to escape the determinations of theory. Kant explains that however much critics may 'adduce' the more definite prescriptions of '*Batteux* or *Lessing*',

> There is neither a science of the beautiful [*Wissenschaft des Schönen*], only a critique, nor beautiful science [*schöne Wissenschaft*], only beautiful art. For if the former existed, then it would be determined in it scientifically, i.e., by means of proofs, whether something should be held to be beautiful or not; thus the judgment about beauty, if it belonged to a science, would not be a judgment of taste.[53]

---

52. Immanuel Kant, *Kritik der Urtheilskraft*, Berlin and Libau, 1790; quoted from *Critique of the Power of Judgment*, ed. Paul Guyer, trans. Paul Guyer and Eric Matthews, Cambridge, 2000, p. 113.

53. Kant, *Critique*, pp. 165, 184 [*Werkausgabe*, ed. Wilhelm Weischedel, vol. X, Frankfurt on Main, 1974, p. 239].

After the *Third Critique*, both aesthetic textbooks and new work in the field focus firmly on poetry and the fine arts as the proper categories of aesthetic practice (so that Hegel, for instance, makes 'poetry' and not 'literature' the relevant term). As a result, modern *literature* derives its formative intellectual claim from the abortive interests of aesthetic 'belles lettres'. From this defunct discussion, modern *literature* draws whatever focus it has: both the perpetual sense that this is in some way a specific category, and the suggestion that it has aesthetic interests at its centre. But once 'letters' are decisively sidelined from aesthetic reflection, the initial, formative interest of *literature* becomes for us the concept's abortive legacy, and the cause of its persistent weakness as an analytic tool.

As part of an aesthetic lexicon, we might long have forgotten about 'literature', and on the strength of its first formative debate, the category looks an unlikely candidate for future academic prominence. But at the same time as eighteenth-century writers on aesthetics discuss the sensory potential of 'belles lettres', the considerably wider development of literary historiography lends a pervasive presence to 'letters' as a novel, retrospective focus for cultural self-understanding. This separate, simultaneous stage of formation defines a new historical object. Here, 'literature' is for the first time understood as a substantial body of writing – waiting to be read, interpreted and studied.

In the late eighteenth century, history becomes its own, independent source of explanation to rival synchronic analysis, and 'literature' – now in the sense of a semantic archive of evolving linguistic cultures – is constantly presented as one of the most productive objects of emphatically historical thought. J. G. A. Pocock suggests that 'the historicist revolution of the eighteenth and nineteenth centuries, which transformed our awareness of society and culture into an historical awareness of an unprecedented kind', is a revolution 'of the concepts used to organise and control the whole body of information about the past'. And *literature* is a prime example of how, as Pocock writes, 'the history of historicism is that of the process by which these concepts became in the full sense historical'.[54]

---

54. J. G. A. Pocock, 'The Origins of Study of the Past: A Comparative Approach', *Comparative Studies in Society and History*, vol. 4, no. 2, 1961, pp. 210, 246. On the

In an ever larger number of narrative histories, 'literature' becomes an historical archive of writing, and embodies qualitative change over time. The assumption that the archive of literary works takes different forms in every age and culture, that it offers condensed, and indeed exemplary, bodies of social and cultural documentation, underlies all of the first recognizably modern literary histories by Friedrich Schlegel, Madame de Staël or Jean François de La Harpe. But Johann Gottfried Herder's 1767 fragments 'On Recent German Literature' are a particularly eloquent early example of how 'literature' settles as a concrete historical fact. Herder envisions a comprehensive, periodical review of intellectual life that would contain 'more than letters, excerpts, and interpretations serving as diversions; a work that draws the outline of a complete and entire portrait of literature, in which no line is without importance for the whole, whether it be hidden in the shadow or standing out in the light.' To be able to grasp its object, Herder suggests, it is crucial that 'this universal and unique work would be based upon a *History of Literature*, from which it would draw support. Which stage has this nation attained? And which might and should it attain? What are its talents and what is its aesthetic sense? What is its extrinsic state in the sciences and in the arts?'[55] For Herder, 'language, *aesthetics*, history, and philosophy are the four provinces of literature, which reinforce each other mutually, and which are all but inseparable'.[56] Language, however, figures not just as a 'tool' of intellectual culture,[57] but as its 'repository' or 'quintessence', and consequently a significant 'form' that shapes the archives which different cultures leave behind.[58] To some degree, Herder insists, written sources all resist translation, and, viewed as 'literature', the traces of intellectual history must in a strong sense be read.

---

development of a strictly historical mode of explanation, see Reinhart Koselleck, 'Historia Magistra Vitae: The Dissolution of the Topos into the Perspective of a Modernized Historical Process', in *Futures Past: On the Semantics of Historical Time*, trans. Keith Tribe, Cambridge, MA, 1985, pp. 21–38.

55. Johann Gottfried Herder, 'On Recent German Literature: First Collection of Fragments', in *Selected Early Works 1764–1767: Addresses, Essays and Drafts; 'Fragments on Recent German Literature'*, ed. Ernest A. Menze and Karl Menges, trans. Ernest A. Menze with Michael Palma, University Park, PA, 1992, p. 94.

56. Ibid., p. 95.

57. Ibid., p. 101.

58. 'Erste Sammlung. Zweite völlig umgearbeitete Ausgabe', in *Werke in zehn Bänden*, ed. Martin Bollacher et al., vol. I, Frankfurt on Main, 1985, p. 548.

'Literature' and literary texts are necessarily historical objects, and Herder appeals: 'Reader! Let history speak.'[59]

There is no space here to illustrate how these two separate, formative stages of a closed discussion of aesthetic 'belles lettres', on the one hand, and a thriving new literary history, on the other, begin to interact once *literature* secures its field around the 1820s. But the basic pattern should be familiar, or at least recognizable. On the one hand, *literature* in literary history presents an inclusive archive of past writing whose hermeneutic interest, authority and coherence – not least in opposition to other texts and sources – announce themselves as permanently pre-established. In this fundamental regard, 'literature' is simply the range of cultural objects which forms the object of literary history. And because such built-in evaluations are at once circular and automatic, the category is hard to beat in any cultural or institutional context where stability is in demand. Theoretically, on the other hand, *literature*'s formative, historically failed and consistently inarticulate reference to the aesthetic seems to intimate a conceptual core. Yet together with its promise to explain what all these texts and interests – as viewed within that concept – truly are, *literature* can itself offer little help in thinking about what if anything that shared coherence might be. As a conceptual history, this argument does nothing to prejudge whether or not the discipline should retain some account of 'literature'. Historically divided and critically flawed, however, the influential profile of *literature* is worth recalling.

Questions or Archives?

No less than other commentators, Goethe draws on the dominant use of *literature* as soon as the modern concept secures its role. Reviewing one of the many new literary histories, his only complaint about the work's archival claim is that it fails to be even more exhaustive. 'How little of what has happened has been written', he reflects, and even then: 'how little of what has been written has been saved!' Their modern concept recommends these objects as the concrete relays of a cultural past, but Goethe reminds his readers that in this role, 'literature is essentially

---

59. 'Dritte Sammlung', in Herder, *Werke*, vol. I, p. 372.

fragmentary, it contains monuments of the human spirit only insofar as they have been devised in writing, and have ultimately remained.'[60] In line with *literature*, Goethe suggests that aesthetic or imaginative interests might organize these sources, and continues to keep informed about their burgeoning historiography.[61]

From 1827, however, his concern with 'world literature' turns to quite different questions, and the ensuing statements predict a new epoch of intellectual exchange. Notwithstanding Koselleck's stress on Goethe's detachment from teleology, these global observations trace an historical logic of education and enlightenment. Yet in relation to modern *literature* itself, the orientation of 'world literature' is indeed untimely. As if to revive 'letters' in their dated classical sense, Goethe explores an emergent learning, while in the dominant line, engagements with *literature* follow different rules. Given this personal divergence, it is perhaps not surprising that from the outset Goethe's speculations find no constructive response.

For one thing, most of his relevant suggestions are made in private, and only the posthumous publication of the conversations with Eckermann lends the term its wider national and European currency.[62] Circulation alone, however, can hardly explain the lack of any considered response to Goethe's often urgent proposals. Even amongst his associates, 'world literature' finds no active audience, and Hartmut Steinecke has rightly asked why even those who knew the unpublished statements, and 'otherwise often

---

60. *Kunst und Alterthum*, vol. 5, no. 2, 1825, p. 166.

61. When Goethe looks back on the eighteenth century in his autobiographical *Poetry and Truth* (1812), he makes the fate of 'cheerful, self-sufficient, lively poetry' speak for a broader 'condition of German literature' (MA, vol. XVI, 1985, p. 282). As early as 1795 he contemplates writing his own 'history of the development of our pre-eminent writers, as shown in their works' ('Literarischer Sansculottismus' [1795], in MA, vol. IV.2, 1986, p. 19). On Goethe's familiarity with the genre, see Klaus C. Haase, 'Goethe und die Anfänge der deutschen Literaturgeschichte', *Goethe*, vol. 26, 1964, pp. 231–52.

62. The first German edition, Johann Peter Eckermann, *Gespräche mit Goethe in den letzten Jahren seines Lebens: 1823–1832*, 2 vols, Leipzig, 1836, is followed by *Conversations with Goethe in the Last Years of his Life*, trans. Margaret Fuller, Boston, 1839; and Eckermann and Fréderic Jacob Soret, *Conversations of Goethe with Eckermann and Soret*, trans. John Oxenford, 2 vols, London, 1850. Both *Entretiens de Goethe et d'Eckermann, pensées sur la littérature, les moeurs et les arts*, trans. Joseph-Numa Charles, Paris, 1862, p. 116, and *Conversations de Goethe pendant les dernières années de sa vie, 1822–1832, recueillies par Eckermann*, trans. Émile Délerot, intro. Sainte-Beuve, vol. I, Paris, 1863, p. 298, translate 'Welt-Literatur' as 'litterature universelle'.

adopted and distributed his keywords and ideas', nonetheless 'showed no interest in discussing the concept which was so important for the author'.[63] Alongside *literature*'s formative profile, this failure can be reconstructed.

In 1831, Carlyle prepared to review William Taylor's *Historic Survey of German Poetry*, and promised his revered correspondent 'some concluding speculations' on 'what I have named *World-Literature*, after you'.[64] Taylor gains praise for contributing to 'a new era in the spiritual intercourse of Europe', but even as Carlyle adopts Goethe's term, he suggests that 'instead of isolated, mutually repulsive National Literatures, a World-Literature may one day be looked for'. Notwithstanding Goethe's separate interests, Carlyle looks to a more integral, cosmopolitan archive whose selections would abstract from contingent localisms. Endorsing the new standard, his comments bolster the historico-aesthetic claim that *literature* presents a heritage of lasting significance. In modern society, Carlyle explains, 'Literature is fast becoming all in all to us; our Church, our Senate, our whole Social Constitution.' But in its new-found centrality, concrete texts now compose this institution:

> In these times of ours, all Intellect has fused itself into Literature: Literature, Printed Thought, is the molten sea and wonder-bearing Chaos, into which mind after mind casts forth its opinion, its feeling, to be molten into the general mass, and to work there; Interest after Interest is engulfed in it, or embarked on it: higher, higher it rises round all the Edifices of Existence; they must all be molten into it, and anew bodied forth from it, or stand unconsumed among its fiery surges.[65]

---

63. Hartmut Steinecke, ' "Weltliteratur" – Zur Diskussion der Goetheschen "Idee" im Jungen Deutschland', in Joseph A. Kruse and Bernd Kortländer, eds, *Das Junge Deutschland. Kolloquium zum 150. Jahrestag des Verbots vom 10. Dezember 1835. Düsseldorf 17.–19. Februar 1986*, Hamburg, 1987, p. 156.

64. Letter to Goethe, 22 January 1831, in *The Collected Letters of Thomas and Jane Welsh Carlyle*, ed. Kenneth J. Fielding et al., vol. V, Durham, NC, 1976, p. 220.

65. Thomas Carlyle, review of William Taylor, *Historic Survey of German Poetry*, 3 vols, London, 1828–30, *The Edinburgh Review*, vol. 53, no. 105, 1831, pp. 179–80. Carlyle himself tried to write a history of German literature (of which his famous essay 'On History' was to form the first chapter) and later lectured on the subject in London. In his drafts, Carlyle notes the novelty of *literature* as a key concept, commenting that 'Literature, the strange, composite set of Agencies which men designate by that word, has in late times, as we see, obtained a specific name; so that we can now say an Author, as we say a Carpenter or Smith, and talk of the Literary world, as we do of the Clerical, Medical, Legal' (*Carlyle's Unfinished History of German Literature*, ed. Hill Shine, New York, 1973, p. 1).

Over time, this inscrutable process transforms and incorporates intellectual history into a distinctive range of objects. Like others who argue with *literature*, Carlyle points to poetry, where he seeks to centre his claims, but the centrality of his construction depends on a comprehensive archive.[66]

On all these points, even Goethe's confidant promptly falsifies his interests. And once 'world literature' is more widely used, the dominant concept further assimilates Goethe's abstract views. Rather than respond to his predictions for inquiry, readers take account of the conversation with Eckermann to provide a larger, retrospective 'mirror and expression of intellectual life'.[67] For another enthusiastic supporter, this magnified perspective on significant writing will provide 'young producers' with a compelling 'law' of composition.[68] For his part, Karl Gutzkow predicts that patriotic interests will soon object to the very 'principle of a world literature', since its new selections must necessarily act as a 'thoroughgoing and simple regulator' of traditional 'aesthetic assessments'. Although such a global canon would include everything 'worthy of being translated into foreign languages', the 'small yield of such productions' cannot but conflict with national preferences.[69] Soon, the *Communist Manifesto*'s discussion of an increasingly global marketplace equally magnifies *literature* to explain the analogy between 'material' and 'intellectual production'. For Marx and Engels, exotic materials and desires everywhere inspire new commodities, and as 'from the numerous national and local literatures, there arises a world literature', this new transnational body similarly provides consumers with a literary range of 'cosmopolitan' goods.[70]

More than any other genre, literary history at once propagates and thrives on this misreading. From the mid-nineteenth century,

---

66. 'Literature is now nearly all in all to us', he writes to Goethe, 'our best Priest must henceforth be our Poet' (letter to Goethe, 22 January 1831, *Collected Letters*, vol. V, p. 220).

67. 'Ueberblick über französische, englische und deutsche Literatur', *Blätter zur Kunde der Literatur des Auslands*, vol. 1, no. 1, 1836, p. 1.

68. Ludolf Wienbarg, 'Goethe und die Welt-Literatur', in *Zur neuesten Literatur*, Mannheim, 1835, p. 1.

69. Karl Gutzkow, 'Ueber Goethe im Wendepunkte zweier Jahrhunderte' (1836), in *Gesammelte Werke*, 2nd edn, vol. XII, Jena, 1881, p. 80.

70. Karl Marx and Friedrich Engels, *The Communist Manifesto* (1848), ed. Gareth Stedman Jones, trans. Samuel Moor, London, 2002, pp. 223–4.

its surveys present comprehensive bodies of 'world literature', and their suggestion of an historically articulate, global object firmly secures the category where the new comparative studies will soon take it up. To avoid a true 'monster of a book', Johannes Scherr excludes all prose from his *Picture-Gallery of World Literature*,[71] but the work's successive editions still pursue 'a comprehensive representation of humanity's poetic production' by means of standard 'chronological order' and 'gradual development'.[72] Given the 'express desire' of publishers to see more works 'of this content', others 'join the ranks of guidebooks that have quickly gained popularity', and help further to extend the genre's compass.[73] Goethe's ideas can never check the pull of *literature*, and when Georg Brandes reconsiders 'the concept of a world literature' in 1899, he objects only to its aesthetic bent. While 'time itself' must judge poetic or imaginative writings, the global archive should incorporate 'scientific works' before all others since their significance can be 'definitive'. Brandes is aware 'that this term originates with Goethe', but the dominance of *literature* has long obscured its initial nexus of ideas. By now, even this informed commentator 'cannot presently recall in what context he used it', and Brandes debates the global inequities of translation and literary fame 'without regard for the word's great author'.[74]

In spite of Goethe's directions, 'world literature' has helped literary studies to represent their textual objects, while doing little to frame specific questions. In his attempt to clarify its role, Fritz Strich confirms that in this established function the term 'only finds wholly unambiguous expression in these so-called "histories of world literature"'. Whether arguments seek to extend or to restrict the global canon, this heading presents modern debate with an investment in 'nothing but the writings of all times and

---

71. Johannes Scherr, *Bildersaal der Weltliteratur*, 3rd edn, vol. I, Stuttgart, 1884, p. 7.

72. Ibid., p. vi.

73. Adolf Schwarz, *Brevier der Weltliteratur. Vorführung der bedeutendsten poetischen Schriftsätze der hervorragendsten Völker*, Leipzig, 1878, p. vi. Other examples include Adolf Stern, *Geschichte der Weltliteratur in übersichtlicher Darstellung*, Stuttgart, 1888; Julius Hart, *Geschichte der Weltliteratur und des Theaters aller Zeiten und Völker*, 2 vols, Neudamm, 1894–96; and Alexander Baumgartner, *Geschichte der Weltliteratur*, 7 vols, Freiburg, 1897–1912.

74. Georg Brandes, 'Weltlitteratur', *Das litterarische Echo*, vol. 2, no. 1, 1899, p. 1.

peoples, the writings of the world, these series of national literary histories of Germany, England, France, Italy, China, India strung together'.[75] As *literature* writ large, that is, its assurance of pre-existing objects relegates intellectually distinctive questions to a subordinate role. Precisely to defend a more problem-oriented 'perspective' against such curatorial premises, Mieke Bal submits that conventional 'disciplines, as we all know, tend to be primarily defined by their object, or subject matter'.[76] Max Weber, by contrast, argued that the 'scope' of any particular discipline must be defined by 'the *conceptual* interconnection of *problems*', and not prefigured by an ostensibly '"actual" interconnection of "things"'.[77]

Goethe's reflections on emergent 'world literature' remain both too varied and too fragmentary to define such a project. But the conceptual nature of his response supports Weber's insistence that 'a new "science" emerges where new problems are pursued by a new method'. Following Goethe, literary studies would contest their questions rather than pursue a stable archive, and such cognitive reforms would 'open up significant new points of view' before addressing their concrete objects.[78] Drawing on both Goethe and Weber, Franco Moretti concludes that if comparative literature is ever to redeem its global promise, 'the sheer enormity of the task makes it clear that world literature cannot be literature, bigger; what we are already doing, just more of it'.[79] Instead, 'the *categories* have to be different', and in contrast with *literature*'s dominant profile, Goethe's own departure turns out to endorse this bid. Misread as extending their dominant frame, 'world literature' has helped to shape literary studies around a primary choice of objects. Yet Goethe exemplifies a strictly conceptual response to change, and his conjectures suggest how the subject might come to revise its questions. Rather than telling us what to read, 'world literature' would first explore what its study sets out to know.

---

75. Strich, 'Weltliteratur', p. 423.
76. Mieke Bal, 'Semiotic Elements in Academic Practices', *Critical Inquiry*, vol. 22, no. 3, 1996, p. 585.
77. Max Weber, 'Objectivity in Social Science and Social Policy' (1904), in *The Methodology of the Social Sciences*, ed. and trans. Edward A. Shils and Henry A. Finch, New York 1949, p. 68.
78. Ibid.
79. See Moretti's 'Conjectures on World Literature', in this volume.

World Literature and World Thoughts:
Brandes/Auerbach

Peter Madsen

'In any event, our philological home is the earth: it can no longer be the nation.' (17/310)[1] These are the words of one of the greatest literary scholars of the twentieth century, Erich Auerbach. Some forty years ago he asked what the meaning of the term 'world literature' could be: 'Our earth, the domain of *Weltliteratur*, is growing smaller and losing its diversity. Yet *Weltliteratur*, as it was conceived by Goethe, does not merely refer to what is generically common and human; rather it considers humanity to be the product of fruitful intercourse between its members' (1/301). The precondition for world literature in Goethe's sense was, so to speak, Babylonian confusion, a multitude of cultures each with its characteristic features. But the historical process, as Auerbach saw it, was about to wipe out these differences: 'human life is becoming standardized', a 'process of imposed uniformity' is undermining the specificity of cultural formations. Life on the planet was becoming modern, along with standardization as the dominant tendency.

---

1. References are, first, to the English translation of the essay, 'Philology and *Weltliteratur*, by Maire and Edward W. Said in *Centennial Review*, vol. XIII, no. I, Winter 1969, and, second, to the German text: 'Philologie der Weltliteratur', in Erich Auerbach, *Gesammelte Aufsätze zur romanischen Philologie*, Bern, 1967.

A decade earlier, Horkheimer and Adorno had traced a similar tendency in their masterpiece *Dialectic of Enlightenment*, and Heidegger had in his peculiar manner been obsessed with similar themes (before the war these considerations underpinned his support of the cause of the National Socialists). Standardization, the reign of the abstract general, is one of the major themes in twentieth-century European culture, particularly, perhaps, in its middle part, from the twenties through to the seventies. The responses have been of many kinds, but often with somewhat apocalyptic overtones. This is also the case with Auerbach's essay 'Philology and *Weltliteratur*', the text with which I am here concerned. If this process of standardization and concentration is fully realized, 'man will have to accustom himself to existence in a standardized world, to a single literary culture, only a few literary languages, and perhaps even a single literary language. And herewith the notion of *Weltliteratur* would be at once realized and destroyed' (3/301). There is of course a very precise political context for this bleak imagining. Auerbach, like Horkheimer and Adorno, belonged to a generation and group of intellectuals which experienced Germany's rapid, although in many respects superficial, modernization in the period between the wars, and subsequently underwent the experience of the modern United States. In between, the historical unfolding of Nazi Germany's hyperrational realization of irrational concerns had cast its shadow on any *blind* belief in Reason (for Horkheimer and Adorno, self-reflective reason came to take the place of 'enlightenment' *tout court*). In any case, in these circumstances, the abstract and the general could appear in themselves as nothing other than the intellectual reproduction of an ominous tendency situated in the actual historical process of 'modernization' itself.

Looking back at the tradition of philologically informed studies in the humanities, Auerbach singles out as the distinguishing feature what he calls 'penetration and evaluation' of the historical material 'so that an inner history of mankind – which thereby created a conception of man unified in his multiplicity – could be written' (4/302). Variegation, unification and the idea of inner history are the key terms here. The question for Auerbach was whether a similar set of terms made sense for his own time, in a situation that seemed to be entirely determined by the process of modernization. History as a humanistic discipline was for Auerbach the only mode of inquiry that could provide a total picture of humanity. In phrasing that is close to Hegel's formulation of the idea of world history, he describes 'the inner history of the last millennia' – and 'this is what philology, a historicist discipline, treats' – as 'the history of mankind achieving self-expression', a history that demonstrates 'man's mighty, adventurous advance to a consciousness of his human condition and to the realization of his given potential' (5/303). A hidden plan seems to become visible that was not accessible at earlier stages. Auerbach's own time is to him a privileged historical moment, 'a time (*Kairos*) when the fullest potential of reflective historiography is capable of being realized' (5–6/303), since it is an historical moment when humanity is highly developed but still has the experience of a variety of cultures. Future generations will perhaps no longer have a lived experience of this variegation.

> Whatever we are, we became in history, and only in history can we remain the way we are and develop therefrom: it is the task of philologists, whose province is the world of human history, to demonstrate this so that it penetrates our lives unforgettably. (6/303)

On Auerbach's own account, the historical moment he experienced was at once a closure and a turning point, and as such it offered the chance of forming a general view of history. He was clearly steeped in the tradition of the nineteenth century and of its heirs in the twentieth. We, perhaps, are not. Nevertheless, Auerbach's daring generalizations might ring a bell in our present historical situation, and point to some potential tasks for the humanities in the age of accelerated globalization.

Yet Auerbach's main concern is not general history, it is the study of literature, 'philology of world literature'. In earlier times, this field of inquiry could aspire to making an active contribution to spiritual exchange, refinement of morals and international understanding. This surely was crucial to what Goethe meant by *Weltliteratur*. Some of the early contributions to comparative literature were motivated by a wish to overcome hostility between nations (notably Germany and France). In his programmatic essay 'Le Cosmopolitisme et les littératures nationales' (1895) the prominent French literary scholar Ferdinand Brunetière stressed: 'A European spirit is on its way in our age', and with an eye to the recent French–German war as well as the unfolding of the

Dreyfus affair, he wrote that 'the hatred between races and peoples, which is even more horrible than other types of hatred, has an animal, a particularly inhuman aspect'.[2] Against the background of the Second World War and the Nazi regime, however, it is no wonder that Auerbach concluded that the ideals of mutual understanding had been undermined by the historical events – although his scepticism at this point should not be taken as a model for later generations.

In a somewhat strange move he declares as a general task the creation of *historical myths*, or rather the synthesizing of the history of world culture at this turning point (when the particular seemed to surrender to the abstract and general), in such a way that the synthesis can become a 'myth' 'for those people [*Völker*] who are in the midst of the terminal phase of fruitful multiplicity': 'In this manner, the full range of the spiritual movements of the last millennia will not atrophy within them' (7/304).

This view of the task of literary studies is, of course, decisively marked by a deeply pessimistic and anti-modern view of the historical process: more than two thousand years of European culture seemed to be about to withdraw into the past together with the cultures of the rest of the world under pressure from an abstract unifying modern culture and as a result of the wounds inflicted by the Nazi regime. These words, however, came from a man who – as an exiled German scholar in Istanbul during the war – identified it as his task to synthesize the tradition of Western literature from a specific point of view, namely its 'representation of reality', in what is perhaps the most important contribution to literary studies in the twentieth century, his book *Mimesis*. It is, as it were, his own accomplished work he recommends as exemplary to his professional readers in his late essay on 'Philology of World Literature'. Remote and strange as Auerbach's idea of history and myth may seem to many, there is a great deal of sanity in his reflection on the conditions of the kind of study he recommends.

Extended to the world-stage, the project is of course awesome. The material is immense, endless, and no-one could possibly master the literatures of the world in any other than a compilatory

---

2. Quoted from Carl Fehrman, *Litteraturhistorien i Europaperspektiv*, Lund, 1999, p. 42. 'Race' referred not only to its meaning in contemporary usage, but also to a 'people' in the national sense, thus the translation 'races and people'.

and superficial way. Since Auerbach's time a new way of mastering
the field has developed as an academic culture; in a word: theory.
It has been a problematic turn, since what is mastered is not so
much the material field of study as the professional academic
enterprise cast in the form of an institutional culture. The trick is
that a 'theory' in principle covers everything, a very tempting idea
for a student or a scholar who is confronted with an immense
amount of potential reading, if no other principle of organization
seems to be available.

Auerbach's suggestion is to stay firmly on the ground of
literature. 'Durchdringung und Gestaltung' (to 'penetrate' and
'construct an adequate presentation') of the material, these are
his key terms (8/304); the result should be 'historical synthesis',
'a synthetic history-from-within' ('einer synthetisch-inneren Ge-
schichtsschreibung', 12/307). To provide a similar representation
of world literature in general is impossible, if only for practical
reasons. A selection has to be made, a particular viewpoint must
provide a principle of selection. In our own time, the two most
prominent temptations are perhaps to grasp hold of a theory or
to seek out periodization. A theory may come in handy as a
principle of selection, but Auerbach's basic criterion is that the
organization of the material should be concrete, it should bring
out some 'inner' features of the relevant body of material. A
period-concept is also handy as the basis for identifying 'typical'
historical features. But this too would be another version of the
abstract-general subsuming the specific. Auerbach rightly rejects
'the desire to master a great mass of material through the
introduction of hypostatized, abstract concepts of order; this leads
to the effacement of what is being studied, to the discussion of
illusory problems and finally to a bare nothing' (10/306). Unfortunately what he leaves us with are merely 'intuition' and 'art' as
the bases of good scholarship. Yet, although these terms may
appear somewhat old-fashioned, their main function in his argument is to clear the decks for some interesting and, it seems to
me, fruitful, if problematic, framings of the central problem. In
this respect, we should note three important moves.

First, Auerbach points to historical experience – 'We have
participated – indeed, we are still participating – in a practical
seminar on world history' (11/306) – as an incentive to a broad-
ening of horizon and a deeper understanding of 'the structure of

interhuman processes'. Historical phenomena are now appreci-
ated with more 'insight and imagination' than was the case in
earlier contributions to historical philology; despite their merits,
pre-First World War contributions appeared to Auerbach as
'unrealistic and restricted in the positing of the problems they set
themselves'. We, I would add, have no less reason to pay attention
to the practical seminar on world history in which we are all – in
more or less comfortable fashion – enrolled.

Secondly, Auerbach raises the question of 'synthesis'. His own
answer to this question is that even if general standards of
scholarly research should be upheld, the individual scholar must
rely on his intuition in order to find what the Germans call an
Ansatz, a grip, a handhold, a way of grasping: a point of departure
that is simultaneously a preliminary outline, the result of initial
research and the outcome of some personal commitment.[3] The
personal commitment is grounded in historical experience.

Thirdly, Auerbach delineates some of the characteristics of
what he calls the 'good *Ansatz*'. There are basically two such
characteristics. On one hand the point of departure must be
concrete and vigorous. Besides the general meaning, which cor-
responds to the English usage of the word, 'concrete' in German
has specific associations. For a description to be 'concrete' means
in the Hegelian tradition that it has to provide a synthesis of
conceptual determinations. On the other hand: 'The point of
departure [*Ansatz*] must be the election of a firmly circumscribed,
easily comprehensible set of phenomena whose interpretation is
a radiation from them and which orders and interprets a greater
region than they themselves occupy' (14/308). The interpretation
should have *Strahlkraft*, 'a potential for radiance'. This second
criterion is important, but problematic. It is important because it
points to the indubitable fact that no study of literature would be
interesting if it did not open on to significant historical perspectives. But it is problematic because it may imply a view of history
steeped in the nineteenth-century tradition of *Geistesgeschichte*, the
kind of history promoted by Hegel and, in a different vein, but
with greater academic success in the twentieth century, by Dilthey.

---

3. The word *Ansatz* has a variety of meanings in German, among them a germ, a
personal inclination, a sediment, an estimate, a disposition. Auerbach also uses the
term *Handhabe*, handhold.

The point of departure must, says Auerbach, 'have radiating power, so that with it we can deal with world history' [so das von ihm aus Weltgeschichte getrieben werden kann] (15/309). A good *Ansatz* must be precise and intrinsically related to its object (*gegenständlich*). It should open up general perspectives, but it should not be 'abstract' in itself, it should not 'be a generality imposed on a theme from the outside' (16/309).

Auerbach's warnings against abstract generalization are still compelling: 'Ready-made, through rarely suitable concepts, whose appeal is deceptive because it is based upon their attractive sound and their modishness, lie in wait, ready to spring in on the work of a scholar who has lost contact with the energy of the object of study' (16/309). These warnings are well worth listening to, even if the idea that every specific study should radiate and illuminate world history is ambiguous. One might construe it in either a weak or a strong version. The strong version would imply the idea of world history as a unity, as in Hegel. The weak, and valid, version would insist on the fact that each and every part of cultural history is embedded in world history, but also on the fact that the particular relations to that history are manifold.[4] 'To make men conscious of themselves in their own history is a great task', as Auerbach has it (17/310).

*

When Goethe coined the word *Weltliteratur*, humanism and the spirit of global citizenship [*Weltbürgergeist*] were still thoughts that were generally entertained. During the last decades of the nineteenth century these thoughts have been forced onto the defensive by a gradually stronger and still more heated national sentiment. Contemporary litera-tures turn increasingly national. I do not hold, though, that

---

4. The Hegelian idea of being concrete is seductive, but ultimately false. It presupposes that world history can be summarized as the unfolding of *Geist* (world spirit) as a conceptual edifice. World history is a heterogeneous process in time which cannot be subsumed under one conceptual construct. But that does not mean that the weak version of Auerbach's approach is obsolete. The increasingly dominant capitalist world system has its logic and thus its own history of expansion. It can be conceptualized, but in the real world the unfolding of this logic presupposes a set of millieux that are not all governed by a uniform logic. A history of this expansion should be a history of the way in which capitalist logic interferes in, but cannot swallow up, differently ordered spheres of life throughout the world.

the spirit of nationality and of global citizenship are mutually exclusive. The world literature of the future will become
so much more captivating the more national specificities
become apparent and the more it becomes heterogeneous,
as long as it maintains a general human aspect. What is
written directly for the world will have no value as a work
of art (XII.28).[5]

My compatriot, the great literary critic and intellectual Georg
Brandes (1842–1927), wrote these words in his essay on 'World
Literature' in 1899. The tendency in the direction of standardization singled out by Auerbach half a century later was already at
that point on Brandes's mind. In his reflections on *Weltliteratur*
Goethe stressed the improvement of the means of communication
as a factor that would facilitate knowledge of the literatures of
foreign countries. To Brandes the creation of a world market for
literature, on the other hand, implied the risk that the incorpor-
ation of concrete specific experience would deteriorate: 'Writers
have started to write for an unlimited, unspecific public, and the
result suffers from these efforts' (28). Zola is Brandes's example:
'In his great series of novels *Les Rougon-Macquart* he wrote for
France, and it is in general densely worked out. . . . At the peak
of his fame he wrote his trilogy *Lourdes–Rome–Paris* for the entire
world, and it has in several sections become more abstract than
earlier. . . . He wrote as Sarah Bernhardt acts, when she is performing in Peru or Chicago' (28). Holding up the torch of
humanism and global citizenship, Brandes keeps an eye on the
way in which literature should be rooted in concrete experience.
In a period of bellicose nationalisms his position is a precarious
act of balance. His early masterwork from the 1870s and onwards,
Main Currents in Nineteenth-Century Literature (i.e. European literature), on the other hand, primarily stressed the universal ideals
inherited from the Enlightenment.

In 'Philologie der Weltliteratur' Auerbach described the broad
historical process as a drama or a play (*Schauspiel*) and he stressed
the moment of artistic talent involved in the making of cultural
history. Brandes used the same terms about his own work.

---

5. References are to Georg Brandes, *Samlede Skrifter* [Collected Works], Copenhagen: Gyldendal, 1902–. This essay was reprinted in vol. XII; quotes are in my
own translation. I am not aware of any translations of the essay.

Throughout the six volumes of *Main Currents* he refers to his
subject as an historic drama; in the concluding remarks he
emphasizes that the last volume should be understood as 'the last
act of a great historic drama' (VI.681/VI.410).[6] The aim of his
work was 'by means of the study of certain main groups and main
movements in European literature, to outline the psychology of
the first half of the nineteenth' (VI.681/VI.410). The year 1848 –
a historical turning point and a preliminary end – sets the limit
to this immense task.

Brandes had to 'single out the main literatures' and to 'find a
pattern or norm in the movements, a beginning and an end'.
These are not the only terms that remind one of the Aristotelian
discussion of the proper chain of events for a tragedy. Brandes is
also looking for 'reversals'. He found the pattern or norm he was
looking for in the 'great rhythmical ebb and flow – the gradual
dying out and disappearing of the ideas and feelings of the
eighteenth century until authority, the hereditary principle, and
ancient custom once more reigned supreme, then the reappear-
ance of the ideas of liberty in ever higher mounting waves'
(VI.682/VI.410). If we recall Auerbach's recommendations, Brandes's approach slots in nicely to the same frame of thought: an
immense material, the search for a specific angle, but also a
personal commitment behind the intuition – in Brandes's case,
the destiny of the idea of freedom. This is Brandes's *Ansatz*, his 'grasp',
his point of departure, which is also a preliminary result of his
reading, as well as the core of his own commitment in his own
time. There was, I might mention in passing, a specific national
side to this: Brandes wanted to show that his own country,
Denmark, was far behind the general development in Europe, in
fact steeped in reaction against the heritage of the Enlightenment. His concluding remarks are concerned with this personal
aspect of the matter:

> It is self-evident that the standpoint here adopted is a personal one. It
> is the personal point of view, the personal treatment, which present
> literary personages and works thus grouped and ordered, thus con-

6. References are, first, to the Danish text, *Hovedstrømninger i det nittende Aarhun-
dredes Litteratur*, in Brandes, *Samlede Skrifter*, vols IV–VI, and, second, to the English
translation in *Main Currents in Nineteenth-Century Literature*, vols I–VI, London:
Heinemann, 1901–05.

trasted, thus thrown into relief or cast into shadow. Regarded impersonally, the literature of a half-century is nothing but a chaos of
hundreds of thousands of books in many languages.

The personal standpoint is not, however, an arbitrary one. It has
been the author's aim to do justice, as far as in him lay, to every single
person and phenomenon he has described. No attempt has been
made to fit any of them into larger or smaller places than they actually
occupied. It is no whim or preconceived intention of the author that
has given the work its shape. The power which has grouped, contrasted, thrown into relief, lengthened or shortened, placed in full
light, in half light, or in shadow, is none other than that never fully
conscious power to which we usually give the name art. (VI.682–3/
VI.411)

Brandes thus counts on 'the power of art' with a view to a
synthesis between the personal (i.e. subjective) viewpoint and
'inner' (i.e. objective) order in the material. Two ideals are at
stake in *Main Currents*. One is the idea of science, the other is the
idea of art. It may be a simplification, but it seems that Brandes
started out conceiving his role very much as that of a scientist,
whereas towards the end of the work he comes rather to display
artistic leanings. What remains in any case is the nexus between
personal commitment and historical material of the kind later
stressed by Auerbach.

From a scientific point of view the task is to reconstruct 'what
really happened'. But not everything that has happened. The
ideal of a complete mapping implicit in hard-core positivism (to
give a shorthand) is absurd. There is always a choice of the
question to ask, what to look for: the 'intuition', according to
Auerbach; the 'power of art', according to Brandes. But this is
not a formula for a pure piece of whimsy or the reflection of a
purely personal intention. Research should be concerned with
significant questions. There is no doubt, of course, that the
destiny of the ideas of the Enlightenment in the nineteenth
century is, by any reasonable standards, intellectually and historically significant. It is no less significant in relation to the twentieth
century or the beginning of the twenty-first. That is one good
reason for considering Brandes's work. Another is that it is an
exercise in literary criticism that has had a truly global
significance.

For Nietzsche, Brandes was 'a good European and missionary

of culture' (it is no wonder Nietzsche was fond of him: Brandes
was one of the first to promote him in Europe). When Brandes
died in 1927, Thomas Mann sent a telegram to the Danish
newspaper *Politiken* (Georg Brandes and his brother Edvard were
among the founders of this newspaper in the 1880s, and it was
here that Brandes published numerous essays and reviews). 'A
master of productive criticism' was the headline of Mann's communication, and looking back Mann maintained:

> His *Main Currents*, this bible for young European intellectuals 30 years
> ago, will remain a classical document in the history of the culture of
> the nineteenth century, and we Germans should never forget the ray
> of light that fell on Nietzsche's icecold solitude when the message
> arrived about the lectures of a certain Georg Brandes at the University
> of Copenhagen on 'The German Philosopher Friedrich Nietzsche'.[7]

The bibliographical details are impressive. The individual volumes
of *Main Currents* were immediately translated into German from
1872, Russian and Polish translations appeared from 1881, translations were published in England and the US from 1901, a
Japanese translation followed in 1915, the first four volumes were
translated into Chinese in 1935–39, a Spanish translation followed
in 1946; as recently as 1975 an English translation was reprinted
in New York, and in 1980 the publication of what I understand is
a complete version was initiated in China.[8] These are the raw
facts. There is no reason to believe that these translations did not
encounter an interested public. The impact of Brandes's work
has thus indeed been truly global. Particularly interesting is
perhaps the Chinese reception.[9] It is no wonder that there was an
interest in Brandes's work. In 1915 the head of the literary faculty
at Peking University, Ch'en Tu-hsiu, wrote in a programmatic
article in the news periodical *New Youth*:

> Due to the rise of science since the end of the nineteenth century, the
> real nature of the universe and human life was discovered. Europe
> was unveiled and entered a new enlightened era; the face of Nature

---

7. In English in Hans Hertel and Sven Møller Kristensen, eds, *The Activist Critic:
A Symposium on the Political Ideas, Literary Methods and International Reception of Georg
Brandes*, Copenhagen 1980 (= *Orbis Litterarum.* Supplement 5)

8. Bibliographical information in ibid. and from the Royal Library, Copenhagen.

9. On the Chinese reception, see Christian Hermann Jensen, in *The Activist
Critic.*

was stripped of the mask which had concealed its mysteries. All the old moral principles, old thoughts, and old institutions handed down from antiquity were destroyed. Literature and the arts followed the current, and passed from romanticism to realism and further to naturalism.

There may be a certain Chinese twist in the reference to institutions handed down from antiquity, but otherwise this is very close to Brandes: the stress on the impact of the natural sciences, the abolition of old thoughts etc. The Danish scholar whose essay on the reception of Brandes in China I am drawing on here traces a passage in an essay by Lu Hsün (Lu Xun) from 1907 back to one of the volumes of *Main Currents* (read by Lu Hsün in German, I suppose). Here is Brandes: 'Human reason, which in every domain had for centuries been compelled to drudge like a serf, which had been intoxicated with legends and lulled to sleep with psalms and set phrases, had been roused as if by the crow of a cock and had leaped up wide awake.'[10] This is a nice specimen of Brandes's prose, which apparently appealed to the 26-year-old Lu Hsün. In 1921 the important journal *The Short Story Magazine* wrote:

> The career of the great critic of our generation, Georg Brandes, has been one of mediation. I need say no more. His imperishable work is *Main Currents in the Literature of the 19th Century*. For a long time we have heard about the fame of this work. His thoughts appeal to us, and we hope that before long there will be someone who will present it to China in its entirety.[11]

It is hard to think of more convincing testimony to the truly global importance of *Main Currents*.

In Brandes's own opinion it was 'a comparative study of European literature' (IV.1/VI.vii). According to the French *Encyclopedia Universalis*, he was 'le père du comparatisme'; although some might look for other possible progenitors, and it has been questioned that *Main Currents* should be seen as an example of comparative literature at all,[12] in the early development of comparative literature as an academic discipline Brandes was widely

---

10. In English in *The Activist Critic*, p. 230, in Danish in *Samlede Skrifter* V, p. 54.

11. *The Activist Critic*, p. 232. The author was the brother of the editor Mao Tun (Mao Dun, real name Shen Yen-ping: Shen Tse-min).

12. For example, L. P. Rømhild in *The Activist Critic*.

regarded as one of its pioneers. Yet it is obvious that Brandes is
thinking in the terms of very broad trends in nineteenth-century
sciences: 'Just as the botanist must handle nettles as well as roses,
so the student of literature must accustom himself to look, with
the unflinching gaze of the naturalist or the physician, upon all
the forms taken by human nature, in their diversity and their
inward affinity' (IV.199/II.3). 'The literary critic passing from one
variety to another of the type of a certain period in a manner
resembles the scientist tracking some structure through its metamorphoses in the different zoological species' (IV.71/I.63). Here
the reference is clearly to Darwin, and elsewhere we find Brandes
referring to 'the comparative study of language, philology as
natural science' (IV.172/I.176 – translation changed by me).

This is, however, only one element in the intellectual pattern.
Brandes – although, again, in this he was by no means alone in
the nineteenth century – associated the idea of evolutionary
development in Darwin with the Hegelian philosophy of history.
In his presentation of Hegel and the Young Hegelians in relation
to Young Germany in the last volume of *Main Currents*, the centre
of attention is Hegel's vision of 'the history of the world [as] one
grand drama of liberation', 'a truly great thought-poem', 'a new
species of poetry'. Only 'a few of the great fundamental thoughts'
remain after the detailed application of the Hegelian method has
lost its spell. 'But he who in his early youth has passed through
the Hegel period in his own mental experience perfectly understands the rapturous enthusiasm of the youth of that day, and the
strength they drew from these cosmic thoughts, these world-ideas'
(VI.529/VI.227). What remains is the idea of an inner development in history towards the realization of freedom, but also the
idea that progress is not unilinear. The approach is dialectical in
the sense that progress is met with reaction: this reaction, however, also serves further progressive steps, in short the Hegelian
sublation or *Aufhebung*: 'true, supplementing and correcting reaction is progress', as Brandes says in his introductory lecture
(IV.4).[13] The turning points that act as reversals in the structure
of drama show up here as dialectical turns in the philosophy of
history.

---

13. The English version I am using here unfortunately only has a very short
version of Brandes's sweeping and provocative introductory lecture.

The idea of history as progressive realization of the ideals of freedom – these 'world thoughts', as Brandes puts it[14] – he absorbed from Hegel, and this idea governs his entire work. This is the transpersonal element in the commitment underlying the 'intuition' (in Auberbach's term). Elsewhere in *Main Currents* there is a discussion of the question of 'taking sides' in poetry. Brandes advocates taking the side of 'a system of ideas which, from their very nature, are not confined to any place [such as a nation] – world-wide thoughts, the great general interests of humanity' (VI.507/VI.201). Realization of the ideas of freedom has a double meaning here, since it includes, on the one hand, free thought and, on the other, freedom in the practical world. It is free thought and in particular freedom of the individual that is at the core of Brandes's commitment, and also at the core of a fundamental ambiguity in his work. Nietzsche was no friend of organized representation of social demands; the scorn he directs against what he calls 'resentment' is also directed against organized labour, as is clearly demonstrated in one of his untimely considerations, *The Uses of History*. How could Brandes, who frequently refers to the ideals of the French Revolution, embrace Nietzsche's thought?

He discusses a related question in his section on Heinrich Heine; the terms of his discussion illuminate his own position. Heine was regarded as a revolutionary. 'But his political animosity is exclusively aroused by medieval conditions, medieval beliefs. He is anti-clerical in good earnest, but not democratic in good earnest' (VI.434/VI.110). Brandes's interpretation is that 'Heine was at one and the same time a passionate lover of liberty and an out-and-out aristocrat. He had the freedom-loving nature's thirst for liberty, pined and languished for it, and loved it with his whole soul; but he had also the great nature's admiration for human greatness, and the refined nature's nervous horror of the rule of mediocrity' (VI.437–8/VI. 114). *Mediocrity* is the key word. Brandes is describing aspects of his own temper here. A detail should be noticed, namely that this aversion is purely *nervous*, it is a matter of refined sensibility, an aristocratic mentality although

14. The Danish word *Verdenstanke* is constructed in analogy to German (the equivalent would be *Weltgedanke*).

in a modern guise, a spontaneous rejection of what may limit the freedom of the aristocrat.

> The apparent contradiction in his political sympathies and tendencies arose from the fact that he loved greatness and beauty as truly as he loved liberty, and that he was not prepared to sacrifice the highest development of humanity on the altar of unreal equality and real mediocrity. (VI.439/VI.116)

Heine predicted a society 'composed of liberated slave souls, who had only exchanged the servility which was their instinct for free indulgence in the envy which lay at the root of their morality' (ibid.). These words could come straight out of Nietzsche's *Genealogy of Morals*. In Brandes's section on Madame de Staël, 'public opinion' (IV.108/I.103) is the enemy. Confronted with public opinion the 'genius is in much the position of the clever headboy in a stupid class' (IV.108–9/I.103). Equality, it will be seen, is not Brandes's major concern and thus has no place inside the animating 'world thought' Brandes both detects within the unfolding of world history and uses as a tool for making sense of that history. He feared and hated mediocrity. To him the ideas of the French Revolution are ambiguous: 'the watchword: Liberty, Equality, and Fraternity . . . contained at least two fundamental principles instead of one. Liberty as a fundamental principle may be regarded as emanating from Voltaire, fraternity from Rousseau. And equality and liberty did not combine well' (V.25).[15] The historical semantics of freedom is a complicated matter.

As an analysis – informed by an idea of freedom – of a huge collection of historical material, Brandes's *Main Currents* thus exemplifies the kind of academic work suggested by Auerbach. A case in point is Goethe's *Werther*, which holds a prominent place in the first volume of the work. In Brandes's account, the search for freedom and an inner relation to nature are the governing traits of Werther. Werther is 'more than the spirit of the new era, he is its genius' (34/20), detesting 'all rules' (35/21); 'he is nature in one of its highest developments, genius' (ibid.). His

---

15. The English version is in this case quoted from Georg Brandes, *Revolution and Reaction in Ninteteenth Century French Literature*, vol. 3 of *Main Currents*, New York: Russell & Russell, 1960, p. 24.

psychological condition and his conflicts with the prejudices and rules of society turn him into a representative character: 'the trouble in his soul is the trouble which heralds and accompanies the birth of a new era' (39/26). 'It seems as if there were a great and terrible discord between the individual and the general condition of things, between heart and reason, between the laws of passion and those of society. The impression that this was so had taken deep hold of that generation' (40/27). The interpretation of Werther in this historical context thus runs along the same lines as the analysis of Heine, except that Werther is taken as representative of the pre-Revolutionary age. The French Revolution is primarily understood in terms of the liberation of the individual, in particular the extraordinary individual: 'Nor was it long before they heard the crash, before the time came when all barriers were broken down and all forms done away with; when the established order was overthrown and distinctions of class suddenly disappeared; when the air was filled with the smoke of gunpowder and the notes of the "Marseillaise" ...' (40/27). Political, social and individual change is one and the same in this version of 'revolution', and Brandes directly links Werther's 'revolutionary ire at conventional society, its prejudices, its compulsory regulations, its terror of genius' (38/24) to the events of 1789. The morning after Werther's suicide a book is found on his desk (Lessing's *Emilia Galotti*). This and other features are taken directly from the account Goethe received in a letter of the suicide of one Karl Wilhelm Jerusalem. Another text is mentioned in this source: a manuscript by Jerusalem of which the first part is entitled 'On Freedom' ('Von der Freiheit').[16] Goethe did not integrate this particular feature, but the theme underlies the entire novel.

However, as it is evident from Brandes's chapter on *Werther* – and *Main Currents* in general – 'freedom' is a complex concept. The late Hungarian scholar Ferenc Feher touched on this question in an essay a decade ago.[17] His example is from the same age: Mozart and Da Ponte's opera *Don Giovanni*. At a certain

---

16. Goethe, *Werke, Jubiläumsausgabe*, vol. 4, ed. W. Vosskamp et al., p. 637, Frankfurt on Main and Leipzig: Insel Verlag, 1998, p. 637.

17. 'Between Relativism and Fundamentalism: Hermeneutic as Europe's Mainstream Political and Moral Tradition', in Feher and Heller, eds, *The Grandeur and Twilight of Radical Universalism*, New Jersey 1991.

point in the opera all the main characters sing together the words 'Viva la libertà'. This extended stress on the word freedom is, says Feher,

> an incommensurable expression of the new age born with the French Revolution and its new concept of the political. Freedom will be the common vocabulary in which the will of all [Rousseau's concept of *la volonté de tous* in his *Social Contract* is alluded to here] is going to express itself. But behind this apparent total consensus, there will be a cornucopia of almost irreconcilable interpretations. . . . Right at its peak, when the unrestrained, sensuous singing of all . . . protagonists celebrates the intoxicating moment of the birth of the new principle, the principle immediately displays its Janus face. We are all one in aspiring to *libertà*; this creates the common *melos* among us, the very possibility of interpreting each other. But we are also different within this common *melos* to the point of mutual indiscernibility. We regularly misread each other, subsume others under our own motivations, over- and underestimate each other. And when interpretation breaks down, in our rage, we solve by violence, or by resorting to transcendental powers (to the Comtur) what we cannot solve by our own this-worldly means. But the blessed predicament of modernity is that we cannot abandon either the common *melos* or the individual difference unless we want to destroy the new modern world, our own creation, with our own hands. (565–6)

The first performance of *Don Giovanni* took place in Prague in 1787, two years before the outbreak of the French Revolution and one year after the American Declaration of Independence. Freedom was not only in the air; action was taken or was about to be taken. The world of this opera is far from the world of politics, but it is permeated by class conflicts and conflicts of attitudes and values. The collective celebration of liberty or freedom, it will be recalled, is sung at the moment Don Giovanni gathers all the main characters in the story at his house party. As Feher points out, in this moment a multitude of aspirations are articulated by the same word.

The world of the characters is a delimited social world, but there is also an historical dynamic at work here. Don Giovanni is the representative of untrammelled libertinage; to him, freedom is the unrestricted aristocratic privilege to be defended if necessary by the sword – not only mortally against Anna's father, but also as a warning against Masetto: 'I tell you, Masetto, if you don't go at once without more argument [*he shows him his sword*] you'll repent it.' This peasant who bows his head before the sword also has his own ideas of freedom, quite contrary to Don Giovanni's. And then there is Zerlina. She has advice for the other peasant girls: ['You maidens whose thoughts dwell on love, don't let time pass you by.'] Freedom is here the imminent, if not immediate, satisfaction of erotic desire, *piacere*. It is the same principle as Giovanni's, although held within the frame of marriage. But the nexus of freedom and desire can also lead astray. All too easily Zerlina tends to believe in Giovanni's promise of marriage, or is it not rather that Zerlina is erotically attracted to Don Giovanni, that it is the principle of *piacer* that governs here? *Vorrei e non verrei* ['I would like and I don't want'], *Mi trema un poco il cor* ['My heart trembles a bit']. And then: *Presto . . . non son più forte* ['Quick then . . . I'm no longer strong']. At this point Zerlina and Giovanni can sing together: '*Andiam, andiam, mio bene, a ristorar la pene d'un innocente amor*' ['Then come, oh come, my dearest, and ease the ache of a chaste love']. Enter Donna Elvira. In fact, in this great opera about libertinage the erotic encounters are constantly interrupted or frustrated, in particular for Ottavio. He is quite eager to marry Anna, but they are not peasants; they are exemplary representatives of the emerging bourgeoisie and its ideal of restraint, Ottavio's sexual frustration being itself part of the bourgeois experience. Anna insists on 'letting the time pass by'. The ultimate frustration of erotic fulfilment is at the symbolic level, of course, namely the appearance of the dead *Commandatore*. He interrupts Giovanni at the graveyard, when he is about to tell Leporello of new adventures, and he shows up at Giovanni's house at the point when at his last supper he declares as his principal belief: '*Viva le femmine! Viva il buon vino! Sostegno e gloria d'umanità*') ['Here's to women and good wine, the support and glory of mankind']. In short: Humanity instead of Divinity, the pleasure of good wine instead of wine as symbol of Christ's blood, and instead of his flesh (symbolized by bread), the female body.

Freedom for Anna means protection of the private sphere, prosecution and punishment of the rapist, but also conformity with public opinion. Her concerns become even more clear when compared to Elvira's quite different attitude. On the one hand, she is enraged because Giovanni has betrayed his promise to marry her, but the fundamental problem is that she is in love with him and can neither help it nor bear it. Her actual behaviour is completely divorced from public concerns; she loves her seducer and declares it. Her love has nothing of Anna's domesticated bourgeois sensibility; she is all fire (*'Son per voi tutta foco'*). In that respect she is as little restrained as Giovanni. What, then, is freedom for her? Since her decision is to go into a convent, it seems like her wish is to free herself from desire, and from the sources of erotic arousal.

Ottavio represents the modern citizen in so far as he wants to discover truth: 'I will pursue every means to discover the truth' (*'Ah, di scoprire il vero ogni mezzo si cerchi'*), while incarnating the virtues of friendship and the obligations of a betrothed. He is governed by 'duty, compassion and affection' (*'dover, pietate, affetto'*) – all of them good bourgeois virtues. But he does not act very much. Basically freedom is for Ottavio the freedom of the citizen in an ordered society where the authorities take care of villains.

Finally Leporello, the servant. He wants to be liberated from the position of an underdog. His idea of freedom is conceived inside the master–slave relation; he wants to become a master himself: 'I'd like to live the life of a gentleman and serve no more' (*'Voglio far il gentiluomo, e non voglio più servir'*). But in the end, he goes to the inn to find a better master. His dream of freedom is only momentary.

There can be disagreements over the interpretation of the various ideas of freedom implied in this opera, and each specific staging will give its own particular interpretation. But there can be no doubt that in singing together of freedom, the characters do not collectively share and endorse one single version of it.

The idea of freedom is, to quote Brandes again, a 'world thought', a global concern. And since his time it has been incorporated in the formulation of principles that are meant to have global application (as enshrined in the first paragraph of the charter of the United Nations). But there have been many disagreements over the meanings and uses of the idea of freedom. These disagreements have enormous consequences when put into practice. They are not only ideas that can be discussed, they are also guidelines for the organization of worldly matters. In this sense too, one might say, they are 'world thoughts'. It is thus all the more important for the humanities to take these differences into account in order to provide antidotes to misunderstandings and misapplications.

Freedom is just an 'example', although, of course, not an arbitrary example, of those 'world thoughts' that it will be the task of the humanities to explore in a global context in the future, whether explicit or implicitly embedded in works of imagination. Culturally speaking, the process of globalization is – just like the process of modernization – multifaceted. On the one hand, it is a threat to the particular, to differences between cultural forma-tions, as was stressed by Auerbach. The meaning and value of such threats are not given a priori; there are after all peculiarities it is worth getting rid of, such as aristocratic prerogatives or arbitrary authority. On the other hand, it is a process that furthers the growth of common ideals, of 'world thoughts' as guidelines in the mastering of an increasingly common global destiny. The meaning and value of these thoughts is not given a priori either. That is what cultural exchange and discussion are about.

Goethe's concept of '*Weltliteratur*' was coined at an earlier stage of globalization; it was, however, intimately linked with global integration as he saw it. In his later years he was fascinated by the prospect of the linking together of the world through the con-struction of both a Panama Canal and a Suez Canal. Trade was the model for cultural exchange and permeated his metaphors: the word *Weltliteratur* was analogous to *Weltverkehr* (global exchange) and parallel to similar constructions like *Weltbildung*. A double concern was involved:[18] on the one hand the global perspective; on the other hand, a turn towards the objective world. *Weltbildung* (world-education) would mean an education in global matters beyond national limitations as well as in matters beyond individual mental and sentimental borders. 'Free trade of concepts and sentiments, just as exchange of products and fruits of the earth, will increase the wealth and the general well-being of mankind.'[19] A crucial task in this 'free spiritual trade' (*freie geistige Handelsverkehr*, cit. 45)' was that of the translator: providing

---

18. As it is stressed by Hans Joachim Schrimpf in his fine essay *Goethes Begriff der Weltliteratur* (Stuttgart: J. B. Metzlersche Verlagsbuchhandlung, 1968), on which I am drawing here. Cf. also Fritz Strich, *Goethe und die Weltliteratur*, Berlin, 1957.

19. Cited in Schrimpf, *Goethes Begriff*, p. 14.

access to the 'spiritual goods' of foreign nations. Whereas Goethe turned his attention to the overcoming of national limitations, among them not the least the limitations of German national culture as it was increasingly developing nationalist traits, later discussions of world literature, like those of Brandes and Auerbach, have stressed the risks involved, the papering over of cultural specificities.

Similar discussions are often permeated by a combination of, on the one hand, a focus on literature as a *linguistic* work of art and, on the other hand, the prominent nineteenth-century cultural theme of the intertwining of national culture and national language. The construction of national identity, however, is in itself a mystifying (and potentially destructive) endeavour. The seemingly natural link between literature as a linguistic art form, national language and national identity is at odds with the fact that literature travels in translation and that all nations are heterogeneous culturally speaking. From the outset the idea of world literature goes against the grain of nationalism.

In 1795 Kant wrote from his viewpoint as a German philosopher in his short book *To Perpetual Peace*:

> Because a (narrower or wider) community widely prevails among the Earth's peoples, a transgression of rights in *one* place in the world is felt *everywhere*; consequently, the idea of a cosmopolitan right [*Weltbürgerrecht*] is not fantastic or exaggerated, but rather an amendment to the unwritten code of national and international rights [*Staatsrecht* and *Völkerrecht*], necessary to the public rights of men [*Menschenrechte*] in general. Only such amendment allows us to flatter ourselves with the thought that we are making continual progress towards perpetual peace. (119/216)[20]

When we consider what has happened in the world since then, Kant's expectations may seem naïve. The principles he advocated have nevertheless developed into principles agreed to, if not followed, by most of the nations of the world. And his remarks on

---

20. References are, first, to Immanuel Kant, *Perpetual Peace and Other Essays*, trans. Ted Humphrey, Indianapolis/Cambridge, MA: Hackett Publishing Company 1983, and, second, to the German text, 'Zum Ewigen Frieden', in Immanuel Kant, *Werke*, vol. VI, Frankfurt on Main: Insel Verlag, 1964.

the way in which even distant violations of human rights catch attention around the world are so much more to the point, as the globalization of communication has taken what might be termed a quantum leap since his time and in particular during the last decades. Here again the multifaceted character of globalization is visible. Global mass communication is certainly one of the most serious threats to the particular, to the specific character of cultural formations, and much is to be said about the heaps of trash that are spread all over the world. But the media have also brought the various communities together and have been vehicles for 'world thoughts': the world market for literature does, in spite of the forebodings expressed by Auerbach, increasingly distribute articulations of a variety of horizons of experience, thereby contributing to mutual understanding.

Kant did find an 'underlying wisdom of a higher cause that directs the human race toward its objective goal and predetermines the world's cause' (120/217). We may have just as much difficulty in finding this wisdom as we have with Hegel's idea of the cunning of reason. Yet despite the disastrous aspects of the twentieth century, it still remains *one* reasonable task for the humanities to follow the history and cultural context – from the past through the present and into the future – of the destiny, on a global scale, of world thoughts like those singled out by Brandes – with all due attention to, but also unperturbed by, the sheer complexity of the matter. Today, no less than in Goethe's time, *Weltliteratur* has its role to play in *Weltbildung*.

4

Global *Translatio*:

The 'Invention' of Comparative Literature, Istanbul, 1933

Emily Apter

Any language is human prior to being national: Turkish, French, and German languages first belong to humanity and then to Turkish, French and German peoples.

Leo Spitzer, 'Learning Turkish' (1934)

In many ways, the rush to globalize the literary canon in recent years may be viewed as the 'comp-lit-ization' of national literatures throughout the humanities. Comparative literature was in principle global from its inception, even if its institutional establishment in the postwar period assigned Europe the lion's share of critical attention and shortchanged non-Western literatures. As

This essay grew out of dialogue with Aamir Mufti, whose own work on 'Auerbach in Istanbul' became a point of departure for my arguments here. I also acknowledge with profound gratitude the work of Tulay Atak, whose discovery and translation of Spitzer's 'Learning Turkish' article was crucial, as was her research assistance at UCLA and in Istanbul. I was fortunate to have had the chance to interview Süyehla Bayrav thanks to Tulay and her friends. Thanks are also due to Fredric Jameson, who put me in touch with Professor Sibel Irzik at the Bosporos University. Gayatri Chakravorty Spivak, Andreas Huyssen and David Damrosch offered invaluable suggestions when a version of this essay was presented at Columbia University. Hans Ulrich Gumbrecht was also kind enough to share his manuscript on 'Leo Spitzer's Style', a rich source of literary history for this period.

many have pointed out, the foundational figures of comparative literature – Leo Spitzer, Erich Auerbach – came as exiles and émigrés from war-torn Europe with a shared suspicion of nationalism. Goethe's ideal of *Weltliteratur*, associated with a commitment to expansive cultural secularism, became a disciplinary premise that has endured, resonating today in, say, Franco Moretti's essay 'Conjectures on World Literature', in which he argues that anti-nationalism is really the only raison d'être for risky forays into 'distant reading'. 'The point,' he asserts, 'is that there is no other justification for the study of world literature [and for the existence of departments of comparative literature] but this: to be a thorn in the side, a permanent intellectual challenge to national literatures – especially the local literature. If comparative literature is not this, it's nothing.'[1]

Anyone who has worked in comparative literature can appreciate Moretti's emphasis on anti-nationalism. The *doxa* of national language departments tend to be more apparent to those accustomed to working across or outside them, while critical tendencies and schools appear more obviously as extensions of national literatures to those committed self-consciously to combining or traducing them. National character ghosts theories and approaches even in an era of cultural anti-essentialism. English departments are identified with a heritage of pragmatism, from practical criticism to the new historicism. Reception and discourse theory are naturalized within German studies. French is associated with deconstruction even after deconstruction's migration elsewhere. Slavic languages retain morphology and dialogism as their theoretical calling cards. 'Third World allegory' lingers as an *appellation contrôlée* in classifying third world literatures, and so on. Lacking a specific country, or single national identity, comparative literature necessarily works toward a non-nationally defined disciplinary locus, pinning high stakes on successfully negotiating the pitfalls of *Weltliteratur*, especially in an increasingly globalized economy governed by transnational exchanges and flows. But as we have seen, the more talk there has been of 'worlding' the canon along lines established by Edward Said, the less consensus there is on how to accomplish the task. As Moretti puts it: 'the literature around us is now unmistakably a planetary system. The

---

1. See Chapter 6, below.

question is not really *what* we should do – the question is *how*.
What does it mean, studying world literature? How do we do it? I
work on West European narrative between 1790 and 1930, and
already feel like a charlatan outside of Britain or France. *World*
literature?'

A number of rubrics have emerged in response to this 'How
to' question, even if they hardly qualify as full-fledged paradigms:
'Global literature' (inflected by Fredric Jameson and Masao
Miyoshi), 'cosmopolitanism' (given its imprimatur by Bruce Robbins and Timothy Brennan), 'world literature' (revived by David
Damrosch and Franco Moretti), 'literary transnationalism'
(indebted to the work of Gayatri Chakravorty Spivak) and comparative postcolonial and diaspora studies (indelibly marked by
Edward Said, Homi Bhabha, Françoise Lionnet and Rey Chow,
among others). While promising vital engagement with non-
Western traditions, these categories offer few methodological
solutions to the pragmatic issue of how to make credible comparisons among radically different languages and literatures. Moretti,
once again, articulates the matter succinctly: 'world literature is
not an object, it's a *problem*, and a problem that asks for a new
critical method; and no-one has ever found a method by just
reading more texts.' Does he himself propose a method? Well,
yes and no. He introduces the promising idea of 'distant reading'
as the foundation of a new epistemology (echoing Benedict
Anderson's notion of distant or e-nationalism), but it is an idea
that potentially risks foundering in a city of bits, where micro and
macro literary units are awash in a global system with no obvious
sorting device. Distance, Moretti pronounces, '*is a condition of
knowledge*: it allows you to focus on units that are much smaller or
much larger than the text: devices, themes, tropes – or genres
and systems. And if, between the very small and the very large,
the text itself disappears, well, it is one of those cases when one
can justifiably say, Less is more.'

If, in this formulation, distant reading seems scarcely distinct
from the old tropes, themes and genres emphasis familiar from
comparative literature of yesteryear, Moretti, to give him his due,
is proselytizing for something more radical. Acknowledging the
daunting prospect of what Margaret Cohen has called 'the great
unread', and frankly admitting that in his own area of expertise
he has dealt only with literature's 'canonical fraction', Moretti

advocates a kind of lit crit heresy that dispenses with close reading, relies unabashedly on second-hand material, and subordinates intellectual energies to the achievement of a 'day of synthesis'. Following Immanuel Wallerstein, the champion of world-systems theory, Moretti sets his hopes on the synthetic flash of insight that produces a shape-shifting paradigm of global relevance. His examples emphasize a socially vested formalism – 'forms as abstracts of social relationships' – ranging from Roberto Schwarz's formal reading of foreign debt in the Brazilian novel, to Henry Zhao's concept of 'the uneasy narrator' as the congealed expression of East–West 'interpretive diversification', to Ato Quayson's use of genre – Nigerian post-realism – as the narrative guise assumed by imperial interference.

Moretti's attempt to assign renewed importance to plot, character, voice and genre as load-bearing units of global literature has much to recommend it, as does his political formalism in the expanded field of world-systems theory, which bluntly recognizes the uneven playing field of global symbolic capital. Like the work of Perry Anderson, and other affiliates of the *New Left Review*, his 'macro' approach is clearly indebted to Jameson's *Marxism and Form*. But it is an approach that ignores the extent to which 'High Theory', with its internationalist circulation, already functioned as a form of distant reading. It also favours narrative over linguistic engagement, and this, I would surmise, is ultimately the dangling participle of Moretti's revamped *Weltliteratur*.

The problem left unresolved by Moretti – the need for a full-throttle globalism that would valorize textual closeness while refusing to sacrifice distance – was confronted earlier in literary history by Leo Spitzer when he was charged by the Turkish government to devise a philological curriculum in Istanbul in 1933. In looking not just at what Spitzer preached – a universal Eurocentrism – but more at what he practised – a staged cacophony of multilingual encounters – one finds an example of comparatism that sustains at once global reach and textual closeness.

Spitzer in Istanbul

It is by now something of a commonplace in the history of comparative literary studies to cite Erich Auerbach's melancholy

postscript in *Mimesis* in which he describes the circumstances of
the book's preparation during the period of his exile in Turkey
from 1933 to 1945.

> I may also mention that the book was written during the war and at
> Istanbul, where the libraries are not well equipped for European
> studies. International communications were impeded; I had to dis-
> pense with almost all periodicals, with almost all the more recent
> investigations, and in some cases with reliable critical editions of my
> texts. Hence it is possible and even probable that I overlooked things
> which I ought to have considered. . . . On the other hand it is quite
> possible that the book owes its existence to just this lack of a rich and
> specialized library. If it had been possible for me to acquaint myself
> with all the work that has been done on so many subjects, I might
> never have reached the point of writing.[2]

Equally famous is the use to which Edward Said put this passage,
making it not just the cornerstone of a critique of the Orientalist
worm gnawing the internal organs of Eurocentric literary criticism, but also the foundation of his own particular brand of exilic
humanism: 'The book owed its very existence to the very fact of
Oriental, non-Occidental exile and homelessness,' he would write
in *The World, the Text and the Critic*.[3] Auerbach, as many have
remarked, remained a consistent *point de repère* for Said, starting
with his translation (with Maire Said) of Auerbach's seminal essay
'Philology and *Weltliteratur*' at the outset of his career in 1969,
and continuing through to his 1999 PMLA presidential column
titled 'Humanism?' where he chastises Auerbach for being 'mystified' by the 'explosion' of 'new' languages after the Second World
War. But even in this critical sally, Said recuperates the Auerbachian project in his vision of humanism: 'In any case,' he concludes, 'I don't believe that humanism as a subject for us can be
evaded.'[4]

In his astute essay 'Auerbach in Istanbul: Edward Said, Secular
Criticism, and the Question of Minority Culture', Aamir Mufti
uses the Auerbachian Said as a point of departure for rethinking
comparative literature in a postcolonial world, by firmly ground-

---

2. Erich Auerbach, *Mimesis: The Representation of Reality in Western Literature*, trans.
Willard R. Trask, Princeton, 1953, p. 557.
3. Edward Said, *The World, the Text and the Critic*, Cambridge, MA, p. 8.
4. Edward Said, 'Humanism?', *MLA Newsletter*, Fall 1999, p. 4.

ing it in the experience of the minority.[5] Where Said, according to Mufti, took the condition of Auerbach's exile as a goad to 'questioning received notions of "nation, home, community and belonging"', Mufti proposes moving from the politics of un-homing to the politics of statelessness, with all that implies: the loss of human dignity, the stripping of rights and the reduction of an ethnic identity to the faceless category of the minority (Mufti is borrowing here from Hannah Arendt's analysis of the Jews as paradigmatic minority in her *The Origins of Totalitarianism*) (AI 103).

> Said's insistence on the critical imperative of the secular can appear elitist and hence paradoxical only if we fail to recognize this minority and exilic thrust in his work, if we forget the haunting figure of Auerbach in Turkish exile that he repeatedly evokes. It is in this sense that we must read Said when he himself speaks of exile not as 'privilege' but as permanent critique of 'the mass institutions that dominate modern life'. Saidian secular criticism points insistently to the dilemmas and the terrors, but also, above all, to the ethical possibilities, of minority existence in modernity. (AI 107)

Arguing against Ahjaz Ahmad, according to whom, Mufti maintains, Auerbach is shorthand for a High Humanist, '"Tory" orientation' locked into permanent battle with Foucauldian anti-humanism, Mufti underscores parallels between Auerbach's 'synthetic' critical practice and the holistic aspects of Saidian Orientalism. He discerns, in the Auerbach of Said's invention, an ethics of coexistence; an ethical ideal of *Weltliteratur* that acknowledges the fragility of worldliness and refuses to be threatened by the spectre of 'other' languages crowding the floor of European languages and literatures.

But what happens to this ethical paradigm of global comparatism if we are compelled to revise the foundation myth of exile? Does the picture change, does the way we read Auerbach's melancholy postscript and self-described intellectual isolation shift, when we reckon fully with the fact that Spitzer had already been in Istanbul for several years by the time Auerbach got there? There are few traces of the Istanbul chapter of literary history in

---

5. Aamir Mufti, 'Auerbach in Istanbul: Edward Said, Secular Criticism, and the Question of Minority Culture', *Critical Inquiry*, 25, Autumn 1998. Further references to this essay will appear in the text abbreviated AI.

the annals of early comparative literature; there are scant references to the intellectual collaborations among émigré colleagues
and Turkish teaching assistants at the University of Istanbul in the
1930s, and there are really no full accounts of what happened to
European philological pedagogy when it was transplanted to
Turkey.[6] I would like to suggest that the fact that Spitzer had
established a lively philological school in Istanbul, and learned
Turkish along the way, might have significant bearing on attempts
to redefine comparative literature today as a 'worlded' minoritar-
ian comparatism. My point is that in globalizing literary studies,
there is a selective forgetting of ways in which early comparative
literature was always and already globalized. Spitzer in Istanbul,
before Auerbach, tells the story not just of exilic humanism, but of
worldly linguistic exchanges containing the seeds of a transnational humanism or global *translatio.* As the status of European
traditions within postcolonial studies continues to be negotiated,
this transnational humanism may be construed as a critical practice that reckons with the uncertain status of European thought
in the future global marketplace of culture. It questions the
default to European models in hermeneutic practices, and yet
recognizes, as Said so clearly does, that the legacy of philological
humanism is not and never was a Western versus non-Western
problematic; it was, and remains, a history of intellectual import
and export in which the provenance labels have been torn off.
René Étiemble clearly intuited this legacy, when, in 1966 he called
for recasting comparative literature to accommodate future
demographics:

> . . . one or two billion Chinese who will claim to be of the first rank
> among the great powers; Moslems in hundreds of millions who, after
> having asserted their will to independence, will re-assert (as indeed

---

6. The most complete account of Spitzer and Auerbach's Istanbul careers may
be Geoffrey Green's *Literary Criticism and the Structures of History: Erich Auerbach and
Leo Spitzer,* Lincoln, NE and London, 1982. Green maintains that Istanbul was not
a place of hardship for Spitzer. While there, he maintains, Spitzer 'concentrated
upon "the inner form": with the "brazen confidence" that comes from placing
one's faith in Providence, he viewed his surroundings – despite their shortcomings
– as being vitalized by a divine spirit' (p. 105). Thomas R. Hart's essay 'Literature
as Language: Auerbach, Spitzer, Jakobson' is one of the few to credit the influence
of Istanbul and Turkish alphabetization on Auerbach's œuvre. In Seth Lerer, ed.,
Literary History and the Challenge of Philology: The Legacy of Erich Auerbach, Stanford,
1996. See pp. 227–30.

they are already doing) their religious imperialism; an India where hundreds of millions will speak, some Tamil, others Hindi, still others Bengali, others Marathi, etc.; in Latin America tens of millions of Indians who will clamor for the right to become men again, and men with full rights; at least one hundred and twenty million Japanese, besides the two present great powers, Russia and the United States, who perhaps will have become allies in order to counterbalance new ambitions; a huge Brazil, a Latin America perhaps at long last rid of United States imperialism; a Black Africa exalting or disputing *négritude*, etc. As for us Frenchmen, we are quite willing to create an *Agrégation* of Modern Letters, provided, however, that it does not include China or the Arab World.[7]

Étiemble's prescient vision of contemporary literary politics extends to his disciplinary reformation of comparative literature in the year 2050. The topics he came up with – 'Contacts between Jews, Christians and Moslems in Andalusia; Western influences during the Meiji era; Role of the discovery of Japan on the formation of liberal ideas in the century of the Enlightenment; Evolution of racist ideas in Europe since the discovery of America and Black Africa; Bilingualism in colonized countries; The influence of bilingualism on literatures', and so on – are profoundly in step with the kind of work being done today in transnational and postcolonial literary studies.[8] If Étiemble fashioned a futuristic global comparatism for the 1960s relevant to us now, he inherited a vision that had already been put into pedagogical practice in the 1930s by Leo Spitzer. The story of Spitzer's Istanbul seminar, and the model of global *translatio* that it affords, thus has special bearing on comparative literature today.

Most famous in the United States for a group of essays on stylistics published in 1967 under the title of the leading essay, *Linguistics and Literary History*, Leo Spitzer was rivalled only by Auerbach in his breadth of erudition and role in the academy as the teacher of multiple generations of comparatists. Paul de Man placed him squarely in an 'outstanding group of Romanic scholars of German origin' that included Hugo Friedrich, Karl Vossler,

---

7. René Étiemble, *The Crisis of Comparative Literature*, trans. Georges Joyaux and Herbert Weisinger, East Lansing, MI, 1966, p. 56.

8. Ibid., p. 57.

Ernst Robert Curtius, and Auerbach.[9] In his introduction to the
collection *Leo Spitzer: Representative Essays*, Spitzer's former student
at Johns Hopkins, John Freccero, acknowledged Spitzer as the
premier forerunner of deconstruction.[10] Spitzer preferred her-
meneutical demonstrations to books devoted to single authors.
His œuvre was sprawling and unsystematic, unified primarily by
his consistent attention to heuristics, and by a preoccupation with
select writers of the Spanish Golden Age, the Italian Renaissance,
the French Enlightenment and with the Decadents (Cervantes,
Gongora, Lope de Vega, Dante, Diderot, Baudelaire, Charles-
Louis Philippe).

Spitzer was profoundly unprepared for the institutionalization
of antisemitism in the Nazi years preceding the Second World
War. Like Victor Klemperer, he assumed he would have immunity
from political persecution as a result of his distinguished record
of military service during the First World War (his experience as
a censor of Italian prisoners' letters formed the basis of an early
publication on periphrasis and the multiple 'words for hunger').[11]
Unlike Klemperer, who stayed in Dresden throughout the war –
somehow managing to survive and keeping himself from suicidal
despair with the help of a 'philologist's notebook' in which he
documented the perversion of the German language by Nazi
usage – Spitzer fled to Istanbul in 1933. On 2 May 1933 the
Ministry of Education approved his replacement at the University
of Cologne by Ernst Robert Curtius and in July of that year he
was denounced along with other Jewish faculty members in a
report submitted to the University president that was authored

---

9. Paul de Man, *Blindness and Insight: Essays in the Rhetoric of Contemporary Criticism*,
Minneapolis, 1971, p. 171.

Several recent publications attest to renewed interest in the Romance philolog-
ical tradition prior to and during the Second World War. See Hans Ulrich
Gumbrecht, *Vom Leben und Sterben der grossen Romanisten: Karl Vossler, Ernst Robert
Curtius, Leo Spitzer, Erich Auerbach, Werner Krauss*, Munich, 2002, and Peter Jehle,
Werner Krauss und die Romanistik im NS-Staat, Hamburg, 1996. For a fine review of
Jehle's book, emphasizing the timeliness of re-examining the career of Werner
Krauss, the 'militant humanist' and Enlightenment scholar who joined the party
in 1945 and emigrated east to become chair of the Romance Institute at Leipzig,
see Darko Suvin, 'Auerbach's Assistant', *New Left Review*, 15, May–June 2002,
pp. 157–64.

10. John Freccero, 'Foreword' to *Leo Spitzer: Representative Essays*, ed, Alban
Forcione et al., Stanford, 1988, pp. xvi–xvii.

11. See Leo Spitzer, *Die Umschreibungen des Begriffes 'Hunger' im Italienischen*, Verlag
von Max Niemeyer, 1921.

by the head of a National Socialist student group.[12] With the writing on the wall, Spitzer resigned shortly after receiving invitations to teach at the University of Manchester and the University of Istanbul. As he sailed for Turkey, his entourage included his wife, his children and his teaching assistant, Rosemarie Burkart. Burkart and Spitzer enjoyed a passionate liaison in Istanbul.[13] By all accounts a gifted philologist in her own right with a passion for sports, art and music, and judging from her photograph, a thoroughly 'modern woman', with cropped hair, Burkart helped alleviate the melancholy that one would expect to have accompanied Spitzer's expulsion. It is perhaps no accident that in his article 'Learning Turkish' he employed the language of love when describing what it felt like to learn a foreign language late in life.

Spitzer's situation in 1933 was comparable to that of hundreds of Jewish academics dismissed from their posts at the time. Many emigrated to Palestine, others found asylum in unoccupied European capitals (the case of art historians Fritz Saxl, Nikolaus Pevsner, Gertrud Bing and Otto Pächt in London), and quite a few landed in Latin America (especially Brazil, Peru and Mexico). The United States was a destination of choice, but unless they were internationally renowned scholars like Einstein or Panofsky, many who fled to the United States discovered limited employment opportunities in their adoptive country, largely because of antisemitism in the American academy. As the recent documen-

---

12. Curtius's careerist opportunism vis-à-vis Spitzer's vacated post has been read as evidence of his compromised position with respect to the bureaucracy of National Socialism. The debate is still on with respect to Curtius's vision of Europeans as citizens of humanity. Earl Jeffrey Richards frames these concerns in terms of a series of important questions: Was Curtius's vision of a supranational Europe, captured in his 1948 masterwork *European Literature and the Latin Middle Ages*, a dangerous rampart offered to Himmler's ideology of 'Fortress Europe' or to the Nazi vision of a new Germania built on romantic neo-mediaevalism? Was Curtius politically naïve to assume that his ideal of European humanism would remain untainted by historical circumstances? Or was he simply the scapegoat for all the German Romanic scholars who continued to work unscathed or who profited from the émigré departures under the Third Reich? Was Curtius unfairly misread given his consistent and, some would say, courageous refutation of national character theory? See Earl Jeffrey Richards, 'La Conscience européenne chez Curtius et chez ses détracteurs', in Jeanne Bem and André Guyaux, eds, *Ernst Robert Curtius et l'idée d'Europe*, Paris, 1995, pp. 260–1.

13. Though Spitzer received an offer from Harvard in 1934, Rosemarie Burkart was unable to obtain US residency papers, and they stayed in Turkey for another two years.

tary film *From Swastika to Jim Crow* effectively demonstrates, it was America's black colleges in the South who often extended a helping hand, creating a generation of black academics trained by Jewish émigrés who would later attest to a sense of shared history as persecuted minorities. One of the lucky few, Spitzer secured job offers easily and spent three years, 1933–36, at the University of Istanbul as the first professor of Latin Languages and Literature in the Faculty of Literature and as Director of the School of Foreign Languages. It was at Spitzer's invitation that Auerbach joined the department in 1936, not quite the isolation from Europe that he would have us believe in the afterword to *Mimesis*. On closer inspection of the intellectual community congregated in Istanbul in the twenties and thirties,[14] Auerbach's jaundiced depiction of his loneliness in the wilderness really appears to be a distorted picture of what it was like to live and work there.

When I interviewed Süheyla Bayrav, a distinguished 86-year-old emeritus professor of literature at the University of Istanbul and a member of Spitzer's seminar in 1933, it became clear that a familial atmosphere prevailed.[15] Turkish students – Nesteren Dirvana, Mina Urgan, Sabbattin Eyuboglu, Safinaz Duruman – joined in discussion with the émigrés – Heinz Anstock, Eva Buck, Herbert and Lieselotte Dieckmann, Traugott Fuchs, Hans Marchand, Robert Anhegger, Ernst Engelburg, Kurt Laqueur, Andreas Tietze and Karl Weiner. The teaching sessions frequently took place in Spitzer's apartment, which was equipped with an extensive personal library of literature and reference works. When the young Süheyla (Sabri) Bayrav (who did a thesis with Spitzer on the *Chanson de Roland*) solved an etymological mystery that Spitzer had been wrestling with for some years, he instantly confirmed that her intuition was accurate with the help of volumes on his shelf. From then on, she was anointed a serious philologist, and eventually joined the ranks of Spitzer's department as a faculty member. Bayrav belonged to the first generation of Turkish

---

14. Despite Auerbach's oft-repeated criticism of the bibliographical shortcomings of the Istanbul library, he managed to edit a Romanology seminar publication around 1944 that included well-referenced essays on Shakespeare, Péguy, Shelley, Marlowe, Rilke and Jakobsonian linguistics.

15. The interview took place in the summer of 2001. It was conducted in French at Süheyla Bayrav's house, located in a suburb on the Asian side of Istanbul.

women to attend university and pursue professional academic careers. Spitzer's seminar, though intimidating, professionally launched a number of women scholars: Rosemarie Burkhart played an active and productive role as a Romance philology professor; Eva Buck, a translator of German origin brought up in China and educated by British nuns, used her comparative background in languages to compose an anthology of European literature in Turkish; Azra Ahat, a Belgian-educated humanist, edited a dictionary of Greek mythology and became a well-known translator; and Bayrav forged a transition between philology and structural semiotics through her work on linguistic literary criticism, in addition to becoming an intellectual magnet for Turkish writers and visiting intellectuals such as Barthes and Foucault.

Bayrav and her cohort carried on the tradition of East–West exchange and commitment to translation fostered by the Spitzer seminar well into the seventies and eighties. By contrast, Auerbach and his students, most of whom, like Walter Kranz or Herbert Dieckmann, hailed from Germany and concentrated on European languages and literatures, seem to have been relatively uninterested in the potential for an enlarged vision of world literature presented by the conditions of their exile. On meeting Harry Levin in America for the first time, Auerbach discredited the scholarship of his Turkish colleagues, pointing to the case of a Turkish translator of Dante who admitted to working from a French translation chosen at random.[16] A more important cause of his intellectual dyspepsia was political. He bitterly opposed the climate of burgeoning nationalism in Turkey. In a letter to Walter Benjamin written in 1937, he repudiated the 'fanatically anti-traditional nationalism' that came out of Atatürk's 'struggle against the European democracies on the one hand and the old Mohammedan Pan-Islamic sultan's economy on the other'. The émigrés, he conjectured (in an argument that has become familiar in the wake of 9/11), were in Istanbul as part of the Turkish

---

16. Harry Levin, 'Two *Romanisten* in America: Spitzer and Auerbach', in *Grounds for Comparison*, Cambridge, 1972, pp. 112–13. Further references to this work will appear in the text abbreviated GC. Levin, in this essay, argues that Spitzer and Auerbach reacted in contrasting ways to 'the lack of scholarly paraphernalia' in Istanbul. He casts the former's *Wortbildungslehre* or word-formation approach as 'infra-scholarship', and the latter's 'sociohistorical rather than strictly stylistic' approach as 'para-scholarship' (GC 118).

government's premeditated scheme to free itself from imperial hegemony; acquiring European technological know-how with the aim of turning it back on Europe:

> . . . rejection of all existing Mohammedan cultural heritage, the establishment of a fantastic relation to a primal Turkish identity, technological modernization in the European sense, in order to triumph against a hated yet admired Europe with its own weapons: hence the preference for European-educated emigrants as teachers, from whom one can learn without the threat of foreign propaganda. Result: nationalism in the extreme accompanied by the simultaneous destruction of the historical national character.[17]

The new Turkish nationalism, and its repressive cultural arm, was certainly in evidence during Auerbach's eleven-year sojourn in Istanbul, but one could argue, without really overstating the case, that it was the volatile crossing of Turkish language politics with European philological humanism that produced the conditions conducive to the invention of comparative literature as a global discipline, at least in its early guise. A fascinating two-way collision occurred in Istanbul between a new-nations ideology dedicated to constructing a modern Turkish identity with the latest European pedagogies, and an ideology of European culture dedicated to preserving ideals of Western humanism against the ravages of nationalism. Auerbach's self-portrait as a lonely European scholar seems increasingly questionable the more one takes account of the sizeable professional, artistic and political European community that was well established in Istanbul (and Ankara) by the time he arrived in Turkey in 1936.[18] The mythographer Georges Dumézil worked in Istanbul between 1925 and 1931, having come at the invitation of Atatürk to help prepare the ground for

---

17. As cited by Karlheinz Barck, 'Walter Benjamin and Erich Auerbach: Fragments of a Correspondence', *Diacritics*, Fall–Winter 1992, p. 82.

18. Hans Ulrich Gumbrecht suggests that the Istanbul period was the culmination of a sense of intellectual melancholia already fully fledged in Auerbach's pre-exile professional life. Gumbrecht wagers 'that his passionate and distanced view of European culture emerged during his exile in Istanbul or even after his emigration to the United States in 1947. At most, the experience of expatriation that the National Socialist regime had inflicted upon him gave Auerbach the opportunity to become fully aware of his distanced and sometimes melancholic perspective on western culture as a culture that had entered its final stage.' See Gumbrecht, '"Pathos of the Earthly Progress": Eric Auerbach's Everydays', in Lerer, ed., *Literary History and the Challenge of Philology*, p. 31.

alphabetization in 1928. Leon Trotsky found safe harbour there between1931 and 1933, as did Gerhard Kessler, the German socialist political exile who helped found the Turkish Workers' Syndicate. Spitzer was preceded by the Romanist Traugott Fuchs, who taught at Roberts College and helped facilitate his appointment at the University of Istanbul, (known, at this time, as the *Emigré Universität*).[19] Shortly after Spitzer's arrival, he was joined by a large number of German-speaking academics and creative artists, including the distinguished philosopher of mind Hans Reichenbach (who taught at the University of Istanbul from 1933 to 1938); Fritz Neumark (economy and law, Istanbul University), Georg Rohde (a classical philologist based in Ankara in 1935, who studied Arabic influences on world literature and initiated a 'Translations from World Literature' series), Wolfram Eberhard (Chinese language and literature in Ankara University), Paul Hindemith (1935–37, who founded the Ankara State Conservatory with Carl Ebert and brought Béla Bartók in 1936), and a host of innovative architects and planners, among them Bruno Taut (who taught between 1936 and 1938 at Istanbul Technical University) and the French urban planner Henri Prost.[20] Later arrivals whose impact was equally significant (in more ways than one, since many of them were apparently engaged in espionage during the war) were the British historians Sir Ronald Syme (a specialist of Rome and Anatolia, appointed Professor of Classical Philology at the University of Istanbul from 1942 to 1945), the classical archaeologist George Bean (at Istanbul University starting in 1944, where he worked on *Aegean Turkey* and *Turkey's Southern Shore*) and the famous historian of Byzantium and the Crusades, Sir Steven Runciman.[21] An essay by Runciman demonstrating the Eastern origins of Western tropes and poetic devices, published in 1959, anticipates many of Said's discussions in *Orientalism* of suppressed Muslim cultural influences.[22] In addition to the

---

19. Anne Dietrich, *Deutschsein in Istanbul*, Opladen, 1998.

20. Other notable visitors included: Cemil Bilsel, Ernst Reuter, Rudolf Nissen, Beyazit Platz, Alexander Rustow, Wilhelm Röpke and Hellmut Ritter.

21. Sources here include *Cogito, sayi*, 23, 2000, and the appendix to Horst Widmann, *Exil und Bildungshilfe: Die deutschsprachige akademische Emigration in die Türkei nach 1933*, Bern, 1973.

22. Sir Steven Runciman, 'Muslim Influences on the Development of European Civilization', *Sarkiyat Mecmuasi* [Oriental Magazine] 3, 1959, pp. 1–12. Runciman's argues that 'The medieval French romance, *Floire et Blanchefleur*, is an eastern story;

presence of these renowned British scholars, the black American
writer James Baldwin, and the structural linguists Émile Benveniste and A. J. Greimas also worked in Istanbul in the 1950s.
According to Fredric Jameson's recollection, Greimas, Michel de
Certeau and Louis Marin claimed to have 'invented semiotics'
when they overlapped in Istanbul in that decade. These successive
generations of scholars and critics appear as so many *couches*
added to the city's historic role as a magnet for diaspora, migration and cultural fusion, and as a capital of world-historical power,
from the Holy Roman Empire to the Ottoman Empire.

Istanbul's tradition as a cultural cross-roads, combined with the
fact that it already had established Jewish and German enclaves
(and had served as a way-station for Jews immigrating to Palestine), made university posts there in the early thirties especially
coveted by European exiles.[23] When financial hardship took a
turn for the worse in July 1936 a year after his dismissal at the
Dresden Technical University in 1935, Victor Klemperer recorded
in his diaries the extent to which jobs at the University of Istanbul
were jealously monitored. After noting that 'Spitzer's post in
Istanbul has finally been given to Auerbach', he confided with a
touch of pique the story of how Auerbach had lobbied Benedetto
Croce to secure the position, succeeding despite his inadequate
fluency in French:

> This morning, with a recommendation from 'Vosslaiir', I was visited
> by Edmondo Cione, a little librarian from Florence, amico del Croce,
> anti-fascista. Would like to be a lecturer in Germany, did not know
> that I had lost my post. I recommended him to Gelzer in Jena. He will

---

while one of the most famous and lovely of all European romances, *Aucassin et
Nicolète*, betrays its Muslim origin. The hero's name is really al-Q-asim, while the
heroine is stated to be a Muslim princess of Tunis. It seems, also, that the use of
rhyme in medieval European verse was inspired by Arabic models. Long before
Europe knew of the collection of short stories which we call the *Arabian Nights*,
Muslim romance and poetry were making a mark on European literature' (p. 22).

23. Despite Turkey's neutrality, the Nazis also maintained a significant foothold
in the city, taking over the banking and administrative structure of the *Deutschen
Kolonie* once they assumed power. There were branches of the Hitler Youth,
German press outlets for propaganda, and a programme of Nazification in the
German schools in Istanbul. The tensions between these two German-speaking
communities – proximate yet offshore – were, needless to say, rife. For an account,
based in part on the documentation of Liselotte Dieckmann (who worked with
Spitzer as a lecturer), see Dietrich, *Deutschsein in Istanbul*, Chapter IV. Dieckmann
also echoes the fears expressed by Auerbach that modern Turkish nationalism
would come to resemble National Socialism.

see if he can be of assistance to me in Italy. He told me how Auerbach came to the Istanbul appointment. He had already been in Florence for a year, and Croce provided an opinion on him. . . . Now Auerbach is brushing up his French in Geneva. And Spitzer had been saying in Italy that only someone who could really speak French would get the appointment! If I go off to Geneva for a couple of months then I too could 'really speak French' again.[24]

Istanbul was particularly popular because it *was* Europe as far as many of the Austrian and German émigrés were concerned. As Klemperer's friend the physicist Harry Dember wrote in a letter of 12 August 1935 on learning he had been appointed at the university: 'It is certainly right on the edge – you can see across to Asia – but it is still in Europe.'[25]

The influx of émigrés to Istanbul grew as the dire need of employment by victims of Nazism who had been fired from their jobs in Germany and Austria converged with the opportunism of a young Turkish republic (1923–30) eager to Westernize by instituting 'reforms' within the academy (often at the expense of scholars already there). It is nothing short of historical irony that in many cases a Turk's job lost was a German's job gained. Firings, at both ends, were crucial to the formation of this humanism at large. In hindsight, one wonders whether émigré professors in Turkey were aware of the Turkish government's manipulation of their circumstances. Did they know, for example, that in 1932 the government had commissioned a Swiss pedagogue named Albert Malche to write a report on the state of the Istanbul Darülfünun (as it was then called), used to justify mass dismissals of Turkish faculty in 1933?[26] Malche's scathing report recommended complete overhaul of the university, citing insufficient publications, inferior foreign language training and inadequate scientific instruction. In his agenda for reform, he envisioned a cosmopolitan university with professors from 'Berlin, Leipzig, Paris or

24. Victor Klemperer, *I Will Bear Witness: A Diary of the Nazi Years*, vol. I (1933–41), trans. Martin Chalmers, New York, 1999, pp. 175 and 178, respectively.
25. Harry Dember to Victor Klemperer in Victor Klemperer, *The Language of the Third Reich: LTI – Lingua Tertii Imperii A Philologist's Notebook*, trans. Martin Brady, London, 2000, p. 159. Further references to this work will appear in the text abbreviated LTI.
26. For an account of Malche's role in the reform, see Horst Widmann, *Exil und Bildungshilfe: Die deutschsprachige akademische Emigration in die Türkei nach 1933*, pp. 45–8.

Chicago'. This cosmopolitan culture, he insisted, would be the only guarantor against single schools becoming dominant. Charged with a global recruitment mission, he received acceptances of his offers mainly from German or German-speaking professors.[27] It was Malche, working closely with an organization charged with placing German scholars abroad – 'Notgemeinschaft deutscher Wissenschaftler in Ausland' – who helped bring Spitzer to Istanbul. Spitzer's initial mandate was daunting: 'he was in charge of coordinating classes in four languages for several thousand students', 'lectured to his classes – through an interpreter – in French and used a multitude of other languages to communicate with his teaching staff'.[28]

Though the department that Spitzer built was in many respects an island of Eurocentric insularity, he was clearly more open than Auerbach was to engaging with Turkish culture, publishing an article, 'Learning Turkish' ('Turkceyi Ogrenirken'), in the journal *Varlik* (*Being*) in 1934. Though Auerbach spent over a decade in Istanbul,[29] he apparently never mastered the Turkish language, and there is little evidence to suggest seepage of his 'foreign' surround into *Mimesis*, or into his textbook *Introduction to Romance Languages and Literatures*, the latter 'written at Istanbul in 1943 in order to provide my Turkish students with a framework which would permit better to understand the origin and meaning of their studies'.[30] One can readily appreciate how Herbert Dieckmann (one of the 'star' German students formed by Auerbach in this period who later went on to a distinguished career as a literary critic, co-authoring the influential *Essays in Comparative*

27. Ibid.

28. Geoffrey Green, basing these assertions on an interview published by Spitzer in *The Johns Hopkins Magazine* April 1952. See *Literary Criticism and the Structures of History*, p. 105.

29. It is strange that Paul Bové does so little with the impact of Istanbul on Auerbach's work given his criticism of the inattention paid to 'the cultural and political roots' of Auerbach's work, and his argument that 'Auerbach's project of writing "a synthetic history-from-within" owes much to its own academic cultural context.' Ideally one would match Bové's useful reappraisal of the impact of Weimar culture and German modernism on Auerbach's thought with a discussion of the influence of Turkish alphabetization on Auerbach's analysis of literary language and its public. See Paul Bové, *Intellectuals in Power: A Genealogy of Critical Humanism*, New York, 1986, p. 79.

30. Erich Auerbach, *Introduction to Romance Languages and Literatures*, trans. from French by Guy Daniels, New York, 1961. The Turkish edition, translated by Süheyla Bayrav, appeared in 1944.

Literature with Harry Levin in 1961) could become an Enlightenment specialist in a purely European mould. Unless they went on
to become Turcologists (like Robert Anhegger or Andreas Tietze,
who founded Turkish studies at UCLA after working at Istanbul
University from 1938 to 1958), the non-Turkish students and
faculty in literature tended to hew to a standard European
curriculum. On the one hand, Auerbach endorsed the enlarged
cultural purview of his own generation of European philologists
(Vossler, Curtius and Spitzer), but, on the other, he was concerned to maintain exclusive boundaries around European civilization, keeping it 'from being engulfed in another, more
comprehensive unity', a unity that in today's parlance might
correspond to global comparatism.[31]

It comes as no surprise that Auerbach's *Introduction to Romance
Languages and Literatures* packages the Romance syllabus with few
concessions to his Turkish audience beyond the addition of a
chapter on Christianity. And yet, on closer inspection, the attention paid in this work to Romanization and the long-term impact
of Roman linguistic colonization on the history of European
languages might well be attributed to the fact that Auerbach bore
witness to the process of Romanization in Turkey.[32] Auerbach

---

31. Erich Auerbach, *Literatursprache und Publikum in der lateinischen Spätantike und
im Mittelalter*, Bern, 1958. Published in English as *Literary Language and its Public in
Late Latin Antiquity and in the Middle Ages*, trans. Ralph Mannheim, Princeton, 1965.
Adopting the same gloomy tone that one finds in the afterword to *Mimesis*,
Auerbach articulates his profoundly pessimistic fear that Western civilization would
be subsumed by modern global culture: 'European civilization is approaching the
term of its existence; its history as a distinct entity would seem to be at an end, for
already it is beginning to be engulfed in another, more comprehensive unity.
Today, however, European civilization is still a living reality within the range of
our perception. Consequently – so it seemed to me when I wrote these articles
and so I still believe – we must today attempt to form a lucid and coherent picture
of this civilization and its unity' (p. 6).

32. Thomas Hart has surmised that the break with tradition induced by the
banning of Arabic script 'may have reminded Auerbach of the loss entailed by the
decline of classical studies in the West', and in support of this claim he cites a
letter sent by Auerbach to Benjamin shortly after his arrival in Istanbul in
December 1936: 'Here all traditions have been thrown overboard in an attempt to
build a thoroughly rationalized state that will be both European and extremely
Turco-nationalistic. The whole process is being carried out with a fantastic and
unearthly speed [*es geht phantastisch und gespenstisch schnell*]; already it is hard to
find anyone who can read Arabic or Persian or even Turkish texts written in the
last century, since the language has been modernized and reoriented along purely
Turkish lines and is now written in roman letters.' Thomas R. Hart, 'Literature as
Language', pp. 230–1.

greeted the massive literacy campaign in which he himself was a participant with extreme pessimism (placing it in the wider context of a global standardization of culture – 'an International of triviality and a culture of Esperanto'),[33] but the issue of literacy became a crucial theme in his 1958 masterwork *Literary Language and its Public in Late Latin Antiquity and in the Middle Ages*. Here he showed how linguistic 'conservatism' – the grammatical stability of literary Latin that resulted from efforts made during the late Roman republic to standardize spelling and grammar – helped form a literary public that in turn guaranteed the legacy of Western culture. Though it remains a matter of speculation as to whether or not the standardization of modern Turkish directly inspired Auerbach's *Literary Language and its Public*, it seems safe to assume that Turkey's self-colonizing policy of *translatio imperii* afforded compelling parallels to imperial Rome. Auerbach argues that the stability of Latin as a literary language was crucial to the formation of a literary public during the Empire. After imperial decline, written Latin endured as a language of law and religion because 'there was no other written language and because it had long served, with the same homogeneity and the same conservatism . . . as the specialized language of the various branches of public life'.[34]

Varlik, the journal of art, literature and politics in which Spitzer's 'Learning Turkish' was published, can be seen as a direct outgrowth of the language reforms of 1928 instituted by the newly minted Turkish Republic. It is difficult to overestimate the impact of these reforms on Turkish politics and culture. Abolishing the Arabic alphabet used in Ottoman writing and abruptly introducing a phonetic, Romanized modern Turkish script, Atatürk effectively rendered the older educated classes illiterate, while ensuring that the next generation would be unable to access historical archives, legal documents or the Ottoman literary tradition.[35] Spitzer's article on 'Learning Turkish', appearing as it did under a rubric called 'language debates' that attracted contri-

---

33. As cited by Barck, 'Walter Benjamin and Erich Auerbach', p. 82.

34. Áuerbach, *Literary Language*, p. 252.

35. For a fascinating discussion of how the theme of intergenerational language loss, acquisition and recovery informs the work of a modern Turkish writer living in Germany, see Azade Seyhan's examination of Emine Sevgi Ozadamar's *Mutterzunge* (1994) in *Writing Outside the Nation*, Princeton, 2001, pp. 118–19.

butions from Turkish intellectuals ranging from university professors to the Minister of Education, must thus be situated in the political maelstrom of this literacy revolution.

Spitzer and Auerbach published substantial essays on philology alongside the work of their students in the Istanbul university journal – *Publications de la faculté des lettres de l'Université d'Istanbul* – edited by Auerbach. The table of contents of the 1937 issue, which included Spitzer's Romanology seminar, attests to its cosmopolitan reach:

Azra Ahat, 'Uslup ilminde yeni bir usul'
Eva Buck, ' "Die Fabel" in "Pointed Roofs" von Dorothy Richardson'
Rosemarie Burkart, 'Truchement'
Herbert Dieckmann, 'Diderots Naturempfinden und Lebensgefühl'
Traugott Fuchs, 'La première poésie de Rimbaud'
Hans Marchand, 'Indefinite Pronoun "one" '
Sabahattin Eyüboglu, 'Türk Halk Bilmeceleri'
Leo Spitzer, 'Bemerkungen zu Dantes "Vita Nuova" '
Süheyla Sabri, 'Un passage de "Barlaan y Josaiat" '
Erich Auerbach, 'Über die ernste Nachahmung des Alltäglichen'.[36]

It is tempting to read this table of contents as the *in vitro* paradigm of a genuinely globalized comparative literature, as evidence of critical reading practices that bring the globe inside the text. Though merely a coda of working papers, it offers a glimpse into the way in which European humanism 'Atatürk-style' (that is, attuned to Turkey's modernizing agenda) played a key role in transforming German-based philology into a global discipline that came to be known as comparative literature when it assumed its institutional foothold in postwar humanities departments in the United States.[37] The contributions of young Turkish

---

36. The translated essay titles are: Azra Ahat, 'A New Method in Studies of Style' (a study of Spitzer's word art); Eva Buck, ' "Colour" in Dorothy Richardson's "Pointed Roofs" '; Rosemarie Burkart, 'Go-Between'; Herbert Dieckmann, 'Diderot's Nature-Empathy and Life Feeling'; Traugott Fuchs, 'The Early Poetry of Rimbaud'; Sabahattin Eyüboglu, 'Turkish Anonymous Riddles'; Leo Spitzer, 'Remarks on Dante's "Vita Nuova" '; Süheyla Sabri, 'Un passage from "Barlaan and Josaiat" '; Erich Auerbach, 'On the Serious Imitation of the Everyday'.

37. When comparative literature took root as a postwar discipline in the US, the European traditions were dominant, the Turkish chapter of its life was effaced. What attracted the American academics was European erudition. As Carl Landauer notes, in his consideration of 'Auerbach's Performance and the American Academy, or How New Haven Stole the Idea of *Mimesis*', the idea of the 'virtuoso performer created by the author of *Mimesis* in Istanbul in the 1940s played

scholars to the seminar publications are particularly significant in this regard. Azra Ahat, whose essay treated Spitzer's methodology and word art, dedicated her career to the translation of Greek and Latin classics for a state-sponsored project to create a modern library for the new Turkish Republic. The library formed part of a concerted mission to 'Greekify' Turkey and thereby consolidate the state's efforts to establish non-Islamic, anti-Ottoman cultural foundations on which secular nationalism could be built. Initiatives as far-ranging as the 'Blue Cruises' (boat trips featuring sites of Greco-Roman civilization along Turkish shores) or the government's investment in classical philology in the university system were linked to the myth of Turkey as a new Greece. The appropriation of classicism for the purposes of cultural prestige and national identity is a familiar enough move since imperial Rome, but in the specific context of Atatürk's reforms it took on new implications, forcing comparative literature, in its nascent form, to renegotiate its relation to nationalism (the émigré generation tended to be *anti*-nationalist in reaction against the hyper-nationalist Nazi *Kulturkampf*), and opening up philological humanism to historic debates over 'who claims Greece' in the Balkans, the countries bordering the Black Sea and Asia Minor.[38]

If the complex relationship between classical philology and nationalism was represented in the Spitzer seminar through the work of Ahat and her associates, the seminar also acted as a laboratory for working through what a philological curriculum in literary studies should look like when applied to non-European languages and cultures. Spitzer's assistant Sbahattin Eyuboglu, an

---

perfectly to American audiences of the 1950s'. 'But Auerbach was not alone,' Landauer writes, 'for a number of émigré scholars with their obvious erudition and their mastery of an enormous range of cultural artifacts became prized possessions of their adopted culture, so that reviews of books by Kantorowicz, Panofsky, Cassirer, Jaeger, Spitzer, Kristeller, and Auerbach seem to blend into one another. It was not just an encyclopedic range that marked these scholars but a sense that they brought a certain "depth" to the study of culture and history from which Americans could learn. It was, then, as a masterful scholar and a translator of European "depth" that the author of *Mimesis* made his name in an American academy looking for exactly such exemplars.' in Lerer, ed., *Literary History and the Challenge of Philology*, p. 180.

38. This appropriation of Greek culture in Turkey must be considered against the backdrop of the history of Greek minorities in the region. See Stathis Gregouris, *Dream-Nation: Enlightenment, Colonization and the Institution of Modern Greece*, Stanford, 1996. See also Neal Ascheson's *Black Sea: The Birthplace of Civilization and Barbarism*, London, 1996.

editor of *Varlik* and a strong participant in the language debates, was a crucial player on this front, adapting Spitzer's methods to analyses of folk tales, stories and poems written in Turkish vernacular tongues. Eyuboglu's predilection for linguistic and generic morphology, as well as Süheyla Bayrav's work on morphology, tilted old-school philology towards formalism.[39] With the arrival of Benveniste and Greimas (who introduced the structural linguistics of Roman Jakobson), Istanbul assumes renewed importance in literary history and theory, from philological humanism to semiotics and structuralism.

Philology Wars

Spitzer's seminar in Istanbul was obviously not an inaugural or unique example of global comparatism. The idea is as old as that of culture itself, and extremely widespread, especially if one takes into account successive generations of avant-garde writers and intellectuals working on journals or political initiatives outside the academy and within transnational circuits of exchange. Nonetheless, Spitzer's seminar would seem to afford an example of global *translatio* with contemporary relevance in so far as it furnished the blueprint for departments of comparative literature established in the postwar period. I would like to suggest that comparative literature continues to this day to carry traces of the city in which it took disciplinary form; a site where East–West boundaries were culturally blurry, and where layers of colonial history obfuscated the outlines of indigenous cultures. Edward Said was clearly aware of the importance of Auerbach's location in Istanbul when he chose him as a disciplinary figurehead of *Weltliteratur* in exile. Paul Bové maintains convincingly that Auerbach bequeathed to Said a 'critical humanism', whose 'progressive secular potential' Said would spend much of his career seeking to fulfil.[40] I would add here that Said might have made his case for retaining Auerbach as a precursor of his own brand of secular humanism even stronger had he been more familiar with the story of Spitzer in Istanbul.

---

39. This information is based on an interview with Professor Süyehla Bayrav: see note 15 above.

40. Bové, *Intellectuals in Power*, p. xiii.

It may seem forced to resurrect Spitzer as a figure of transnational humanism *avant la lettre*, but the stakes in construing this figure are high, since laying claim to comparatism's philological heritage is synonymous with securing symbolic capital in the humanities. Carrying the illustrious tradition of Renaissance humanism into modern scholarship, and having, so to speak, mapped the etymological genome, philology claims a long history of shaping literary institutions and national politics.[41] As Bernard Cerquiglini has observed: 'At the dawn of the nineteenth century, extremely diverse phenomena of order, nature, and evolution all seemed to converge, forming a coherent semantics connected with the practice and study of texts. Philology is the most significant expression of this coherence. Its history is the history of our spontaneous philosophy of the textual.'[42] For Michael Holquist, philology and, more broadly, the study of language allowed Wilhelm von Humboldt, Johann Fichte, Friedrich Schleiermacher and Friedrich Schelling to 'resolve the Kantian paradox of how to institutionalize autonomy' in the context of the newly formed Berlin University, itself, of course, the template for the American academy.[43]

Even if one insists, as does Andreas Huyssen, that the Kantian ideal of secular humanism embodied in German philology became irredeemably tainted by the worst kind of German nationalism, philology's history contains distinguished counter-examples. Victor Klemperer kept his will to survive intact during the Second World War by devoting himself to his 'philologist's notebook' (referred to affectionately as his 'SOS sent to myself' or 'secret formula'), a meticulous chronicle of the damages of Nazi diction to everyday life. Klemperer employed the Latin expression *Lingua Tertii Imperii* (or LTI for short) when designating the Language of the Third Reich.[44] By retrieving the Roman legacy of

---

41. On the problem of philology and genetics see my essay, 'The Human in the Humanities', *October*, 96, Spring 2001, pp. 71–85.

42. Bernard Cerquiglini, *In Praise of the Variant: A Critical History of Philology*, trans. Betsy Wing, Baltimore, 1999, p. xiv.

43. Michael Holquist, *Association of Departments of Foreign Languages Bulletin*, vol. 33, no. 2, Winter 2002, p. 18.

44. Klemperer treated LTI almost as if it were a linguistic totem warding off the evil effects that Nazism wrought upon language. In his posthumously published book he wrote: 'The label LTI first appears in my diary as a playful little piece of parody, almost immediately afterwords as a laconic *aide-mémoire*, like a knot in a

translatio imperii and reconnecting it to the *lingua imperii* of the Third Reich, he not only drew an analogy between Nazi and Roman linguistic imperialism, he also emphasized the very particular contempt for original meaning that characterizes translation under conditions of conquest. In this view, he seems to have subscribed to the position of his fellow philologist Hugo Friedrich, who drew on Saint Jerome's assertion that 'The translator considers thought content a prisoner (*quasi captivos sensus*) which he transplants into his own language with the prerogative of a conqueror (*iure victoris*).' 'This', Hugo concluded, 'is one of the most rigorous manifestations of Latin cultural and linguistic imperialism, which despises the foreign word as something alien but appropriates the foreign meaning in order to dominate it through the translator's own language.'[45] For Klemperer, Nazi discourse provided a comparable model of language domination. In examining the term *Strafexpedition* (punitive expedition), a word initially registered in the speech of a former family friend and the first term recognized as being specifically National Socialist, he noted 'the embodiment of brutal arrogance and contempt for people who are in any way different, it sounded so colonial, you could see the encircled Negro village, you could hear the cracking of the hippopotamus whip' (LTI 43). Klemperer discerned in Nazi language a similar pattern of violent semantic usurpation to the one that Friedrich ascribes to Roman translations, even though the language of the original in the Nazi case was one and the same with the target. This *intralingual* or German-to-German translation (in Jakobson's terms a 'rewording', or 'interpretation of verbal signs by means of other signs in the same language'[46]) covered a host of travesties. There was what Klemperer called the 'poisoning of the drinking water of language', an expression applied to the casual adoption of Nazi-sanctioned words by ordinary citizens as in the case of a co-worker who,

---

handkerchief, and then very soon, and for the duration of those terrible years, as an act of self-defence, an SOS sent to myself. A tag with a nice erudite ring – the Third Reich itself after all delighted from time to time in the rich sonority of a foreign expression' (LTI 9).

45. Hugo Friedrich, 'On the Art of Translation' (trans. Rainer Schulte and John Biguenet) in Rainer Schulte and John Biguenet, eds, *Theories of Translation: An Anthology of Essays from Dryden to Derrida*, Chicago, 1992, pp. 12–13.

46. Roman Jakobson, 'On Linguistic Aspects of Translation', Schulte and Biguenet, eds, in *Theories of Translation*, p. 145.

without apparent malice, falls into using words like *artfremd* (alien), *deutschblütig* (of German blood), *niederrassig* (of inferior race) or *Rassenschande* (racial defilement). There was semantic substitution – the replacement of the word *Humanität*, for example (with its 'stench of Jewish liberalism'), by the 'manly' term *Menschlichkeit*) – which went along with the programme of germanicizing lexical roots and stamping out 'foreign' etymons. Klemperer also noted the Nazi technologization of language, the new privileging of a verb like *aufziehen*, meaning 'to wind up a clock or mechanical toy' or 'mount warp on a loom'. In conjuring up automatic, robotic actions that are both comic and deadening, the verb mimicked the hollow, de-animating rhetoric of Nazi speeches or the goose-step march. And then there was the prevalence of pictograms capable of emitting subliminal psychological messages. Klemperer decodes the letters SS sported by the Nazi Storm Troopers as a rune based on the visual appropriation of a common symbol for 'Danger – High Voltage!'[47]

Klemperer's powerful use of philology as a prophylactic against Nazi-think (complementing the strategic use made of philologically trained literary critics such as I. A. Richards and Leo Marx, both deployed as cryptographers during the war) bears directly on the politics behind Spitzer and Auerbach's philological practice during the war. It is a 'resistance' philology with an impeccable ethical pedigree, which is perhaps one reason why the fight over 'who claims philology' continues in the context of contemporary canon and culture wars. Charles Bernheimer's *Comparative Literature in the Age of Multiculturalism* (1995) may be read in this light as a turf battle with Lionel Gossman and Mihai Spariosu's *Building a Profession: Autobiographical Perspectives on the History of Comparative Literature in the United States* (1994). In the former essay collection the critics tend to frame postcolonial theory as the logical outcome of comparative literature's poly-

---

47. Klemperer writes: 'Long before the Nazi SS even existed, its symbol was to be seen painted in red on electricity substations, and below it the warning 'Danger – High Voltage!' In this case the jagged S was obviously a stylized representation of a flash of lightning. That thunderbolt, whose velocity and capacity for storing energy made it such a popular symbol for the Nazis! Thus the SS character was also a direct embodiment, a painterly expression of lightning. Here the double line may well suggest increased energy, because the little black flags of the children's formations only bore one jagged bolt, what you might call a half-SS' (LTI 68–9).

glot, international heritage, whereas in the latter, the postcolonial turn, if recognized at all, is positioned as a reductive politicization of comparative literature's distinguished European foundations.[48] Though the stakes involved in these most recent philology wars appear academic and parochial in comparison to those of Klemperer et al., they are linked to critical problems, ranging from the cultural implications of literary methodology, to rethinking 'world literature' beyond Anglocentric parameters of the 'foreign' languages, to the question of whether European humanism will continue to have traction in the global marketplace of culture.

In the battle zone of Europe pro and con, Saidian humanism has remained a major flashpoint. Said's 1978 watershed book *Orientalism*, together with his notion of 'contrapuntal reading', introduced in *Culture and Imperialism* (which stressed 'simultaneous awareness both of the metropolitan history that is narrated and of those other histories against which [and together with which] the dominating discourse acts'), have been assailed on the grounds that they shortchange aesthetic value by reducing texts to sociological example, while fostering 'victim studies' and anti-humanism.[49] But, as Herbert Lindenberger reminds us, when Auerbach's *Mimesis* was attacked on the left for its Eurocentrism in the early 1980s, it was none other than Edward Said who rescued it as a model work of broad cultural authority and *Weltliteratur*, earning him, at least in Lindenberger's estimation, the Auerbachian mantle.[50]

Saidian humanism views Europe from outside Europe ('provincializing' it, to borrow Dipesh Chakrabarty's phrase), while roundly criticizing the habit of referring to traditions such as Islam in an impacted, monolithic way.[51] 'It is very much the case

48. For more background on the disciplinary schisms within comparative literature induced by the advent of postcolonial theory, see my essay 'Comparative Exile: Competing Margins in the History of Comparative Literature', in Charles Bernheimer, ed., *Comparative Literature in the Age of Multiculturalism*, Baltimore and London, 1995, pp. 86–96.

49. Edward Said, *Culture and Imperialism*, New York, 1993, p. 51.

50. Herbert Lindenberger, 'On the Reception of *Mimesis*', in Lerer, ed., *Literary History and the Challenge of Philology* p. 209. My thanks to Howard Bloch for bringing this article to my attention.

51. Dipesh Chakrabarty, *Provincializing Europe: Postcolonial Thought and Historical Difference*, Princeton, 1999.

today', Said would argue in *Representations of the Intellectual*, 'that
in dealing with the Islamic world – all one billion people in it,
with dozens of different societies, half a dozen major languages
including Arabic, Turkish, Iranian, all of them spread out over
about a third of the globe – American or British academic
intellectuals speak reductively and, in my view, irresponsibly of
something called "Islam." '[52] Taking translingual perspectivalism
as an a priori, Saidian humanism pivots on the vision of the
intellectual who refuses to see languages and cultures in isolation.
What legitimates the intellectual's claim to knowledge and freedom is a sensitivity to the demography of Babel.[53] The radical side
of Saidian humanism – its agitation of the status quo and refusal
of congruence with the contoured, habituated environments
called home – lies, I would suggest, not so much in its philological
ecumenicalism (which could easily become watered-down linguistic multiculturalism), but, rather, in its attachment to the shock
value of cultural comparison.

If, instead of taking Auerbach for its *Ansatzpunkt* (and by
extension, the fetish of 'exile' since the record shows that Auerbach was in pretty good cosmopolitan company during his Istanbul sojourn), Saidian humanism had started with Spitzer, it might
have gleaned from Spitzer's critique of Ernst Robert Curtius – the
scholar who swooped in to take his job just as he was dispatched
to Istanbul – its very own practice of a 'lightened' philology; a
philology that has shed its 'solidity', 'aridity', 'asceticism' and
'mediaeval garb'.[54] Said's memoir *Out of Place* exemplifies this
culturally lightened and globally expanded philology, placing
Shakespeare with Shirley Temple, Kant *avec* Wonderwoman. The
narrative mobilizes a lexicon in which American product labels
are grafted onto Arabic and Anglophone expressions. The anom-
alous acoustic effect of words like Ping Pong and Dinky Toy vie
with Britishisms (BBC, Greenwich Mean Time) and local brand

---

52. Edward Said, *Representations of the Intellectual*, New York, 1994, p. 31.
53. See his statement: 'The intellectual is fundamentally about knowledge and
freedom' (ibid., p. 59).
54. Leo Spitzer, *American Journal of Philology*, 70 (n.d.,) pp. 425–6. As cited by
Hans Ulrich Gumbrecht, '"Zeitlosigkeit, die durchscheint in der Zeit": Über E. R.
Curtius' unhistorisches Verhältnis zur Geschichte', in Walter Berschin and Arnold
Rothe, eds. *Ernst Robert Curtius: Werk, Wirkung, Zukunftperspektiven*, Heidelberg,
1989, pp. 233–4.

names ('Chabrawichi cologne') on a single page.[55] 'Like the objects we carried around and traded, our collective language and thought were dominated by a small handful of perceptibly banal systems deriving from comics, film, serial fiction, advertising and popular lore that was essentially at street level,' Said tells us, as if to dispel any temptation to make humanism the high serious preserve of an indigenous culture untouched by global capitalism and trademark literacy (OP 205). Said's sense of marvel at the way in which the coinage of popular culture interacts with the hard currency of European aesthetics recalls, perhaps not surprisingly, Spitzer's landmark 1949 essay, 'American Advertising Explained as Popular Art', in which he analysed the Sunkist orange juice logo as a modern-day equivalent of mediaeval heraldic insignia.

So, given this Spitzerian lineage, who, for Said, might embody Spitzer in transnational times? In *Out of Place* the author's family friend Charles Malik emerges as the most obvious choice, despite Said's political differences with him. A spokesman for Palestine in the 1940s and a former UN ambassador for Lebanon, he became a professor of philosophy at the American University of Beirut, having studied with Heidegger in Freiburg and Whitehead at Harvard (OP 264). With his 'strong north Lebanese village (Kura) accent affixed to a sonorously European English', Malik becomes, in Said's ascription, a kind of Spitzer of the Middle East, demonstrating fluency in English, Arabic, German, Greek and French, while ranging, in conversation, from Kant, Fichte, Russell, Plotinus and Jesus Christ, to Gromyko, Dulles, Trygve Lie, Rockefeller and Eisenhower (OP 266).

Though Said himself (by his own account) never rivals Malik's language proficiency, his intellectual interests and accomplishments – in music, politics and literary criticism – make him an equally compelling example of the secular humanist. As a 'self-reader' he is mindful of the *translational* transnationalism of humanism, a condition that, I would surmise, is ultimately more significant for the future of humanism than the premium placed on exile throughout many of his writings. Reading the hyphenations of his identity as a 'Palestinian-Arab-Christian-American', or

---

55. Edward Said, *Out of Place: A Memoir*, New York, 1999, p. 205. Hence forward abbreviated as OP in text.

the mutations of his own name at various stations of life, Said is above all a self-translator. In Cairo, he is 'Edward', a symbol of Arab Anglophilia. In his father's stationery store, he is 'Mister Edward' or 'Edward Wadie'. And in Mount Herman boarding school, he is Americanized as 'Ed Said', which on the page begs to have the second name pronounced to rhyme with the first. 'Ed Said' becomes a place-holder for the expectation of speech, as in: 'Ed said . . . what?' What Said says, it turns out, is flush with the polyvalent associations around his name, now, in its own right, a transnationally circulating signifier of global comparatism, ethical militance, exilic humanism and contrapuntal reading practices. But this over-reading of a name begs the question of defining transnational humanism; shifting the burden of definition to identity, and thereby evading the complex issue of how transnational humanism selects for culture; that is to say, how it excludes as well as culls a philological example from an unsorted jumble of texts. To give this problem its due, one must reflect more fully on the role played by philology in reaching for connections across languages, while at the same time respecting the recalcitrance of the original.

Global *Translatio*

Looking again more closely at the table of contents of the Istanbul literary review, a paradigm of *translatio* emerges that emphasizes the critical role of multilingualism within transnational humanism. The juxtaposition of Turkish, German and French attests to a policy of *non-translation* adopted without apology. Spitzer's own contributions are exemplary here; in each individual essay one hears a cacophony of untranslated languages. And as a literary critic in command of French, German, Hebrew, Hungarian, Latin, Greek, Italian, English, Provençal, Spanish, Portuguese, Catalan, Romanian, Gothic, Anglo-Saxon, Sanskrit, Lithuanian, Old Church Slavonic, Albanian, Neo-Greek (and now, we ascertain, Turkish as well), he had many languages to choose from. It was, of course a common practice among highly educated European literary scholars to leave passages and phrases free-standing in a naked state of untranslation. For Spitzer non-translation was a hallowed principle of his method, enunciated most famously in a starred passage of the famous 1948 essay 'Linguistics and Literary History'.

> *The frequent occurrence, in my text, of quotations in the original foreign language (or languages) may prove a difficulty for the English reader. But since it is my purpose to take the word (and the wording) of the poets seriously, and since the convincingness and rigor of my stylistic conclusions depends entirely upon the minute linguistic detail of the original texts, it was impossible to offer translations. [Since the linguistic range of readers of literary criticism is not always as great as Spitzer's, the editors of this volume decided to provide translations.][56]

The editors' remarks in brackets are literally beside the point. Their well-meaning pandering to Anglophone readers may well facilitate accessibility, but it renders moot Spitzer's explicit desire to disturb monolingual complacency. Spitzer inserted this note not just to admonish his readers to refer to the original, but to insist on their confrontation with linguistic strangeness. In allowing the foreign-ness of the original to 'shine through', he resembles the ideal Benjaminian translator for whom the model translation is a scriptural 'interlinear' rewording, proximate to the original to the point of being, almost, no translation at all.[57]

Spitzer's practice of non-translation is not an argument against translation per se, but, rather, a bid to make language acquisition a categorical imperative of *translatio studii*. A profound respect for the foreign-ness of a foreign language – of foreign-ness as the sign of that which is beyond assimilation within language itself – motivated Spitzer's plurilingual dogma, allowing him to be linked, albeit somewhat anomalously, to Benjamin, Adorno and de Man. Adorno's paraphrase of how 'Benjamin spoke of the author inserting the silver rib of the foreign word into the body of language' shows how important this idea of the foreign became to critical theory. The rib represents Hebbel's 'schism of creation': in 'sticking out', Adorno noted, it embodies 'suffering in language' and 'in reality as well'.[58] Adorno's formulation echoes in Paul de Man's idea of translation as 'the suffering of the

---

56. Leo Spitzer, 'Linguistics and Literary History', in *Leo Spitzer: Representative Essays*, p. 35.
57. Walter Benjamin, 'The Task of the Translator', in *Illuminations*, trans. Willard Trask, New York, 1969, p. 82.
58. Theodor Adorno, 'Words from Abroad', in *Notes to Literature*, trans. Shierry Weber Nicholsen, 2 vols, New York, 1991, vol. 2, pp. 187–8.

original' ('die Wehen des eigenen'), by which he refers to the 'bottomless depth of language, something essentially destructive, which is language itself'.[59] Responding to questions posed after a lecture he gave on *The Task of the Translator* at the very end of his career, de Man contended that what was interesting about Benjamin's 'language of historical pathos, language of the messianic, the pathos of exile and so forth', was the fact that it 'really describes linguistic events which are by no means human' (RT 96).[60] De Man then associates Benjamin's 'pains of the original' with 'structural deficiencies which are best analyzed in terms of the inhuman, dehumanized language of linguistics, rather than into the language of imagery, or tropes, of pathos, or drama, which he chooses to use in a very peculiar way' (RT 96). De Man dries out the residual humanism of Benjamin's sacred language (*reine Sprache*), and turns it into something technical, 'purely linguistic'. Though Spitzer's humanist credo of linguistic foreign-ness for its own sake and de Man's theory of linguistic inhuman-ism may seem very far apart, they come together in a common love for linguistic foreign-ness.

Spitzer's abiding respect for the integrity of individual languages resonated in the concluding remarks of his lecture on 'Development of a Method', delivered four months prior to his death in 1960. Adopting a credo of linguistic serial monogamy, he posits that each and every language, at the time of the critic's engagement with it, lays claim absolutely to his or her uncondi-tional love:

> . . . philology is the *love* for works written in a particular *language*. And if the methods of a critic must be applicable to works in all languages in order that the criticism be convincing, the critic, at least at the moment when he is discussing the poem, must love *that* language and *that* poem more than anything else in the world. (RE 448, emphases in the original)

Now even if Spitzer failed to demonstrate the same degree of passion for Turkish as for classical, Germanic and Romance

---

59. Paul de Man, 'Conclusions: Walter Benjamin's "The Task of the Translator"', in *The Resistance to Theory*, Minneapolis, 1986, pp. 84–5. Further references to this work will appear in the text abbreviated RT.

60. For a further discussion of the status of the human in Spitzer and de Man, see my 'The Human in the Humanities'.

languages, he placed Turkish on an equal footing as a language worthy of love. And in his essay 'Learning Turkish', he showed more affection for the language than one might expect, comparing the effort of a linguist in mid-career trying to learn Turkish to 'the situation of an old person learning to ski', a figure of speech connoting, on the one hand, *le démon de midi* (mid-life crisis), and, on the other, the pulse-quickening thrill of dangerous liaisons. Despite the fact that he is no expert in Turcology, and despite his rudimentary grasp of the language, the intrepid philologist throws himself willy-nilly into analysing the word for 'veil' – *Kaçgöç* (meaning 'the flight of women when a man enters the house', 'the necessity for women to hide and escape from men'). Focusing on its usage in a Turkish novel called *Casual Things*, Spitzer draws parallels with Roman carnival masks, and links the word to the expression 'this is no laughing matter' in Balkan languages.

Below its philological surface, Spitzer's explication resembles a classic captivity narrative, in which the European gentleman rescues Turkish womanhood from the clutches of Muslim repression. And Spitzer's conclusion – that the spirit of the Turkish people inclines more towards emotionalism than logic – falls prey to familiar Eurocentric refrains. But the 'love' of Turkish is manifest, evident in the author's admission of 'inferiority' in the face of a language with so old and venerable a tradition, and discernible in the second part of the essay, in which he searches in vain among the European languages for the spiritual equivalent of Turkish expressions of prudence and precaution. By the time we get to Part III, Turkish has become a language uniquely blessed with a quality Spitzer names 'symbolical hearing', or 'psychophonics'. This subtle parallelism between 'real and phonetic resemblances' lends itself to fantastic abilities to represent the mood of reality, emerging, in this regard, as the non-Western corollary of the German *Stimmung* or 'atmosphere', to which Spitzer devoted an entire book. Muting his earlier dismissal of Turkish 'emotionalism', Spitzer, by the time he reaches the essay's third section, is extolling the calibration of abstraction and reality unique to the Turkish language. Though he never states the case in so many words, his reading challenges the shibboleth that Indo-European languages are superior because of their higher incidence of abstraction.

In disrespecting narrowly construed East–West dichotomies, in learning Turkish (in learning, even, to love a non-Romanic language), and in establishing a seminar in which Turkish assumed its place alongside European languages as a subject field of philological research and criticism, Spitzer forged a worldly paradigm of *translatio studii* with strong links to the history, both past and present, of *translatio imperii*. The strange parallelism of Latinization during the Middle Ages, Romanization under Atatürk in the 1920s, and the institutionalization of the Language of the Third Reich under Nazism produced a heightened awareness of the political complexities of linguistic imperialism in the work of European émigré scholars, even when they defined their pedagogical mission around the preservation of High Latinity's cultural remains. Scanning the grammars of the world in search of connections that unlocked the secrets of a cultural unconscious, tracking, to paraphrase Geoffrey Hartman, 'the sources and intentions that turn words into psychic etymologies, even at the risk of destroying the identity of the sign', Spitzer's seminar yielded a linguistically focused world-systems theory that stands as a counterweight to Moretti's narrative-based paradigms of distant reading.[61] If distant reading privileges outsized categories of cultural comparison – national epic, the 'planetary' laws of genre – philology affords its micrological counterpart as close reading with a worldview: word histories as world histories; stylistics and metrics in diaspora. Where Auerbach, according to David Damrosch, established an ethics of textual autonomy in which texts discover order and relationality because they are 'allowed to live freely', Spitzer created a similar ethics for the language of the original, whereby originals are not surrendered to translations, but, instead, find each other freely, attempting connection even at the risk of failure and shock.[62] The practice of global *translatio*, as Spitzer defined it, is patterned after untranslatable affective gaps, the nub of intractable semantic difference, episodes of

---

61. Geoffrey Hartman, *The Fate of Reading*, Chicago, 1975, p. 121. See also, Hartman's *The Fateful Question of Culture* (New York, 1997) for a discussion of the contrast between the idea of culture that arose from émigré cosmopolitanism and culture as it is being defined within a globalized literary studies today.

62. David Damrosch, 'Auerbach in Exile', *Comparative Literature*, vol. 47, no. 2, Spring 1995, p. 109.

violent cultural transference and counter-transference, and unexpected love affairs. In retrospect, Spitzer's invention of comparative literature in Istanbul transformed philology into something recognizable today as the psychic life of transnational humanism.

5

Mapping Identities:
Literature, Nationalism, Colonialism

Timothy J. Reiss

For those who publicly study relations between literature and nation, poetics and imperialism, 'centres' and 'others' and associated matters, the temptation to adopt some high ground of rectitude is matched only by the danger of binary extremism. To have been born and raised in a European 'metropolitan' culture is to wear a mantle of guilt or carry the torch of civilization. Not to have been is to wear an aureole of glory or carry a duty to acquire universal values. Those who still uphold the latter positions believe they argue the good of a common humanity. Those adopting the former assert they argue an actual pluralism of humanity that their antagonists deny and crush beneath a self-serving oppression. For them, to dwell in the centres of high capitalism is to have to find a way to go 'all the way through' its foundational practices 'and out the other side'. So Terry Eagleton puts the matter in his contribution to *Nationalism, Colonialism, and Literature* (23).[1] To be sure, those born in evil must traverse 'the

This essay first appeared as a multi-review in *American Literary History*, vol. 4, no. 4, 1992, pp. 649–77. It is reprinted here (with changes) by permission of Oxford University Press. An expanded version is Chapter 2 of my *Against Autonomy: Global Dialectics of Cultural Exchange*, Stanford, CA: Stanford University Press, 2002.

1. Terry Eagleton, Fredric Jameson and Edward W. Said, *Nationalism, Colonialism, and Literature*, ed. Seamus Deane, Minneapolis: University of Minnesota Press, 1990. Henceforth cited in my text as NCL.

very metaphysical [and social] categories' they hope 'finally to abolish' and cannot 'live sheer irreducible difference *now*' (23–4). Still, although 'we have as yet no proper names' (24) for what that 'other' may be, its existence as the bright future of changed humanity is an attainable dream. It may not be '*now*', but it definitely has a when.

To think of cultural difference as the 'other' of metropolitan practices is a dilemma for all commentators on these topics, however they try to resolve it. And resolve it they must. Otherwise they repeat the colonizing gesture they criticize. In one sense, Eagleton notes, that is simply because the tools of our critical craft have largely been developed 'on a terrain already mapped out by [the] antagonists' in question (24). That is so whether or not the commentator is by origin 'metropolitan': for Homi Bhabha, Sylvia Molloy, Edward Said and Gregory Jusdanis (who claims for modern Greece a 'marginal' status), no less than for Eric Cheyfitz, Eagleton, Fredric Jameson and most authors in Bhabha's collection *Nation and Narration*.[2] For the latter, at least, there is a further complexity, one to which some are blinder than others. It concerns learning to listen, precisely, to differences; with trying to understand cultures in their own terms as wholes, rather than ingesting them as 'our' 'other'; with knowing that diverse cultural processes *do* exist, binding people in different relations and different understandings of being (for example), and that these must change our ideas of literature and criticism just because they question the claim of any culture to centrality or universality.[3] 'To be incapable of seeing that Nature has more than one face, that humans have a variety of ideas and interests,' wrote José Enrique Rodó a century ago, 'is to live in a shadowy dreamworld penetrated by a single ray of light.'[4]

This is not to denigrate the achievements of metropolitan cultures. It is to open up others and to open them up *to* others. To do so entails many tasks. The history of the invention of

---

2. These are the authors primarily under review, footnoted in due time.

3. I think especially of Ngũgĩ wa Thiong'o's *Moving the Centre: The Struggle for Cultural Freedoms*, London: James Currey, 1993. My own *Against Autonomy* (see note 1) tries to follow his spirit and references other works doing the same.

4. José Enrique Rodó, *Ariel*, trans. Margaret Sayers Peden, foreword James W. Symington, Prologue Carlos Fuentes, 1988, rpt Austin: University of Texas Press, 1989, p. 42.

metropolitan cultures has to be explored, to understand their mechanisms and their relation with other cultures, as Jusdanis tries to do for the modern Greek case. The ways in which different cultural arenas function and adopt processes found elsewhere is a subject addressed by Molloy and, to a degree, by Cheyfitz. Furthermore, the manner of such relations needs explaining. Most of the writers discussed here want to do this. But almost without exception, they posit cultural antagonisms taking the form of oppressor and oppressed, of colonizer and colonized. It is important to understand the mechanisms of dispossession, of internalized oppression, of identity bereft, of how cultural territory is mapped (a much-worked concept), but the similarities of explanation and vocabulary become slightly depressing. Further, seen through such spectacles, cultural territories inevitably fall into here and there, self and other. As an explanatory tool, the device may not be unhelpful. As an instrument of change – and that is what *all* these writers rightly want – it is less so. Such conflictual separations, such neat boxes of explanation, correspond neither to the reality of cultural meetings nor to the complexity of their creation.

Said argues in 'Yeats and Decolonization' that imperialism means a loss of the colonized place by its own natives as colonizers 'map' it, 'chart' it for themselves (NCL 77). The place gets a 'second nature'. Once so mapped, it no longer seems a colonial creation. To recover the place, the 'anti-imperialist nationalist' has to 'remap' it, people it with myths and religion, as well as find a language, by 'an almost magically inspired, quasi-alchemical redevelopment of the native language' (79). Such finding, such remapping, has to use the 'second nature' made by previous mappers at the same time as it draws on other cultural memories. What is so made has much to do with conflict, but nothing to do with simple polarities. (Said avers that Yeats never got beyond nativism, accepting imperialism's own defining gloss on the human, in terms of negritude, Irishness, Islam or whatever [89].)

Cultural categories mingle and float. 'Borders' are beyond porous, cultures mutually defining. The fault of European culture was to believe that they are not, that the burden of definition lay wholly on it – Rodó's 'single ray of light'. The challenge for contemporary critics working from within that arena is to avoid the trap of that belief. Simplified binarisms will not do it.

'Tell me, Askar,' asks that protagonist's Uncle Hilaal in Nurud-din Farah's novel *Maps*, 'do you find truth in the maps you draw?' Answered by silence, Hilaal clarifies his question: '[D]o you carve out of your soul the invented truth of the maps you draw? Or does the daily truth match, for you, the reality you draw and the maps others draw?' A pause ensues before Askar replies 'with the confidence of one who's regained possession of a mislaid identity':

> 'Sometimes,' I began to say, 'I identify *a* truth in the maps which I draw. When I identify *this* truth, I label it as such, pickle it as though I were to share it with you, and Salaado. I hope, as dreamers do, that the dreamt dream will match the dreamt reality – that is, the invented truth of one's imagination. My maps invent nothing. They copy a given reality, they map out the roads a dreamer has walked, they identify a notional truth'.[5]

In fact, Askar is mapping a Somalia that includes the Ogaden region and the lands for which the Western Somali Liberation Front is fighting against Ethiopia. His 'notional truth' could become a 'third nature', no less real than the present one. The creation of such national territory depends on people identifying it as such – and no less does their identity depend on it. But the maps with which Askar must perforce start, whether Mercator or decimal, are European in origin.

Farah writes of a quest for national and personal identity, recovery of things dispossessed. But his narrator, a voice switching continually between second, first and third person, traverses frontiers that move, gazes on seas that acquire changing mean-ings, delves into divers tales of his and others' pasts, explores the varieties of culture – why, for example, a long-lived written culture may have no 'single . . . genius of a poet', while one that has had a script for less than a century has 'many hundreds of major poets' – and wonders whether these very varieties let one rank cultures (*Maps* 201). These questions, including the last ethno-centric one (as Hilaal accuses), are those of all the present writers. For Farah, writing in 1986 from an unsettled place of struggle, these issues could only be matter for telling and retelling: 'in the process he became the defendant. He was, at one and the same

---

5. Nuruddin Farah, *Maps*, New York: Pantheon, 1986, p. 216. Henceforth cited in my text.

time, the plaintiff and the juror. Finally, allowing for his different
personae to act as judge, as audience and as witness, Askar told it
to himself' (246). These tellings, as this last sentence of the novel
indicates, can never escape forensic inquiry. No judgement is at
hand. The teller never gets beyond queries, however he and they
cry for resolution. He has nowhere to fix the bounds of an answer,
nowhere from whence to project the lines of an ordered cartography, no 'self' to give a source for the survey: 'no one has ever
explained how to read maps, you see, and I have difficulty
deciphering all the messages' (111).

Our many commentators rarely admit to such perplexities.
Evidently, if you see cultures as oppressors and victims, as sites of
historical conflict between takers and producers, as neatly
bounded spaces of difference, matters do become simpler. Alone,
that neither invalidates arguments nor makes them not worth
repeating. It limits their import. Introducing his anthology *Nationalism, Colonialism, and Literature*, Seamus Deane (like two of his
three authors) thus takes a rather uncomplicated view of Irish
culture and its relation to British nationalism. He notes how
revisionist Irish history, by seeing Irish–English relations in wholly
localized terms, and so too complex for systematic explanation,
tends to play the conqueror's game by veiling the effects of
conquest and denying they can be analysed. The Field Day
Theatre Company's view, he says of the group whose projects
include this anthology, is that culture can be analysed as a whole
and that Britain's imperialist role is essential to that analysis.
(However simplified the arguments of this collection may
become, they have an exact intention: to intervene practically and
theoretically in the politics of [Northern] Irish culture.)

Deane, like his colleagues and everyone else in the books
discussed here, rejects any view that claims a particular art as
universal: it is a 'specific activity indeed, but one in which the
whole history of a culture is deeply inscribed. The interpretation
of culture is not predicated on the notion that there is some
universal quality or essence that culture alone can successfully
pursue and capture. That is itself a political idea that has played
a crucial role in Irish experience' (NCL 7). Just those universalist
claims let one national culture impose itself on another, the latter
inevitably copying the former (7–8). 'At its most powerful, colonialism is a process of racial dispossession. A colonized people is

without a specific history and even, as in Ireland and other cases, without a specific language' (10). As Said says in the same collection, a first step is thus to regain a language of culture. The process is perforce communal, however it is lived in individual cases, and 'often begins with the demolition of the false stereotypes within which it has been entrapped. This is an intricate process, since the stereotypes are successful precisely because they have been interiorized' (12). It is one way, avers Eagleton here, that a hegemonic system 'continues to exert an implacable political force' (24).

For Eagleton agrees that the victim is forced to struggle in terms given by the oppressor (not so simple, Farah implies). So the fight 'will demand a difficult, perhaps ultimately impossible double optic, at once fighting on terrain already mapped out by its antagonists and seeking even now to prefigure within that mundane strategy styles of being and identity for which we have as yet no proper names' (NCL 24). Eagleton calls this double optic 'irony'. Joyce's *Ulysses* and *Finnegans Wake* may perform it. They offer, he asserts, a sardonic 'aesthetic totalization' of the Enlightenment 'opposition' between aesthetic particularity and abstract understanding: Dublin becomes at once an iteration of imperial centres and 'an expression of the rootless conditions of an international monopoly capitalism' (35). Ireland is given a centre that is no centre (34–7). Like Said's Yeats, Eagleton's Joyce reaches a threshold he cannot cross: colonialism 'is a *relation*' and a 'nation cannot live on as some corporate self-identical entity once those political relations have been dismantled' (28).

The point is well taken, but since both Deane and Eagleton start by positing bounded entities in conflict, matters end there. So they do in Jameson's essay in the collection, analysing 'varieties of imperialism' in E. M. Forster and again Joyce. *Howards End* shows imperialism as 'bad' infinity: a constant effort of movement that is 'the bad opposite of place itself': 'cosmopolitanism, London, the nomadic, the stench of motorcars, antibilious pills, all begin to coalesce as a single historical tendency' (NCL 57). In Forster this is 'Empire', a place of finally meaningless endless motion. To Jameson such lack of meaning marks the disjunction between a metropolis and the colonies that enable its life while remaining invisible to it. For the very operation of Empire is hidden from its metropolitan beneficiaries (50–1). In Dublin, however, Joyce finds place: enclosed, always already 'told', as it repeats, in minor key, the habitation of an older imperial dispensation (60) – where encounters and conversations evince 'an older urban life', a totalizing map that turns 'the great imperial space of the Mediterranean' into the closed 'space of the colonial city' (64). The view and polarity echo Eagleton's and Deane's.

Most authors in Bhabha's collection *Nation and Narration* adopt a similar view, though their multitude and variety rather impede commentary.[6] I belittle many subtleties of argument in paring them to a place in mine. They include efforts to show that even in the West's past, forms of patriotism offered a civic arena of debate akin to Habermas's public sphere, quite different from post-eighteenth-century nationalism, and opened ways to 'otherness' blocked by this later development (Simon During, John Barrell). Such views may have shared much with Rousseau's offering narration as an escape from nation-as-nature, relief from its violence and rediscovery of nature before violence: true nation (Geoffrey Bennington). Claims about historical binarisms are repeated, with more or less nuance, of nineteenth-century North American writing (David Simpson, Rachel Bowlby), twentieth-century English writing and criticism (Francis Mulhern, Gillian Beer) and current criticism in Australia, which, Sneja Gunew argues, opposes hegemonic tendencies through a supposedly 'counter-public sphere' (NN 99).

Although I am being reductively unjust to some of the authors, binary claims overwhelm the reader. They point to flaws widespread in this writing. These include neglecting the complications of history, taking parts for wholes and so thinking narrow argument to be broadly validated, confusing words and things, allowing for a certain ease of dogmatic assertion. Something of these practices has already been implied. I shall quickly take three cases, no doubt unfairly to the overall arguments advanced by their authors but indicative with regard to the issues I want to raise about discussions of literature, colonialism, nationalism and such other major bogeys of contemporary academic debate as multiculturalism, pluralism and the canon (all involving understandings of 'otherness').

---

6. Homi K. Bhabha, ed., *Nation and Narration*, London: Routledge, 1990. Henceforth cited in my text as NN.

For the first, trimming historical complexity, I query a claim made in Timothy Brennan's essay in Bhabha's anthology, not because it grounds his topic but because it is an article of faith in analyses concerning metropolitan literature and nationalism/ colonialism (Brennan furnishes such magic names as Mikhail Bakhtin, Eric Hobsbawm and Benedict Anderson). It is that the novel is intimately tied to the idea of the 'nation' and its sustaining myths. As the novel is made a creation of the European eighteenth century, the tie meshes happily with stated implications of a dialectic of Enlightenment and destruction of Reason. The claim gaily fits those of Bennington, Barrell, During and others about a generosity of debate having been lost in the eighteenth century. But the force of the relation depends, Brennan rightly sees, on a claim of novelty (overall, the assertion wants to tie capitalism, nationalism, imperialism and colonialism to new European cultural forms: so many eighteenth-century deviations).

So, Brennan holds, the novel's ancestor, epic, was, unlike the novel, never addressed 'to or for one's contemporaries' (NN 50). The genealogical claim is infirm, its collateral patently false: the *Aeneid, Divine Comedy, Lusiads, Orlando Furioso, Franciade, Gerusalemme Liberata, Faerie Queene, Pucelle* and even *Paradise Lost* all addressed contemporaries in specific ways. Most directly elaborated myths of national origin and achievement. The literary story *has* to be made complicated. Bhabha and his contributors, Deane and his colleagues, Jusdanis and many others, want to fix nation-making basically in the European nineteenth century. History will not allow this: at least not with regard to the cultural narrations that develop the idea – and wider activities, including, I have tried to show, the invention of literature itself.[7] Epics were not just 'ritualistic reaffirmations of a people' (50). They may not have sought to '*create* a people' (50); they most assuredly sought regularly to establish a dynastic legitimacy *for* a people. Some sense of 'national identity', of a localizable, differentiated community with which one could (and did) identify, with its own myths and tales, long pre-existed the European nineteenth century (as did its modern understanding of literature).

How far does this matter? For one thing it queries the blind-

---

7. Timothy J. Reiss, *The Meaning of Literature*, Ithaca: Cornell University Press, 1992.

nesses behind Bruce Robbins recalling in the same collection a question put to Raymond Williams by the editors of *New Left Review*. These signal my second issue: parts taken for wholes. The editors noted that (Williams's) literary criticism did not cope with the Irish famine or the 1848 revolutions and that this showed there was no path from novels to structures of feeling, real experience and social structures (NN 213).[8] Williams replied with the case of Dickens. Robbins does not query this reply. Both are emblematic. For while the *New Left Review may* be able to make their assertion of *a* novel, it is meaningless to make it of *the* novel: from Edgeworth and Austen to Balzac and Sue, La Roche and the Brontës to Turgenev and Tolstoy, Sand and Eliot to Melville and Hawthorne, Manzoni and Galdos to Dickens, Chernyshevsky and others named in Bhabha's collection, not to mention their many seventeenth- and eighteenth-century ancestors. The failure is again of the historical imagination (or worse). Somehow, unselfconsciously, all take a reputed English case as both exemplary and all-embracing. I once noted the odd reinscription in Eagleton's *Criticism and Ideology* of familiar but excoriated Great Tradition categories in his explanation of nineteenth-century (English) novels.[9] Jusdanis, in *Belated Modernity*, finds a like blindness in his *Function of Criticism*, which 'assumes the existence of a homogenous criticism and deems it unnecessary to mention that its real subject is English criticism'.[10]

The blindness of critics to their own historical situation and to the historical determinants of their chosen cultural object is not accidental. It is a factor of the very nationalism wherein they operate, at least if we are to believe Ernest Renan, translated in Bhabha's collection. 'Forgetting, I would even go so far as to say historical error, is a crucial factor in the creation of a nation, which is why progress in historical studies often constitutes a

---

8. The editors' main reference for this bizarre positivism must be Raymond Williams, *Marxism and Literature*, Oxford: Oxford University Press, 1977.

9. Terry Eagleton, *Criticism and Ideology: A Study in Marxist Literary Theory*, London: New Left Books, 1976. My remarks are now in Timothy J. Reiss, *The Uncertainty of Analysis: Problems in Truth, Meaning, and Culture*, Ithaca: Cornell University Press, 1988, pp. 192–4.

10. Gregory Jusdanis, *Belated Modernity and Aesthetic Culture: Inventing National Literature*, Minneapolis: University of Minnesota Press, 1991, p. 6. Henceforth cited in my text as BM. The reference here is to Terry Eagleton, *The Function of Criticism: From the Spectator to Post-Structuralism*, London: Verso, 1984.

danger for [the principle of] nationality' (NN 11). For Renan, nation was of course a good thing (indeed a foundation for ranking peoples [12–14]). That the national idea is the result of a particular *story* must therefore be forgotten (18–19). So too, exactly similarly, must the story by which the nation as colonizer violates its victim, naturalizing their pasts into two sides of one same, in a shared 'forgetfulness'. For the colonizer, forgetfulness creates the idea of historically inevitable progress, springing from a 'timeless and perpetual' nation, 'an ontological presence that has, somehow or other, always already existed'.[11] For the colonized, it means 'our people losing grip on their history, being swept out of the current of their history into somebody else's history, becoming a footnote' – or becoming negritude to whiteness, spirituality to materialism. That the 'history of Africa became the history of alien races in Africa, and the real history . . . was virtually forgotten' were necessary consequences of the retelling.[12] Only by forgetting can nations and their oppressions become natural: the 'second nature' of which Said writes. Renan's forgetting of the story of origins at the same time makes a space *and* lays a base for creating 'a rich legacy of memories', a storied tradition that allows present consent to the heritage (NN 19). Beyond nationalism, at issue is the functioning of a whole cultural environment.

This is why some obfuscation is needed on the part of dogmatic metropolitan critics. We need to deny claims sapping our 'rich legacy', our Great Tradition, and accounts arguing that our metropolis is established simultaneously with the forgetting of that establishment. Our comprehension of other cultural traditions requires a stability of cultural distinctness (at the very least to enable apprehension of contrast). My third issue about binary claims concerns this. For it is, I think, to save the possibility of such claims, even as he seeks to discuss abstractly their sociopolitical establishment, that Eagleton continues in *Ideology: An Introduction* his attacks on Foucault and others. This work's overt aim is to analyse the meanings of the word and idea of 'ideology' and trace their history from the eighteenth century to the twentieth.

---

11. Stathis Gourgouris, *Dream Nation: Enlightenment, Colonization and the Institution of Modern Greece*, Stanford: Stanford University Press, 1996, p. 18.
12. Chinua Achebe, *Conversations with Chinua Achebe*, ed. Bernth Lindfors, Jackson: University Press of Mississippi, 1997, p. 157.

Implicitly, Eagleton also explores arguments enabling the establishment of his own cultural space (my immediate interest here).
Indeed, his focus of debate, setting aside 'ideology''s establishment, is almost wholly within the contemporary British Left.

That Eagleton starts by attacking Foucault's arguments on the
ubiquity of power, on grounds that the claim is so broad as to be
useless as an analytical tool, is revealing.[13] There is much difference between saying that all signifying practices involve power
relations and specifying the nature of the relations. The first is an
axiom to ground projects exploring the second. 'Foucault and his
followers' do not 'effectively abandon the concept of ideology
altogether' (II 8). Rather, they suggest a way to understand what
enables *all* social relations of any kind, at the same time as they
make us aware of what lies in them. The clue to what is behind
Eagleton's criticism is his Popperian claim that this view of
'power' is too capacious: 'For a term to have meaning, it must be
possible to specify what, in particular circumstances, would count
as the other of it' (7). He thinks he qualifies his assertion by
allowing that that 'other' need not be '*always and everywhere* the
other of' the term (7, his italics).

Foucault questions precisely that notion of 'other'. Societies,
the ordered and meaningful relations composing them, *have* no
such an 'other'. Ordered signifying practices *ground* any and all
understanding. So they do societies, known only in the intermesh-
ing organization of such multiple signifying practices, *not* in any
putative contrast to other societies. 'Nature', for example, is
always 'nurture' in some way: the problem is to understand, as
Said and Farah propose, different mappings of nature. There can
be no 'other' as the 'opposite' of such complex processes and
entities. So 'ideology' can be a way of understanding different
functionings of power: it deals not with whether power is present
or not, but with its 'how'. In this regard, the very idea of *otherness*
is an element *within* the functionings of power particular to
Western culture(s). It is the inevitable supplement of the self-
consciousness taken to be the necessary agent of such power.

So Eagleton's argument is not unlike Joan Scott's odd assertion
that if consciousness is always part and parcel of a changing social

---

13. Terry Eagleton, *Ideology: An Introduction*, London: Verso, 1991, p. 7. Henceforth cited in my text as II.

environment (just as different functionings of power will be), it means that 'political differences among women cannot be explained as false consciousness'.[14] It means no such thing. Consciousness, experience, identity, may change, but in given times and places they are constrained by specifiable conditions. It is in relation to such conditions that we speak of 'false consciousness', thereby signifying internalization of a self-understanding that actually betrays the subject's own interests: whether of class, gender, race or whatever. This is what Chinweizu means when he describes a colonized population as one 'with false historical and cultural consciousness'.[15] This *includes* issues of identity per se only as *aspects* of that 'alien' displacement of one history into another of which Achebe writes. It is a nonsense to *oppose* false consciousness to consciousness as self-identity, whether fixed or in flux: the one is a part of the other. This is, indeed, one of Eagleton's understandings of ideology. In both cases, two different levels of analysis have been conflated. Like 'false consciousness', 'ideology' signals diverse orders and relations of power in an overall social environment where power is thus never absent from the signifying practices composing it. These last impose particular forms of activity, but their precise nature will vary from society to society.

Human consciousness may have been different in ancient Greece from its 'counterpart' in modern Europe, among the Hopi or in contemporary China, but in each environment no analytical difficulty is involved in grasping oppositional functions and practices. One understands, for instance, that in most or all American Indian cultures, autobiography as a continuous story of a contained and possessive self has not been possible. This is because individual consciousness did not precede community or make a possession of its 'self'; it has not been a bounded and enclosed place or entity. But that does not mean there is no process internal to such cultures playing on that 'communal' comprehension in conflictive ways, maybe organizing it in terms of some dominant (or subordinate) interest. A similar sense of

---

14. Joan Wallach Scott, *Gender and the Politics of History*, New York: Columbia University Press, 1988, p. 4.

15. Timothy J. Reiss, 'History, Criticism, and Theory: Fact and Fantasy', *Canadian Review of Comparative Literature*, vol. 16, 1989, pp. 136–53, here pp. 149–50; Chinweizu, *Decolonising the African Mind*, Lagos: Pero Press, 1987, p. 219.

'who-ness' pervades many cultures. One needs to feel for such conflictive processes within unfamiliar parameters (unfamiliar to those in different cultures), but that is quite different from arguing that these conflicts either cannot be analysed if all are taken as matters of power relations or are not in question if consciousness is a social construct. Since all social order necessarily involves inclusions and exclusions, there is no doubt that such processes exist. Foucault's point is that we need first to try to grasp wholes in their own particular forms of functioning. Where societies and cultures are concerned, we can best do so by seeing them as ways of organizing events, meanings and activities, ways always imbricated in specific and local relations of power, titles of interest. Eagleton wants rather to know them, first, from *here*, and then what 'second' is possible? One could hardly find a clearer instance of the Western dilemma with which I began: using instruments presupposing confrontation, separateness and isolation, how are the spaces between cultural places to be bridged? How can one even envision homes, places and times in their own particularities?

Eagleton's repeated attack on Foucault's reminder of Marxism's embedding in nineteenth-century argument (NCL 27) also has a kind of ironic poignancy. The reminder itself, if its import is to be thoroughly understood and put to work, needs grasping in its own political context.[16] Foucault always saw the need to work through the 'presentness' of one's own discursive practice (quoted in Jusdanis, BM xv). Eagleton himself notes that hegemonies have to be lived and worked through – one cannot grope around them – although the abstract language of his 'coming out on the other side', as if ideology and hegemony were reified places, rooms through which one passes, gives pause. For it seems that Eagleton, like others here, is unable to do that working through, suffering from a blind spot, fixed in opposition of self and other. That is surely why he re-establishes categories of a familiar English Great Tradition and why, Jusdanis again observes, when he writes an essay on 'Literature's Romantic Era', the titular universalism turns out to lie entirely within 'the boundaries of England' (BM 6). In *The Function of Criticism,* his eye lighting on Habermas, Eagleton calls for an idea of criticism as 'a counter-

---

16. 'History, Criticism, and Theory', p. 141.

public sphere'.[17] The thought is used by Gunew in her contribution to *Nation and Narration*, although she admits that it has been criticized as meaningless in Habermas's terms: the 'counter' is already in his public sphere, partly characterizes it. The point is that the public sphere is *not a* place but a practice: again Eagleton is caught in the trap – trope – of his 'other'.

Eagleton's reiterated criticisms of Foucault's reminder may be thought of as his scratching at a symptomatic itch. Foucault's not very hidden intent (his taking aim at the analyses behind the Stalinist excesses of the French Communist Party aside) was at least twofold: first, Marx had analysed a particular socioeconomic order at a particular moment of development; second, the analysis was nonetheless taken (by Marx and his successors) as universally valid. The first means that new analyses are continually needed and that they are themselves an aspect of the issues they analyse and a part of the solution of their impasses: we analyse our own practices from within, as Cheyfitz carefully observes in his introduction to *The Poetics of Imperialism*.[18] Such analyses are among and made from the signifying practices which compose our cultural home.

The second should act as a warning: to beware of belief, not in totalizing analyses (which do not per se exclude difference) but in the universal validity of any one topical analysis. Historical materialism rested on the analysis of a specific moment in a particular industrial society. In *Marxism and Literature*, Williams explored the processes of its foundation and some ways of extending and adjusting them to an understanding of cultural practices in different times and places. The inevitable fluidity and even vagueness that result are consequences Eagleton and others resist.[19] His bent is for more foursquare analysis: he knows where he is, he wants clarity of outcome. He may have doubts as to what exactly he may find when he opens the door on the other side of the room we (Europeans) now, and everyone will, occupy. He has no doubts of the room, or that it has familiar-looking doors or that when he finally steps through the *right* one (that with the

---

17. *The Function of Criticism*, p. 123.
18. Eric Cheyfitz, *The Poetics of Imperialism: Translation and Colonization from The Tempest to Tarzan*, New York: Oxford University Press, 1991. Henceforth cited in my text as PI.
19. See my *Uncertainty of Analysis*, pp. 179–203.

'proper name') there will be another room probably not *so very* different: its form already predicated by the analysis and by the material of the room which *had* to precede it in the narrow house trailer of time. You speak, many have said, from where you live, but that is a far cry from saying everyone else should, or should want to, live there too (which is what *Ideology* is ostensibly all about, entirely polemically so).

This may be a bit parodic and less than just. But Eagleton's figure, and figuring, are so ubiquitous in these debates (not least because of the ready analysis and answer he is taken to provide) as to require observation of their danger. These blindnesses reinscribe the very processes they query. What is the function of criticism? To query the dominant claims of cultural hegemonies? Or maintain them? To make a 'counter'-public sphere? Or rest in the same? The questions and choices are not unfamiliar. That is not the point. The irascible inability to question the ground is. Eagleton stands here as the figuring of danger just because his work has proven so seductive. To use his name would be ungracious and gratuitous were the peril not, I have tried to show, general: that of making one culture central, deriving from it all 'other' cultures, valorizing universally one standard of taste, analysis of worth and imperative of order, without determining the grounds and sources of the valorization or marking the limits of application or of the very grounds of application. The danger is not that one speaks from within 'the formative places of Enlightenment': one has no choice in *that*. Rather it is that without knowing the grounds of the practices from within which we speak, we may do so without being able, as Günter Grass has put it, to tell the 'old story . . . altogether differently'.[20]

The object, really, of all those examined here is to try to find ways of carrying out Grass's suggestion to tell an old story differently, rework ways of seeing and open up a Western enclosure. I put it thus because most analyse cultural relations of power in that enclosure and want to change them, although they perforce do so from a position, as it were, 'on top'. Most of the authors work, like myself, in metropolitan universities and publish with metropolitan presses (Cambridge, Oxford, Routledge, Verso, Minnesota) for a chiefly academic audience. That, again, is why I

---

20. Quoted in my *Meaning of Literature*, p. 347.

have taken Eagleton as an emblem of the dangers of enclosure. To speak of the 'other' is *not*, is *never*, to step outside. It is just to project an other in the image of the self.

So one of the major ways to start telling the tale differently is to examine the construction of the enclosure. That is what Jusdanis seeks to do in *Belated Modernity*. The case of modern Greece that he takes is an especially interesting one. Marginalized from a Western European sphere more or less after Hellenistic times, Greek culture had a quite separate development through the Byzantine period and was absorbed, after 1453, into the Ottoman Empire. Earlier Western indifference came closer to wilful ignorance (BM 15). At the same time, Western European cultures were busy making old Greece into one of their two founding pillars. By the late eighteenth century, many Greek intellectuals were aware of this and, as they began to conceive 'the idea of a national community distinguished by language' (25), turned to this West for cultural aid, unabashedly using its nostalgia for the grandeur of antiquity. By the 1821 revolts (33), a Westernizing intellectual establishment was already publishing newspapers and literary works abroad, mostly in the German-speaking lands.

Jusdanis argues that modern Greek literature sought to consti-tute itself a bulwark, indeed seal and guarantor of a nation-state being established in the struggle against the Ottoman Empire, by deliberately modelling itself on the aforementioned metropolitan cultures. Already complicated by argument over the several vari-eties of Greek language, however, relations with Western models were further confused by the fact that whereas in Western cases it could be argued that modern literature was associated with 'bour-geois individualism', in Greece the association of literary culture with the 1821 revolts against the Ottoman Empire made it a buttress of Greek 'feudalism', however different 'clientelistic' relations between 'the oligarchy of landlords and military men' and the peasants may have been from an older Western European dispensation (BM 32–3). In modern times, Jusdanis says, this has given a cast to Greek literature quite different from that of its Western European counterparts: not a 'compensatory' practice offering 'a space of deliverance from the consequences of social fragmentation' (103) but a cultural product resisting 'autonomi-zation' until very late in the twentieth century and, in its efforts to stay part of 'social and political life', offering a critique of 'modernity' (113–21). Here, Stathis Gourgouris sees 'Greece's ever-receding position in the race toward modern civilization, its irredeemable belatedness in the formation and function of modern institutions, its ever more breathless anxiety for the international prestige of bourgeois regularity'.[21]

With regard to how a national literature – and indeed nation – may be established, the case is fascinating, and Jusdanis seems quite right to believe it holds lessons for many other cultural centres: not least in the play of metropolis and 'margin', of how the last may change the first in using it, and of how unfamiliar forms of analysis may be needed to interpret texts and understand their functioning. Jusdanis seems to avoid the danger observed by Gyan Prakash that the story of an 'aborted or failed modernity defers the conclusion of the modernization narrative but does not eliminate the [Western] teleological vision'.[22] With his story of 'belated' modernity, Jusdanis shows how Greece diverted and changed the instruments it took over, once they were inserted into a different cultural arena and a different history. Even so, the question of how the occupants of any cultural place could conceivably see themselves as 'marginal' evidently requires asking, although it cannot be explored here.[23]

Other dilemmas exist. One concerns a kind of ethnocentrism. For a century and a half, with geographic reason, the German lands were the chief cultural reference for Greek intellectuals. So Jusdanis takes their development of literary culture as exemplary. From Lessing and Schiller, Goethe and Hegel, it is easy to develop a thought that literature in Western modernity has been a cultural practice compensating for 'social fragmentation'. But the German case (differently from but no less than the Greek) was also one of 'belated modernity'. For various reasons, so were the Russian, Italian and Spanish. However much the last two had been originators of concepts of literary modernism in the sixteenth and early seventeenth centuries, there was a kind of later dispersal: occasional peaks, but little sustained depth of 'organic' produc-

---

21. *Dream Nation*, pp. 70–1.

22. Gyan Prakash, 'Writing Post-Orientalist Histories of the Third World: Indian Historiography Is Good to Think', in Nicholas B. Dirks, ed., *Colonialism and Culture*, Ann Arbor: University of Michigan Press, 1992, pp. 353–88, here p. 367.

23. *Against Autonomy* confronts it at some length.

tion until much later – probably as late as the Greek ('organic' naming an originating bond with social processes *in toto*). The nation-state may have a constitutional relation with 'literature' as a whole, rather than with the novel alone. Furthermore, the very idea of 'modernity', with its divers exclusions and Europeanist claims, is itself problematic.

Whatever the Italian and Spanish cases, quite other were those of the models taken by the eighteenth-century German-speaking writers, the English and French. Here (and they did become models, direct or indirect, angel or demon, for many later establishments), literature was emphatically not compensatory. It was a way to vanquish a sense of disaster and justify establishment of new social and political sureties. In its first establishment, modern literature was so far from compensating for society's incapacities as to assure its stabilizing benefits. When German thinkers adopted these claims a century later, they did so first in terms enabling establishment, not in compensation of failures. To misread German establishment may be to misread Greek. If literature *always* played an establishing role in 'social and political life', how are we to understand its differences? The issue has again to do with Renan's (and Eagleton's) forgetting. Literature may be an instrument that not only enables such forgetting but goes far to forge it. We have to make every effort to know the details of history, which are necessarily always those of *specific* histories, tied to places and times, to particular homes.

We must also avoid confusing words and things. That the word *nation* was not used in its modern sense until the nineteenth century would *not* mean its referent was not yet at issue. That the word *literature* did not obtain its modern nuances until Johnson's *Dictionary*, say, does *not* mean its familiar practice did not exist. While Jusdanis's work deals extensively with critics, there is virtually no study of 'literary' works. One needs some sense of a fit between what is said and what is done. This is a flaw I want to try to avoid in this essay. An occasional problem also arises from using secondary sources: *pace* Habermas (BM 185n8), the term *public* was used in England and France in a quite modern sense well before the mid- or late seventeenth century.[24] This matters

---

24. Claims of usage are always dubious. As to 'nation', Jusdanis and all the others named earlier are just wrong. What of Richard Hakluyt's celebrated 1589 work,

because it is rightly taken to be at issue in the establishment of literary culture.

The case Jusdanis probes is of special interest because it raises issues of the relation between metropolis and 'margin', literature and national identity, possession and variety, of a kind that most of these critics should find particularly fruitful. Modern Greece confronted and adopted Western European cultural forms. Furthermore, Greece is a bridge for those forms and their practitioners both to *their* adopted past and to wholly unfamiliar cultures. With Aimé Césaire, one must insist 'that it is a good thing to place different civilizations in contact with each other; that it is an excellent thing to blend different worlds; that whatever its own particular genius may be, a civilization that withdraws into itself atrophies; that for civilizations, exchange is oxygen'.[25] For metropolitan critics, the Greek case offers a special sort of unfamiliar familiarity.

There is another way to tell different stories. Simply by starting with the knowledge that one is in a place with its own interests and concerns or even in a place somehow relieved of local entanglement, one can avoid catching oneself in traps of self and other. In the modern world, one may be caught in the webs of powerful cultural hegemonies, but one's adoption of elements from another (metropolitan) culture remains just that, an adoption. Jusdanis tries to show how a developing Greek aesthetic culture played ambivalently off Western Europe to elaborate its own national cultural character. Molloy, astutely using centrally

---

hugely expanded in 1598–1600: *The Principal Navigations, Voyages, Traffiques and Discoveries of the English Nation?* Hakluyt meant to assert the mercantile authority and history of the English and establish political, social and commercial parameters of their 'Nation'. What of the Parliamentarian Henry Parker's 1642 argument against Charles I, that 'it is unnatural for any Nation to give away its owne proprietie in it selfe absolutely . . .' (*Observations Upon Some of His Majesties Later Answers and Expresses 1642*, in William Haller, ed., *Tracts on Liberty in the Puritan Revolution 1638–1647*, 3 vols, New York: Columbia University Press, 1934, vol. 2, pp. 165–213, here p. 186)? The terms, *nature, nation, property, self* and their association were not to startle but to explain in ways that Parker assumed his readers recognized. I have explored 'literature' in *Meaning of Literature*. The very complex terms *private* and *public* are discussed in my *Mirages of the Selfe: Patterns of Personhood in Ancient and Early Modern Europe*, Stanford: Stanford University Press, 2003.

25. Aimé Césaire, *Discourse on Colonialism*, trans. Joan Pinkham, New York: Monthly Review Press, 1972, p. 11. (Translation of *Discours sur le colonialisme*, 1955.) Henceforth cited as *Discourse*.

problematic tales of personal identity, shows how autobiographical stories can be ambiguous establishments of *political* actuality.

I earlier mentioned that autobiography is no easy idea for some cultures. This has been no issue for Latin American writers, at least as to personal identity. What is, however, matter for arduous debate is the tie between person and political role, individual and community. It is not accidental that most of the autobiographers discussed by Molloy in *At Face Value* are fairly considerable political or cultural figures in various (mostly Argentine) new sociopolitical establishments.[26] Equivocal as particular writers may be, individual identity is always constituted by way of political institution. This so differs from 'norms' of Western European establishments of identity as hardly to need remark. At least from the seventeenth century, such identity was based in an idea of self whose independent rights were owed entirely to the individual. It would be hard to find a European autobiography that did not make such an assumption, even when seeking to muddy the waters (André Malraux, for instance).

Molloy's persons, even when not major political figures, think themselves only in a communal political arena. This is true of Argentina's founding figure, Domingo Faustino Sarmiento, as it is of the Cuban slave Juan Francisco Manzano; the Argentine intellectual Victoria Ocampo; the Cuban exile the Condesa de Merlin; the Venezuelan Mariano Picón Salas; the Argentines Norah Lange and Lucio Victorio Mansilla; or the Mexican José Vasconcelos. Almost all make a kind of genealogy for their (written) identity by alluding to their reading of European books. All without exception establish their current sense of stable identity by embedding it, however often tentatively and ambivalently, in a national story: one they have actually created or helped create (Sarmiento or Vasconcelos) or one they see as defining the persona worthy of autobiography. Making identity by catching it in the books of Europe and places of Latin America, identity that is at once personal and national, nicely enacts the treachery and fluidity of the frontier between metropolitan artefact and elsewhere. Such identities match Said's establishments of different 'natures'. Like Farah, they use known maps in a territory whose

---

26. Sylvia Molloy, *At Face Value: Autobiographical Writing in Spanish America*, Cambridge: Cambridge University Press, 1991.

nature and boundaries will be made by someone other than their first makers.

The idea of personal identity, as made, for example, in Western autobiography, is thus altered, once taken in different cultures: thoughts that Molloy has explored also in fiction. Just as the mostly public figures of her scholarly work fix their being by binding it in recorded political annals, so the private characters of *Certificate of Absence* try to grasp a sense of themselves in small acts of mutual violence. Only in communal antagonisms, grand political conflict set in a minor key, can a protagonist find being: 'What she writes does not constitute, and will never constitute, an autobiography: rather, it tries to reproduce a disjointed series of acts of violence that befell her, that also befell others.'[27] The historical figures explored in *At Face Value* had to fuse the artefacts of metropolitan cultures with the constitutions of their own history to establish their identity. The persons of *Certificate of Absence*, displaced as they are from the arena of that constitution, trace something like the failure of such an establishment. They remain 'ill at ease in [their] skin' (CA 5, 70), simulacra of containment that show themselves tired efforts to set one's 'own order on what [one] transcribes' (8), fitful bids 'to correct the image, or perhaps to restore some kind of order' (8). 'Order is what she wants to impose whenever she feels the threat of a shared vagueness, of an emptiness invading her emptiness' (10).

Like Farah, Molloy tracks the attempt to establish a sort of cartography of identity. Here, too, it can be sifted only in fugitive tellings: 'Her words, herself: broken up, pieced together. . . . Her body and her phrase will tear again, but not at the old scars: they will split open in a different way, revealing new fractures. She accepts this future violence as something not necessarily negative, as a sign, perhaps, of a secret order.' Yet words that 'imply an order . . . also lead astray' (CA 48). One is caught between a need for maps and tales that may always, somehow, belong already to others and a need for one's own place of customary habit, requiring 'the support of others' in familiarity (76). Whatever the small local violences, it is they who help 'define [one's] existence'

---

27. Sylvia Molloy, *Certificate of Absence*, trans. Daniel Balderston and Sylvia Molloy, Austin: University of Texas Press, 1989, p. 49. (Translation of *En breve cárcel*, 1981.) Henceforth cited in my text as CA.

(95): 'I wanted all of you – mother, sister, lovers – to be here, I live only in you' (116). The unending need to write is an effort somehow to make oneself into the safely continuous place of history. But 'how to bring forth violence, how to write it down?' (86). As words escape, so does continuity: in the present ('she feels divided, wavering, suspended before a choice she does not control' [71]); of the past ('How can one return to what one has already seen, what one thought one already knew, and look at it afresh?' [70]).

I am reminded of no novel so much as of Witold Gombrowicz's *Cosmos*, which also tracks dissolution of identity and of telling, often in language almost identical. *Cosmos*, also written by an exile (spending years in Molloy's homeland of Argentina before coming, like her, to France), ends in banality.[28] *Certificate of Absence* ends in an airport: 'She is alone: she is very frightened' (CA 125). I am reminded, too, of a novel some of our commentators see as addressing from a blunt metropolitan side these hard issues of national culture, colonialism, order and identity: Rudyard Kipling's *Kim*. But so far from being blunt, the novel approaches these puzzles with haunted wariness, avoiding simplistic snares of self and other in its careful wrestling with fluidities of frontiers and identity.

In the essay I commented on before, Jameson, opposing *Howards End* to *Passage to India*, makes a useful point about the different ways the 'colonizer' inhabits a home world and a colonized one. Introducing *Kim*, Said echoes the point by means of a comparison between Dorothea Brooke's 'reawakening' to the world at the end of *Middlemarch* and Kim's at the end of his story.[29] Where Dorothea feels part of an 'involuntary, palpitating life', Kim's 'wheels' of being 'lock up anew on the world without': 'roads were meant to be walked upon, houses to be lived in, cattle to be driven, fields to be tilled, and men and women to be talked to. They were all real and true – solidly planted upon the feet –

---

28. See Timothy J. Reiss, 'The *Cosmos* Rag, or: How Mean Can You Be?' *Discours social/Social Discourse*, vol. 4, no. 1–2, 1992, pp. 117–46. Reworked and expanded into Chapter 7 of *Against Autonomy*.

29. Edward W. Said, 'Introduction' to Rudyard Kipling, *Kim*, Harmondsworth: Penguin, 1987, pp. 7–46, here p. 20. Henceforth cited in my text as Intro. or *Kim*. The essay is reworked in Said's *Culture and Imperialism*, New York: Knopf, 1993.

perfectly comprehensible – clay of his clay, neither more nor less' (*Kim* 331).

'For the European or American women in Europe', says Said (who has spoken too of James's *Portrait of a Lady*), 'the world is to be discovered anew; it requires no one in particular to direct it, or to exert sovereignty over it. [Molloy might adjust this idea.] This is not the case in India, which would pass into chaos or insurrection unless roads were walked upon properly, houses lived in in the right way, men and women talked to in correct tones' (Intro. 21). But it is Said who adds 'properly', 'the right way' and 'in correct tones'. That surely puts him in the wrong. It reduces *Kim*, as so often, to mere opposition of Empire and victim. First, to take Said's own terms, Kim's reawakening is no more voluntary than Dorothea's or Isabel Archer's: 'He *did not want to cry – had never felt less like* crying in his life – but of a sudden easy, *stupid* tears trickled down his nose, and with an almost audible click *he felt* the wheels of his being lock up anew on the world without' (*Kim* 331, my italics).

In fact Kim, contrary to what Said asserts, is, *was always*, *both* native and non-native: far more the first than the last. Moreover, his place in Empire would be ambivalent even were that not so: his father, after all, was Irish; his own name is 'Kimball O'Hara'. Not by chance does a turning point in Kim's *Bildungsroman* occur in the high Himalayas in the company of his Tibetan spiritual guide, near and at the very Irish-sounding 'Shamlegh-midden' (Ch. 14). Kim's wilfulness always regards, we learn at the start (*Kim* 51), the pleasures of the game, not the interests of politics. That is why it is *not* ludicrous for him to combine the (Buddhist) Way and the Great Game of imperial intelligence: both are forms of mapping. One has the lama's chart, the other a surveyor's mensuration. This may be, as Said opines, 'ahistorical' (Intro. 22), but one can hardly bypass that difficulty in the novel by changing Kim. If we read him as a sign of a moment when 'India was already well into the dynamic of outright opposition to British rule' (10), his ambivalence may be the more revealing. He embodies the struggle Eagleton calls 'ironic', the struggle neither Joyce nor Yeats, according to Said and Jameson, ever got out *of*. In many ways, *Kim* was autobiographical of a Kipling who always felt closer ties with India and Indians where and with whom he was born and first raised than with England and the English, where he felt outcast not only because his sensibility set him apart from the sportingly virile ideal of public school manhood but also, as Ashis Nandy notes, because his dark skin made him look 'noticeably a non-white'.[30]

This is not the place to elaborate a reading of *Kim*, but a few remarks may highlight elements suggesting that even writers from 'the formative places of Enlightenment' may begin to tell the tale otherwise, to touch hands, as it were, with Farah, Molloy and others. This matters because it disables the choice of unambiguous opposition. For *Kim* too deals with maps of identity. Travelling the Great Trunk Road with the Buddhist abbot, Kim finds himself part of the teeming colours of India, not, *pace* Said, potential chaos, but ordered 'left and right', composed of villagers purposefully dispersing 'by twos and threes across the level plain. Kim felt these things, though he could not give tongue to his feelings' (*Kim* 111). 'Who is Kim?' is an ever-reiterated question, from the time he feels himself one 'insignificant person in all this roaring whirl of India' (166). He is, it is true, caught here between the uncharted free places of his native life (and land, for he *is* native) – unmade no doubt by colonization – and something else. For him, those places were a game until *threatened*, as the novel does indeed show in its heavy-handed opposite: imperialist militarism, religion and education at their most brutally oppressive. But Kim slides away from that opposition towards some new making.

His heroes are those who reject simplicities. Neither Mahbub Ali nor Colonel Creighton is quite Pathan or Sahib. Each plays an equivocal role in the clash of oppressor and oppressed. Mahbub works for imperial order (inasmuch as divers imperial powers confront each other on Indian soil), but his dealing lies in the life and welfare of the bazaar. Creighton works for imperial order, but is utterly absorbed in the life of India. The ('correct') Pathans' insurgent nationalism (Intro. 26) has its direct counter in the brutal colonization of the regiment of Mavericks and its red bull ensign. Mahbub and Creighton play different roles, approaching Kim's eventual 'middle way', which is why Mahbub and Kim can exchange pejorative 'Sahib', 'blackman' and 'Pathan,' as mockingly affectionate 'insults'. In irony the words

---

30. Ashis Nandy, *The Intimate Enemy: Loss and Recovery of Self under Colonialism*, Delhi: Oxford University Press, 1983, p. 67. Henceforth cited as Nandy.

lose their colonizing bite. Like the words Molloy's protagonists use or the maps put in Askar's hands, the colonizers' epithets get such recast meanings as come from altering 'cultural priorities on both sides', remaking 'subcultures previously recessive or subordinate' and sapping those 'previously salient' (Nandy 2). Kim rejects the hyper-masculinity and paternalism represented by the Mavericks and Raj bureaucrats for a 'softer side' emphasizing 'speculation, intellection and *caritas*' (Nandy 32). To be sure, much of Kim's instruction will now be in how to measure, map and order place on behalf of the rulers of the Great Game – so much so that Kim's search for personal identity *does* become caught up in mapping territory.

Likewise, the lama's quest for enlightenment requires he draw in 'clearest, severest outline' a chart of the 'Great Wheel' (*Kim* 240). The angry tearing of this chart by the Russian agent results in the 'collapse of their Great Game', brought about not by any 'craft' or 'contrivance' of their opponents but 'simply, beautifully, and inevitably' (297) – words earlier ascribed to India itself: 'it was beautiful to behold' (111). There is a clear lesson here, as there also is in the abbot's discovery that he no longer needs his chart, when he can tell a 'fantastic piled narrative of bewitchment and miracles that set Shamlegh a-gasping' (307) and ultimately find that he 'has reached Knowledge' (333). There is a lesson, too, in the fact that Kim now hears tales of the Sahibs from the Indians' viewpoint, 'every detail lighted from behind' (306), and has thrown his fine surveyor's instruments over the 2000-foot cliff of Shamlegh-midden; as if this backlighting had indeed overturned 'all the familiar landmarks of thought – ours: that which has our age and our geography – unsettling all the ordered surfaces and all the planes that temper the profusion of beings, disturbing and upsetting for a long time our millennial practice of the Same and the Other'.[31] Kim has listened so well to the abbot's culture that he has to cast away the instruments that embody the vehement measuring priorities of European culture.

We may adopt Said's proposal that the museum keeper's gift of spectacles to the lama at the novel's start to help him see better

---

31. Michel Foucault, *Les mots et les choses: Une archéologie des sciences humaines*, Paris: Gallimard, 1966, p. 7.

(*Kim* 60) stands for 'Britain's benevolent sway' (Intro. 15) – not to mention an arrogant supposal that their eye problem is the same! But we must then attend to the end: 'even his spectacles do not make my eyes see' (*Kim* 320). Similarly, Said avers that the lama's living on Kim's 'strength as an old tree lives on the lime of a new wall' (321) marks dependence on Empire. He ignores not only Kim's ambiguous role, but his answer that 'Thou leanest on me in the body, Holy One, but I lean on thee for some other things' (321): spiritual growth and the changes we are tracing. To adopt a proverb Nandy turns somewhere to depict how the colonized may reassert cultural control in the face of the colonizer's force, this gives another twist to the maxim about the spirit being strong but the flesh weak. 'Weakness' can itself become means to reassert a cultural home (Nandy 64–113). It is no surprise that the lama closes the novel: 'he crossed his hands on his lap and smiled, as a man may who has won salvation for himself and his beloved' (338). This is the abbot's victory, not the Raj's. The 'colonial system' may have 'acquired the status of a fact of nature', from whose colonizing side Kipling partly wrote (Intro. 10). Its interests are finally the lesser.

Perhaps that makes no difference on the ground really mapped by and for those interests. In objective economic and political praxis, the lama's gesture may be one of withdrawal: power, wealth and benefit are the colonizers'. To see these as 'illusion' is to cede all hold on it. Kim's quest, you may say, now upheld by the lama's assurance, remains that of colonial adventurism, a game of 'glory' which has in some way co-opted the way of the other. (What does it *mean* that Kim wakes to spiritual renewal, not unlike the Buddha, from sleep under 'a young banyan tree' [*Kim* 332]?) Still, of his Way, the Teshoo Lama is *not* dispossessed, even if he images all other dispossession: chart destroyed, body beaten, bereft of worldly goods – religion as opiate. But *that* interpretation makes the novel a critique of everything British India stood for. So does Kim's wending a path between the Game and the Way, West and East, reason and spirit. And may not the ruin of Russia's part in the Great Game prefigure that of Britain's? The lama's mapping in his head can be India's of itself.

For one may interpret quite differently the fact that *Kim* ends with the abbot's contentment. His smiling wisdom reflects Partha Chatterjee's argument about the 'strategies one encounters in the

emergence of the disciplines in colonial society. The claim is not
that the field of knowledge is marked out into separate domains
by the fact of cultural difference' or that one is excluded from
knowledge. It is 'a claim for an alternative science [way of
knowing] directed at the same objects of knowledge'.[32] It happens
that Chatterjee is writing of work in Calcutta just contemporary
with Kipling's experience in India, as is Nandy in making virtually
the same point about figures like Sri Aurobindo (Nandy 85–100)
or Mahatma Gandhi (48–63, 100–7). Such alternative ways work
cumulatively, in time hatching new cultural configurations. That,
too, *Kim* plainly shows. Whatever others do, Kim himself reveres
Lurgan (no European), Creighton, Mahbub, the Babu and above
all the lama. The first four inhabit a twilight world of equivocal
mappings. The last we have seen. For the reader, it is Kim's
judgement, eponymous hero that he is, that must finally set
interpretation.

A novel cannot change objective realities of economic and
political relations. It can elaborate their patterns. It may not only
make us aware of differences of life, custom, culture, and
language, but provide – require, it may be – access to them.
Indeed, it is surely products of the fictive imagination that as
much as any others transform cultural understandings and practices. Edward Gibbon, admired eighteenth-century predecessor of
Kipling, had, no less ambiguously, proposed something similar:

> An Iroquois work, even were it full of absurdities, would be an
> invaluable treasure; it would offer an unique specimen of the workings
> of the human mind, when placed in circumstances which we have
> never experienced, and influenced by manners and religious opinions
> entirely contrary to our own. We should be sometimes astonished and
> instructed by the contrariety of ideas thus produced; we should
> investigate the causes of their existence; and should trace the progress
> of the mind from one error to another. Sometimes, also, we should
> be delighted at recognizing our own principles recurring, but dis-
> covered in other ways, and almost always modified and altered. We
> should there learn not only to own, but also to feel the power of

---

32. Partha Chatterjee, 'The Disciplines in Colonial Bengal', in Partha Chatterjee,
ed., *Texts of Power: Emerging Disciplines in Colonial Bengal*, Minneapolis: University of
Minnesota Press, 1995, pp. 1–29, here pp. 18–19.

prejudices, not to be astonished at what appears most absurd, and often to distrust what seems best established.[33]

Maybe there was much here of Kipling's own, 'What do they know of England, / Who only England know?': the idea that foreign customs, practices and artefacts exist to service metropolitan culture, to make the places of cultural differences into inverted or identical echoes of one supposed centre. Whether and how this map is new are grave questions. Exclusion, appropriation, interweaving, are scales on an ample spectrum. To judge distances from one to another is not hard, but to evaluate intentions, where one shades into another, is fruitless. For whatever a Gibbon may have come to think in later, more conservative work, here at least, in this youthful *Essai* (first written and published in French in 1761), he offers that real contact with other cultures must change our views of our own, make us 'distrust' many of our clearest certainties. 'Absurdities', 'prejudices' and 'error' are as much ours as the Iroquois'. We learn 'the power of prejudice' by not holding to our monologue, as Césaire (after Rodó) put it. The self/other polarity is a form of that monologue, continuation of the 'colonial enterprise'. 'The truth is', Césaire went on,

> that this policy *cannot but bring about the ruin of Europe itself* and that Europe, if it is not careful, will perish from the void it has created around itself. They thought they were only slaughtering Indians, or Hindus, or South Sea Islanders, or Africans. They have in fact overthrown, one after another, the ramparts behind which European civilization could have developed freely. (*Discourse* 57–8)

Gibbon's astonishment, instruction and delight, his urge that we probe 'contrarieties', modifications, alterations and differences, are no more to be belittled than *Kim*'s new patterns. The lama refuses to be caught in 'limits set by' the 'rulers', to lose his 'soul' to 'internalization of [his] victor', forced to fight 'according to the victor's values, within his model of dissent' (Nandy 3, 111). So does Kim.

Cultural meetings produce as much questioning of known

---

33. Edward Gibbon, 'An Essay on the Study of Literature', in *The Miscellaneous Works. . . . With Memoirs of His Life and Writings, Composed by Himself; Illustrated from His Letters, with Occasional Notes and Narrative*, by John, Lord Sheffield, London, B. Blake, 1837, pp. 631–70, here p. 654.

traditions as exploration of different ones. Or they may produce a new hybrid, a second, a third nature. Of course, such hybrids may signal cultural imposition, as Cheyfitz argues they did and do in official documents of English and American imperialism, incapable of the effort of understanding indigenous peoples 'as integral, different entities' (PI 11). Such documents have their own imaginative interest. Their imperial work demands reduction. It may do so just because their writers recognize difference as irreducible. You make silhouettes or demons of those whose place you wish to take because you know they have rights like yours, because they must not be given the right to do the same to you and because to strive to detail difference would be to acknowledge the first and deny your wish. '[I]n dealing with this subject, the commonest curse is to be the dupe in good faith of a collective hypocrisy that clearly misrepresents problems, the better to legitimize the hateful solutions provided for them' (Césaire, *Discourse* 10).

Cheyfitz's imperial documents are tools that trail the acts they justify. For colonization is not

> evangelization, nor a philanthropic enterprise, nor a desire to push back the frontiers of ignorance, disease, and tyranny, nor an attempt to extend the rule of law.... The decisive actors here are the adventurer and the pirate, the wholesale grocer and the ship owner, the gold digger and the merchant ... I find that hypocrisy is of recent date; that neither Cortez discovering Mexico from the top of the great teocalli, nor Pizarro before Cusco (much less Marco Polo before Cambaluc), claims that he is the harbinger of a superior order; that they kill; that they plunder; that they have helmets, lances, cupidities; that the slavering apologists come later. (Césaire, *Discourse* 10–11)

The imperial justifying documents still reveal an awareness that the critics of otherness obfuscate (not quite innocently no doubt). The documents make no secret of their denial or of its reasons. The critics seek to assimilate difference to their own perception of legitimacy. But a Gikũyũ or a Nez Percé is not some 'other' of European claim: constituent of a benign *Gemeinschaft* 'alternative' to malignant *Gesellschaft*, an ecohuman reply to the stripped reason of Enlightenment.

In 1971, Roberto Fernández Retamar published his now classic essay 'Caliban: Notes Toward a Discussion of Culture in Our

America'.[34] Like others, he insisted on home cultures before accepting any need to adjust to imposition (as had Rodó in *Ariel*), a view also adopted in Césaire's clash of collaborating Ariel and resisting Caliban in his 1969 play, *A Tempest*. They urged finding lineaments of an earlier map before using its overlay. Although naming Retamar but once, Cheyfitz effectively dilated his 'notes' into a book. I do not demean its gloss on 'Caliban', from Shakespeare, *Tarzan* and colonialism to Montaigne, cannibals and translation's powers. Expanding Retamar's hints, Cheyfitz's *Poetics* explores, with *The Tempest* as sounding board, how European literature made the 'different' of imperial expansion (foretold in Gibbon?) into the 'other' of aesthetic and political imagining. The first is brute imposition. (Kipling's perception of *that* is what makes *Kim* a poor object for critical othering.) The second, whether in *Tarzan*, James Fenimore Cooper's *The Pioneers* or *The Tempest*, sets out 'to rationalize the policy of dispossession' (PI 14).

To this end it has at least two philosophical tools. One involves ancient ideas of translation and metaphor: *translatio* making the foreign familiar; metaphor doing the reverse and, by definition, from Aristotle to later Western tradition, using the play between them. The figured is the foreign, the proper is the national and normal (PI 36: *vide* Eagleton). Throughout the tradition Cheyfitz examines, the very commentaries explained translation as 'an act of violence' (37). Not for nothing were those whose language one did not know called barbarians. The theory and politics of translation were those of deprivation. So, for example, 'this process of translation . . . prepares the way for and is forever involved in the dispossession by which Native American land was *translated* (the term is used in English common law to refer to transfers of real estate) into the European identity of *property*' (43).

The second tool was of newer vintage but directly tied to this last aspect. Holding property to be the mark of political citizenship as of civilized humanity, as Locke did in the *Second Treatise of Government* (PI 55), made those lacking a concept of alienable property (as all Native Americans) or those lacking property

---

34. Roberto Fernández Retamar, 'Caliban: Notes Toward a Discussion of Culture in Our America', trans. Lynn Garafola, David Arthur MacMurray and Roberto Marquez, in *Caliban and Other Essays*, trans. Edward Baker, Minneapolis: University of Minnesota Press, 1989, pp. 3–45.

(European lower classes) not just pre-civilized but not yet fully human: to be that one had to have traversed the civil contract, passing from the monstrous state of nature to the rational order of civil society. The Lockian warrant of property served the needs of a domestic social hierarchy and justified *pari passu* colonialism's hierarchical relations. 'The failure of dialogue, figured as a genetic inability in the other, rather than as a problem of cultural difference' (16), acquired a dual explanation and alibi. The one, involving property, justified a claim of ontological inferiority as well as of political disablement. The other, involving language, legitimized a violent imposition of right speech (but never so simply or one-dimensionally as the 'correct talking' of Said's *Kim*).

These tools still prop the happy binaries of critical seizures of cultural difference. Throughout his work, but especially at the end, Cheyfitz shows *The Tempest* using or predicting these strategies of property and dispossession (PI 157–72). He also shows, in a pretty discussion of Montaigne's 'Des cannibales', how these very terms could be made equivocal. Shorn of its violence, translation became a riddle. Talking with Indians, Montaigne found he needed 'a translator to translate between himself and the translator' (153). Yet he somehow 'understands' the Indians to whom he 'speaks' as living in a culture and language essentially 'democratic', where property, possession and exploitation are literally inexpressible (155–6). By a curious leap of imagination, Cheyfitz implies, Montaigne grasped not just the violence *translatio* did to its victims but the difference it sought to hide. 'Indian people', writes Paula Gunn Allen in a passage Cheyfitz uses as an epigraph (22), 'don't believe in metaphor. Very few of us even understand what that term means.' The claim is odd; the differentiating reasons for it are not. Montaigne would somehow have instantly intuited them.

Metaphor, *translatio*, is the absorbing of the other in the one. Montaigne would have seen that multiplying levels of translation denies such possession, though Cheyfitz's elision of the meaning of that dispersion with a critique of later colonialisms is at least anachronistic, and one suspects aspects of *Gemeinschaft* in his reading of Montaigne. Certainly something of such a myth lies in Montaigne's own understanding, just because he had no direct access to Indians' culture. He could write only from 'common opinion', analogy of 'ancient sources' or second- or third-

hand translated 'contemporary information'.[35] None of these are
a different culture's voice; all reproduce their own Other. This
is so even though Montaigne, relating his meeting with the Indians, assures us of the presence of his 'own man', who had lived
long among Americans and who, being 'simple and crude' and
so not given to interpretation, bore 'true witness'.[36] The perfec-
tion and contentment of the Indians' life and culture was supposedly discussed by them through an interpreter (although
elsewhere Montaigne wrote that their language was unknown to
any French person there) and experienced directly by his man
(445–6: 2.12). The language problem suggests that when Montaigne related their criticisms of France at the end of his essay,
it had more to do with otherness than with any grounded reality
(212–13: 1.31).

Still, ambiguities are many. What attracts in Gibbon's putative
'Iroquois work' is that it would have been the actual voice of the
different culture. Its idea put ambivalence and instability in
Gibbon's writing just because it would not be 'inaccessible'.
Absurdities, errors, prejudices and doubts work in both directions.
Potentially, Gibbon was hearing the Iroquois' voice, accepting the
interference it would introduce into his own no-longer-mastered
(or master) discourse. Montaigne's 'man', with his physical
experience of the Americans, their culture and land, was meant
to give similarly direct access. If he clearly did not, the sceptical
Montaigne had material to *imagine* Americans' speech and set its
difference against his French sufficiently to perturb the sureties
of his own discourse, if not to know the realities of theirs. In his
essay in *Nation and Narration,* James Snead makes a similar point
about contemporary African and African-American writers by
speaking of 'a certain linguistic and cultural eclecticism or *misceg-
enation*', of something 'hybrid' (NN 232, 234). Cheyfitz cites
Walter Benjamin (PI 133–6) explaining how all languages 'supplement' each other by expressing different 'intentions'. In a
'Letter to the Author' before Gibbon's 'Essay', Matthew Maty
denied 'the unsociable genius of different languages' and argued

35. Michel de Certeau, *Heterologies: Discourse on the Other,* trans. Brian Massumi,
foreword Wlad Godzich, Minneapolis: University of Minnesota Press, 1986, pp. 69;
cf. pp. 70–3.
36. Michel Eyquem de Montaigne, *Œuvres complètes,* ed. Albert Thibaudet and
Maurice Rat, Paris: Gallimard, 1962, pp. 200, 202: *Essai* 1.31.

that while 'every language, when complete within itself, is limited', all 'enriched' by 'admixtures': 'Like those lakes whose waters grow purer and clearer by mixture and agitation with those they receive from neighbouring rivers, so modern tongues can only live by intercommunication, and I might venture to say, by their reciprocal clashings.'[37]

A century later, Augustin Cournot lamented our inability 'to arrange all spoken languages to suit . . . the need of the moment'. Victoria Welby soon added that 'what we do want is a really plastic language', one able to 'store up all our precious means of mutual speaking' and let us 'master the many dialects of thought'.[38] These may be closer to Snead's idea. In the same collection, Brennan recalls Salman Rushdie noting how the English language has been transformed by 'those whom it once colonized' (NN 48). From Martinique, Édouard Glissant adds a Caribbean voice to this swelling chorus, calling for a 'multilingualism' to counter 'the arrogant imperialism of monolingualism': less an 'ability to speak several languages' than a 'passionate desire to accept and understand our neighbor's language and to confront the massive leveling force of language continuously imposed by the West . . . with a multiplicity of languages and their mutual comprehension'.[39] Kamau Brathwaite's search for and use of 'nation language' echoes the point. Ngũgĩ's wa Thiong'o's efforts to create as many different language centres as there are cultures using them and to forge multiple bonds among them based on the surety of their *home* language furthers it.

These hopes, visions, questings, reflect the desperate need to escape ideas of otherness, and not only make terms with difference but welcome the hybrid(s). Carlos Fuentes adds: 'One of the wonders of our menaced globe is the variety of its experiences, its memories, and its desire. Any attempt to impose a uniform politics on this diversity is like a prelude to death.'[40] An issue may be that *hybridity* implies a fusion of differences whose result would

---

37. Matthew Maty, 'Letter to the Author', in Gibbon, 'An Essay' (see note 33), pp. 627–31, here pp. 629–30.

38. Both quoted in my *Uncertainty*, p. 34.

39. Édouard Glissant, *Caribbean Discourse: Selected Essays*, trans. J. Michael Dash, 1989, rpt Charlottesville: University Press of Virginia, 1992, p. 249.

40. Carlos Fuentes, 'A Harvard Commencement', in *Myself with Others: Selected Essays*, New York: Farrar, 1988, pp. 199–214, here p. 199.

be a flattening, homogenization or entropy of the political diversities which Fuentes names. One needs to remember that there are many kinds, arrangements and forgings of hybrids. *Interweavings*, Fuentes's own *alternativities* or Wilson Harris's *mutualities* are better terms for processes that must involve recognition and maintenance of diversities, even as they rub against and off one another.

One thinks of Ngũgĩ's bid to make a Gikũyũ literature in the language of and from the store of his own culture's tales, bringing to it elements and processes from many cultures and languages; or of Brathwaite's to make an identity (*X/Self*) from within a history of the voice that recognizes its colonized and its autonomous past, as well as its multiple present. This may not always be welcomed: 'the fifth world had become entangled with European names: the names of the rivers, the hills, the names of the animals and the plants – all of creation suddenly had two names: an Indian name and a white name'.[41] Only recently have these instabilities come to matter to many who write from within so-called 'metropolitan' spaces. Too many readily fall back on familiar sources of response, on habitual ideas of frontier, on known schemas of conflict. For Farah, for Molloy, for Leslie Marmon Silko, for so many others in a world whose order was (once thought to be) constructed by outsiders, things have fallen, are falling, apart, have no ready means of repair. The local models are no longer at hand, only second natures that exist on someone else's maps (in an outsider's dream). Indeed, those who would repair them have yet fully to identify themselves. Questions of power remain unresolved where you have neither identity nor a way of knowing what 'identity' might be.

Issues of who maps whom, of avoiding absorption as a second nature, of negotiating one's own home, were those on which Frantz Fanon, in *Black Skin, White Masks*, took Jean-Paul Sartre to task following his famous 'Orphée noir' preface to Léopold Sédar Senghor's *négritude* anthology.[42] Sartre saw *négritude* as the Hegelian antithesis, essential *other* of Western culture's thesis in a

---

41. Leslie Marmon Silko, *Ceremony*, 1977, rpt Harmondsworth: Penguin, 1986, p. 68.

42. Léopold Sédar Senghor, ed., *Anthologie de la nouvelle poésie nègre et malgache de langue française*, 1948, rpt Paris: PUF, 1969.

conflict to be sublated in a later synthesis. 'I felt that I had been robbed of my last chance,' said Fanon in the hurt surprise of his initial reaction:

> Help had been sought from a friend of the colored peoples, and that friend had found no better response than to point out the relativity of what they were doing. For once, that born Hegelian had forgotten that consciousness has to lose itself in the night of the absolute, the only condition to attain the consciousness of self. In opposition to rationalism, he summoned up the negative side, but he forgot that this negativity draws its worth from an almost substantive absoluteness. A consciousness committed to experience is ignorant, has to be ignorant, of the essences and the determination of its being.[43]

Sartre was stealing actual event, real memory, felt experience, to make them the abstracted other of Western meaning and 'History'. The living and lived urgency of the poetry presented, said Fanon, became an ineluctable moment in someone else's history: 'And so it is not I who make meaning for myself, but it is the meaning that was already there, pre-existing, waiting for me' (BS 134).

Fanon made clear that the gap between himself and Sartre was the gap between colonized and colonizer, black and white. Sartre could *only* speak from outside an experience he could not know. The alternative would be not to write 'Orphée noir': a worse, cowardly choice. Sartre elected to put his Western meaning and morality on the line. Meaning, as Fanon showed, is *simultaneously* in history or, rather, histories, made by as much as given to one. He was not yet possessor of any authoritative discourse whose perturbance should or could be sought: 'I *needed* not to know' (BS 135). He needed to be able to *live* the experience 'in ignorance' of any prescribed meaning. He needed to be able to make his own meaning. But – and the 'but' is a mighty one – *négritude*'s meaning and event were inevitably caught (by the very history of colonization) in white exegesis. As Achebe spoke of Western critics for African writers: 'we have brought home ant-ridden faggots and must be ready for the visit of lizards'. Lizards

---

43. Frantz Fanon, *Black Skin, White Masks*, trans. Charles Lam Markmann, 1967, rpt New York: Grove Weidenfeld, 1968, pp. 133–4. Henceforth cited as BS.

are not all bad. They stop ants from filling your home as the faggots burn.[44]

Sartre's dialectical reading and other Western reactions were always part of its experience, partly ignorant, partly knowing. Sartre saw *négritude* poetry from his outside, inside the colonizers' home: there he was acerbically replying to Hegel's infamous contention that Africa was out of history, including African cultures in a Hegelian dialectic of History in Hegel's own terms. Lest this seem an exercise in pure intellectualism, we should not forget that in 1948 African liberation movements had not got very far (even when they existed), and colonialism in Africa remained much as it had been for far longer than the sixty years since Fashoda. Sartre's case was aimed more at Western claims than at African interests – could he do otherwise? Fanon resisted this appropriation to others' purpose, even (maybe especially) when its author's heart was in the right place: it was no less appropriation.

This working of experience, meaning, interpretation and life is what Fanon achieves in his remarkable reading of Sartre, making Sartre's exegesis itself part of ignorant lived experience, working through and beyond Western interpretation to absorb it into political *négritude*. For Sartre had not forgotten that white and black 'suffer in [their] body quite differently', and Fanon stresses that he had not (BS 138–9). Quite simply, they speak from different places. Fanon's quarrel with Sartre is essential for that reason. White meaning has to be incorporated, appropriated by black life into its own meanings. When Fanon published *Peau noire, masques blancs* (1952), an essential part of that latter 'meaning' had to be to make white exegeses an aspect of the colonization rejected; but used in that rejection, incorporated into a *political* response and responsibility:

> I feel in myself a soul as immense as the world, truly a soul as deep as the deepest of rivers, my chest has the power to expand without limit. . . . Yesterday, awakening to the world, I saw the sky turn upon itself utterly and wholly. I wanted to rise, but the disemboweled silence fell back upon me, its wings paralyzed. Without responsibility, straddling Nothingness and Infinity, I began to weep. (140)

---

44. Chinua Achebe, *Morning Yet on Creation Day: Essays*, 1975, rpt Garden City, NY: Doubleday Anchor, 1976, pp. 62, 81.

'Orphée noir' was part of yesterday's weeping. *Black Skin* was a rousing from Western universals to realities of South Africa's violent segregation, destruction of Bantu society, Parisian racism ... (186). It was 'a mirror ... in which it [would] be possible to discuss the Negro on the road to disalienation' (184), to replace and absorb others' abstractions and 'ideals' with and into one's own experiences.

Complexities of exchange build endless levels of anxious fear of the other, no less real in one culture than another. 'They are afraid, Tayo,' says the Mexican dancer in Silko's *Ceremony*. 'They feel something happening, they can see something happening around them, and it scares them. Indians or Mexicans or whites – most people are afraid of change ... They are fools. They blame us, the ones who look different. That way they don't have to think about what has happened inside themselves' (99–100). The ones who look different are those already 'hybrid', cross-blood, inter-woven. But they are not, never have been or will be 'our' others. Of them, something of a model is found in works like Silko's own *Storyteller*, Gloria Anzaldúa's *Borderlands* or Patricia Penn Hilden's *When Nickels Were Indians*, whose speakers are already elsewhere, frontiers down.[45] They mix East/West, North/South borders, white/Native American, male/female or other bounds. They weave a web from these different places, making a new space of action. Proper metropolitan critics could do some learning here.

No doubt, as in the case of *Kim*, to do this in fiction is different from doing it on the ground. But when Abraham Lincoln 'greeted [Harriet Beecher] Stowe in 1863 as "the little lady who made this big war"',[46] whatever his irony, he was quite serious about the burning focus and sentiment her novel brought to already moving passions, an enigmatic consequence of fictive imagining of which Mark McWatt exclaims:

> To right
> the historical wrongs

---

45. Leslie Marmon Silko, *Storyteller*, New York: Arcade, 1981; Gloria Anzaldúa, *Borderlands/La Frontera: The New Mestiza*, San Francisco: Aunt Lute, 1987; Patricia Penn Hilden, *When Nickels Were Indians: An Urban, Mixed-Blood Story*, Washington, DC: Smithsonian Institution Press, 1995.

46. Ann Douglas, 'Introduction' to Harriet Beecher Stowe, *Uncle Tom's Cabin or, Life Among the Lowly*, ed. Ann Douglas, 1981, rpt Harmondsworth: Penguin, 1986, pp. 7–34, here p. 19.

of all traffic in tongues
is beyond the power
of sentence, story,
novel-writing – and yet . . .
Olive reading *Summer Lightning*!
And yet . . . Bob Marley's songs![47]

47. Mark A. McWatt, 'Enigma', in *The Language of Eldorado*, Sydney: Dangaroo Press, 1994, p. 62.

6

Conjectures on World Literature

Franco Moretti

'Nowadays, national literature doesn't mean much: the age of world literature is beginning, and everybody should contribute to hasten its advent.' This was Goethe, of course, talking to Eckermann in 1827; and these are Marx and Engels, twenty-one years later, in 1848: 'National one-sidedness and narrow-mindedness become more and more impossible, and from the many national and local literatures, a world literature arises.' *Weltliteratur*: this is what Goethe and Marx have in mind. Not what later became 'comparative' literature, but *world* literature: the Chinese novel that Goethe was reading at the time of that exchange, or the bourgeoisie of the *Manifesto*, that has 'given a cosmopolitan character to production and consumption in every country'. Well, let me put it very simply, we have not lived up to these beginnings: the study of comparative or international literature has been a much more modest intellectual enterprise, fundamentally limited to Western Europe, and mostly revolving around the river Rhine (German philologists working on French literature). Not much more.

This is also my own intellectual formation, and scientific work always has limits. But limits change, and I think it's time we return to that old ambition of *Weltliteratur*: after all, the literature around us is now unmistakably a planetary system. The question is not really *what* we should do – the question is *how*. What does it mean, studying world literature? How do we do it? I work on West European narrative between 1790 and 1930, and already feel like a charlatan outside of Britain or France. *World* literature? Many people have read more and better than I have, of course, but still, we are talking of hundreds of languages and literatures here. Reading 'more' seems hardly to be the solution. Especially because we've just started rediscovering what Margaret Cohen calls the 'great unread': I work on West European narrative, etc., etc. . . . not really, I work on its canonical fraction, which is not even one per cent of published literature. And again, some people have read more, but the point is that there are thirty thousand nineteenth-century British novels out there, forty, fifty, sixty thousand – no-one really knows, no-one has read them, no one ever will. And then there are French novels, Chinese, Argentinian, American . . . Reading 'more' is always a good thing, but not the solution.[1]

And perhaps it's too much, tackling the world and the unread at the same time. But I actually think that it's our greatest chance, because the sheer enormity of the task makes it clear that world literature cannot be literature, bigger; what we are already doing, just more of it. It has to be different. The *categories* have to be different. 'It is not the "actual" interconnection of "things",' Max Weber wrote, 'but the *conceptual* interconnection of *problems* which define the scope of the various sciences. A new "science" emerges where a new problem is pursued by a new method.'[2] That's the point: world literature is not an object, it's a *problem*, and a problem that asks for a new critical method; and no-one has ever found a method by just reading more texts. That's not how theories come into being; they need a leap, a wager – a hypothesis – to get started.

I will borrow this initial hypothesis from the world-system school of economic history, for which international capitalism is a system that is simultaneously *one*, and *unequal*: with a core, and a periphery (and a semi-periphery) that are bound together in a relationship of growing inequality. One, and unequal: *one* litera- ture (*Weltliteratur*, singular, as in Goethe and Marx), or, perhaps better, one world literary system (of inter-related literatures); but

---

1. I address the problem of the great unread in a companion piece to this essay, 'The Slaughterhouse of Literature', *Modern Language Quarterly*, vol. 61, no. 1, March 2000. (Special issue on 'Formalism and Literary History').

2. Max Weber, 'Objectivity in Social Science and Social Policy' (1904), in *The Methodology of the Social Sciences*, New York: Free Press, 1949, p. 68.

a system which is different from what Goethe and Marx had
hoped for, because it's profoundly *unequal*. 'Foreign debt is as
inevitable in Brazilian letters as in any other field,' writes Roberto
Schwarz in a splendid essay on 'The Importing of the Novel to
Brazil': 'it's not simply an easily dispensable part of the work in
which it appears, but a complex feature of it;'[3] and Itamar Even-
Zohar, reflecting on Hebrew literature:

> Interference [is] a relationship between literatures, whereby a . . .
> source literature may become a source of direct or indirect loans
> [*Importing* of the novel, direct and indirect *loans*, foreign *debt*: see how
> economic metaphors have been subterraneously at work in literary
> history] – a source of loans for . . . a target literature. . . . *There is no
> symmetry in literary interference. A target literature is, more often than not,
> interfered with by a source literature which completely ignores it.*[4]

This is what one and unequal means: the destiny of a culture
(usually a culture of the periphery, as Montserrat Iglesias Santos
has specified[5]) is intersected and altered by another culture (from
the core) that 'completely ignores it'. A familiar scenario, this
asymmetry in international power – and later I will say more about
Schwarz's 'foreign debt' as a complex literary feature. Right now,
let me spell out the consequences of taking an explanatory matrix
from social history and applying it to literary history.

Writing about comparative social history, Marc Bloch once
coined a lovely 'slogan', as he himself called it: 'years of analysis
for a day of synthesis';[6] and if you read Braudel or Wallerstein
you immediately see what Bloch had in mind, the text which is
strictly Wallerstein's, his 'day of synthesis', occupies one third of a
page, one quarter, maybe half; the rest are quotations (fourteen
hundred, in the first volume of *The Modern World-System*). Years of

---

3. Roberto Schwarz, 'The Importing of the Novel to Brazil and Its Contradictions
in the Work of Roberto Alencar' (1977), in *Misplaced Ideas*, London: Verso, 1992,
p. 50.

4. Itamar Even-Zohar, 'Laws of Literary Interference', *Poetics Today*, vol. 11, no. 1,
1990, pp. 54, 62.

5. Montserrat Iglesias Santos, 'El sistema literario: Teoría empírica y teoría de
los polisistemas', in Dario Villanueva, ed., *Avances en teoría de la literatura*, Universi-
tad de Santiago de Compostela, 1994, p. 339: 'It is important to emphasize that
interferences occur most often at the periphery of the system.'

6. Marc Bloch, 'Pour une histoire comparée des sociétés européennes', *Revue de
synthèse historique*, 1928.

analysis; other people's analysis, which Wallerstein's page synthe-
sizes into a system.

Now, if we take this model seriously, the study of world
literature will somehow have to reproduce this 'page' – which is
to say: this relationship between analysis and synthesis – for the
literary field. But in that case, literary history will quickly become
very different from what it is now: it will become 'second hand': a
patchwork of other people's research, *without a single direct textual
reading*. Still ambitious, and actually even more so than before
(world literature!); but the ambition is now directly proportional
to the distance from the text: the more ambitious the project, the
greater must the distance be.

The United States (where I write this) is the country of close
reading, so I don't expect this idea to be particularly popular. But
the trouble with close reading (in all of its incarnations, from the
new criticism to deconstruction) is that it necessarily depends on
an extremely small canon. This may have become an unconscious
and invisible premise by now, but is an iron one nonetheless: you
invest so much in individual texts *only if* you think that very few of
them really matter. Otherwise, it doesn't make sense. And if you
want to look beyond the canon (and of course world literature
will do so: it would be absurd if it didn't!) close reading will not
do it. It's not designed to do it, it's designed to do the opposite.
At bottom, it's a theological exercise – very solemn treatment of
very few texts taken very seriously – whereas what we really need
is a little pact with the devil; we know how to read texts, now let's
learn how *not* to read them. Distant reading: where distance, let
me repeat it, *is a condition of knowledge*: it allows you to focus on
units that are much smaller or much larger than the text: devices,
themes, tropes – or genres and systems. And if, between the very
small and the very large, the text itself disappears, well, it is one
of those cases when one can justifiably say, Less is more. If we
want to understand the system in its entirety, we must accept to
lose something. We always pay a price for theoretical knowledge:
reality is infinitely rich; concepts are abstract, are poor. But it's
precisely this 'poverty' that makes it possible to handle them, and
therefore to know. This is why less is actually more.[7]

---

7. Or to quote Weber again: 'concepts are primarily analytical instruments for
the intellectual mastery of empirical data'. ('Objectivity in Social Science and

Let me give you an example of the conjunction of distant reading and world literature. An example, not a model; and of course my example, based on the field I know (elsewhere, things may be very different). A few years ago, introducing Kojin Karatani's *Origins of Modern Japanese Literature*, Fredric Jameson noticed that in the take-off of the modern Japanese novel, 'the raw material of Japanese social experience and the abstract formal patterns of Western novel construction cannot always be welded together seamlessly'; and he referred in this respect to Masao Miyoshi's *Accomplices of Silence*, and Meenakshi Mukherjee's *Realism and Reality* (a study of the early Indian novel).[8] And it's true, these books return quite often to the complicated 'problems' (Mukherjee's term) arising from the encounter of Western form and Japanese or Indian reality.

Now, that the same configuration should occur in such different cultures as India and Japan – this was curious; and it became even more curious when I realized that Roberto Schwarz had independently discovered very much the same pattern in Brazil. So, eventually, I started using these pieces of evidence to reflect on the relationship between markets and forms, and then, without really knowing what I was doing, begun to treat Jameson's insight as if it were – one should always be cautious with these claims, but there is really no other way to say it – as if it were a *law of literary evolution*: in cultures that belong to the periphery of the literary system (which means: almost *all* cultures, inside and outside Europe), the modern novel first arises not as an autonomous development, but as a compromise between a Western formal influence (usually French or English) and local materials.

This first idea expanded into a little cluster of laws, which I can't discuss here,[9] and it was all very interesting, but . . . it was

---

Social Policy', p. 106). Inevitably, the larger the field one wants to study, the greater the need for abstract 'instruments' capable of mastering empirical reality.

8. Fredric Jameson, 'In the Mirror of Alternate Modernities', in Karatani Kojin, *Origins of Modern Japanese Literature*, Durham and London: Duke University Press, 1993, p. xiii.

9. I have begun to sketch them out in the last chapter of the *Atlas of the European Novel 1800–1900* (London: Verso, 1998), and this is more or less how they sound: second, the formal compromise is usually prepared by a massive wave of West European translations; third, the compromise itself is generally unstable (Miyoshi has a great image for this: the 'impossible programme' of Japanese novels); but fourth, in those rare instances when the impossible programme succeeds, we have genuine formal revolutions.

still just an idea; a conjecture that had to be tested, possibly on a large scale, and so I decided to follow the wave of diffusion of the modern novel (roughly: from 1750 to 1950) in the pages of literary history. Gasperetti and Goscilo on late eighteenth-century Eastern Europe;[10] Toschi and Martí-López on early nineteenth-century Southern Europe;[11] Franco and Sommer on mid-century Latin America;[12] Frieden on the Yiddish novels of the 1860s;[13] Moosa, Said and Allen on the Arabic novels of the 1870s;[14] Evin

10. 'Given the history of its formative stage, it is no surprise that the early Russian novel contains a host of conventions popularized in French and British literature,' writes David Gasperetti in *The Rise of the Russian Novel* (De Kalb: Northern Illinois University Press, 1998, p. 5). And Helena Goscilo, in her 'Introduction' to Krasicki's *Adventures of Mr. Nicholas Wisdom*: '*The Adventures* is read most fruitfully in the context of the West European literature on which it drew heavily for inspiration'. (Ignacy Krasicki, *The Adventures of Mr. Nicholas Wisdom* (1776), Evanston, IL: Northwestern University Press, p. xv).

11. 'There was a demand for foreign products, and production had to comply,' explains Luca Toschi speaking of the Italian narrative market around 1800 ('Alle origini della narrativa di romanzo in Italia', in Massimo Saltafuso, ed., *Il viaggio del narrare*, Florence: La Giuntina, 1989, p. 19). A generation later, in Spain, 'readers are not interested in the originality of the Spanish novel; their only desire is that it would adhere to those foreign models with which they have become familiar'; and so, concludes Elisa Martí-López, one may well say that between 1800 and 1850 'the Spanish novel is being written in France' (Elisa Martí-López, 'La orfandad de la novela española: Politica editorial y creacion literaria a mediados del siglo XIX', *Bulletin Hispanique*, 1997).

12. 'Obviously, lofty ambitions were not enough. All too often the 19th-century Spanish-American novel is clumsy and inept, with a plot derived at second hand from the contemporary European Romantic novel' (Jean Franco, *Spanish-American Literature*, Cambridge: Cambridge University Press, 1969, p. 56). 'If heroes and heroines in mid-nineteenth-century Latin American novels were passionately desiring one another across traditional lines ... those passions might not have prospered a generation earlier. In fact, modernizing lovers were learning how to dream their erotic fantasies by reading the European romances they hoped to realize' (Doris Sommer, *Foundational Fictions: The National Romances of Latin America*, Berkeley: University of California Press, 1991, pp. 31–2).

13. 'Yiddish writers parodied – appropriated, incorporated, and modified – diverse elements from European novels and stories' (Ken Frieden, *Classic Yiddish Fiction*, Albany: State University of New York, 1995, p. x).

14. Matti Moosa quotes the novelist Yahya Haqqi: 'there is no harm in admitting that the modern story came to us from the West. Those who laid down its foundations were persons influenced by European literature, particularly French literature. Although masterpieces of English literature were translated into Arabic, French literature was the fountain of our story' (Matti Moosa, *The Origins of Modern Arabic Fiction* (1970), 2nd edn, 1997, p. 93). For Edward Said, 'at some point writers in Arabic became aware of European novels and began to write works like them' (Edward Said, *Beginnings* (1975), New York: Columbia University Press, 1985, p. 81). And Roger Allen: 'In more literary terms, increasing contacts with Western literatures led to translations of works of European fiction into Arabic, followed by their adaptation and imitation, and culminating in the appearance of

and Parla on the Turkish novels of the same years;[15] Anderson on
the Filipino *Noli Me Tangere*, of 1887; Zhao and Wang on turn-of-
the-century Qing fiction;[16] Obiechina, Irele and Quayson on West
African novels between the 1920s and the 1950s[17] (plus of course
Karatani, Miyoshi, Mukherjee and Schwarz). Four continents, two
hundred years, over twenty independent critical studies, and they
all agreed: when a culture starts moving towards the modern
novel, it's *always* as a compromise between foreign form and local
materials. Jameson's 'law'[18] had passed the test – the first test,

---

an indigenous tradition of modern fiction in Arabic' (Roger Allen, *The Arabic
Novel*, New York: Syracuse University Press, 1995, p. 12).

15. 'The first novels in Turkey were written by members of the new intelligentsia,
trained in government service and well-exposed to French literature,' writes Ahmet
O. Evin (*Origins and Development of the Turkish Novel*, Minneapolis: Bibliotheca
Islamica, 1983, p. 10); and Jale Parla: 'the early Turkish novelists combined the
traditional narrative forms with the examples of the western novel' ('Desiring
Tellers, Fugitive Tales: Don Quixote Rides Again, This Time in Istanbul',
forthcoming).

16. 'The narrative dislocation of the sequential order of events is perhaps the
most outstanding impression late Qing writers received when they read or translated Western fiction. At first, they tried to tidy up the sequence of the events back
into their pre-narrated order. When such tidying was not feasible during translation, an apologetic note would be inserted. . . . Paradoxically, when he alters rather
than follows the original, the translator does not feel it necessary to add an
apologetic note' (Henry Y. H. Zhao, *The Uneasy Narrator: Chinese Fiction from the
Traditional to the Modern*, Oxford: Oxford University Press, 1995, p. 150). 'Late
Qing writers enthusiastically renewed their heritage with the help of foreign
models,' writes David Der-wei Wang: 'I see the late Qing as the beginning of the
Chinese literary "modern" because writers' pursuit of novelty was no longer
contained within indigenously defined barriers but was inextricably defined by the
multilingual, crosscultural trafficking of ideas, technologies, and powers in the
wake of nineteenth-century Western expansionism' (*Fin-de-siècle Splendor: Repressed
Modernities of Late Qing Fiction, 1849–1911*, Stanford: Stanford University Press,
1997, pp. 5, 19).

17. 'One essential factor shaping West African novels by indigenous writers was
the fact that they appeared after the novels on Africa written by non-Africans. . . .
the foreign novels embody elements which indigenous writers had to react against
when they set out to write' (Emmanuel Obiechina, *Culture, Tradition and Society in
the West African Novel*, Cambridge: Cambridge University Press, 1975, p. 17). '[The
first Dahomean novel,] *Doguicimi* . . . is interesting as an experiment in recasting
the oral literature of Africa within the form of a French novel' (Abiola Irele, *The
African Experience in Literature and Ideology*, Bloomington: Indiana University Press,
1990, p. 147). 'It was the rationality of realism that seemed adequate to the task of
forging a national identity at the conjuncture of global realities . . . the rationalism
of realism dispersed in texts as varied as newspapers, Onitsha market literature,
and in the earliest titles of the African Writers Series that dominated the discourses
of the period' (Ato Quayson, *Strategic Transformations in Nigerian Writing*, Bloomington: Indiana University Press, 1997, p. 162).

18. In the seminar where I first presented this 'second-hand' criticism, Sarah
Goldstein asked a very good, Candide-like question: You decide to rely on another

anyway.[19] And actually more than that: it had completely reversed
the received historical explanation of these matters: because if
the compromise between the foreign and the local is so ubiquitous, then those independent paths that are usually taken to be
the rule of the rise of the novel (the Spanish, the French and
especially the British case) – *well, they're not the rule at all, they're the
exception*. They come first, yes, but they're not at all typical. The
'typical' rise of the novel is Krasicki, Kemal, Rizal, Maran – not
Defoe.

See the beauty of distant reading plus world literature: they go
against the grain of national historiography. And they do so in
the form of *an experiment*. You define a unit of analysis (like here
the formal compromise),[20] and then follow its metamorphoses in
a variety of environments[21] – until, ideally, *all* of literary history
becomes a long chain of related experiments: a 'dialogue between
fact and fancy', as Peter Medawar calls it: 'between what could be
true, and what is in fact the case'.[22] Apt words for this research,
in the course of which, as I was reading my fellow historians, it

---

critic. Fine. But what if he's wrong? If he's wrong, you are wrong too, and you
soon know, because you don't find any corroboration – you don't find Goscilo,
Martí-López, Sommer, Evin, Zhao, Irele . . . And it's not just that you don't find
positive corroboration; sooner or later you find all sorts of facts you cannot
explain, and your hypothesis is falsified, in Popper's famous formulation, and you
must throw it away. Fortunately, this hasn't been the case so far, and Jameson's
insight still stands

19. OK, I confess, in order to test the conjecture I actually did read some of
these 'first novels' in the end (Krasicki's *Adventures of Mr. Nicholas Wisdom*,
Abramowitsch's *Little Man*, Rizal's *Noli Me Tangere*, Futabatei's *Ukigumo*, René
Maran's *Batouala*, Paul Hazoumé's *Doguicimi*). This kind of 'reading', however, no
longer produces interpretations but merely *tests* them: it's not the beginning of
the critical enterprise, but its appendix. And then, here you don't really read the
text anymore, but rather *through* the text, looking for your unit of analysis. The task
is constrained from the start; it's a reading without freedom.

20. For practical purposes, the larger the geographical space one wants to study,
the smaller should the unit of analysis be: a concept (in our case), a device, a
trope, a limited narrative unit – something like this. In a follow-up paper, I hope
to sketch out the diffusion of stylistic 'seriousness' (Auerbach's keyword in *Mimesis*)
in nineteenth- and twentieth-century novels.

21. How to set up a reliable sample – that is to say, what series of national
literatures and individual novels provide a satisfactory test of a theory's predictions
– is of course quite a complex issue. In this preliminary sketch, my sample (and its
justification) leave much to be desired.

22. Scientific research 'begins as a story about a Possible World', Medawar goes
on, 'and ends by being, as nearly as we can make it, a story about real life'. His
words are quoted by James Bird in *The Changing World of Geography*, Oxford:
Clarendon, 1993, p. 5. Bird himself offers a very elegant version of the experimen-
tal model.

became clear that the encounter of Western forms and local reality did indeed produce everywhere a structural compromise – as the law predicted – but also that the compromise itself was taking rather different forms. At times, especially in the second half of the nineteenth century and in Asia, it tended to be very unstable:[23] an 'impossible programme', as Miyoshi says of Japan.[24]

---

23. Aside from Miyoshi and Karatani (for Japan), Mukherjee (for India) and Schwarz (for Brazil), the compositional paradoxes and the instability of the formal compromise are often mentioned in the literature on the Turkish, Chinese and Arabic novel. Discussing Namik Kemal's *Intibah*, Ahmet Evin points out how 'the merger of the two themes, one based on the traditional family life and the other on the yearnings of a prostitute, constitute the first attempt in Turkish fiction to achieve a type of psychological dimension observed in European novels within a thematic framework based on Turkish life. *However, due both to the incompatibility of the themes and to the difference in the degree of emphasis placed on each, the unity of the novel is blemished. The structural defects of Intibah are symptomatic of the differences between the methodology and concerns of the Turkish literary tradition on the one hand and those of the European novel on the other*' (Evin, *Origins and Development of the Turkish Novel*, p. 68, emphasis mine). Jale Parla's evaluation of the Tanzimat period sounds a similar note: 'behind the inclination towards renovation stood a dominant and dominating Ottoman ideology that recast the new ideas into a mold fit for the Ottoman society. The mold, however, was supposed to hold two different epistemologies that rested on irreconcilable axioms. *It was inevitable that this mold would crack and literature, in one way or another, reflects the cracks*' ('Desiring Tellers, Fugitive Tales', emphasis mine). In his discussion of the 1913 novel *Zaynab*, by Husayn Haykal, Roger Allen echoes Schwarz and Mukherjee: '*it is all too easy to point to the problems of psychological fallacy here*, as Hamid, the student in Cairo acquainted with Western works on liberty and justice such as those of John Stuart Mill and Herbert Spencer, proceeds to discuss the question of marriage in Egyptian society on such a lofty plane with his parents, who have always lived deep in the Egyptian countryside' (*The Arabic Novel*, p. 34, emphasis mine). Henry Zhao emphasizes from his very title (The *Uneasy* Narrator: and see the splendid discussion of uneasiness that opens the book) the complications generated by the encounter of Western plots and Chinese narrative: 'A salient feature of late Qing fiction', he writes, 'is the greater frequency of narrative intrusions than in any previous period of Chinese vernacular fiction. . . . The huge amount of directions trying to explain the newly adopted techniques betrays the narrator's uneasiness about the instability of his status. . . . the narrator feels the threat of interpretive diversification. . . . moral commentaries become more tendentious to make the judgments unequivocal', and at times the drift towards narratorial overkill is so overpowering that a writer may sacrifice narrative suspense 'to show that he is morally impeccable' (*The Uneasy Narrator*, pp. 69–71).

24. In some cases, even *translations* of European novels went through all sorts of incredible somersaults. In Japan, in 1880, Tsubouchi's translation of *The Bride of Lammermoor* appeared under the title *Shumpu jowa* [*Spring Breeze Love Story*], and Tsubouchi himself 'was not beyond excising the original text when the material proved inappropriate for his audience, or converting Scott's imagery into expressions corresponding more closely to the language of traditional Japanese literature' (Marleigh Grayer Ryan, 'Commentary' to Futabatei Shimei's *Ukigumo*, New York: Columbia University Press, 1967, pp. 41–2). In the Arabic world, writes Matti Moosa, 'in many instances the translators of Western fiction took extensive

At other times it was not so: at the beginning and at the end of
the wave, for instance (Poland, Italy and Spain at one extreme;
and West Africa on the other), historians described novels that
had certainly their own problems – but not problems arising from
the clash of irreconcilable elements.[25]

I hadn't expected such a spectrum of outcomes, so at first I
was taken aback, and only later realized that this was probably the
most valuable finding of them all, because it showed that world
literature was indeed a system – but a system *of variations*. The
system was one, not uniform. The pressure from the Anglo-French
core *tried* to make it uniform, but it could never fully erase the

---

and sometimes unwarranted liberties with the original text of a work. Yaqub Sarruf
not only changed the title of Scott's *Talisman* to *Qalb al-Asad wa Salah al-Din* (*The
Lion Heart and Saladin*), but also admitted that he had taken the liberty of omitting,
adding, and changing parts of this romance to suit what he believed to be his
audience's taste.... Other translators changed the titles and the names of the
characters and the contents, in order, they claimed, to make the translated work
more acceptable to their readers and more consistent with the native literary
tradition' (*The Origins of Modern Arabic Fiction*, p. 106). The same general pattern
holds for late Qing literature, where 'translations were almost without exception
tampered with.... the most serious way of tampering was to paraphrase the whole
novel to make it a story with Chinese chracters and Chinese background....
Almost all of these translations suffered from abridgment.... Western novels
became sketchy and speedy, and looked more like Chinese traditional fiction'
(Zhao, *The Uneasy Narrator*, p. 229).

25. Why this difference? Probably, because in Southern Europe the wave of
French translations encountered a local reality (and local narrative traditions) that
wasn't that different after all, and, as a consequence, the composition of foreign
form and local material proved easy. In West Africa, the opposite situation:
although the novelists themselves had been influenced by Western literature, the
wave of translations had been much weaker than elsewhere, and local narrative
conventions were for their part extremely different from European ones (just
think of orality); as the desire for the 'foreign technology' was relatively bland –
and further discouraged, of course, by the anti-colonial politics of the 1950s – local
conventions could play their role relatively undisturbed.

Obiechina and Quayson emphasize the polemical relationship of early West
African novels vis-à-vis European narrative: 'The most noticeable difference
between novels by native West Africans and those by non-native using the West
African setting, is the important position which the representation of oral tradition
is given by the first, and its almost total absence in the second' (Obiechina, *Culture,
Tradition and Society in the West African Novel*, p. 25). 'Continuity in the literary
strategic formation we have identified is best defined in terms of the continuing
affirmation of mythopeia rather than of realism for the definition of identity....
That this derives from a conceptual opposition to what is perceived as a Western
form of realism is difficult to doubt. It is even pertinent to note in this regard that
in the work of major African writers such as Achebe, Armah, and Ngũgĩ, the
movement of their work has been from protocols of realist representation to those
of mythopeic experimentation' (Quayson, *Strategic Transformations in Nigerian
Writing*, p. 164).

reality of difference. (See here, by the way, how the study of world literature is – inevitably – a study of the struggle for symbolic hegemony across the world.) The system was one, not uniform. And, retrospectively, of course it had to be like this: if after 1750 the novel arises just about everywhere as a compromise between West European patterns and local reality – well, local reality *was* different in the various places, just as Western influence was also very uneven: much stronger in Southern Europe around 1800, to return to my example, than in West Africa around 1940. The forces in play kept changing, and so did the compromise that resulted from their interaction. And this, incidentally, opens a fantastic field of inquiry for comparative morphology (the systematic study of how forms vary in space and time, which is also the only reason to keep the adjective 'comparative' in comparative literature); but comparative morphology is a complex issue that deserves its own paper.

Let me now add a few words on that term 'compromise' – by which I mean something a little different from what Jameson had in mind in his introduction to Karatani. For him, the relationship is fundamentally a binary one: 'the abstract formal patterns of Western novel construction' and 'the raw material of Japanese social experience': form and content, basically.[26] For me, it's more of a triangle: foreign form, local material – *and local form*. Simplifying somewhat: foreign *plot*, local *characters* and then local *narrative voice*; and it's precisely in this third dimension that these novels seem to be most unstable – most uneasy, as Zhao says of the late Qing narrator. Which makes sense: the narrator is the pole of comment, of explanation, of evaluation, and when foreign 'formal patterns' (or actual foreign presence, for that matter) make characters behave in strange ways (like Bunzo, or Ibarra, or Brás Cubas), then of course comment becomes uneasy – garrulous, erratic, rudderless.

---

26. The same point is made in a great article by António Cândido: 'We [Latin American literatures] never create original expressive forms or basic expressive techniques, in the sense that we mean by romanticism, on the level of literary movements; the psychological novel, on the level of genres; free indirect style, on that of writing. . . . the various nativisms never rejected the use of the imported literary *forms* . . . what was demanded was the choice of new *themes*, of different *sentiments*' ('Literature and Underdevelopment', in César Fernández Moreno, Julio Ortega and Ivan A. Shulman, eds, *Latin America in Its Literature*, New York: Holmes & Meier, 1980, pp. 272–3).

'Interferences', Even-Zohar calls them: powerful literatures making life hard for the others – making *structure* hard. And Schwarz: 'a part of the original historical conditions reappears as a sociological form. . . . In this sense, forms are the abstract of specific social relationships.'[27] Yes, and in our case the historical conditions reappear as a sort of 'crack' in the form; as a faultline running between story and discourse, world and worldview: the world goes in the strange direction dictated by an outside power; the worldview tries to make sense of it, and is thrown off balance all the time. Like Rizal's voice (oscillating between Catholic melodrama and Enlightenment sarcasm),[28] or Futabatei's (caught between Bunzo's 'Russian' behaviour, and the Japanese audience inscribed in the text), or Zhao's hypertrophic narrator (who has completely lost control of the plot, but still tries to dominate it at all costs). This is what Schwarz meant with that 'foreign debt' that becomes a 'complex feature' of the text: the foreign presence 'interferes' with the very *utterance* of the novel.[29] The one-and-unequal literary system is not just an external network here; it doesn't remain *outside* the text: it's embedded well into its form.

Forms are the abstract of social relationships; so, formal analysis is in its own modest way an analysis of power. (That's why comparative morphology is such a fascinating field: studying how forms vary, you discover how symbolic *power* varies from place to place.) And indeed, sociological formalism has always been my interpretive method, and I think that it's particularly appropriate

27. 'The Importing of the Novel To Brazil', p. 53.
28. Rizal's solution, or lack thereof, is probably also related to his extraordinarily wide social spectrum (*Noli Me Tangere*, among other things, is the text that inspired Benedict Anderson to link the novel and the nation-state): in a nation with no independence, an ill-defined ruling class, no common language and hundreds of disparate characters, it's hard to speak 'for the whole', and the narrator's voice cracks under the effort.
29. In a few lucky cases, the structural weakness may turn into a strength, as in Schwarz's interpretation of Machado, where the 'volatility' of the narrator becomes 'the stylization of the behavior of the Brazilian ruling class': not a flaw any longer, but the very point of the novel: 'Everything in Machado de Assis's novels is colored by the *volatility* – used and abused in different degrees – of their narrators. The critics usually look at it from the point of view of literary technique or of the author's humor. There are great advantages in seeing it as the stylization of the behavior of the Brazilian ruling class. Instead of seeking disinterestedness, and the confidence provided by impartiality, Machado's narrator shows off his impudence, in a gamut which runs from cheap gibes, to literary exhibitionism, and even to critical acts' (Roberto Schwarz, 'The Poor Old Woman and Her Portraitist' [1983], in *Misplaced Ideas*, p. 94).

for world literature . . . but unfortunately at this point I must stop, because my competence stops. Once it became clear that the key variable of the experiment was the narrator's voice, well, a genuine formal analysis was off-limits for me, because it required a linguistic competence that I couldn't even dream of (French, English, Spanish, Russian, Japanese, Chinese and Portuguese, just for the core of the argument). And probably, no matter what the object of analysis is, there will always be a point where the study of world literature must yield to the specialist of the national literature, in a sort of cosmic and inevitable division of labour. Inevitable not just for practical reasons, but for theoretical ones. This is a large issue, but let me at least sketch its outline.

When historians have analysed culture on a world scale (or on a large scale anyway), they have tended to use two basic cognitive metaphors: the tree and the wave. The tree, the phylogenetic tree derived from Darwin, was the tool of comparative philology: language families branching off from each other – Slavo-Germanic from Aryan-Greco-Italo-Celtic, then Balto-Slavic from Germanic, then Lithuanian from Slavic. And this kind of tree allowed comparative philology to solve that great puzzle which was also perhaps the first world-system of culture: Indo-European: a family of languages spreading from India to Ireland (and perhaps not just languages, a common cultural repertoire, too; but here the evidence is notoriously shakier). The other metaphor, the wave, was also used in historical linguistics (as in Schmidt's 'wave hypothesis', which explained certain overlaps among languages), but it played a role in many other fields as well: the study of technological diffusion, for instance, or the fantastic interdisciplinary theory of the 'wave of advance' by Cavalli-Sforza and Ammerman (a geneticist and an archaeologist), which explains how agriculture spread from the fertile crescent in the Middle East towards the North-West and then throughout Europe.

Now, trees and waves are both metaphors – but except for this, they have absolutely nothing in common. The tree describes the passage from unity to diversity: one tree, with many branches: from Indo-European, to dozens of different languages. The wave is the opposite: it observes uniformity engulfing an initial diversity: Hollywood films conquering one market after another (or English swallowing language after language). Trees need geographical *discontinuity* (in order to branch off from each other, languages must first be separated in space, just like animal species); waves dislike barriers, and thrive on geographical *continuity* (from the viewpoint of a wave, the ideal world is a pond). Trees and branches are what nation-states cling to; waves are what markets do. And so on. Nothing in common between the two metaphors. But – *they both work.* Cultural history is made of trees *and* waves – the wave of agricultural advance supporting the tree of Indo-European languages, which is then swept by new waves of linguistic and cultural contact . . . And as world culture oscillates between the two mechanisms, its products are inevitably composite ones. Compromises, as in Jameson's law. That's why the law works: because it intuitively captures the intersection of the two mechanisms. Think of the modern novel: certainly a wave (and I've actually called it a wave a few times) – but a wave that runs into the branches of local traditions,[30] and is always significantly transformed by them.

This, then, is the basis for the division of labour between national and world literature: national literature, for people who see trees; world literature, for people who see waves. Division of labour . . . and challenge; because both metaphors work, yes, but that doesn't mean that they work equally well. The products of cultural history are always composite ones; but which is the dominant mechanism in their composition? The internal, or the external one? The nation or the world? The tree or the wave? There is no way to settle this controversy once and for all – fortunately: because comparatists need controversy. They have always been too shy in the presence of national literatures, too diplomatic: as if one had English, American, German literature – and then, next door, a sort of little parallel universe where comparatists studied a second set of literatures, trying not to disturb the first set. No; the universe is the same, the literatures are the same, we just look at them from a different viewpoint; and you become a comparatist for a very simple reason: *because you are convinced that that viewpoint is better.* It has greater explanatory power; it's conceptually more elegant; it avoids that ugly 'one-sidedness and narrow-mindedness'; whatever. The point is that

---

30. '*Grafting* processes', Miyoshi calls them; Schwarz speaks of 'the *implantation* of the novel, and of its realist *strand* in particular', and Wang of '*transplanting* Western narrative typologies'. And indeed, Belinsky had already described Russian literature as 'a *transplanted* rather than indigenous growth' in 1843.

there is no other justification for the study of world literature but this: to be a thorn in the side, a permanent intellectual challenge to national literatures – especially the local literature. If we cannot do this, we achieve nothing. 'Don't delude yourself", writes Stendhal of his favourite character: 'for you, there is no middle road.' The same is true for us.

7

The Politics of Genre

Stephen Heath

Literature exists as so many kinds of writing: for instance, *poetry* as opposed to *drama*, *lyric* as opposed to *narrative* poetry. We read *novels, sonnets, essays, thrillers, parodies, fables, satires,* and so on; with such groupings both responding to actual literature and organizing its production and reception. To write or read at a given time in a given society is to engage with the current conventions of writing, with the expectations of what forms it can take. Indeed, 'literature' itself, which once referred to the whole body of printed matter in a language, is now most often a term for just such an expectation, serving to identify a particular area of writing and drawing the line between it and everything else (science, journalism, history – all the 'non-literary' areas). What is at stake is the differentiation of writing into writings, the availability of a set of identifying types. The most singular text is never simply in a class of its own but is written and read in relation to such types: there is no *genreless* text.

It is classification into genres that has provided the most powerful identification of kinds of literary writing. As a critical term, 'genre' dates from the nineteenth century (earlier periods had talked precisely of 'kinds') and derives via French from the Latin *genus* meaning 'class' or 'sort', a derivation it shares with 'gender'; in Romance languages, one word covers both, with gender thereby inscribed as prime category, fundamental genre (some non-Western languages have adopted the term: Japanese *janru*, for example). The major source for Western genre thinking is Aristotle's *Poetics*, which set out to treat 'of poetry in itself and of its various kinds'. These kinds are distinguished according to object imitated and mode of imitation (Aristotle is concerned only with poetry as mimetic art): tragedy is the imitation in dramatic mode and epic the imitation in narrative mode of the actions of superior beings; while comedy is the imitation in dramatic mode and burlesque or lampoon the imitation in narrative mode of those of inferior ones. Differentiation can be made too according to the medium of the imitation: both epic and tragedy are in verse but the latter has a variety of metres and includes spectacle and song.

Important here are less the particulars of Aristotle's treatise than its influence. In a complicated history, the concentration on poetry as mimesis was supplemented by considerations of non-mimetic poetry and the addition of another – lyric – mode to accommodate it; this giving the 'Aristotelian' triad: *lyrical, epical, dramatic*. The authority of Aristotle, as more generally of the classical tradition of Greece and Rome, made questions of genre a matter of great concern for nations keen to develop worthy literatures of their own in emulation of that tradition. The neo-classicism of seventeenth- and eighteenth-century France and England, for example, was obsessed with genres as standards of decorum, as fixing proper relations between styles and subjects. The models furnished by the classical tradition were taken as self-evident orders of writing, no more than 'Nature methodized' (to imitate them *was* to imitate nature). Correct knowledge of genres and their rules was thus a necessity for the poet and had its own poetic genre, with Horace's *Ars Poetica* as model and Boileau's *L'Art poétique* and Pope's *An Essay on Criticism* as key examples. Shakespeare then posed a critical problem: his greatness was acknowledged but his plays were regarded as 'mingled drama', mixing tragic with comic elements in breach of genre propriety. Significantly, when this judgement was challenged, a need was felt for new genre identifications that would set aside what Coleridge called 'misapplied names' and do justice to the 'different genus' of the plays.

Generic naming indeed can be an explicit part of the presentation of works, including in their very titles: *Roman de la Rose*, *Isayoi nikki* (Abutsu-ni; *nikki* are personal, 'diary' narratives), *Pagina meditationum* (Marguerite d'Oingt), *Essais* (Montaigne),

Narrative of the Life of Frederick Douglass, an American Slave, Written by Himself, *Duineser Elegien* (Rilke), *Une si longue lettre* (Mariama Bâ). Not that such identifications should be taken for granted: genres are not fixed essences and these names need to be understood each time in their historical context and for the various textual effects they can produce: Douglass's work is indeed the narrative of a life but Bâ's is really a novel (in the form of a letter); *Psalms* suggests a certain unity for a book that may also be seen as made up of a number of different poetic kinds, notably praise poems and supplications (the Hebrew title, *tĕhillîm*, means 'praises'); *Kim Vân Kiêu* (Nguyên Du) is known in English as *The Tale of Kieu*, with 'tale' and its suggestion of folk simplicity serving to familiarize a narrative poem whose title is in fact made up of the names of its main characters (an alternative title, *Doan-Truong Tan-Thanh*, points reflexively to its refashioning of an old – sad – story: literally 'bowels in torment, new style'). *The History of Emily Montague* (Frances Brooke), an epistolary novel, is very different from *Historia de las Indias* (Las Casas), at once chronicle, personal testimony and treatise, and both are very different again from an academic work labelled 'history' or 'historia' today. But then too, what does it mean so confidently to differentiate, to slip works into this or that category – 'really' a novel, 'novel' as opposed to 'history', and so on?

Historically, genres and concern with them are to be found throughout world literature, in all cultures. The *Shih-ching*, the classic anthology of early Chinese poetry, gave rise to a tradition of scholarship whose great achievement was the *Wen-hsin tiao-lung* of the fifth-century literary historian Liu Hsieh: Liu's interest was exactly in the kinds of poetry and his study reflects on the nature of genre before proceeding to a chapter-by-chapter account of the genres to be found in the *Shih-ching*. The palaces of fifteenth- and sixteenth-century Aztec civilization had 'houses of song' attached to them, *cuicacalli* whose function was the strict regulation of the composition and performance of lyric poems (poems such as are recorded in the *Cantares mexicanos* codex). The oral poetry of the Yoruba people traditionally falls into a number of genres – *oríkì* ('praise poetry'), *ofò* ('incantations'), *àló àpamò* ('riddles'), and so on – strictly differentiated by linguistic and semantic features which determine their recognition, allow their identification in performance.

These examples of genre thinking and practice leave open questions as to what we are to understand by the term and as to its relevance for world literature, for moving between literatures. The dramatic is a mode of presentation that can be seen across cultures through history, thought about in connection with Sophocles *and* Bhasa *and* Zeami *and* Goethe. Sonnet and haiku are set poetic forms with a limited cross-cultural reach: sonnets are found in European-language literatures; the haiku is specifically Japanese but is sometimes adapted for other poetries (witness, famously, Ezra Pound's 'In a Station of the Metro'). Elegy and *shishōsetsu* come with ideas of both form and content: a poem mourning a death or meditating on the passing of life; a novel or story aimed at producing the conviction of a faithfully chronicled personal experience (Shiga Naoya's story 'Kinosaki ni te' is an example). Elegy, however, also has a history that includes the initial use of the term in classical Greek and Latin literatures to refer to a particular verse couplet, and a subsequent development in which it comes to refer very generally to poems expressive of some mood of meditative melancholy; the *shishōsetsu*, which has its great moment in the 1920s and 1930s, became influential throughout twentieth-century Japanese literature, going beyond genre boundaries and creating something of a general *perspective* of writing. We could then return to sonnet and haiku, which, while defined formally as particular verse patterns, are also developed historically around specific thematic concerns: introduced in thirteenth-century Italy, the sonnet was fashioned through Petrarch into the medium of a particular Renaissance version of love; originating in fifteenth-century humorous linked-verse or *haikai-renga*, the haiku develops as the representative poetic form of the Edo period, looking to express what Bashō described as 'inner sensibilities in harmony with things' but aiming also at a certain closeness to the city life of the *chônin*, of the new mercantile classes. Both sonnet and haiku continue as forms through to today, but with specific thematic reworkings (including the late nineteenth-century renewal of the haiku which gives the term itself its currency).

A strong account of genre insists in one way or another on an intersection of modes and themes, as for Aristotle tragedy is a particular type of subject dramatically presented. The lyrical–epical–dramatic triad is thus a matter not of genres but rather of

modes of enunciation, ways of presenting that do not in themselves involve any defined content. This can be difficult to grasp
because the Romantic and post-Romantic elaboration of the triad
has recast modes as thematically substantial, indeed as *moods* (so
we often use the word 'dramatic' with no reference to mode, to
mean vivid, compelling, momentous – dramatic colours, dramatic
events). Modes as such, however, belong to the pragmatics of
language, are possibilities of language use; a genre is a characteristic mobilization of one or more of those possibilities to some
specific end: such a definition taking genres as a fact of all
discourse, not of literature alone.

The Russian critic and theorist Mikhail Bakhtin talks of 'speech
genres'. We use language to make individual utterances but those
utterances fall within relatively stable types, generic forms that are
the condition of communication: were each utterance simply
individual, *sui generis*, we would never recognize the finality, the
sense, of what we were hearing or reading. These forms can then
be more or less open to variation: patient–therapist conversations
have greater plasticity than military commands. Literary genres
are examples of such speech genres but differ significantly from
the basic ones of everyday communication: 'The vast majority of
literary genres are secondary, complex genres composed of various transformed primary genres (the rejoinder in dialogue, everyday stories, letters, diaries, minutes, and so forth). As a rule, these
secondary genres of complex cultural communication *play out*
various forms of primary speech communication.' So a novel will
include a number of primary genres but absorbed into another
kind of utterance which removes them from the immediacy of
everyday life, catching them up into its own reality as literary-
artistic event. By virtue of their complexity and their work of
transformation – the playing out – of primary forms, such secondary genres are those that most allow for freedom of individual
expression; a freedom, however, that is not outside but from
within – even as it may challenge and defeat – the resources of
existing genres.

If mode and theme and formal matters of diction, metre, and
so on, are aspects to which we look in distinguishing genres, we
need also to think of audience and effect (so Aristotle characterized tragedy as effecting a purgation of pity and fear). Genres, in
fact, have been and are identified in many ways and by reference

to a variety of aspects in a variety of combinations. Aspects which are crucial in the identification of one genre may not be so in that of another (for example, length plays a fundamental part in distinguishing the short story but not the pastoral poem), while particular features of this or that aspect can be shared by different genres (for example, a certain theme can be common to more than one genre). There are difficulties as to saying what kind of concept 'genre' is and even as to what particular genres are, since it is far from easy to arrive at any definition that will adequately determine which works will or will not fall within a genre (other than by equating genre with technical form, so that the sonnet as a verse form is a genre or the novel is simply the genre of 'a fiction in prose of a certain extent' – which makes for a genre that sets the early eleventh-century *Genji-monogatari* alongside the mid-nineteenth-century *Madame Bovary*). Where neo-classicism assumed fixed identities, leaving it relatively untroubled by problems as to the *theory* of genre, modern Western criticism refuses them, leaving it very much concerned with such theory, finally stressing the looseness or fuzziness of genre definitions and perceptions. The search for a set of features all of which must be found in all works of a genre gives way to the notion of groups of texts linked by 'family resemblance': elements are held in common in the group but are not all present in each of its members. Thus no one work will possess features that can identify all the works in the genre; though some works will seem prototypical, more centrally defining than others: *Madame Bovary* has been such a work for the novel in a way that, say, *Gulliver's Travels* has not). Conversely, no one genre will exhaustively identify an individual work which, to a greater or lesser degree, will be involved in other genres (beginning with Bakhtin's primary genres), be able to belong to more than one genre (Spenser's *Faerie Queene* is epic, romance, political allegory, moral treatise), and be available for genre redefinition (Proust's *À la recherche du temps perdu* read now through gay studies as a charter-text 'in that most intriguing of genres, the coming-out story that doesn't come out').

The family resemblance account should not be taken to mean that genres have no substantial reality. To look at literature through genres is to grasp the former historically inasmuch as the latter are precisely not 'natural' forms or abstract categories, but specific socio-historical operations of language by speakers and listeners, writers and readers: orders of discourse that change, shift, travel, lose force, come and go over time and cultures. That there may be no statically enclosing *is* definition of a genre does not leave it as some nominalist fancy, just some arbitrary grouping of texts by literary critics. As Bakhtin suggests, there is a necessary practice of genres whether or not there is any elaborated account of them: the reality of linguistic communication is always that of *kinds of utterance*. If these kinds are constructed in the descriptions and analyses of linguists, historians, critics and others, they are also practical forms of recognition: horizons of expectation for listeners or readers, models of production for speakers or writers. Genres, in other words, are *representative*, typical codifications of discursive properties corresponding to typical situations of communication and with typical conceptions of who is being addressed, whether this be in terms of particular subjectivity, community membership, religious adherence, sexual orientation, class position or whatever (thus romance fiction today has typically identified its readers as female, heterosexual, working and lower-middle class, a commercial audience). Such genre address, moreover, *appeals*, is an envisaged mobilization of desire, holding reader or listener to 'pleasures' which define her or his generic participation (the romance envisages strong heroine identification, release into fantasy, romantic-erotic stimulation).

Genres are stabilizations of relations of communication. Necessarily conservative inasmuch as they depend on the reworking of recognized ways of making sense, they are also possible sites for a conservatism that turns recognition and reworking into regulation and repetition, into laws which are institutionally supported in one way of another; the prescriptive rules of French neo-classicism and the supervised composition of Aztec poetry are examples. They are conservative too in their potential to function as a kind of memory through the process of recollection they involve. The genres of Yoruba oral poetry stretch through time to provide a remembering that is a constructive part of the very existence of the community. Milton knows epic as a genre that runs back over two thousand years; *Paradise Lost* recalls Homer and Virgil and Tasso, rewrites epic tradition with Christian matter. But also vice versa: the Bible itself is read through and for the genre, so that the Book of Job for Milton is 'a brief model' of 'the epic form' (where biblical scholars today usually include Job among 'wisdom writings', identified as a characteristic genre of the ancient Near East).

If genres are forms of history, they are also, of course, as this last example indicates, historical forms, articulated within socio-historical contexts. The generic memory the epic brings is taken up by Milton in a quite specific moment of writing, a moment that includes exactly this long-scale, transcultural imagination of the epic form and its models. As socio-historical operations, genres are open-ended, subject to modification as new utterances change understanding of them (*Paradise Lost* is written in relation to a generic model that it then *newly* exemplifies; the epic is not an essence that Homer's *Iliad* first embodies but the articulation and perception historically of a kind of writing that Milton, as it were, makes up again in his poem) and as the cultural conditions supporting their continuation significantly alter (the development of middle-class industrial societies in nineteenth-century Europe accompanies a secularized, bourgeois culture which finds its meaning in ordinary social terms rather than epic and heroic ones; the epic loses force, the novel emerges as the new genre of this new world – prosaic, realistic, *anti*-epic).

Generic continuities are matched by discontinuities, memory by invention, in complex processes of change. New genres are constantly formed from old ones as additional texts with shifting textual practices problematize the genre conception or as available discourses are brought together into a different form of writing (so Montaigne 'invents' the essay). Different contexts of reading or listening produce new or altered genre identifications as kinds of writing with little or no formal recognition become accredited as genres in response to changing socio-historical pressures (so African-American slave narratives gain acknowledge-ment and are read as a specific genre in the light of contemporary awareness of matters of race and identity and the renegotiation of history and the literary canon). Equally they produce new genres and generic transformations, as classes or groups define and redefine the conditions and understanding of their existence (so rap emerged in the United States as a powerful genre of young African-Americans' social expression).

We can grasp the politics of genre here as a politics of representation, with change and innovation implicated in crises as to who and what is represented and how and to whom.

Typically such crises involve disturbance of and resistance to existing genres from the perception of and appeal to a reality that the resulting new or transformed genres will help precisely to *know*, to bring into meaning. Genres, that is, are attempts to make representational and representative sense. Faced with the 'new' world of the Americas, the European missionaries and colonialists experience something 'so extraordinary', as Las Casas put it, that their genres – chronicle, natural history, legal deposition, epistle – are marshalled *and confronted* with contradictory discourses of 'what they saw', their testimony producing tensions of 'like' and 'unlike', 'same' and 'other', and initiating a work of representation that carries through the centuries in the renewed practices of colonial discourse. Faced with the contemporary United States, Toni Morrison has described a politically contradictory relation of the black woman writer to the novel, necessary genre of the claiming of identity (its historical function for the middle class and then for other groups in the modern world) and, as genre, necessarily to be challenged in a deconstructive, dialogical refusal of the terms of representation it sets (the novel as formally, generically, representative of a specific moment of subjectivity with specific and limiting race and gender terms).

A genre exists only in conjunction with other genres, is distinguished by virtue of its differences from those others to which it is related in what at any given moment is a system of genres. Issues of the politics of genre carry through directly from this. Bakhtin's account of genres as 'literary' in terms of elaboration and complexity, as against immediacy and everydayness, brings with it a particular systematic assumption of literature involving *secondary* over *primary* genres. The relations of these 'primary' speech genres to literature and *its* genres, however, are culturally variable and subject to quite distinct terms of understanding. Genres of oral poetry, for instance, may well depend on and demand recognition of relations between the community's speech genres for which such oppositions as complex/everyday or immediacy/mediation will be damagingly irrelevant. Indeed the very idea of literature here, its habitual confinement to the written, is part of the problem; precisely to counter which, the Kenyan novelist Ngũgĩ wa Thiong'o has proposed the term 'orature' to refer to all the kinds of oral utterances in African culture, poetry included. But we need cultural caution too when looking at the stories of a writer such as the Nigerian Amos Tutuola, whose works create a 'written orality' that has been described as Yoruba speech using English words and that invokes proverbs, riddles, tales and songs in a way which is not just some Western literary 'playing-out': the works can be taken as 'novels' but are in tension with the assumptions of that genre identification, and first and foremost with those of any primary/secondary mastery of discourses. To grasp – to *read* – such tension is central to the study of world literature today, to the reality of writings that exist in a situation of the extensive influence of Western forms and of the struggle for other definitions, new generic terms within and against them.

The politics of genre turns on the distinctions it makes and the hierarchies those distinctions readily support: between high and low, sacred and secular, poetic and prosaic, literary and non-literary genres. To challenge and transform such hierarchies involves a range of shifts in perception and genre judgement, notably as to what counts as the proper matter and language of literature, as to what to *recognize*. The development of the novel provides a powerful middle class with a genre that seeks to represent the terms of its world in defiance of traditional genre views of the actual social life of men and women as fitting only for comedy or satire (the supreme genres are conceived as universal, expressing essential truths in abstraction from the contingencies of the everyday). Diaries, domestic journals, personal narratives, are examples of genres that recent feminist theory and practice has been concerned to accredit, calling into question the gender-ideological bases of existing genre assumptions (distinctions between objective and subjective, public and private, political and personal).

The various forms of the writing of women's lives could be seen as inferior genres because 'female'; the novel as low genre because of its readership (taking in the lower-middle and working classes and importantly including women) and the commercial nature of its production for this readership, the new 'public' (it was often attacked as 'democratic'). 'The public is so stupid,' commented Flaubert, whose own work marks a significant moment in the development of a split between high and low within the genre itself: on the one hand, the 'literary' or 'serious' novel; on the other, 'popular' or 'mass' fiction, the market standardization of genre products – romance, mystery, science fiction, crime, best-sellers (all the drugstore shelf-headings). The split was increasingly supported by an academic institution of literature that elaborated canons of *works* and defined quality, while the power of genre conceptions in consumer mass cultural production only increased in importance. Nowhere is this more visible than in television with its host of recognized – *expected* – genres: sitcoms, news, game shows, reality shows, talk shows, et al. Such genre domination is at once part of the hierarchization process – high genres are seen as full of *individual* works – and a fact of an 'entertainment industry' that aims to maximize profit by organizing production around a limited number of models. Non-standard programmes, those that cross over or upset genre distinctions, can quickly become sites of disquiet and political sensitivity (witness the need felt to keep documentary and drama separate, the controversies surrounding their 'confusion').

This strength of genre classifications is simultaneous with a theory and practice of writing that seeks to undermine them because of that strength, the hold of ready-made expectations of meaning. 'A book no longer belongs to a genre; every book answers to literature alone,' asserted French writer and critic Maurice Blanchot. Or, abandoning 'literature' as itself another genre, the point is to shift from *work* to *text*. Where a work *resembles*, is readable within genre limits that it follows as a condition of its representation to the reader, the text *differs*, transgresses these limits in order to implicate the reader in a writing that disturbs representations. Where the work is on the side of pleasure, modulating a subject's cultural expectations to fulfilment, the text is on the other, that of *jouissance*, coming off from any stability of self in an abruptness of dispersal, the reader pushed out of genres. But then, inevitably, into a new one, that of the writing of the process of the subject in language; a genre that can be given a history from Mallarmé and Joyce through to the present and the texts of Blanchot himself or the deconstructive writings of Jacques Derrida, disturbingly attentive to genre laws and limits. It is this new genre that is invoked by a book such as Abdelkebir Khatibi's *Amour bilingue*, with its scansion of language as 'bilingual', always run through by another 'that asserts and destroys itself as what is incommunicable [*l'incommunicable*]'. Similarly, the 'writing from the body' proposed by Hélène Cixous can be understood as bound up with this same textual focus on subject and language.

These last examples point to the importance today of ideas of the need for resistance to genre terms in a way that takes us beyond a particular French theoretical development of *le texte* as genre. Khatibi's book has 'bilingualism' as a site of exploration at once in language and across languages and nations and histories and sexes: French and Arabic, France and Morocco, colonizer and colonized, man and woman, in a difficult narration of criss-crossing stories, inter-reacting texts. Cixous's textual practices – in novel or play or essay or dialogue – bear on the recognition and creation of a feminine writing – and those genre terms become problematic, impossible in the project of her work as it confronts generic inscriptions of gender (remember the shared etymology). A contemporary politics of genre, that is, runs askew of the lines drawn, the 'legitimate' separations, discordantly mixes kinds to put literature *on the border*, the reality and metaphor of which are perhaps nowhere better exemplified than in contemporary Chicano writing with its cross-mixing border narratives (Rolando Hinojosa) and performances (Carolina Gomez-Peña) and aesthetics (*Criticism in the Borderlands* is the significant title of a recent work in this area).

Writing a year or so after the *fatwah* calling for the suppression of the book and its author, Salman Rushdie described the case of *The Satanic Verses* as perhaps 'one of the biggest category mistakes in literary history'. He was insisting on 'the fictionality of fiction' and on the error of ignoring the genre of his book and reading it not as a novel but as history or anti-religious pamphlet. But then the writing of *The Satanic Verses* goes contrary to an acceptance of genre orthodoxies, including those that would circumscribe the novel – 'only a novel'. Radically dissenting from genre segregations, its claim is for hybridity as force for change: 'It rejoices in mongrelization and fears the absolutism of the Pure. Mélange, hotch-potch, a bit of this and a bit of that is *how newness enters the world.*' The very idea of the study *now* of *world literature* is involved in the hybrid: reading not merely comparatively and generically, this novel from here next to that one from there, but migrationally and impurely, writings intermingled with one another, against the grain of ready – legitimate – identities. To look at genre politically is to read with just such a migrant's-eye view, which is another definition of 'world literature', the newness *its study makes.*

8

Literary History without Literature:
Reading Practices in the Ancient World

Simon Goldhill

'Literature' began, as Auden might have put it, in 1823, along with 'Art' and the other shibboleths of Romantic aesthetics. The rise of 'Literature' as a category is paralleled by the fall of Rhetoric as the privileged discipline of the liberal arts, and, with a beguilingly neat symmetry, as twentieth-century modernism has challenged the category 'literature', so rhetoric has regained its place as a master discourse in the modern academy. If we accept this narrative – at least in such broad terms – it leaves the classicist with something of a problem, however. A literary history that did not recognize that Homer is first and Virgil second (and closer to first than third, as Quintilian put it) would be a strangely truncated affair. While Terry Eagleton[1] can write an account of the ideology of aesthetics that finds its *fons et origo* in the eighteenth century, could such an account be satisfactory for what is called 'literature', with its constant reappropriation of the writing of the past? It would be a naïve nominalism that asserted that the nineteenth-century invention of the term 'literature' is necessarily testimony to some sort of Foucauldian rupture in the history of writing. Nor do I wish to resort to the common gesture of turning to 'textuality' as a passe-partout: it would obscure the crucial lines of ideology and cultural systems that I wish to investigate. My

1. T. Eagleton, *The Ideology of the Aesthetic*, Oxford, 1990.

question, simply put, is 'What is at stake in the category "literature" for literary history?' What happens if we do use the category
'literature' for the ancient world? Can we do literary history
without literature?

That 'literature' is not a category in the ancient world is clear
enough. There is no equivalent term, certainly in Greek writing,
which tends to have a highly developed and structured sense of
the discreteness of genres. There is no term that sensibly or
seriously links prose and verse, for example. Even when education
becomes increasingly institutionalized and internationalized
especially in the Roman Empire, where *enkuklios paideia* – the full
circle of a gentleman's education – could include a reading list of
both prose and verse writers, there is little question but that
contemporary writing is excluded: 'modern literature' is in this
system a contradiction in terms. The lack of a term for 'literature'
here is a sign of the lack of a significant category, the lack of an
institutional and cultural frame.

'Classical Literary Criticism': Inventing a History

Perhaps the clearest way to see what is at stake in the reimporta-
tion of this category can be seen in what is taught as the 'history
of literary criticism'. There is – inevitably – a volume called *The
Cambridge History of Literary Criticism. Vol. 1: Classical Criticism.*
There is also a justly renowned and widely used collection of
sources by Russell and Winterbottom called *Ancient Literary Criticism.*[2] It's fascinating to see what goes into and what gets left out
of this lengthy and influential collection. 'The authors must speak
for themselves,' say the editors, with the all-too-familiar conceal-
ment of the absolutely determinative gestures of selection and
juxtaposition. Indeed, it is clear that the principle of selection is
one of coincidence with the modern category of literature. So to
take a single but paradigmatic example, a small piece by Plutarch
on humour is extracted from his *Table Talk* (a set of questions,
problems and discussions about dinner party etiquette, history
and practice) focusing on the opinion that you should not quote
Aristophanes at parties because his jokes are disgustingly rude, on

---

2. D. Russell and M. Winterbottom, eds, *Ancient Literary Criticism*, Oxford, 1972.

the one hand, and so obscure, on the other, that one would need a personal tutor for explanations. This is juxtaposed to a comparison of Menander and Aristophanes from a different work (existing only in epitome) that compares the two comic playwrights, praising the elegance and smoothness of Menander and excoriating the vulgarity of Aristophanes. Plutarch's comments, however, are an aside in a lengthy discussion of joking and humour in general, in which he suggests that *any* joke is out of place for a proper citizen, since not only do jokes depend on an aggression unsuitable for the collectivity of a symposium, they also destabilize by laughter the self-control of the listener and the dignity of the speaker. Plutarch's remarks need to be placed in a long tradition of writing about the social and epistemological place of humour, which attempts to control the place of humour's unruliness within the regulated life of the citizen and his pals.[3] By abstracting the aesthetic object 'Literature' as the defining characteristic for inclusion, the editors have seriously distorted what Plutarch's discussion is about, what sort of criticism it is. The very judgement on Aristophanes – that he is crude and obscure – must be seen in light not only of the overall discussion of the place of the unruly, but also of Aristophanes' cultural capital as a school text and his frequent quotation in idealized representations of an intellectual dinner party. Plutarch's limit-case reading of Aristophanes cannot 'speak for itself'. It must be understood as part of a very particular construction of propriety and language and citizenship. The aesthetic object *qua* aesthetic object is simply not at stake.

Criticism and the Politics of Citizenship

Indeed, it is generally true that what is taken as ancient 'literary criticism' is aimed not at a discrete body of textual material, but, rather, at the formation of a good citizen. Even the study of grammar, as we will see, is part of this politics. Quintilian famously defines an orator as *vir bonus dicendi peritus*, a 'good man skilled at speaking', and the idea of 'the good man' is taken so seriously that Quintilian argues that a bad man *cannot* be a good speaker,

---

3. S. Goldhill, *Foucault's Virginity*, Cambridge, 1995, pp. 14–20 with bibliography.

and that even if – *per impossibile* – a bad man did have the same speaking skill as a good man, he would still necessarily be a worse orator. Plato's attack on poetry and art in the *polis* is first and foremost an ideological question about which discipline should be the master discourse of the *polis*, and which types of poetry, song and art make a better citizen. Because of poetry's role in education, because of rhetoric's role in the performance of citizenship, because of art's role in the politics of civic representation, to limit such discussions by the sphere of the aesthetic is to ignore how reading and performing and learning is part of the *askesis* of the citizen, part of the policing of the boundaries of sociopolitical engagement. This tradition of the critical discussion of poetry or other writing is not *literary* criticism. The use of the word 'literary' seems designed to obscure the political subject.

The imposition of the category of 'the literary' thus cuts across the social and cultural significance of the discipline of reading and writing in the ancient world. What is being ignored is the very scene of reading – as the scene of the engagement of the political subject. For ancient texts are to be performed – whether it be the event of drama, the philosophical treatise, the erotic epigram – as part of the formulation of the citizen as speaking subject.

What I shall discuss in this essay, therefore, is the historically and culturally specific construction of the subject in and through the scene of reading. By 'the scene of reading' I want to discuss the very broadest sense of reading, whereby one person self-consciously articulates an interpretive response to the performance of a speaking subject, particularly a response to the performance of a rhetorical display, to a lecture, poem or, finally, to a painting or a speech of praise. How is this exchange conceptualized, represented, enacted? How does this process of reading relate to the body of the performer and the reader? How does it relate to the political frame of social interaction between members of a society? In short, is there a history of (this) reading? The hazard of this essay is that the history of this reading will show up the insufficiencies of the 'history of literature'.

Overview

There are three fundamental elements in this nexus of questions, and I shall be looking at them in three different periods. The first element is the cultural and political construction of the citizen: I shall be moving from Athens in the fourth century BCE, with its democratic community of adult males engaged in the political exchanges of citizenship, through the Greeks of the Roman Empire, with their cultural capital but political disenfranchisement and intensely ambivalent self-presentation of status, to, finally, the monastery of Eastern Greeks in the fifth century CE, a paradoxical community of people on their own – *monoi* – reading for God.

Demosthenes could declare in the fourth century BCE that the *politeia* (political constitution) of Athens depended on *logoi* (speeches, arguments); indeed, not only are the major institutions of democracy sites for the display of competitive speech making – lawcourt, assembly, theatre – but also performance in these institutions was the major route to political power. The citizen performs his citizenship as a speaking subject within the city of words. For the Greek citizen of the Roman Empire, however, although rhetorical performance, particularly in the legal arena, could bring great rewards, an engagement in culture also meant an engagement with the lost world of classical Athens via the intellectual methods of Hellenistic scholarship, and, specifically, a heightened consciousness of linguistic performance as a key to elite identity. The protocols of proper speech are central to a politics of class and status. For the Christians, in practising a religion of the book, reading and interpreting the written word are integral to the reception of the *Logos* – and define the person. Thus Augustine's *Confessions* not only records engagements with texts as central moments in the narrative of his and others' spiritual growth – from a soldier's reading of the *Life of Anthony* to his own move away from Manichaean interpretations of the Bible (it is not by chance that he is reading in the garden at the moment of his conversion) – but also discusses the nature of reading itself theoretically as well as theologically. In each of these cases, there is an integral connection between the social and political formation of the citizen and the scene of reading.

The second crucial element might be called the cultural politics of reading. My broad sense of reading implies a space mapped at one pole by the business of teaching how to read at all levels in schools, and, at another, by the production of meaning in the exchanges of cultural life. This requires institutions and practices that are regulated and normative. I shall be moving from the circle of a distinguished orator in classical Athens, where a master teaches his paying pupils about political rhetoric; through the institutionalized Greekness of the empire's education system, where the school-room, lecture hall and patron's house form an arena for the display and surveillance of the proprieties of social exchange; to the Christian world, where in church, in reading groups, with teachers or alone, you read for life, and an incorrect choice, a *heresy* of interpretation, leads to death in this life and the next. These different frames promote and require different practices.

The third element is the body. I need not emphasize after Michel Foucault and Peter Brown that there is a history of the body. And it is, of course, not by chance that the broad sweep of my account travels Foucault's route from the classical *polis* to Christian homiletics. Reading requires the body, but it is, remarkably, part of the history of the body all too rarely articulated, even or especially in Foucault's account of how the normative texts on the body function in society. I will be moving from the orator who must stand upright, not move his hand outside his cloak, via instructions on how to sit in a lecture, to the humble, intense and even prostrated reading of the monk. From the upright orator, then, to the prostrate body, eyes fixed on the wounded body of Christ.

Athens's Orator: Working on Words

Let us begin with the classical city. Now, classical Athens is a performance culture, where democracy formulates the role of the viewing, judging, voting citizen as integral to social and political practice.[4] It is within such a frame that I wish to place my opening

---

4. S. Goldhill and R. Osborne, eds, *Performance Culture and Athenian Democracy*, Cambridge, 1998.

text, which gives a remarkable sense of how performance, politics and the cultural strategies of verbal exchange may be represented and discussed.

This is Isocrates' great speech, the *Panathenaicus*, begun in 342 BCE when the author was 93, it is claimed. The speech begins as a eulogy of Athens, the writer's city, and goes into an attack on Sparta.[5] Both praise and attack are conducted in terms of political policy, constitution and national character. After some 199 chapters of this, the writer turns suddenly and quite remarkably to the moment of writing itself:

> I had just written what you have just read, and was revising it with three or four young men who customarily spend time with me. As we went through it, it seemed good to us and lacking just its conclusion, when it occurred to me to call one of my former students who had lived under an oligarchy, so he could point out any mistakes I had made. (200)

Although poets sometimes represent the moment of creation or inspiration, it is odd indeed for a political pamphlet, especially after two hundred chapters of argument *in persona*, suddenly to represent its own composition in this way. We are invited into the teacher's study with his pupils around him. The student is duly called and, the teacher reports, praises the speech lavishly (201), but, when pushed, attempts to argue that the representation of Sparta is ridiculously biased (202). Isocrates again reflects on the moment of composition and the effect of his pupil's comment (203): 'This brief and brusque assertion was the reason why I did not conclude my speech where I had intended. I thought it would be shameful and terrible for me if when present I should overlook one of my pupils using poor arguments.' The orator's response to the audience's criticism is to turn immediately to counter-attack and the author promptly launches into a violent tirade (204–15) against his pupil (who accepts it with good grace, as fictional pupils do). Indeed, the pupil confesses that he had spoken only in praise of Spartan athletic practices and was motivated by his own perplexity (*aporia*) because he could not simply praise his master as he was accustomed to do.

---

5. See V. Gray, 'Image of Sparta: Writer and Audience in Isocrates' *Panathenaicus*', in A. Powell and S. Hodkinson eds, *The Shadow of Sparta*, London, 1993.

It may look as if the figure of the pupil has been introduced
merely to dramatize a possible objection to the previous argument
and to crush it. (In other words, dramatizing the 'you may object',
or the 'someone might say' strategy typical of forensic oratory.)
But there is much more. For Isocrates goes on to say that he has
an even more crushing attack to make on Spartan training
practices, which he then demonstrates at length (218–29). This
reduces 'the widely experienced and highly trained student' (219)
to silence and departure – in turn prompting a further extraordinary commentary on audience response:

> The young men present did not have the same judgement on the
> scene as I. They praised me for speaking more vigorously than they
> had expected, and for competing nobly. They also despised him.
> Their judgement, however, was faulty and they were wrong about both
> of us. (219–20)

The orator rejects his rhetorical success as an audience's misreading. (Reading the audience – part of an orator's skill, according
to the handbooks – is thus masterfully demonstrated here.) His
reasons: the young man had gone away wiser not merely about
the Spartans' nature, but also about himself ('he had experienced
the message of the inscription at Delphi to "know yourself"'),
whereas he himself had spoken effectively but without the wisdom
of his years – all too like a rash youth. Indeed, after dictating the
speech to an amanuensis, and re-reading it more calmly after
three or four days, not only is he distressed about what he said
immoderately about the Spartans, but he also confesses that 'I
had spoken with contempt and extreme bitterness and altogether
without understanding' (232). The crushing retort to the pupil –
with what rhetorical disingenuousness? – is partially withdrawn
because of its extreme tone. Although tempted to rub it out or
burn it, out of consideration for his old age and the work he had
put in, he decides to invite his pupils to hear the whole speech
with its new ending, and to judge whether it should be destroyed
or circulated. At first, perhaps unsurprisingly, it simply receives
the praise and applause 'such as successful epideictic displays win'
(233).

    In the following audience discussion, however, the same pro-
Spartan pupil nervously opens a further debate, and offers a long
speech (235–63) in which he, too, regrets his former reaction,

and offers a lengthy counter-reading of the speech, claiming that *his own* first reading had been wrong. The voice of the audience gets to perform a critique – a reading – both of a previous reaction, and of the master's further and previous performance. (The *Panathenaicus* gives the lie to the frequently seen assumption that an audience has one direct, immediate response to a performance, and that this response should be privileged.) Although at first sight Isocrates was attacking Sparta, he claims, on closer reading, it was clear that Isocrates was also praising Sparta for precisely what Spartans themselves were proud of. I wish to focus not on the substance nor the *politesse* of the pupil's re-reading, but on a passage where he comments on his strategy of re-reading. The problem is that the orator's rhetoric could be mis-read: lazy readers will miss the political point; sophisticated readers will see how hard it all is:

> To those who read lazily, it would seem simple and easy to comprehend. To those who go through it with care, trying to see what others have missed, it would clearly be hard to comprehend, and full of much history and philosophy, and of all sorts of complexity and fiction, not the fiction which, with evil, usually harms fellow citizens, but that which, with education and culture, benefits and pleasures the listeners. (244–7)

Now, orators traditionally invent opponents' words, often imagining responses to a speech, but here we have a fully dramatized version of an exchange, in which a fictional character discusses the strategies of fiction adopted by the author and encourages – but worries about – a practice of 'non-lazy' reading, and recognizes 'simplicity' and 'singleness' as a lure for those without knowledge, but concludes, nonetheless, that in democracy, it is better to be direct about policy. Yet look at the response, as once again Isocrates dramatizes an audience's engagement with a speech and his masterful comprehension of the scene:

> When he had spoken and asked those present to declare their opinion on the question about which they had been summoned, they did not merely applaud as they usually did for a speech which pleased them, but shouted out that he had spoken remarkably, and thronged around him and praised him, envied him, congratulated him, and had nothing to add or take away from what he had said. They agreed with him and advised me to do what he had urged. Nor did I stand by in

silence, but praised his nature and training. As for the rest, I uttered not a word about what he had said, neither how his interpretations [*huponoiai*] had hit upon my concept [*dianoia*], nor how he had missed, but I let him stay with the position he had formed for himself. (264–5)

First, all the other pupils tumultuously acclaim the pupil's version of the master's discourse, and the master himself praises his nature and training. But the master then distances himself from the collective praise: 'But beyond that I uttered not a word about the sentiments he had expressed, neither how his interpretations had hit upon my concept, nor how it had missed it; but I allowed him stay with the position he had formed for himself.' Asked as a matter of policy for a clear expression of his concept, the author dramatizes the appeal, and his own studied and continued ambivalence towards such a claim.

The oration self-reflexively and self-consciously *performs*, as it discusses, the ambivalence of reading practice within the politics of democratic openness, on the one hand, and the rhetorical and philosophical recognition of the deceptiveness of *logos*, on the other. The movement towards *dianoia*, the meaning, the concept, the intention, of a speech, is framed by the pedagogic exchange, but also by what could be called a politics of reading. As Athens and Sparta are compared and contrasted, the speech dramatizes the possibilities of different political reactions to its own rhetoric, and, in a strikingly self-reflexive manner, sets in motion not merely counter-readings within the text but also an explicit discussion of the strategies of representation themselves. We are shown the community at work over *logoi* – reading as a politically led and politically framed activity. And at the crucial moment, the ironic master withdraws from an authorizing gesture – thus turning back on the reader the task of using his or her interpretive skill, *huponoia*, to determine the sense of the speech. Or, rather, he invites the reader to engage in the community of readers reading – the *agon* of meaning – under his tutelage and indirect direction.

This extraordinary text, which has scarcely entered the history of literary criticism despite its important representation and discussion of interpretation, offers a picture of the orator and his circle engaged in both (re-)reading and the teaching of (re-)reading.

Its frame is the group of citizens as a model for the *polis* in its deliberative procedures. It assumes that the *politeia*, the constitution of a *polis*, is a necessary but contested ground of the citizens' experience. It brings together political understanding, political affiliation and political positioning in the drama of reading the orator's politics. It represents the performance of political reading to engage the reader in – and teach him about – the politics of being a citizen in the city of words.

Rome: Plutarch and the Cultured Citizen

For my second instance, I want to move to the Roman Empire and the Greeks of the Second Sophistic, and in particular to Plutarch, a Greek whose investment in the cultural world of Greekness is in direct and reverse proportion to his engagement in the imperial power of the court at Rome. Plutarch's understanding of how reading and education inter-relate is of most concern for my argument here. By the first century CE, education via what the Greeks call *enkuklios paideia* had become firmly institutionalized throughout the empire, and the emphasis on *paideia* – what constitutes a cultured person – is central to any sense of self-formation in this period.[6] To be a *pepaideumenos*, a 'cultured', 'educated' person, is the aim of training, and the role of a carefully regulated sense of linguistic purity for this culture has been well discussed by recent critics.[7] Plutarch writes a series of treatises on education and language that are paradigmatic of how the scene of reading is fundamental to this sense of the cultured citizen – but in a way that is strikingly different from Isocrates.

I begin with a passage from one of the many discussions of vocal training in the ancient world. It is taken from Plutarch's treatise 'Health Precepts', under the heading 'Exercises suitable for Scholars'. Plutarch declares (130a–b): 'the daily use of the

---

6. C. Anderson, 'The *Pepaideumenos* in Action: Sophists and their Outlook in the Early Empire', *ANRWii*, vol. 33, no. 1, 1989, pp. 79–208; T. Morgan, *Literate Education in the Hellenistic and Roman World*, Cambridge, 1998; T. Whitmarsh, *Greek Literature and the Roman Empire*, Oxford, 2001.

7. S. Swain, *Hellenism and Empire: Language, Classicism and Power in the Greek World, AD 50–250*, Oxford, 1996, pp. 17–100.

voice in speaking aloud is marvellous exercise, not only for health but also for strength', though if you are concerned that your body is not 'up to the mark or is rather tired' (130c), you should restrict yourself to practising 'reading aloud or lecturing'. Excessive straining of the voice should be avoided at all costs, and after a voice exercise you should have a warm oil massage. This exercise indeed should be a regular part of each day: 'Wherefore', he counsels, 'neither a sea voyage nor a stay in a hotel should be an excuse for silence, not even if everyone laughs at you.' It would be rather shameful, he adds, if one were put off by the laughter of 'inn-keepers, sailors and muleteers, who don't find ball-players and shadow-boxers funny, but laugh at someone who exercises his voice, although he is teaching, enquiring, learning and memorizing.'

The suggestion that people might laugh at the voice exercises of the budding orator suggests that this health advice was not just a validated practice. Indeed, Cicero, in a blast of Romanitas, complains that such training is the work of 'Greek actors and their sort', and where Caelius Aurelianus is happy for any set of scales to be practised, the younger Seneca suggests that such scales are effeminate, a worry of Quintilian too – whereas vocal exercise 'while being carried in a litter' is the perfect compromise, since the body can get additional exercise by being jiggled on the road. As Maud Gleason has shown, this obsessive care for the voice is a constitutive element of the *askesis* of the male body in the public gaze: the construction of the citizen as speaking subject.[8] The production of voice, and the discussions of the production of voice, are a dominant feature in the criticism of the role and function of language in society.

This is crucial background to Plutarch's most well-known treatise on 'reading', *How to Study Poetry*. Plutarch's interest here is in 'literature' as a preparation for philosophy and as a means to turn the young towards the useful, and away from the distractions of pleasure. The piece spends much time on the precisions of vocabulary and on how to produce in the young a correct moral understanding. It draws on both Platonic and Aristotelian theory, and it is this combination of systems that also produces the work's

---

8. M. Gleason, *Making Men: Sophists and Self-Presentation in Ancient Rome*, Princeton, 1994, esp. pp. 82–130.

central tension. This tension is produced by two opposing lines of argument. In the first, the structures of mimesis are seen as the source of pleasure in poetry and painting. This explains our delight in the representation of what is inherently ugly, so that the imitation of a pig's squealing (the party trick of one Parmeno) is pleasant, whereas a pig's squealing per se is unpleasant (18c) – or, more grandly, why we enjoy actors representing Philoctetes or Jocasta. The second strand of Plutarch's argument, however, maintains that poetry contains in its positive and negative exempla the test-cases by which a pupil's moral faculties are trained, and, like fruit hidden by foliage (15f), has jewels of expressive statement by which a man might live. Poetical utterances 'lead towards virtue and have the power to mould character' (28e), and make 'learning light and pleasing for the young' (15f). The treatise *How to Study Poetry* is written to negotiate this tension between the deceptive and pleasurable lies of poetry, and the nuggets of instruction to be found in the great writers of the past. It is written to explain how the seductive guiles of poetry can be monitored and directed into becoming the lure for philosophy, and to demonstrate how, as Plutarch concludes, the young man 'prepared by education may be transported by poetry into philosophy'.

Plutarch's strategy of instruction involves two particular techniques. First, he encourages a moralizing appreciation of literature. Each utterance should be evaluated as to whether it is spoken 'rightly, moderately, suitably' – the dictates of a predetermined propriety, dependent on a set of social norms about character and position. By outlining the good and bad through the examples of literary figures, 'we shall prevent the young from any leanings towards the base aspects of characters, but encourage emulation and choice of the better' (27e). This often requires apt counter-quotation; careful reinterpretation (24bff) to bring poetical expressions in line with morality or philosophical principle; or glossing (22c). This process of 'rectification' pictures a world where the educated exchange classical quotations as a sign of cultured behaviour and acculturate the young through this tissue of moralizing tags into a regulated social normativity, where the protocols of propriety are constantly scrutinized and become the means and matter of social exchange. The second technique promoted by Plutarch is closely related. For he repeatedly

demands a particular attention of his readers, a care for the
niceties of language and expression, opposed to 'a lazy and
inattentive listening' (30e). The young man should 'listen wide
awake' (32a); 'close attention must be paid' (19a); the young man
ought not to let the useful 'escape him', or 'wander from the
business, but cling close' (28e). Where for Isocrates 'lazy reading'
meant a misinterpretation of the political intentions of the orator,
for Plutarch, inattentive reading means missing the impropriety
of a poetical expression.

This central worry over recognizing the danger of poetry's
seduction and the need for philosophical self-control is, then, far
from a simply aesthetic or epistemological concern, but closely
linked to what I have been calling a training in the social
engagement with language. Another educational treatise, *On Listening to Lectures*, will help make this point. The central tension of
this work can be expressed in a way analogous to that of *How to
Study Poetry*. On the one hand, no young man can be properly
educated unless he listens and learns from his elders and betters
(like the author); indeed he must learn how to sit, paying proper
attention to the speaker, not rustling and coughing and giggling
– if he wants to become a good citizen. Education depends on
the deep absorption of the lesson: one must

> sit in an upright position without lounging or sprawling; look directly
> at the speaker; maintain a pose of active attention; with a clear
> expression on the face, without sign not merely of insolence or bad-
> temper, but also of other thoughts or pastimes. . . . Not only are
> frowning, a sour face, a roving glance, twisting the body, crossing the
> legs, unseemly behaviour, but also nodding, whispering to another,
> smiling, sleepy yawns, lowering the head, and everything like this, are
> accountable and need much care to be avoided. (45c)

A full physiognomics of the face and body is itemized and banned
in the name of proportion, harmony – in short, propriety. Your
body shows how you have been and are being educated. The
lecture room is a place for scrutinizing the bodily practice of an
audience: for 'the person who is accustomed to listen with self-
control and with respect learns and absorbs the useful lecture'
(39c). So, listen attentively.

On the other hand, the aim of rhetoric is the persuasive
seduction of the listener, and to be won over is to be mastered, to

be emasculated, to lose control. Not to be a good citizen. For hearing can be risky, since:

> Virtue's only hold on the young is the ears, if they are guarded pure, unpolluted by flattery and untouched by base language. Wherefore Xenocrates ordered ear-guards to be worn by children rather than athletes, because athletes have their ears distorted by blows, but children have their characters distorted by words.

The ears are a dangerous part of the body, through which corruption enters, and so Xenocrates advised putting ear protectors – like old football gear – on children rather than athletes. Until philosophy has adequately trained the young, there is always a danger of 'influence and persuasion'. When you listen do not give yourself over. The self-controlled and respectful listener receives the useful discourse, but must also 'see through and detect the uselessness of lying discourse' (39c).

The listener who is to absorb the lesson is also the listener who has to absorb the lesson about a *critical* listening that does not simply absorb but resists. Rhetorical training brings with it the paradox of the self-conscious awareness that rhetoric's mastery over the audience depends not on the following of rules but on an active dialectic between audience and speaker, which is itself the subject of scrutiny and criticism. Subject and object of language's power, the citizen is always engaged in an uneasy dialectic between being the master and victim of words. It is with this that Plutarch's pedagogy engages. Listening has become a central element in the *askesis* of the critical subject. How words enter and leave your body needs training, control and submission to the regulation of propriety, informed by the regime of philosophy. From voice production to ear-guards, the embodiment of language exchange has become a site of what Foucault would call 'care for the self'. Or as Plutarch concludes the treatise: 'right listening is the beginning of right living' (48d).

This process of scrutinizing the somatics of social exchange and concern for its properties takes a crucial sociopolitical turn in my final Plutarchean example, the treatise *How to Tell a Flatterer from a Friend*. Flattery becomes a major topic throughout the Greek writing of the empire, a concern that develops the Aristotelian attempt to define true friendship into the hierarchical world of client and patron with its repeated return to the physiognomics and linguistics of social exchange. The flatterer is the person for whom imitation – mimesis – is the route to plausibility, and whose words need to be listened to with especial care. The worry is discovering whether your 'friend' is true or not. Here, reading the signs is a critical exercise:

> This is the most criminal of all his behaviour. Since he recognizes that frankness of speech is said to be and seems to be the personal voice of friendship, as an animal has a particular cry; and also that lack of frankness of speech is not the mark of a friend, and ignoble, he does not leave this quality unimitated; but as clever cooks use bitter infusions and dry flavours to remove a cloying sweetness, so flatterers apply a frankness which is not true or helpful but which, as it were, leers from beneath its brow and simply tickles. Thus the man is hard to detect. . . . (51c)

The flatterer is most dangerous when imitating the frankness of the friend. Frankness is the special voice, the special enunciation – *phônê* – of a friend: this is the voice adopted by the flatterer. But, continues Plutarch, a flatterer's frankness is not true or useful (the crucial determinants of genuine friendship) but, 'as it were, it leers from beneath its brow and simply tickles, itches'. Even so, the flatterer is extremely hard to catch. The flatterer's false *phônê* is depicted as the distortion of a face, 'leering from the brow and tickling' – itself a distorted expression of extremely rare words. The leering and tickling of the flatterer's face is designed to mark the lack of good order in his character. But – and it's a big but – the 'as it were' remains to mark the slippage of Plutarch's desire. Plutarch can only declare the flatterer to be 'as if', 'like' the corruption he would have hoped to be able to see. The 'as it were' underlines how the flatterer's mimesis is dangerous precisely because his body escapes the inscriptions of such clear signs, such propriety.

Critical reading of language – language as it is embodied – is part of the sociopolitical engagement of the world of client and patron that makes up the empire. A training in poetry is part of a continuum that runs from lectures to the very business of social life with its hierarchical power relations, where an educated man's deportment, his placement in and through language, is subject to constant scrutiny. The hearing and using – the exchange – of language is critical (in all senses) in the exchanges of this world of letters. From guarding the ears of youth in a lecture to trying to catch the giveaway tickle in a friend's voice, learning to read 'embodied language' is a requirement of *paideia*, a shared nego-tiation of the cultural elite of the empire.

In the hierarchical social world of the empire, then, where the cultured Greek's engagement in the spheres of power, politics and education is so different from that of the citizen of the classical *polis*, the questions of reading and of the body and reading have become differently formulated and differently artic-ulated. To put it most apophthegmatically, the focus of protocol has shifted from *politeia* to *paideia*.

The Christian Reader and His Miserable Body

For my third and final moment, I want to look very briefly at the Christian movement growing alongside and in competition with the elites of the empire, eventually to become its dominant cultural frame. Here, the fractures of community and schisms of commit-ments and beliefs require especial nuance. The invention of theology, with its claims that correct reading is necessary for life while incorrect reading is punishable even to the point of death, and the concomitant development of the cult of the holy book (largely new to mainstream classical culture, if not to the Jewish roots of Christianity) fundamentally alter the conceptualization of reading and the body. The growth of theology as a fundamental element of religious observance – the injunction always to care an iota – is as much a factor in the development of Christianity as the recently emphasized focus on the body and asceticism. The inter-play between the two makes up the body of the Christian. In this light, I want to look at one fourth-century Latin poem, the ninth of Prudentius' collection, the *Liber Peristephanon*, a poem in cel-ebration of St Cassian of Imola, which will offer a particularly striking image of the Christian reader and his body.

The narrative structure of *Peristephanon* 9 can be briefly expressed. The poet arrives from Spain in Forum Cornelii (mod-ern Imola) on his way to Rome on a mission of petition (the details of which are not indicated). He prays at the tomb of the saint and sees a picture of Cassian's martyrdom. A sacristan explains the story of the picture. This central passage takes up

most of the poem with a splendid account of how the shorthand
teacher Cassian was killed by being stabbed slowly by his pupils
with their pens. (The boys' animus is not explained.) Prudentius
then completes his prayer for help to the martyr, and, the poet
finally declares, his mission was successful and he returned to
Spain to praise Cassian – praise instantiated in this poem. The
poem thus narrates the trip of petition to Rome and back via
three frames: first, the scene at the tomb between poet and
sacristan; second (inset into the first), the account of the martyrdom; third (framing the first two), the recollection of the journey
from the position of a successful return to Spain.

I want to focus here on two inter-related questions: the
emotional/intellectual response to the picture, and the body of
the pilgrim, reader of images and writer of poems. At the time
Prudentius is writing, the Church's reaction to art and especially
to 'pagan' art is a topic of some debate. It is worth bearing this
intellectual background in mind in turning to Prudentius'
encounter with the painting of St Cassian. The scene of an arrival
at a religious site (or art gallery) and having a painting explained
by an exegete is very familiar from the pagan world.[9] So, Prudentius writes here: 'I consulted the sacristan, who said "what you see,
stranger, is no empty old-wive's tale. The picture recounts a
history that is recorded in books and demonstrates the true faith
of olden times"' (17–19). Although both the appeal to the
authority of the book and the reference to the faith of past times
give a specifically Christian gloss, the exchange establishes a
typical moment of exposition. This is, however, the only poem of
the *Peristephanon* thus to make the narrator a listener to another's
tale of a martyrdom – and this means that for the first time in the
Peristephanon we are watching the scene of response to a martyr
narrative: a reading. How does Prudentius respond? The standard
responses to art in the pagan world are wonder, amazement and
a stunned sense of art's power. Here is Prudentius' opening
description of himself before the painting:

I was stretched out on the ground, prostrate before the tomb,
    which holy

---

9. See S. Goldhill, 'The Naïve and Knowing Eye: Ecphrasis and the Culture of
Viewing in the Hellenistic World', in S. Goldhill and R. Osborne, eds, *Art and Text
in Ancient Greek Culture*, Cambridge, 1994.

> Cassian, the martyr, honours with his consecrated body.
> While in tears I reflected on my wounds and all the labours
>> Of my life and the pricks of grief,
> I lifted my face to heaven, and there stood opposite me
>> An image of the martyr painted in coloured hues,
> Bearing a thousand blows, torn over all his limbs,
>> Showing his skin ripped with minute points.
> Countless boys round him – pitiful sight! –
>> Stabbed and dug into his limbs with their styluses . . . (5–14)

He is lying on the ground, prostrate, and crying, reflecting on his own suffering, when he turns his countenance to heaven and sees the picture of the martyr's suffering. So, after the ecphrasis, he reacts in a similarly emotionally charged way:

> I embraced the tomb, I poured tears too,
> The altar was warmed by my lips, the rock by my breast.
> Then I reflected on all the hidden parts of my distress,
>> Then on what I sought, what I feared, murmuring. (99–101)

Unlike the Greek or Roman professor and exegete strutting and expounding before a work of art, Prudentius depicts himself as in emotional turmoil, weeping, humbled, prostrate and begging. Self-abasement – *tapeinôsis* – is good for Christians. Christianity redrafts an attitude to the body by reversing standard assumptions and valorizing suffering (*paschein*), being prostrate, submissive, humble, slavish. As Shaw writes: 'To be low, base, prone, and exposed was now at the heart of the definition of being good.'[10] So, indeed, Prudentius himself offers a fully normative image of a Christian worshipper of St Lawrence (*Perist.* 2 529–36): 'O three and four and seven times blessed is . . . he who prostrates himself by your bones, who sprinkles the place with tears, who presses his breast to the earth, who pours out his prayer, murmuring.' Tearful Prudentius, abased before the martyr's picture, is therefore representing himself in the authoritative physical and mental position for a Christian.

Prudentius indeed, in his reaction to Cassian, hints strongly at an analogy between himself and the martyr. He suffers from *acumina dolorum* ('pricks of grief' [8]), as the saint feels *acumina*

---

10. B. Shaw, 'Body/Power/Identity: Passions of the Martyrs', *Journal of Early Christian Studies*, vol. 4, no. 3, 1996, pp. 269–312; see also J. Perkins, *The Suffering Self*, London and New York, 1995.

ferrea ('iron pricks' [51]); he describes the miseries of life as *vulnera* ('wounds'), as we are displayed the wounded body (*vulnera* [58]) of the martyr in his grief (*dolorum spicula* [62]). Yet his is a tearful response to the triumphant tale of transcendence and victory. The question might be phrased like this: in what posture, with what expression, is one to read the story of Prudentius prostrate before the tomb of Cassian? With what joy, what embrace? What tears? If the tearful poet imitates the torn martyr, and yet that scene is recalled from the vantage point of a successful return to Spain (established by the inset and framed narrative), how are the different claims of joy and grief, for poet and martyr, to be experienced?

A further contrast will help focus this question. When Eulalia is martyred in *Peristephanon* 3, she typifies the power of the Christian sufferer by her wit and triumph. The executioner is cutting off her breasts:

> and he cut to the bone
> As Eulalia counted the marks.
> 'See, Lord, you are being written on me.
> How it pleases me to read these letters,
> Which mark, Christ, the record of your victory!
> The very purple of the blood as it is drawn
> Speaks your holy name.' (134–40)

Eulalia perceives the torture of her body as the writing of Christ's glorious name. She controls the scene by expressing the marks on her body as signs of victory; and wittily seeing the purple blood as the royal signature, she reads her own body as inscribed with a martyr's record. Suffering becomes glory by virtue of its reading of the body; and pleasure in the poem's language matches – underscores – (our) pleasure and awe in the virgin's triumph. Yet Cassian's death – equally a grim writing on the body – affords wit only for the torturers (69–72): 'Why do you complain,' one cries, 'you our teacher gave us this iron and put this weapon in our hands. See, we are giving you back the many thousands of marks [*milia multa notarum*] which we took from your teaching in tears.' The rhetorician is hoisted by the petard of the well-taught student, as his cheeks, face and whole body are pierced and lacerated. 'See if we have made any mistakes for you to correct in our letter formation,' asks one stabbing boy (79–80) in this textual criticism of the flesh. As the skin of the shorthand teacher is scored and scratched with the *notae* of his pupils' pens, he becomes a noted text of instruction for the faithful. Michael Roberts describes this aspect of the poem's self-reflexivity well: 'shorthand notes have that synecdochal quality of embodying in a small compass a larger whole', so a narrative of martyrdom or a relic 'encapsulates in a few characters the whole passion'.[11] The writing on the body and the writing of the poem are analogous testaments in brief to the glory of the martyr's passion. Yet unlike Eulalia, Cassian is also the object of wit. The poem offers its cruel wit as a further sadistic twist to the suffering of the martyr. A reader's pleasure in the language of the poem is harder to assimilate simply to the celebration of the martyr's triumph. There remains a difficult interplay between pleasure and tears here.

The staging not just of a narrative of martyrdom but also of a weepy response by the poet to the picture and its story, recollected afterwards from the position of a successful return, creates a layered scene of reading that not merely offers the prostrated and crying Christian imitator of the passion of a saint as a model of response, but also engages the reader of the poem in a complex dynamic of responding to this response. How tearfully, how joyfully is Prudentius to be read?

Conclusion

This question will do to mark how far this essay has tried to travel – from the politics of the rhetoric school of the *polis*, via the proprieties of the Empire lecture hall and academy, to the theology and control of the body in the community of monks. From upright orator to prostrate Christian. Through these different pictures of men teaching younger men about language, and about the social exchange of language; and through these different exemplary pictures of men performing the multiform acts of reading, I hope to have outlined at least why reading itself needs a history that goes beyond book production and vocalization and

---

11. M. Roberts, *Poetry and the Cult of the Martyrs*, Ann Arbor, 1993; see also A.-M. Palmer, *Prudentius on the Martyrs*, Oxford, 1989.

literacy, and why it provides a more culturally nuanced history than the 'history of literature'. Reading and self-formation are deeply interconnected: the conceptualization of the citizen as a speaking subject, the cultural frames of interpretation and the idea(l)s of the body each inform the notion of reading in antiquity, and the models of reading are markedly different in different periods and offer important expressions of major cultural change.

What I hope to have shown in outline at least is the destructive poverty of the category of 'literature' for the way in which the critical engagement with language production and consumption functions in the ancient world. The establishment of the sphere of the literary with its various exclusions does not merely distort the interconnections between the texts of poetry, say, and the other textual productions of the ancient world, but also thoroughly twists the connections between those texts and the culture in which and for which they were produced. In short, the seventeenth and eighteenth centuries may turn out to be better guides for the classical world than the nineteenth and twentieth – and the literary history that I would like to see written may well exclude 'literature' altogether.

9

The Rooster's Egg:
Pioneering World Folklore
in the Philippines

Benedict Anderson

In 1887, at the Madrid Exposición Filipina, a 23-year-old *indio* named Isabelo de los Reyes, living in colonial Manila, won a silver medal for a huge Spanish-language manuscript which he called *El Folk-Lore Filipino*. He composed this text in unwitting tandem with José Rizal (then aged 25), who was wandering around continental Europe composing the incendiary novel *Noli Me Tangere*, which earned him martyrdom in 1896 and, later, eternal status as Father of His Country and First Filipino.

Who was Isabelo? He was born in 1864 in the Northern Luzon archiepiscopal town of Vigan, to parents of the Ilocano ethnic group, the vast majority of whom were, in those days, illiterate. His mother, however, was evidently a poet of some quality, so that at the Madrid and later expositions her poetry was displayed for Spaniards, Parisians, and people in St. Louis. This accomplishment did not save her marriage, and the young Isabelo was entrusted to a well-off relative who sent him to a seminary in Vigan, where he organized a demonstration against abusive behaviour by the peninsular-Spanish Augustinians; then on to the College of San Juan de Letran and finally, for a degree as Notary Public, to the only colonial university then existent in Southeast Asia, the Dominicans' Santo Tomás in Manila. Meanwhile Isabelo's father had died, and the young man plunged into the burgeoning world of journalism. It is said that he eventually published, in 1889, the first newspaper in a Filipino vernacular.

But while still a teenager, Isabelo read an appeal in Manila's Spanish-language newspaper *La Oceania Española* (founded in 1877), asking readers to contribute articles to develop a new science, named *el folk-lore*, followed by a simple sketch of how this was to be done. He immediately contacted the Spanish editor, who gave him a collection of 'folklore books', and asked him to write about the customs of his native Ilocos. Two months later Isabelo set to work, and soon thereafter started publishing – not merely on Ilocos, but on his wife's township of Malabon, the Central Luzon province of Zambales, and in general terms on what he called *el folk-lore filipino*. It became, for a time, the passion of his life. The question, naturally, is why? What was the meaning of *el folk-lore* for a clerically educated native youth in 1884? Much can be learnt from the Introduction and the first pages of his youthful masterwork.[1]

Isabelo described *el folk-lore* here, albeit with some hesitations, as a *ciencia nueva* (a new science), perhaps consciously echoing Giambattista Vico's *Sienza Nueva*, which had burst on the trans-European scene in the mid-nineteenth century, thanks to the efforts of Michelet and others. Isabelo explained to his readers, in both the Philippines and Spain, that the word 'folklore' – which he translated pungently as *saber popular* – had only been invented in 1846, by the English antiquarian William Thoms, in an article published in the London *Athenaeum*. The first folklore society in the world had been organized in London as recently as 1878 – a mere six years before he started his own research.[2] The French had followed suit nationally only in 1886 – just as Isabelo was starting to write. The Spanish had been caught intellectually napping; when their turn came, they had no thought but to incorporate the Anglo-Saxon coinage into Castilian as *el folk-lore*.

---

1. References hereafter will be mainly to the original text, published in Manila in 1889 by the publisher Tipo-Lithografia de Chofré y C. Where relevant, comparisons will be made with a recent reprint combined with English translation by Salud C. Dizon and Maria Elinora P. Imson (Quezon City, 1994), to be referred to in abbreviated fashion as Dizon–Imson. This new version, a valuable endeavour in many ways, is nonetheless marred by hundreds of errors of translation, and some mistakes in the Spanish transcription.

2. *El Folk-Lore Filipino* (henceforward *EFF*), p. 8.

Like his contemporary Rizal, Isabelo was starting to position himself alongside pioneering Britain, above and ahead of the tag-along colonial metropole. He was like a fast surfer on the crest of the wave of world science's progress, something never previously imaginable for any native of what he himself called this 'remote Spanish colony on which the light of civilization shines only tenuously'.[3] This position he reinforced in several instructive ways.

On the one hand, he was quick to mention in his Introduction that some of his research had already been translated into German – then *the* language of advanced scholarly thinking – and published in journals (*Ausland* and *Globus*) which, he claimed, were the leading European organs in the field. *El Folk-Lore Filipino* also judiciously discussed the opinions of leading Anglo-Saxon contemporaries on the status of the *ciencia nueva*, politely suggesting that they were more serious that those of peninsular-Spanish *folkloristas*. He must also have enjoyed commenting that 'Sir George Fox' had been in conceptual error in confusing Folklore with Mythology, and some Castilian contemporaries in muddling Mythology and Theogony.[4]

On the other hand, the newness of this *ciencia* had a special colonial aspect to it, which he did not hesitate to underline. He dedicated his book to '*Los folk-loristas españoles de la Peninsula, que me han dispensada toda clase de atenciones* [the Spanish folklorists of the peninsula, who have tendered me every manner of consideration]'. His Introduction spoke warmly of 'colleagues' in Spain – the directors of *El Folk-Lore Español* and of the *Boletin de la Enseñanza Libre de Madrid* in the imperial capital, and of the *Boletin Folklorico* in Seville – who had kept him abreast of research in the peninsula which ran parallel to his own work on *El Folk-Lore Filipino*.

The peninsularity, so to speak, of these colleagues was regularly underlined, as well as the peninsularity of their research. Without explicitly saying so, Isabelo (rightly) insinuated that no colonial Spaniards or creoles were doing anything comparable in the Philippines. This, of course, permitted him to position himself as a far-ahead-of-the-colonial-masters scientific pioneer of the new universal science. To explain this peculiar situation Isabelo

---

3. Ibid., p. 19.
4. Dizon–Imson, p. 30.

resorted to an ingenious device – certainly made necessary by the violent, reactionary character of the clerically dominated colonial regime at the time. He described a series of courtly exchanges in the Manila press with a liberal-minded (almost certainly peninsular) medical doctor and amateur littérateur, who had contributed to local newspapers under the penname Astoll.[5] This move allowed him to quote the peninsular as admiring Isabelo's courage and imagination, but feeling deeply pessimistic about his chances of success in the face of the overwhelming indifference, indolence and mental stupor in the colony. 'Here the only things that grow luxuriantly are cogon-grass and molave – two tenacious local weeds.'[6] And when Astoll finally broke off their exchange in despair, Isabelo, who had indirectly raised the question of why 'certain corporations' (meaning the religious orders) had contributed nothing, commented that in the circumstances 'prudence warrants no other course'. Into the mental darkness of the colonial regime, then, Isabelo saw himself as bringing the light of modern Europe.

Newness, however, came in still another guise in *El Folk-Lore Filipino*, and this was related to the idea of *ciencia*. The Introduction contains a most interesting discussion of the larger debate on the scientific status of folklore studies. Isabelo had fun noting that one faction of the peninsular *folkloristas* were so impatient to turn *el folk-lore* into a theoretical science that they soon could no longer understand one another – opening the way for a much-needed international discussion, in which the Anglo-Saxons appeared more modest and more practical. At the other extreme were those Spanish folklorists who were merely sentimental collectors of vanishing customs and conceptions for some future museum of the past.

Isabelo made clear what he thought folklore was about, and how he saw its social value. In the first place, it offered an opportunity for a reconstruction of the indigenous past which was impossible in the Philippines by any other means, given the absence of pre-Spanish monuments, inscriptions or, indeed, of any written records at all. (When Rizal tried to do the same thing

---

5. Isabelo identified him as José Lacalle y Sanchez, a professor of medicine at the University of Manila (Sto. Tomás). *EFF*, p. 13.
6. Ibid., p. 14.

a little later, he saw no other way to proceed than to read between the lines of the best of the early Spanish administrators' writings.) Serious research on customs, beliefs, superstitions, adages, tongue-twisters, incantations, and so on, would throw light on what he referred to as the 'primitive religion' of the pre-Spanish past. But – and here he sharply distinguished himself from amateur *costumbristas* – he also underlined the importance of comparisons. He confessed that until he had completed his research he had been sure that the neighbouring Tagalogs and Ilocanos were *razas distintas* – distinct races – on account of their different languages, physiognomies, behaviour, and so on. But comparison had proved to him that he had been wrong and that the two ethnicities clearly derived from a common source. The implication of the title *El Folk-Lore Filipino* was that further research would show that all the indigenous inhabitants of the archipelago had a common origin, no matter how many languages they now spoke or how different their present customs and religious affiliations. All this meant that, *contra* the colony's clerical historiographers, who began their narratives with the sixteenth-century conquest, the real history of the archipelago and its *pueblo/pueblos* (here he hesitated often) stretched far further back in time, and could not be framed by coloniality.

On the other hand – and here Isabelo made a move that radically distanced him from his peninsular colleagues – the new science could not and should not be confined to sentimental excavations of the quaint. *El Folk-Lore* is above all the study of the contemporary, in particular what he termed *el saber popular*. This *saber* was real knowledge, not 'lore' with its musty, antiquarian connotations. He offered the hypothetical example of a *selvaje* (wild man, perhaps a savage) in the forests near his home region of South Ilocos who might, any day (accidentally, Isabelo said) discover that a certain local fruit provided a better antidote to the cholera virus than that currently manufactured at the instance of the Spanish medical scientist Dr Ferran.[7] The framing for such claims was the absence of serious scientific knowledge about almost everything in the Philippines. The recent Augustinian friars' compilation *Flora de Filipinas* [The Flora of the Philippines]

---

7. Dizon–Imson, p. 24.

was, for example, very far from complete.[8] The indigenes had a
much deeper knowledge of medicinal plants, of flora and fauna,
of soils and climatic variations than did the colonialists, and this
huge reservoir of knowledge, contained in the *saber popular*, was
still unknown to the world. The Philippines thus appeared not
merely as a region containing a mass of exotica unknown to
Europeans, but also as the site for a significant future contribution
to mankind, springing from what the common people knew, in
their own languages, but of which Spanish had no conception. It
was exactly the 'unknownness' of the Philippines which gave its
folklore a future-oriented character that was necessarily absent in
the folklore of peninsular Spain. It was also, however, the living
specificity of the Philippines that positioned it to offer something,
parallel and equal to that of any other *país*, to humanity. This is
the logic which would much later make the United Nations both
possible and plausible.

So far, so clear. Too clear, in fact. For Isabelo's text, under the
bright lights of its major themes, is also not without its shadowy
complications. We might provisionally think about them under
three rubrics.

Firstly, what was Isabelo to himself? To begin with, it is necessary to underline an ambiguity within the Spanish word *filipino*
itself. In Isabelo's time this adjective had two distinct senses in
common parlance: (1) belonging to, located in, originating from
Las Islas Filipinas; (2) creole, of the locally born but 'pure
Spanish' social group. What it did not mean is what Filipino
means today, an indigenous national-ethnicity. One can see how
much things have changed over the past century if one compares
just one sentence in Isabelo's Introduction with its recent translation into American by two Philippine scholars. Isabelo wrote:

> Para recoger del saco roto la organización del Folk-Lore regional
> filipino, juzgué oportuno contestar al revistero del *Comercio* y, aprove-
> chando su indirecta, aparenté sostener que en Filipinas había personas
> ilustradas y estudiosas que pudieran acometer la empresa.[9]

This literally means: 'To save the organization of the Folklore of
the region of the Philippines, I judged it the right moment to

---

8. Ibid., p. 11. The editors say that the book, a compilation by various hands,
and edited by Fr. Andres Naves, was published in Manila in 1877 by Plana y C.
9. *EFF*, p. 13.

contest the view of *El Comercio*'s reviewer, and taking advantage of his insinuation, I pretended [??] to maintain that in the Philippines there exist enlightened [*ilustradas*] and studious persons capable of undertaking the task.'

The published translation – completely anachronistic – has: 'I tried to defend the establishment of Filipino Folklore by answering the accusation of the columnist of *El Comercio*, by bravely stating that there are indeed Filipino scholars ready and capable of undertaking the task.'[10] Where Isabelo was thinking of a sort of global folklore which included the regional portion of the Philippines Islands, and spoke of enlightened persons in the Philippines – no ethnicity specified – the translators have omitted 'regional' to create a folklore of the Filipinos, and 'enlightened persons' to imagine 'Filipino scholars'.

In *El Folk-Lore*, Isabelo never described himself as a Filipino, for the modern usage did not seriously exist in his time. Besides, Filipinos were then exactly what he was not: a creole. He did, however, describe himself in other ways: sometimes, for example, as an indigene (but never by the contemptuous Spanish term *indio*), and sometimes as an Ilocano. In a remarkable passage he wrote: 'Speaking of patriotism, has it not frequently been said in the newspapers that for me only Ilocos and Ilocanos are good? . . . Everyone serves his *pueblo* to his own manner of thinking. I believe I am here contributing to the illumination of the past of my own *pueblo*.' Elsewhere, however, he insisted that so strict had been his objectivity that he had 'sacrificed to science the affections of the Ilocanos, who complain that I have publicized their least attractive practices'. Luckily, however, 'I have received an enthusiastic response from various intellectuals [*sabios*] in Europe, who say that, by setting aside a misguided patriotism, I have offered signal services to Ilocos *mi patria adorada* because I have provided scholars with abundant materials for studying its prehistory and other scientific topics relating to that *province*.'[11]

Rizal opened his enraged novel *Noli Me Tangere* with a celebrated Preface addressed to his motherland, which included these words: 'Desiring your well-being, which is our own, and searching for the best cure [for your disease], I will do with you

---

10. Dizon–Imson, p. 13.
11. *EFF*, pp. 18, 17. Emphasis added.

as the ancients did with their afflicted: expose them on the steps
of the temple so that each one who came to invoke the Divinity
would propose a cure for them.' And in the last poem he wrote
before his execution in 1896, he too spoke of his *patria adorada*.
But was it Isabelo's?

There is a beautiful sentence in the Introduction to *El Folk-Lore
Filipino* in which Isabelo described himself as *hermano de los
selváticos, aetas, igorrotes y tinguianes* (brother of the forest-peoples,
the Aeta, the Igorots and the Tinguians). These so-called primitive peoples, most of them pagan before the twentieth century
dawned, and many never subjugated by the Spanish colonial
regime, lived and live in the high Cordillera that flanks the
narrow coastal plain of Ilocos. In his boyhood, Isabelo would have
seen them coming down from the forests in their 'outlandish
garb' to trade their products for lowland commodities. To this
day, a form of Ilocano is the *lingua franca* of the Gran Cordillera.
No-one else in Isabelo's time, certainly no-one who counted
himself an *ilustrado*, would have spoken in such terms of these
forest-dwellers, who seemed, in their untamed fastnesses, utterly
remote from any urban, Hispanicized, Catholic or deist milieux.
(And Isabelo never spoke of any other ethnic groups in Las
Filipinas as his *hermanos*.)

Here one sees how it was possible for him to think of his
province as a big *pueblo*, and as a *patria adorada*, since in the most
concrete way it linked as brothers the 'wild' pagans of the
mountains and a man who won prizes in Madrid. Here also one
detects an underlying reason why, in his proto-nationalist striv-
ings, Isabelo went to folklore, rather than the novel or the
broadsheet. Folklore – comparative folklore – enabled him to
bridge the deepest chasm in colonial society, which lay not
between colonized and colonizers – they all lived in the lowlands,
they were all Catholics, and they dealt with one another all the
time. It was the abyss between all of these and those whom we
would today call 'tribal minorities' – hill-people, hunters and
gatherers, 'head-hunters'; men, women and children facing a
future of – possibly violent – assimilation, even extermination.
Out of *el folk-lore*, child of William Thoms, there thus emerged a
strange new brotherhood, and an adored father/motherland for
the young Isabelo.

What were the deeper purposes of the *folklorista*'s work in Las

Islas Filipinas? Apart from its potential contributions to the modern sciences, and to the reconstruction of the character of 'primitive man', we can detect three which have a clear political character. First, there is the possibility – the hope – of cultural renaissance. With a certain sly prudence, Isabelo allowed Astoll to speak on his behalf here:

> Perhaps Folklore will provide the fount for a Philippine poetry [*poesía filipina*], a poetry inspired by Philippine subjects, and born in the mind of Philippine bards [*vates*]. I can already hear the mocking laughter of those braggarts who have made such fun of you. But let them laugh, for they also laughed at other manifestations of the *pueblo*'s genius [*ingenio*], and then had to bow their heads in confusion before the laurels of [Juan] Luna and [Félix] Resurrección. [Two 'native' painters – one of them from Ilocos – who had just won prizes at exhibitions in Madrid.] And these traditions and superstitious practices which you are making known could one day inspire great poets, and enthusiastic lovers of the strange beauties of this rich garden.[12]

Elsewhere Isabelo quoted Astoll once again: 'If Sr de los Reyes's studies and investigations make connections to *pueblos* [people] like the Philippine one [or is it the Filipino one? – *como el filipino*] where the character of the indigenes [*naturales*] has been depicted solely by the brushstrokes of dullwitted daubers, one can see how much potential value they have *for the future*.'[13] Here Isabelo's work, printed in Manila, could open up the possibility of a great flowering of literary and poetic talent for the *naturales*, a talent before which boorish peninsulars and creoles would have to hang their heads in confusion. This is the normal hope and strategy of anti-colonial nationalists: to 'equalize themselves up' with the imperial power.

The second theme would be to subvert the dominance of the reactionary Church in the colony, best shown in a wonderfully deadpan chapter entitled 'Ilocano Superstitions that are Found in Europe'. It opens in this vein:

> Taking advantage of the folkloric materials gathered by D. Alejandro Guichot and D. Luis Montoto in Andalusia, by D. Eugenio de Olavarría y Huarte in Madrid, by D. José Perez Ballesteros in Catalonia, by

---

12. Ibid., p. 15.
13. Ibid., p. 14. Emphasis added.

D. Luis Giner Arivau in Asturias, by Consigliere Pedroso, with his *Tradiçoes populares portuguezas*, in Portugal, as well as others, I have drawn up the following list of superstitions which I believe were introduced here by the Spaniards in past centuries. The list should not surprise anyone, given that in the early days of Spanish domination, the most ridiculous beliefs [*las creencias más absurdas*] were in vogue on the Peninsula.[14]

Mischievously, the list begins:

When roosters reach old age or have spent seven years in someone's house, they lay an egg from which hatches a certain green lizard that kills the master of that house; according to the Portuguese and French, however, what hatches is a snake. If it spots the master first, the latter will die, but that fate will strike the former if the master sees the snake first. The Italians and the English, as well as some Central Europeans, believe it is a basilisk that is hatched. Father Feijóo says: 'It is true, the rooster, in old age, really does lay an egg.' The Portuguese and the Ilocanos, however, agree that what is in the egg is a scorpion.[15]

Other irresistible examples are these: 'To make sure visitors do not overstay, Ilocanos put salt on their guests' chairs. Spaniards place a broom vertically behind a door, while the Portuguese put a shoe on a bench in the same spot, or throw salt on the fire.' 'In Castile as in Ilocos, teeth that have fallen out are thrown onto the roof, so that new ones will grow.' 'According to the people of Galicia, if a cat washes its face, it means that rain is coming; the Ilocanos say it will rain if we give the animal a bath.' 'The people of Galicia say that a gale is coming when cats run about like mad; people in the Philippines substitute cockroaches for these cats.' Finally: 'Sleeping with the headboard facing the east is bad for Ilocanos. But for Peninsulars (Spaniards and Portuguese) it is good. All three agree that facing the headboard south is unlucky.'

One can see why Isabelo felt a *singular placer* in dedicating his

---

14. Ibid., p. 74. In successive footnotes Isabelo gives the titles of these authors' works: *El Folk-Lore Andaluz; Costumbres populares andaluzas; El Folk-Lore de Madrid; Folk-Lore Gallego; Folk-Lore de Asturias*. He also casually mentions an earlier work of his own, described as a *largo juguete literario* (long literary skit), entitled *El Diablo en Filipinas, según rezan nuestras crónicas* (The Devil in the Philippines, as Our Chronicles Tell It).

15. *EFF*, p. 75. Sources given are: Pedroso's above-cited work; Rolland's *Faune populaire de la France*; Castelli's *Credenze ed usi populari siciliani*; V. Gregor's *Notes on the Folk-Lore of the North-East Scotland* [*sic*]; and Larousse's *Grande dictionnaire encyclopédique du XIX siècle*.

book to peninsular folklorists, since they had offered him the scientific materials that would demonstrate the 'ridiculous beliefs' of the conquistadors, and prove that, if the colonialists sneered at Ilocano supersitions, they should recognize many of them as importations of their own: any bizarreness in Ilocano folk beliefs had easy analogues in the bizarreries of Iberia, Italy, Central Europe, even England.

The third theme is political self-criticism. Isabelo wrote that he was trying to show, through his systematic display of *el saber popular*, those reforms in the ideas and everyday practices of the *pueblo* that must be undertaken in a self-critical spirit. He spoke of his work as being about 'something much more serious than mocking my *paisanos*, who actually will learn to correct themselves once they see themselves described'. In this light, folklore would be a mirror held up before a people, so that, *in the future*, they could move along the great highway of human progress. It is clear, then, that Isabelo was writing for one and a half audiences: Spaniards, whose language he was using, and his own *pueblo*, whose language he was not using, and of whom only a tiny minority could read his work.

Where did Isabelo position himself in undertaking this task? At this juncture we finally come to perhaps the most interesting part of our inquiry. For most of the hundreds of pages of his book, Isabelo spoke as if he were not an Ilocano himself, or, at least, as if he were standing outside his people. The Ilocanos almost always appear as 'they', not 'we'. For example, 'There is a belief among *los Ilocanos* that fire produced by lightning can only be extinguished by vinegar, not by water.' Better still:

> Los ilocanos no pueden darnos perfecta idea acerca de la naturaleza de los mangmangkík, y dicen que *no son demonios*, asegún la idea que los católicos tienen de los demonios.

('The Ilocanos cannot give *us* a complete idea about the nature of the *mangmangkík*, and they say that *they are not devils* according to the Catholics' idea of what devils are.'][16] Isabelo here placed himself in the ranks of world folklore's savants, peering down at 'the Ilocanos' from above, and dispassionately distinguishing their superstitions from the parallel credulities of 'the Catholics'.

16. Dizon–Imson, p. 32.

At the same time, there are a number of passages which have a rather different tonality. At the start of the exposition of his research results Isabelo wrote:

> The Ilocanos, especially those from Ilocos Norte/Northern Ilocos, before starting to cut down trees in the mountains, sing the following verse:

> Barí, barí!
> Dika Agunget pári
> Ta pumukan kamí
> Iti pabakirda kamí

> Literally translated these lines mean: barí-barí (an Ilocano interjection for which there is no equivalent in Spanish), do not get upset, *compadre*, for we are only cutting because we have been ordered to do so.

Here Isabelo positions himself firmly within the Ilocano world. He knows what the Ilocano words mean, but his readers do not: for them (and by this he intends not only Spaniards, but also Europeans, as well as non-Ilocano natives of the archipelago) this experience is closed. But Isabelo is a kindly and scientific man, who wishes to tell the outsiders something of this world; and yet, he does not proceed by smooth paraphrase. The reader is confronted by an eruption of the incomprehensible original Ilocano, before being tendered a translation. Better yet, something is still withheld, in the words *barí-barí*, for which Spanish has no equivalent. The untranslatable, no less; and perhaps, beyond that, the incommensurable.

Isabelo suspected, I am sure, that his Spanish was by no means perfect, and might be laughed at by Astoll's 'dullwitted daubers' and 'braggarts'. He probably was also aware that the particular folklore methodology he was using might be doubtful in its systematics, and perhaps was soon to be superseded as science continued its grand world progress. But he had *barí-barí* in particular, and Ilocano in general, safely up his intellectual sleeve. On this ground he could not be contested. However, he needed to show, or half-show, his trump. This is the satisfaction of the tease: Dear readers, here is Ilocano for you to view, but you can only see what I permit you to see; and there are some things that you are actually incapable of seeing.

There is still a third position, which complicates matters yet
again. In a chapter on 'Music, Songs and Dances', Isabelo wrote:

> The lyrics of the *dal-lot* are well worth knowing. The *dal-lot* is composed
> of eight-line stanzas, with a special Ilocano rhyming scheme which you
> can see from the following refrain:
>
> > Dal-lang ayá daldal-lut
> > Dal-lang ayá dumidinal-lot.
>
> I transcribe it for you, because I do not know how to translate it, and
> I do not even understand it, even though I am an Ilocano. It seems to
> me to have no meaning.[17]

But it remains 'well worth knowing', because it is authentically
Ilocano, perhaps even because it is inaccessible to the frustrated
bilingual author himself. Isabelo leaves it at that. There are no
speculations. But there is an intimation, nonetheless, of the
vastness of the *saber popular*.

Three ill-fitting situations therefore: Outside (*they* can not give
us a complete idea); Inside (there is no Spanish equivalent of
bari-bari); and Outside Inside (even though I am an Ilocano
myself, I do not understand this Ilocano-language refrain; but I
am telling this to 'you', not to 'us').

What can be said by way of conclusions? I would propose four
points.

1

From the end of the eighteenth century on up into the twentieth,
'folklore studies', even if not yet defined as such, were a fundamental resource for nationalist movements. In Europe, in particular, they provided a powerful impulse in the democratizing
development of vernacular national cultures – spreading through
poetry, and other literary forms, to music, painting and dance.
One could broadly generalize by saying that the impulse had the
effect of aligning the language of folklore studies with that of a
popular nationalism: Norwegian folklorists would write in 'New
Norse' (not Danish and not Swedish) to recuperate the Norwegian *saber popular*; Finns would write in Finnish, not Swedish or

---

17. Dizon–Imson, pp. 258–9.

Russian; and this pattern would be paralleled in Bohemia, Hungary, Romania, and so on. Even where this was not entirely the case – a striking example is the Irish revivalist movement which operated both through Gaelic and through a colonially imposed English, well understood by most Irish men and women – the ultimate object was national 'awakening' and liberation.

At first sight, Isabelo's endeavour strikes one as quite different, because he was writing as much as anything for his non-nationals, in an imperial language which perhaps 3 per cent of the *indios* of the Philippines understood, and maybe only 1 per cent of his fellow Ilocanos could follow. In Europe folklorists wrote mostly for their *paisanos*, to show them their common and authentic origins. By contrast, *folklorista* Isabelo wrote mostly for the modern world – Germany, Spain, England – to show how Ilocanos and other *indios* were fully able and eager to enter that world, on a basis of equal and autonomous contribution.

2

Isabelo's study also marks his country off from the many neighbouring colonies in the Southeast Asian region. In these other colonies, most of what we can informally classify as 'folklore studies' was carried on by intelligent colonial officials with too much time on their hands, in an age still innocent of radio and television; and it was intended mainly to be of use to the colonial rulers, not to the studied populations themselves. Even after independence, these other folklore studies have led a marginal existence, while they have done significantly better in the postcolonial Philippines. Why should this have been so?

One answer is that in all the other colonies there survived a substantial written record from precolonial times – royal chronicles, Buddhist cosmologies, monastic inscriptions, Sufi tracts, court literatures – and it was these, not folklore, that provided the fount of aboriginal and glorious authenticity when nationalist movements got under way. The remote Philippines had never had powerful, centralized and literate states, and had been so thinly touched by Islam and Buddhism that they were Christianized with remarkably little violence or revolt. Seen from this angle, folklore substituted for Ancient Grandeur.

Another answer, at least as good, lies in the nature of nineteenth-century Iberian imperialism. Spain and Portugal, once great imperial centres of Europe, had been in decline since the mid-seventeenth century. With the loss of Latin America, the Spanish empire had been drastically reduced – to Cuba, Rio de Oro and the Philippines. Throughout the nineteenth century, Spain had been rent by the most violent internal conflicts as it struggled to make the transition from feudal past to industrial modernity. In the eyes of many of its own inhabitants, Spain itself was 'backward', superstitious, barely industrializing; and this understanding was widely shared not only in Europe, but also by the young intellectuals of the residual Spanish colonies. (This is why Isabelo was proud to have his writings published in Germany, while his equivalents elsewhere sought publication in the imperial metropoles.) The banner of progress was thus the flag of an Enlightenment (*Ilustración*) which had scarcely begun to conquer in Spain. Isabelo saw himself as an *ilustrado*, great-grandson of Denis Diderot; and thus involved in a common struggle with substantial numbers of Spaniards in the peninsula itself. In the colonial Philippines, the Enlightenment idea (so regularly denounced today by scholars originating from the former British colonies) was experienced as a project of human emancipation which linked forces in both colony and metropole. It thus seemed quite normal to the youthful Isabelo to dedicate his work to his colleagues in Spain.

At the same time, the 'backward Philippines' was the one colony in nineteenth-century Southeast Asia to have a real university – even if it was dominated by the Dominican Order. From this university graduated Isabelo and many of his nationalist companions; here, ultimately, lay the reason why the Philippines became, at the century's end, the site of the first nationalist revolution in the whole of Asia.

3

Enlightment came to the Philippines through the language of 'backward' Spain, and its prime agents, in every sense of the word, were therefore necessarily (at least) bilingual. (Many of the first generation of intellectuals also learned Latin in Manila and, if

they went abroad, acquired some French and English and
German as well.) Nowhere does one detect any marked aversion
or distrust towards this Romance language so heavily marked by
Arabic, the common vehicle of both reaction and enlightenment.
Why this should have been so is a very interesting question. One
reason is certainly that, in complete contrast to almost all of Latin
America, Spanish was never even close to being a 'majority'
language in the Philippines. Dozens of mainly oral local languages
flourished then, as indeed they do today; nothing in Isabelo's
writing suggests that he thought of Spanish as a deep menace to
Ilocano or its future survival. Furthermore, Spanish appeared to
him as the linguistic vehicle for speaking not only to Spain but
also, through Spain, to all the centres of modernity, science and
civilization. It was an 'international language' more than it was a
colonial one. What also undergirded this approach was the fact
that the Philippines had had no earlier 'language of power' –
potential rival of Spanish – based in the dynastic speech of a
precolonial political order.

It is striking that Isabelo never considered the possibility that,
by writing in Spanish, he had somehow betrayed his *pueblo* or had
been sucked into a 'dominant culture'. I think the reason for this
seemingly innocent stance is that, in the 1880s, the future status
of Las Islas Filipinas was visibly unstable, and some kind of
political emancipation was looming on the horizon. This instability had everything to do with local circumstances, but it was
ultimately grounded on the emancipation of Latin America more
than half a century before. Spain was the only imperial power
which 'lost' its empire in the nineteenth century. Nowhere else in
the colonial world did the colonized have such examples of
achieved liberation before their eyes. Here one sees a situation
wholly different from that of the present-day New World, where
Spanish has become both the 'eternal' majoritarian master over
all the indigenous languages in Latin America, and an equally
'eternal' oppressed minority in the expansive/expansionist
United States. No emancipation visible on the horizon in either
case.

4

Nonetheless, as we have had occasion to indicate above, there are
instructive reticences in Isabelo's youthful work, marked by the
uneasy pronominal slippages between 'I' and 'they', 'we' and
'you'. He was always thinking about two audiences, even when
writing for one and a half. 'The worst of men is the wretch who is
not endowed with that noble and sacred sentiment which they
call patriotism,' he wrote. Spanish was not for him a national
language; merely international. But was there a national language
in which Spanish could be opposed? Was there a clearcut *patria*
to which this national language was attached – a hypothetical
Ilocano-land? He never spoke of them as such. Besides, there
were those Aetas and Igorots who were his *hermanos*. There were
also those Tagalogs who, his investigations had shown him, were
not of a 'race distinct' from the Ilocanos; but he knew, as its
discoverer, that as yet no Tagalogs or Ilocanos were aware of this
scientific truth. It was this state of fluidity that led him back, at 23
years old, to the obscurely bordered culture out of which he grew,
and which, he sensed, he had partly outgrown. Ilocano popular
knowledge, or culture, thus came to its young patriot as something authentic, to be displayed to the whole world, as well as
something to be corrected – of course, by the Ilocanos themselves.
His mother tongue, Ilocano, thus became something to be translated, while also partially untranslatable. And at some points it
even slipped quietly away beyond the sunlit horizon of the
Enlightened young bilingual himself.

10

Hearing Voices:

Ricardo Palma's Contextualization
of Colonial Peru

Elisa Sampson Vera Tudela

No hemos encontrado comprobante alguno que garantice
la autenticidad de lo que vamos a referir, pero es tradición
popularísima en Lima, y como tal la apuntamos. Algo de
verdad habrá en el fondo, y sobre todo *si non e vero e ben
trovato.* [*sic*]

[We have not found any proof to guarantee the authenticity
of what we are about to recount, but it is a very popular tale
in Lima, and as such we note it down. There must be a
grain of truth in it and, above all even if it's not true, it's a
at least a good find.][1]

Ricardo Palma's (1833–1911) nonchalant disregard for historical
accuracy and insistence that a story's popularity and its narrative
charm justify reproducing it place him in the familiar Romantic

---

1. Vítores in *Tradiciones Peruanas completas,* ed. Edith Palma, Madrid: Aguilar,
1952, p. 294. All quotations are from this edition. Hereafter *Tradiciones.* All
translations are mine.

role of secretary to 'the people'.[2] Palma's position as bard is fairly degraded, however, for he never appears as a noble bearded figure intoning the secrets of Peruvian nationality to the nation's 'children'. Instead, we have a much more domestic scene with Palma as national grandfather, sitting by the fire and spinning yarns. We should not take his dismissal of historical proof too seriously, however, for Palma was fascinated by history and spent a good deal of time in the archives as well as listening to old wives' tales. In the story 'Mujer y tigre' the narrative is anchored around an anecdote told by a grandmother and heard by Palma as a child. As an adult, he investigates the historical background of the story and comes up with the archival proof that confirms the 'truth' of what he overheard, which he then writes up in his distinctive informal style, inserting it into another text as he simultaneously injects his particular brand of 'orality' into it.[3] The questions I am interested in looking at in this essay centre on how precisely Palma contextualizes the past and why such an imaginative exercise should have been so successful and have imposed itself on such large sectors of Peruvian society for such a long period.[4] None of these activities are as benign as the grandfatherly

---

2. The Romantic motif of secretary is commonplace in Palma's work. In 'Los tres motivos del oidor' he tells us that the proverbial phrase he is describing is still in current usage and that he has picked it up 'de boca de muchos viejos' ['from the mouths of many old people'] Ibid., p. 78. For a very similar appraisal of the types of stories Palma chooses to tell, see 'Franciscanos y Jesuitas' where Palma goes to his friend 'don Aeodato de la Mentirola' ['Mr. I. Love-Fibbing'], who says his grandmother told him the story. Palma asks if it is 'cuento o sucedido histórico' ['a story or a historical fact'] and receives the reply that, 'llámelo usted como quiera; pero ello ha de ser verdad, que mi abuela no supo inventar ni mentir' ['call it what you will, but it must be true for my grandmother did not know how to invent stories or tell lies']. Ibid., p. 277. In *Resurrecciones* he mounts a direct appeal to the reader to substantiate the 'tradicionality' of a story, insisting that everyone, including the reader, has heard it told. Ibid., p. 78.

3. Perhaps the best confirmation of Palma's genius for recording the voice of 'the people' is that his own work has become the focus of studies of folklore. Shirley L. Arora's conclusion that 'the ways in which Palma modified proverbial expressions have much in common with the process of variation found in oral tradition' seems to confirm that Palma not only records folkloric tradition, he somehow becomes it himself. *Proverbial Comparisons in Ricardo Palma's Tradiciones peruanas*, Folklore Studies 16, Berkeley: University of California Press, 1966, p. 4. Newspaper publication ensured a diffusion and fame that can be considered as being so extensive as to have resulted in a 'reinsertion' of Palma into the oral culture he attempted to represent.

4. Palma's *Tradiciones* (over 1500 pages of them) have been bowdlerized in pirate anthologies, transformed into strip cartoons and quoted in history textbooks. They

image would suggest. In this respect, it is useful to consider Latin America as undergoing an 'uneven' modernization in the period Palma writes his most well-known works, the series of short stories known as *tradiciones* (1827–1918). Unlike Europe, where the gradual definition of art and literature as discrete fields can be considered as coinciding with a rationalization of political functions, in Latin America the same dynamic 'generated a literary field whose separation from the political sphere was incomplete and uneven – even today'.[5]

Folklore, and more precisely its manifestations in oral narratives and poems, first becomes the privileged site for the 'soul' of a people in Romantic ideology.[6] In Latin America, the logic of this model would be to imagine the 'soul' of these nations being incarnated in indigenous peoples and their cultures. Although there were attempts in Peru in the early nineteenth century to write an *incaísta* literature, they were not very successful. Most works were inspired by Inca Garcilaso de la Vega,[7] but were themselves aesthetically poor and received little or no support, no doubt because they highlighted too many profound historical ruptures to be successful.[8] Vastly more popular were the *costum-*

---

continue to form the basis of what most Peruvians know about their colonial past and what they retransmit and circulate as stories and anecdotes.

5. Julio Ramos, *Divergent Modernities: Culture and Politics in Nineteenth-Century Latin America*, trans. John D. Blanco, Durham, NC and London: Duke University Press, 2001, p. xlii.

6. For Herder, popular traditions constituted the origin of all culture and historical development in a nation. They are the soul and 'genius' of a people. The interest in folklore was driven strongly by liberal historiography. Authors such as Augustin Thierry quarrelled with a conservative historiography that gave power only to heroes. Instead, they argued for putting 'the people' at the centre. Accompanying this bias for the popular was a call for the renewal of the rhetoric of history and an admiration for historical novelists, seen as great minds who could divine history using their imagination. See Lionel Gosman, *Between History and Literature*, Cambridge, MA: Harvard University Press, 1990, p. 94.

7. Inca Garcilaso de la Vega (1539–1616). Son of a Spanish captain and an Inca princess. One of the first of the *mestizo* elite who was brought up speaking both Quechua and Spanish. Considered the first great Hispanic American writer and quickly salvaged by the nineteenth century as a precursor of cultural and intellectual emancipation. Translator of neoplatonic works from Italian into Spanish, author of historical chronicles and most well known for his two histories of Peru: *Historia General de Perú* (1617) and *Comentarios Reales* (1609).

8. Here, a comparison with Isabelo de los Reyes, the subject of Benedict Anderson's essay in this volume, is instructive. Reyes' book on folkore in the Phillipines is published in 1887 – at the height of Palma's production of *Tradiciones* – and the importance both writers assign to the 'new science' is significant. As a member of the Ilocano ethnic group, Reyes' primordial task is to represent the

brista works, which concentrated on contemporary national 'types' and were very much inspired by Romantic interpretations of Herder.[9] Both these approaches, although radically different in their treatment of history, shared one characteristic: a total disregard for and avoidance of the colonial period as a subject. Palma himself avoids the colonial theme on occasion by marrying the *tradición* with *incaísmo* in a number of works which he sets in pre-conquest times ('Palla Huarcuna', 'La Achirana del Inca', 'La gruta de las maravillas'). It would be fair to say these are some of the least successful *tradiciones*, relying on romantic stereotyping of the noble Inca characters. Palma's genius seems only really to have been inspired by the colony.[10] What then is the significance of his choice to contextualize folklore and oral tradition predominantly in the colonial period?

Although the colonial legacy was not something that the newly independent nations of Latin America particularly liked to dwell upon, it is clear that from the legal system to the economy, the colony continued living on in large sections of the republican social body.[11] This had two very obvious implications: that the colonial legacy was a barrier both to progress and change, and that it also constituted an important source of stability in what

Ilocanos using this new tool. His political use of folkore as an emancipatory genre is quite apparent: it is used to consign the 'colonial' to history, an enormously daring act as Reyes writes as a colonial subject. Palma, writing after independence, is in a very different subject position as a writer. Not being an indian himself, he has no authority with which to represent indigenous folklore. He turns instead to constructing the folkore of the *mestizo* or mixed-race population of Peru. For this project the the tools of pure folklore are soon abandoned and instead the new science is rapidly mixed with fiction and history in narratives which necessarily have the colony at their very centre for before the colonial period their subject/s did not exist. Here, as in so many instances in Palma's work, the hybridity of post-independence would seem to blur the neat divisions being exported by enlightened thought from the European centre.

9. *Costumbrismo* developed an image of the nation focused on the rural or on virgin landscapes and illustrated them with suitable 'national' types designed for maximum didactic effect. See Beatriz González Stephan, *La historiografía literaria del liberalismo hispanoamericano del XIX*, Cuba: Editorial Casa de las Américas, 1987.

10. *Tradiciones* with Inca themes are in the end only a small part of Palma's literary production. Another small number of stories are set in independent Peru.

11. Antonio Cornejo Polar, 'Ajenidad y apropiación nacional de las letras coloniales: reflexiones sobre el caso peruano', in *Crítica y descolonización: el sujeto colonial en la cultura latinoamericana*, ed. Beatríz González Stephan and Lucía Helena Costigan, Caracas: Universidad Simón Bolívar and Ohio State University, 1992, pp. 598–606 (p. 599).

otherwise were very chaotic times.[12] Such an elusive and ambiguous space sociopolitically was equally awkward in cultural terms. Perhaps the best example of these kinds of difficulties is the polemic about historiography which raged during the mid-1840s between José Victorino Lastarria and Andrés Bello. Herder was quoted liberally by both sides of the debate.[13] It becomes clear, then, that Palma's choice of subject was anything but neutral politically, and that his 'historical' approach was embroiled in a pan-American intellectual debate about the role of historiography in the new American nations. His stories spoke directly to the question of whether a more philosophical (Lastarria) or a predominantly narrative (Bello) approach should be taken to the retelling of history.

Although from the above description it would seem that Palma aligned himself with the more 'conservative' forces of debate, it is well to remember that his gaze on the colony was not at all that of an antiquarian.[14] For Palma, history was alive, and he wrote about it with many of the narrative elements of style which he learned as a journalist.[15] As a result, his representation of the

---

12. On the legal system in particular, see Andrés Bello's project to draft a new civil law code for Chile. Bello argued that the legislation that governed Latin America was fundamentally Spanish, even decades after independence, and that this should not be changed. The notion was that Roman law had stood the test of time and grown with the country. It was not a foreign imposition that would generate conflict, unlike the Napoleonic code favoured by other reformers. The analogous application of this argument to the cultural realm was not lost on contemporaries. See Iván Jaksíc, *Andrés Bello: Scholarship and Nation Building in Nineteenth-Century Latin America*, Cambridge: Cambridge University Press, 2001, p. 113.

13. Ibid., pp. 137–42. *Ideen zur Philosophie der Geschichte der Menschheit* was known in Chile through the French translation of Edgar Quinet (1827).

14. The difficulty of distinguishing 'liberals' from 'conservatives' in this period is enormous. González Stephan suggests that this may be due to the fact that both sides were variants of the dominant sectors of society (the new or the old oligarchies), and thus labelling them so distinctly is often misleading. González Stephan, *La historiografía literaria*, pp. 93–4.

15. For the key role of journalism in the literature of this period, see Aníbal González, *Journalism and the Development of Spanish American Narrative*, Cambridge: Cambridge University Press, 1993, and Ramos, *Divergent Modernities*. Ramos's comments on how the new journalists came from the middle classes and had no symbolic capital or oligarchic filiation are particularly pertinent. José Carlos Mariátegui comments in a very similar way on Palma's middle-class background and how it made him profoundly republican in outlook. José Carlos Mariátegui, 'El proceso de la literatura', in *Mariátegui total*, Lima: Amauta, 1994, pp. 103–57. It was in fact in literature that the aristocracy was most taken to task in this period. For example, *costumbrista* sketches often complained that the aristocracy was not open to merit or luck and that it claimed a birthright that did not exist. On the

colony is curiously contemporary; not only in the most obvious sense that Palma as narrator inserts comparisons with the present (invariably driven by some didactic urge), but in more profound and subtle temporal negotiations which will be explored later.

Palma was not the first in Peru to 'rediscover' the colony, and this has been linked to specific historical events which highlighted the colonial past.[16] The mid-nineteenth century was certainly a period of intense interest which saw the publication of historical texts as well as of colonial accounts themselves.[17] Already in 1844 José Manuel Valdez y Palacios chose to include some colonial writers for the first book to be written about Peru's literary tradition, though all were admittedly from the end of the colonial period and were rescued as *ilustrados* or precursors of emancipation. A mere eighteen years later (1862), though, José Toribio Polo managed to reclaim the whole of colonial literature as 'Peruvian' (though he was not very complimentary about it).[18] None of these gazes directed at the colonial past were exotic gestures invoking strange and faraway things. They were, rather, a recognition 'de un hecho macizo: la tenaz persistencia colonial en el tejido más hondo de la vida republicana y – por consiguiente – del lazo que une ambas etapas como segmentos de un solo proceso'. ['of a solid fact; the strong and unrelenting presence of the colony at the most profound levels of republican life – and as a result – of the tie that united both historical moments into segments of a single continuous process.'][19]

This recognition of the 'living' power of the colonial past is at the centre of Palma's contextualizing project. For him, neither

role of newspapers as critically important for a concept of civil literature which was in turn essential for the production of sense of nationality, see Benedict Anderson's seminal thesis in *Imagined Communities: Reflections on the Origin and Spread of Nationalism*, London: Verso, 1991.

16. Antonio Cornejo Polar describes nineteenth-century land disputes where Peru invoked colonial documents and saw fit to boast about its 'viceregal' character, and also mentions the new 'guano' wealth which was distributed, administered and spent in the best 'colonial' fashion. In *La formación de la tradición literaria en el Perú*, Lima: Centro de estudios y publicaciones, 1989, pp. 40–2.

17. Cobo's 1639 *Historia de la fundación de Lima* was first published in 1882. Also chronicles by Zárate, Gómara and Cieza appeared for the first time in the nineteenth century. See Fernando Unzueta, 'Las tradiciones Peruanas y la cuestión nacional', in Julio Ortega, ed., *Tradiciones peruanas*, Madrid: Colección archivos, 1993, pp. 503–19.

18. See ibid., p. 504.

19. Cornejo Polar, *La formación*, p. 50.

literary history nor philology is a static or isolated study concerned only to fix an origin or define a past. In relation to philology, for example, Palma's interest in questions of language manifested itself in many forms: historical, political and creative. He was the Peruvian representative to the Real Academia de la lengua Española and lobbied it in a self-conscious battle modelled on the Wars of Independence. He also wrote about his skirmishes with this institution in the form of a *tradición* ('Barchilón'), ensuring that they passed into the Peruvian cultural imaginary.[20] Palma is determined to construct a dynamic sequence that moves across and through not only fields of expertise and literary genres but also temporalities, extending into the future as well as back into the past. According to Benedict Anderson, it is exactly in this sense that Isabelo de los Reyes conceives the science of folklore – as a project that will not exoticize its subject or otherwise fix it but which enables a fully political engagement with the present and the future. Palma's political aims are less immediately obvious, but, as we shall see, the concern with dynamism in his case also signals a desire to engage actively with the present and future.

Palma's contextualization of the colonial legacy was characterized by this mixture of methods and effects, but can be broadly understood to take three forms: the archival, the historical and the literary – all of them marked by fluidity, dynamism and creativity.[21] In 1884 Palma was appointed as director of Peru's National Library.[22] This came in the aftermath of the war with

20. *Tradiciones*, pp. 129–31. Details of these quarrels can be found in *Boletín de la Academia Peruana de la Lengua* 20, Lima: Nueva Epoca, 1985. Their general drift was Palma's insistence that certain Peruvian words be included in the Academia's dictionary, a request which was refused on the grounds of purity. Curiously, Palma's position was in fact not so different from the Academia's, for he also believed in the power of standardization and the need to regulate spelling and grammar in Spanish. Nevertheless, he also clearly saw room in this project for the specificities of Peruvian Spanish. For the centrality of linguistic cohesion to arguments about independence in Latin America, Bello's thoughts are instructive: that without control, Spanish would shatter into a thousand dialects along the model of that other imperial language, Latin. See Ramos, *Divergent Modernities*, p. 36 and Jaksic, *Andrés Bello*, more generally.

21. In this respect, Palma's relation to the work of Juan del Valle Caviedes, an eighteenth-century satirist, is exemplary. Palma not only edits Caviedes's work, he writes a *tradición* about it, cites it frequently in his own writings, occasionally takes on Caviedes's satirical persona himself, invents Caviedes's biography and corrects some of his poetry.

22. Palma held this position until 1912.

Chile (1879–84), which had devastated the country, and it was his responsibility to build up the library from virtually nothing. Palma described himself as the *bibliotecario mendigo* (begging librarian) and he did indeed initiate a flurry of epistolary relationships with other librarians and government officials throughout Latin America and Europe, designed to reclaim books that had been lost during the wars and political upheavals following independence. It is a certainty that this work put Palma in contact with a hugely varied number of colonial manuscripts and books, and no doubt it is from here that his fascination springs. As well as acquiring books for the library, Palma was also involved in the re-edition of many colonial manuscripts.[23] This should not be considered a dry philological exercise, but is more correctly read as part of his desire to circulate a large and varied 'archive' of colonial knowledge, thus generating new and enriching readings of the period.[24] Palma was also the author of an historical work, *Anales de la inquisición de Lima* (1863), based on research he carried out on Inquisition manuscripts. In *Anales*, the colonial material inspires Palma to write something much more complex than an objective historical account, and it is certainly possible to see his history as containing the beginnings of the style that would eventually mature into the trademark of the *tradiciones*.[25]

This 'new' genre, the *tradición*, became the exclusive vehicle for Palma's literary contextualization of the colony. The purported 'novelty' of the *tradiciones* highlights their generic slipperiness and is best illustrated by Palma's own unwillingness to define them in any substantial or coherent way, preferring instead to tantalize his readers with many allusive references to their literary identity.[26] Perhaps the most interesting thing about this 'problem' of definition is precisely its problematic nature.

---

23. Valle y Caviedes, as mentioned, the Ciego de la Merced, various viceregal poets and editions of popular *coplas* and *romances*.

24. Cf. Cornejo Polar's theory that one reason for the increase in interest in satire in the late nineteenth century in Peru is due precisely to Palma's recycling of colonial diatribes, graffitti, satirical rhymes and *pasquines*. In 'Ajenidad y apropiación', p. 604.

25. See my 'Pyrotechnic History and Phosphorescent Literature: Ricardo Palma's "Anales de la Inquisición de Lima"', in *Romance Quarterly*, 47, 2000, pp. 215–26.

26. The question of genre has of course been central to Palma studies. Here, I will confine myself to indicating that such disorder and generic confusion is in fact characteristic of the period. See Emilio Carilla, *El Romanticismo en la América Hispana*, Madrid: Gredos, 1958, p. 76.

Palma invests heavily in making his narratives difficult to cat-
egorize, in questioning every kind of boundary or label placed
on them, and in quite openly ridiculing these critical desires.
A large part of the generic instability of the *tradiciones* can
certainly be seen as stemming from their circumstances of production and publication. Palma wrote them over forty-six years
and published them serially in newspapers.[27] They were only
posthumously organized into monograph collections. The most
important collection remains that edited by Palma's daughter,
Edith. In her edition, Edith Palma orders the *tradiciones* chronologically, imposing a teleological logic which would no doubt
have infuriated her father, whose vision of historical change was
much more impious than his daughter's inevitable pageant from
colony to independence.

Along with this delight in confusing generic categories and
satirizing the desire to order and systematize literature went
Palma's very political disdain for the same hierarchizing and
ordering tendencies in the social sphere (which he identified with
the oligarchy in the present and the aristocracy in the past). He
identifies genealogy as one of the main hierarchizing mechanisms
in society and he is both fascinated and repelled by it. 'Un libro
condenado' is devoted to the story of how a man in high Limeño
society who is slighted at a party revenges himself through the
publication of a book slandering all the city's families by telling
stories about their impure backgrounds (their 'bastardía, villano
abolengo, impureza de sangre' [illegitemacy, ignoble linage and
impure blood'].[28] The book is quickly banned by the establishment and the author escapes to Mexico, but not before having
wreaked havoc on the social organization of the colonial city. In
his review of the book Palma's admiration is barely veiled.
Throughout the *tradiciones* as a whole, his satire of the colonial
fascination with genealogy is unremitting.[29] He positions himself

---

27. Eleven 'series' of *tradiciones*, each of varying numbers, were published in
total.

28. *Tradiciones*, pp. 314–17.

29. In 'Los alcaldes de Arica' Palma quotes Simón Rodríguez, Bolívar's teacher,
on how this obsession with rank and with inventing genealogies is a particularly
New World malady: 'El descendiente de un moro de Africa venía de España
diciendo que en su familia no se habían conocido negros; y el hombre más soez
se presentaba con un cartucho de papeles, llenos de arabescos y garabatos, para
probar que descendía de la casa más noble de Asturias o Vizcaya' ['the descendant

very clearly as *el demócrata* who understands nothing of heraldry, which he dismisses as 'pergaminos y títulos de Castilla y danzas y medias anatas y escudos y demás pamplinas heráldicas' [certificates and titles from Castille, certificates of sinecures, coats of armour, shields and other heraldic thingummies], his vocabulary giving away that he has in fact read enough about the subject to have picked up the jargon.[30]

This mixture of deep acquaintance and interest with a powerful emotive investment is a striking feature of his contextualization of many aspects of the colony. For example, it drives the strong contemporary edge which is central to Palma's satire.[31] It is not insignificant that the catalyst for criticism throughout the *tradiciones* is invariably superficial. This is persistently the way Palma presents history: from upside down, from the margins to the centre. As a result of this disconnection from 'big' politics, Palma is often accused of producing a saccharin image of the colony.[32] In this interpretation, the middle classes caught in the difficulties of the post-independence period would find in Palma's vision something of a lost childhood. As Cornejo Polar has argued however, Palma's interpretation is not quite so comforting or

---

of an African moor would come from Spain saying that there had never been any black people in his family and the most vulgar man would present himself bearing a file of papers full of arabesques and scribbles in order to prove he descended from the most noble house of Asturias or Vizcaya']. Ibid., p. 303.

30. Ibid., p. 152. See 'El ahijado de la providencia', ibid., pp. 151–3 and 'Felíz barbero', ibid., pp. 309–12, for similar appraisals of colonial aristocracy.

31. Similarly, Reyes's self-criticism is an important aspect of his folkoric studies of the Iloco. The aim, for both authors, is to empower the subjects of their criticism. See Benedict Anderson, 'The Rooster's Egg', in this volume.

32. Critics depict Palma as having created a 'colonial utopia' where life is sumptuous, refined and even decadent; a world away from the grim realities of post-independence. See Julio Ortega's introduction to *Tradiciones peruanas* for a review of the criticism. Contemporary critics essentially expressed a similar opinion. Palma's writing was seen as a minor literature, nothing grand or epic, neither tragic nor noble and designed to purvey a base fantasy. In the words of González Prada, Palma's arch critic, the *tradiciones* were 'falsificaciones agridulcetes de la historia y la caricatura miscroscópica de la novela' ['sweet'n'sour falsifications of history and the microscopic caricature of the novel']. Quoted in Jaime Martínez Tolentino, *Literatura hispánica e hispanoamericana: tres autores reveladores: Ricardo Palma, Julián del Casal y Jacinto Benavente*, Kassel: Reichenberger, 1992, p. 3. In relation to the 'parodic' character of the *tradiciones* as a genre, compare with Lukács on Merimée and Vitet not having any heroes or heroism in their works because they chose to write anecdotes and memoirs rather than novels. Georg Lukács, *The Historical Novel*, trans. Hannah and Stanley Mitchel, London: Merlin, 1962.

comfortable. It has much more to do with a desire to create a fantasy of homogeneity and to project this onto the past in the hope that somehow its effect will filter down into the present and the future.[33] This narrative mechanism characteristically pays no respect to the usual way history is read or considered to influence the time outside its subject.

In Palma's rendition of the past, attention is given over to the quotidian, to the domestic underside of life, to the small people of history, and the emotion driving such a revelation is best characterized as affectionate and intimate rather than desiring. Palma's intention is to make the reader feel at home in the past. The mechanisms by which this is achieved in the *tradiciones* are manifold and it would be impossible to provide a comprehensive survey in an essay of this length. Nonetheless, it is useful to provide an overview. The most obvious is clearly the choice of subject matter. Palma invariably goes for what in terms of nine-teenth-century historiography would certainly be considered mar-ginal but which is the staple of the folkloric interest in history: the people. So, in 'El que pagó el pato' the story is set at a monumental historical moment: the mock-trial of the last Inca, Atahualpa, by the conquistadores. This ludicrously illegal and spectacular ploy spelt the end of indigenous rule in Peru. In Palma's version we hear nothing of the trial itself but instead follow the biographies of the twenty-four judges who tried the Inca king. Similarly, in 'Aceituna, una' we are treated to a cultural history of the olive in the New World, a 'history' which allows Palma to range over etymology, botany and acculturation, giving an interpretation of the colonial world designed to appeal to every reader's range of knowledge and experience. This type of approach does not mean that Palma ignores more traditional historical questions; simply that he focuses on them differently. In some *tradiciones*, for example in 'Quizá quiero, quizá no quiero', which deals with the consequences of one of the first marriages between an indian woman and a conquistador in the colony, Palma is careful to weave his romantic story-line into a wider historical plot of what was going on at the time. Thus, the hero (a 'real' historical figure) is introduced with Palma's usual blend of documented facts, hearsay and embroidered detail. He

33. Cornejo Polar, 'Ajenidad y apropriación', p. 605.

then interjects a long factual description of what was actually happening in the colony at the time – 'a la sazón encontrábanse los conquistadores en atrenzos feroces' [at the time the conquistadores were in frenzied battles] – a historical lesson sweetened by the preceding rhetorical show.[34] Interestingly, Palma tends to keep the two types of narration quite distinct, using the narratorial voice to signal a change from one to the other. Thus, in 'La monja de la llave' the reader is told it is time to throw in 'el obligado parrafillo histórico' 'the obligatory little historical paragraph'.[35] Most of the *tradiciones* do precisely this; ceremoniously consign the voice of official history to a distinct paragraph or paragraphs while the unofficial history is narrated with drama, humour and plenty of licence in the main part of the story. Often, the very plot is sufficient to give an indication of Palma's penchant for the unofficial side of the historical process. In 'Los amantes del real orden' the analysis of colonial history and political life concentrates on socio-demographic and psychological factors. At the centre of the story is the order given by the King of Spain that unmarried conquistadores should wed any suitable widows and not remain single. The King's analysis is that the civil wars ravaging his prized overseas possession are set off by too much sexual licence. Palma dryly draws similar conclusions for the present but regrets that such a solution is not so easily enforceable now.

Giving women roles as protagonists is the most clear 'upside-down' representation of history in the *tradiciones*. Mainstream historiographical thought in the nineteenth century did not consider women to be significant historical agents. Palma does this consistently throughout the *tradiciones* (he is fascinated by witches and nuns), but most directly in a series of stories which have the *tapadas* as their subject. *Tapadas* (the covered ones) are the traditionally veiled women of Lima, and throughout the colonial period their dress is represented as causing trouble because it made it difficult to ascertain the identity or rank of the wearer and so gave women enormous freedom to engage in all kinds of scandalous behaviour in public. Various attempts were

---

34. *Tradiciones*, p. 33.
35. Ibid., p. 202. Palma makes some kind of reference to this obligatory 'historical' paragraph in almost every *tradición*.

made by different viceroys to reform this dress and Palma's stories focus on the reaction of the *tapadas*. In his rewriting it is clear that the women hold the real power of the kingdom and that the men are in awe and terror of them. Moreover, his wry comment is that these rebellions could really be considered the beginning of the independence movement in Peru as they are the first serious challenge to viceregal authority.[36]

Palma's desire to represent those voices usually excluded from grand literary and historical narratives is also revealed in the plotting of the *tradiciones*. All the *tradiciones* have a fulcrum in terms of the plot. It is often an anecdote (sometimes taken from a historical source, sometimes invented, often a combination of both) or a proverb (again, sometimes substantiated, often not). The anecdotal or proverbial nature of the fulcrum means that it does not serve to produce a coherent and stable plot-line but rather it emphasizes the fragmentary nature of the majority of the *tradiciones*.[37] Even *tradiciones* such as 'Una carta de indias' which appear to have a predictable story-line – the biography of the main character – behave quite differently in Palma's hands. Here, the narrative of the 'life' is constantly derailed by seemingly marginal details (how golden tweezers are sent to the Spanish court in an attempt to bribe the noble ladies, how the name *America* is in fact an Amerindian one and not connected to Amerigo Vespucci). As usual, it is the voice of the narrator which provides some coherence rather than any structural device such as plot.[38] The narrator does not act alone, however. His assistants include the devil, witches, miracles and superstition. It is as if the literature of the 'pure' nineteenth century (of liberalism, rationalism, science, etc.) is simply not literature at all for Palma. Colonial documents, and especially ecclesiastical ones, proved an enormous source of inspiration, and Palma 'lifts' many of his best stories of naughty nuns, wicked witches and deluded young girls

---

36. *La conspiración de la saya y manto*, ibid., pp. 159–62, and *Motín de Limeñas*, ibid., pp. 228–30. Palma's habitual misogyny is sometimes offset by a more pressing desire to criticize other sectors of society.

37. On the plots of the *tradiciones* and their relationship to the *fait divers* in journalism, see González, *Journalism*, p. 75.

38. Similarly, Palma's 'biography' of Francisco de Carvajal, 'el demonio de los andes' ['the demon of the Andes'], also abandons the obvious structure provided by the life story and instead presents fragmentary episodes, not chronologically ordered, in twelve different *tradiciones*.

from these pages.[39] This certainly goes some way towards explaining his 'nostalgia', for the colony as in it he seems to locate many of the elements that make a 'good story', namely manifestations of inexplicable causalities and bizarre coincidences.

A multiplicity of historical voices cohabit in the *tradiciones* (occasionally even along with the official version of events) and their relations are not always stable or harmonious. They are saved from complete atomization, however, by the voice of the narrator himself, who steps in to lend authority and to clear up confusions, though, as we shall also see, he usually quickly sabotages whatever authority is established and plants material for more confusions. As González remarks, few nineteenth-century literary genres require the textual 'presence' of their author or simultaneously have as much of their authority undermined by him as the *tradición*.[40] There is no doubt that the authorial voice in the *tradiciones* tends to question its own authority, revealing at every opportunity the textual mechanisms that underlie it and the 'unfinished' character of them. The majority of Palma's descriptions of his own writing practice, as we have seen, are modest dismissals. Writing of a series of shorter *tradiciones* he calls *hilachas* (worn threads), Palma describes them as

> apuntaciones históricas y chismografía de viejas. Hay en ellas cosas frívolas al lado de noticias curiosas. El autor ha deshilachado tela de algodón y tela de seda y formado un ovillo o pelota de hilachas.

> [Historical notes and the gossipography of old ladies. Frivolous things lie next to curious items in them. The author has unstitched cotton and silk in order to make a ball or spool of worn threads.][41]

Here, the metaphor is a carefully chosen domestic one, the author literally spinning a yarn, and not of very fine quality. The humility of the narratorial tone in relation to literary status is difficult to judge, however, for often, as González states, 'there is

---

39. The material Palma uses is incredibly rich and varied. Inquisition files, for example, are often in the form of transcripts of trials, recording the actual words spoken. These are some of the historical voices Palma listens to, transcribes and reinserts into texts.

40. González, *Journalism*, p. 65.

41. *Tradiciones*, p. x. Cf. 'Hermosa entre las hermosas', ibid., p. 196. 'Dice usted, amigo mío, que con cuatro paliques, dos mentiras y una verdad hilvano una tradición' ['You say, my friend, that I can stitch up a *tradición* with four little sticks, two fibs and one truth'].

a tantalizing play between orality and textuality that intensifies the slippery, indefinable nature of the text, and suggests that Palma's *tradición* contains, from the very beginning, its own self-criticism'.[42] In 'El que se ahogó en poca agua' the story begins with a list of proverbs which the narrator claims will be proved true by the unfolding of events he is to retell. This weight of 'proverbial knowledge' is complemented in the story by the invocation of a more literary type of authority. Palma quotes directly from Inca Garcilaso and states that the truth of his *tradición* is unimpeachable given this source.[43] These two invocations must shore up the anecdotes that form the 'plot' of the *tradición* (which concentrates on the bizarre and ridiculous deaths met by various conquistadores). More accurately, it is not the authority invoked, but the invoking of authority, the sonority of the narrator's own voice in its quest to secure belief, that knits the story together.[44]

Palma's *tradiciones*, quoting and misquoting some colonial sources, creatively rewriting some and still more creatively inventing others, generate a genuine 'intertext': a fluid and consistent reimagination of the past in meticulous detail. In terms of quotation from extant colonial sources, his repertoire is vast.[45] The play of citation extends into cross-referencing his own writings, turning himself into one of his own 'sources'. In 'Pasquín y contrapasquín', Palma quotes a proverb, then points the reader to an elucidation of it he has made in another *tradición*. In 'El

---

42. González, *Journalism*, p. 66.

43. It is interesting to note that Palma is not always so respectful of Garcilaso's reputation, and in 'Quiza quiero, quiza no quiero' he says of him: 'Garcilaso (no el poeta, sino el cronista del Perú, que a veces es más embustero que el telégrafo)' ['Garcilaso (not the poet but the historian of Peru, who is sometimes as tricky as the telegraph']. *Tradiciones*, p. 33.

44. In this essay I have only examined the very broad outlines of Palma's project. For a closer reading that seems to support some of the arguments here, see Escobar on 'critical negativity', where he claims that there is a frequent presence in Palma's mature style of 'asseveration by the exclusion of opposites'. Escobar notes, 'instead of categorical statements, Palma prefers the suggestive statement that, eliminating its opposite, leaves some margin to the imagination. For example: "the Pearl no longer had an orient"; "myself not being yet an old man."' Quoted in González, *Journalism*, p. 65.

45. A few examples must suffice: Palma quotes from the anonymous text *La monja alférez*; another much cited author is Calancha, who wrote one of the first chronicles about Peru. The references to Garcilaso Inca have already been noted. Other sources include private letters, inquisition files, official viceregal correspondence and miscellaneous documents.

tamborcito del pirata', though the narrator may not have seen the events, he claims a spurious patriotic tie to the colonial source he quotes as an authority, adopting its author as his 'countryman':

> Yo no lo vi, por supuesto, pero sí lo vio mi paisano el padre Juan Meléndez, autor de la curiosa Crónica dominicana, impresa en Roma en 1681, y a mi paisano me atengo, que fué fraile veraz si los hubo y muy serio y formalote.

> [I, of course, did not see it but my countryman father Juan Meléndez, author of the curious Dominincan chronicle printed in Rome in 1681, did, and I trust in my compatriot for he was a very true friar, if ever there was one, and very serious and very ceremonious.][46]

More significantly, Palma's sympathy with the period extends to his dramatization of events and – notably – speech. In 'Franciscanos y Jesuitas', the story comes to life as Palma describes the everyday actions of a witch as she sets about welcoming her guests, a Franciscan friar and a Jesuit priest, in a tone that juggles serious historical detail with the ridiculous:

> La vieja que en este momento se ocupaba en clavetear con alfileres un muñequito de trapo, dentro del cual había puesto, a guisa de alma, un trozo de rabo de lagartija, abandonó tan interesante faena, y después de guardar el maniquí bajo una olla de la cocina, salió presurosa a recibir a sus huéspedes.

> [The old woman, who at that moment was busy stabbing a cloth dolly (in which she had put a bit of lizard's tail to represent the soul) with pins, abandoned such an interesting task, and after hiding the doll under a pan in the kitchen, hurriedly went out to meet her guests.][47]

Innumerable *tradiciones* go further with the scene-setting and transcribe the speech of historical characters. In 'Los Azulejos de San Francisco' Palma re-creates the 'crowd scene' when the mob hears the town crier announcing the death penalty for a man who has killed a woman.

> Oigamos los que se charlaba en un grupo de ociosos y noticieros, reunidos en el tendejón de un pasamanero.
>   ¡Por la cruz de mis calzones, qué guapo mozo se pierde – decía un

---

46. *Tradiciones*, p. 267.
47. Ibid., p. 278.

mozalbete andaluz bien encarado – por culpa de una mala pécora,
casquivana y rabicortona! . . .

[Let's listen to what was being chatted about in a group of layabouts
and gossips who were gathered in the shopdoor of an upholsterer's.
   'By the cross of my pants, what a lovely man is to be lost,' said a
good-looking young guy from Andalucía, 'and all the fault of this
black sheep, a flirt and a slattern.][48]

Palma's 'intertext', however, is even more complex than this
already complex re-weaving and re-imagining of the past for it
also activates contemporary sources and voices, injecting these
into the past to produce what we have described previously as a
'contemporaneity effect'. Perhaps the most radical consequence
of this fluid intertext is the relativization of all knowledge: Palma's
is not an ideological discourse but a discourse about ideologies.[49]
In 'Los refranes mentirosos' there is a nice undoing of 'traditional' knowledge when the story challenges various old proverbs and yet generates new ones in the process. In 'El tamborcito
del pirata' very predictable comments on religious beliefs in the
colony and how their blindness has been superseded in the
modern age are undone by the exasperated dismissal of enlightenment as a 'tall story' too: '!Es mucho cuento la ilustración de
nuestro siglo escéptico, materialista y volteriano!' ['The enlightenment of our sceptical, materialistic and Voltaire-inspired time
is also a tall story'].[50]

   The creativity of this approach is impossible to transmit in
isolated quotation; rather it is an effect that permeates each

---

48. Ibid., p. 306.
49. The primal ideological clash between indigenous and European cultures is
material for relativization with Palma, who finds the undercutting of Spanish
superiority particularly funny. See how in 'El abad de Lunahuaná' indigenous
superstition proves more effective than the imported Catholic one. Ibid.,
pp. 193–4.
50. Ibid., p. 270. The most obvious manifestation of the 'contemporaneity effect'
is when Palma comments directly on the past. So, in 'Entre jesuitas, agustinianos y
dominicos' the narrator criticizes the Jesuit Order by underlining how different
(and more superior) the values of contemporary secular society are. Ibid., p. 212.
Similarly, in 'Vítores' the narrator cannot help but compare the rigging of
elections in convents by influential elite families in the colonial period to how
contemporary presidential elections are also rigged. His jaded conclusion is valid
for both periods: money runs the '(mis)government' of the country. Ibid., p. 291.
More usually, the effect is achieved much more subtly: the narrator interjecting a
comparison or temporal 'tag' in the midst of many other observations. Cf. 'Los
ratones de fray Martín', ibid., p. 258.

tradición individually and also the body of *tradiciones* as a whole, constituting a concerted, methodical and hugely ambitious project. The core of the 'contemporaneity effect' is usually tied to a documentary fragment, though often also to a folkloric 'document' (a proverb, a saying, etc.) which lies buried at the heart of the nineteenth-century retelling. By virtue of its immersion in the modern *tradición*, this fragment immediately acquires not only new meanings but also a new historical dimension. This is not to say that the fragment becomes detached from its original timeframe (in fact the opposite is true, for in order to achieve its 'historical' effect the *tradición* relies on the fragment to have temporal depth) but that the fragment totally modifies the very character of the 'past' that it signifies.[51] Palma's *tradiciones* were written during a period of incredible social change in Peru. Lima, the city which is the main 'character' of so many of the stories, is estimated to have doubled in size between 1880 and 1930, transforming itself from a *ciudad patricia* to a *ciudad burguesa* in Romero's terms.[52] There would have been greatly increased social mobility, changes in the economy, new opportunities of every kind; all of which would have exploded traditional hierarchies and demanded more and different things from the cultural sphere. However much they might have the past as a subject matter Palma's texts are very much of this modern period. His concern for the 'oral' in general and for subtle changes in linguistic usage in particular allows him to collect new literary resources and means that he founds his entire writing practice on the moving and unfinished character of language.[53] Transcribing

---

51. Cornejo Polar, 'Ajenidad y apropriación', p. 605.
52. José Luis Romero, *Latinoamérica: la ciudad y las ideas*, Mexico: Siglo XXI, 1976, p. 252.
53. The appropriation of oral literatures for the quick construction of national literary heritages was a common Romantic strategy. Cf. José López Portillo's invocation of the traditional cornucopian image of America when writing about potential cultural wealth in 1898: 'Nuestra vida nacional está aún tan poco explotada por el arte, como nuestra naturaleza por la industria; todo es virgen entre nosotros, las selvas y las costumbres, la tierra material y el mundo moral que nos rodea' ['Our national life remains as underexploited by art as our natural resources by industry: everything amongst us is virgin: forests and customs, the material world and the moral world which surrounds us']. Quoted in Norma Klahn and Wilfredo H. Corral, eds, *Los novelistas como críticos*, Mexico: Fondo de cultura económica, 1991, p. 123. See also Enrique Pupo Walker on how colonial documents fed this Romantic love of legend as Latin America had *cantidades inagotables* (infinite quantities) of this kind of material. In *La vocación literaria del*

these unofficial and oral elements into writing and injecting them
with his own version of 'orality' in order to recirculate them
allows Palma to explore what lies outside the theoretical certainties of his own age. His fascination with the relation of the 'voice'
to the 'letter' and with 'the people' to a particularized hero or
heroine is linked to the wish to represent what enlightened/
rational discourse usually leaves out or explains away. Palma in
this sense can genuinely be thought of as exploring the underside
of the rationalizing projects of his own century through literary
creation.

From a narrowly literary perspective, Palma's achievement was
to create a 'literary tradition' whose basic sequence of prehis-
panic–conquest–colony–emancipation–republican present may
now seem entirely natural but was in reality the product of a
complicated and much disputed historical choice.[54] More broadly,
however, what Palma achieves is that he transforms the colony
into a period which contemporary Peruvians recognized (and
continue to recognize) as their 'own' past. This sense of belonging and genealogy is, then, extremely significant and constitutes
the creation of a *tradición* in the sense of popular history or
folklore. The invention of tradition, of a common memory, and
the mediation between modernity and the areas that modernity
has excluded or run over is one of the great strategies of legitimation instituted by modern Latin American literature.[55] Palma's
complex archival contextualization of the colony can be considered a quite startling inauguration of this.

---

*pensamiento histórico en América: desarrollo de la prosa de ficción: siglos XVI, XVII, XVIII
y XIX,* Madrid: Gredos, 1982, p. 191.

54. Cornejo Polar, 'Ajenidad y apropriación', p. 602. It is worth noting that this
creation of a literary tradition serves to legitimate and 'place' Palma's own writings
in an historical and cultural context, through a 'self-fathering' strategy. For a nice
illustration of Palma's own invocation of this literary tradition, see 'Orgullo de
cacique', *Tradiciones,* pp. 181–2. Palma places himself as an 'heroic' republican
listener (his battleship is shipwrecked) who lands and hears a story from the
mouth of an indian, but who also knows that a different version is retold by
Garcilaso. Here Palma is the privileged secretary of indigenous folklore and also
the retransmitter of a prestigious *mestizo* written tradition.

55. Ramos, *Divergent Modernities,* p. 120.

The Order of Oriental Knowledge:
The Making of D'Herbelot's
Bibliothèque Orientale

Nicholas Dew

To the ordinary man of letters, this book is a kind of new world: new histories, new politics, new manners, new poetry; in a word, a new heaven, a new earth.

Charles Perrault, *Les Hommes illustres*, 'Barthélemy d'Herbelot'

Now I had in my hands a vast methodical fragment of the total history of an unknown planet, with its architectures and its quarrels, with the terror of its mythologies and the murmur of its languages, with its emperors and its seas, with its minerals and its birds and its fishes, with its algebra and its fire, with its theological and metaphysical controversies.

Jorge Luis Borges, *Ficciones*, 'Tlön, Uqbar, Orbis Tertius'

Borges begins a study of Dante by comparing the *Divine Comedy* to a panel on the wall of an Oriental library, inscribed with 'all the legends of the *Thousand and One Nights*'.[1] This image – of a poem that is both a map of a universe and a catalogue of

---

For their help with earlier versions of this essay, I would like to thank Ann Blair, Luce Giard, Gottfried Hagen, Neil Kenny, Jim Watt, and members of the Research Centre at King's College, Cambridge.

1. Jorge Luis Borges, 'Nine Dantesque Essays', in *The Total Library: Non-Fiction 1922–1986*, Harmondsworth, 1999, p. 267.

fables – might equally stand for those early modern texts that claimed to give a complete account of a distant region or continent (whether real or not, since for readers the difference was not always clear). One such text – and one for which Borges's metaphor could almost have been coined – was the *Bibliothèque orientale* of Barthélemy d'Herbelot, first published in 1697 and destined to become the eighteenth century's nearest thing to an encyclopaedia of the Islamic world.[2] The first edition was a large folio volume of a thousand and sixty densely printed pages, containing over eight thousand alphabetically ordered entries on the history and geography of the Turkish-, Persian- and Arabic-speaking world. Then as now, European readers knew little about the history or literatures of the East. The sheer size of the book, and the amount of new knowledge it contained, inspired its readers with a kind of vertigo: as Charles Perrault noted in his life of d'Herbelot, even for the learned, the *Bibliothèque orientale* represented a 'new world: new histories, new politics, new manners, new poetry; in a word, a new heaven, a new earth'.[3]

Because the book was edited after d'Herbelot's death by his friend and fellow Orientalist Antoine Galland, some have seen the *Bibliothèque orientale* as somehow related to Galland's more famous work, his translation – the first into a Western European language – of the *Thousand and One Nights*.[4] It does seem that many readers valued d'Herbelot's book as a source of Oriental tales. Voltaire, using it to research his universal history the *Essai sur les mœurs*, called it 'the Arab and Tartar tales that go by the

---

2. Barthélemy d'Herbelot, *Bibliothèque orientale, ou Dictionaire universel contenant généralement tout ce qui regarde la connoissance des peuples de l'Orient*, ed. and preface by Antoine Galland, Paris, 1697. A revised and augmented edition appeared in 4 vols, The Hague, 1777–79; there was also a reprint of the first edition, Maastricht, 1776, a popularized version, 6 vols, Paris, 1781–83, and a German translation, 4 vols, Halle, 1785–90. For a fuller treatment of d'Herbelot, see my *Oriental Learning in Louis XIV's France*, Oxford, forthcoming; and Henry Laurens, *Aux sources de l'orientalisme: La Bibliothèque Orientale de Barthélemi d'Herbelot*, Paris, 1978.

3. Charles Perrault, *Les Hommes illustres qui ont paru en France pendant ce siècle, avec leurs portraits au naturel*, 2 vols, Paris, 1696–1700, vol. 2, pp. 71–2.

4. See, for instance, Robert Irwin, *The Arabian Nights: A Companion*, Harmondsworth, 1994, p. 19; Maxime Rodinson, *La Fascination de l'Islam*, Paris, 1982, p. 70. On Galland, see Mohamed Abdel-Halim, *Antoine Galland: sa vie et son œuvre*, Paris, 1964; his translation of the *Mille et une nuits* appeared Paris, 1704–17; cf. Borges, 'The Translators of *The Thousand and One Nights*', in *The Total Library*, pp. 92–109.

name of the *Bibliothèque orientale*.[5] Later in the century, William Beckford was to find in d'Herbelot the inspiration for his novel *Vathek*. Edward Gibbon, using the *Bibliothèque orientale* for the later volumes of his *Decline and Fall of the Roman Empire*, admitted that without the guidance of 'two learned Frenchmen' – Joseph de Guignes and d'Herbelot – he 'should be blind indeed in the Eastern world'.[6] However, when he introduces d'Herbelot in a footnote, Gibbon complains that 'his work is an agreeable miscellany, which must gratify every taste; but I never can digest the alphabetical order'.[7] The tension between the desire for narrative history and the frustrations of alphabetic order – summed up in the contrast between Voltaire's assessment and that of Gibbon, and found repeatedly in responses to d'Herbelot – provides a framework for discussing the relationship between how the *Bibliothèque orientale* is structured and how it represents the Orient.

Probably the best known recent analysis of d'Herbelot's book is that put forward by Edward Said in his path-breaking *Orientalism*. In Said's view, d'Herbelot did not intend to 'revise commonly received ideas about the Orient': the work 'confirms' readers' prejudices, setting forth the Orient for the European reader to behold: it creates 'the Orient' as an enclosed 'stage on which the whole East is confined'. This sense of theatre and confinement suggests that the *Bibliothèque orientale* allowed European readers to discover their 'capacities for encompassing and Orientalizing the Orient' by means of the Orientalist's expertise. Said argues that the *Bibliothèque orientale* forces the reader to approach the Orient through the filtering 'grids and codes' imposed by the Oriental scholar: 'truth . . . becomes a function of learned judgement, not of the material itself, which in time seems to owe even its existence to the Orientalist'. For Said, d'Herbelot's book expresses the 'power and effectiveness' of scholarly Orientalism,

5. Voltaire to René-Louis d'Argenson, 11 Dec. 1742, letter D 2698 in Voltaire, *Correspondence*, ed. Theodore Besterman, 51 vols, Geneva and Oxford, 1968–77, vol. 8, p. 310: 'les contes arabes et tartares sous le nom de la Bibliothèque orientale'.

6. Edward Gibbon, *The History of the Decline and Fall of the Roman Empire*, ed. David Womersley, 3 vols, Harmondsworth, 1994, vol. 3, p. 541 n. 41 (ch. 57). Gibbon relies heavily on d'Herbelot in chapters 42, 46, 50–2, 57, 65; see Rolando Minuti, 'Gibbon and the Asiatic Barbarians: Notes on the French Sources of *The Decline and Fall*', in David Womersley, ed., *Edward Gibbon: Bicentenary Essays*, Oxford, 1997, pp. 21–44.

7. Gibbon, *Decline and Fall*, vol. 3, pp. 238–9 n. 15 (ch. 51).

'the triumphant technique for taking the immense fecundity of the Orient and making it systematically, even alphabetically, knowable by Western laymen'. The fact that the work is organized as a series of articles arranged alphabetically is important: 'what may have been a loose collection of randomly acquired facts . . . were transformed into a rational Oriental panorama, from A to Z'. This emphasis on the alphabetical ordering – 'what the printed page delivers is an ordered, disciplined judgement of the material' – presupposes a conception of the *Bibliothèque orientale* as a stable, typographically reliable text.[8]

As his use of terms like 'disciplinary order' and 'discursive confinement' reveals, Said's view of d'Herbelot, like much of *Orientalism*, is inspired by Foucault. It seems fair to suggest that Said's view of the *Bibliothèque orientale* can be encapsulated in the Foucauldian emblem of the 'Panopticon': Said uses the metaphor of Bentham's prison design later in the book, when discussing Sylvestre de Sacy, who was roughly the Panopticon's contemporary.[9] For Said, the *Bibliothèque orientale* is a well-tempered instrument of the Western will to represent the East. Not only does this model imply that a book like d'Herbelot's effortlessly imposes its meaning upon a body of docile readers, it also implies that all agency is gathered in the hands of European scholars in their metropolitan institutions.

The aim of this essay is to challenge such a portrayal of the *Bibliothèque orientale*: to explore how it was made; to show how it was produced through a network of interactions linking Paris to Istanbul; to emphasize that the agency involved in its production was distributed throughout that network; and, perhaps most importantly, to caution against overestimating the 'efficacy' of d'Herbelot's book. What emerges is that the *Bibliothèque orientale* was by no means a trouble-free instrument or a 'rational panorama'. Partly because of d'Herbelot's decisions, partly because of the accidents of its production, it was, in Gibbon's image, a dish that sought to 'gratify every taste' and yet remained indigestible.[10]

*

8. Edward W. Said, *Orientalism: Western Conceptions of the Orient*, reprinted with a new Afterword, Harmondsworth, 1995 (first edn 1978), pp. 63–7.
9. Ibid., p. 127.
10. To be fair to Said, his account of the *Bibliothèque orientale* is concerned largely

Even by seventeenth-century standards, the title page of the *Bibliothèque orientale* made rather impressive claims. The long list of topics covered was clearly supposed to suggest an encyclopedic classificatory scheme:

BIBLIOTHEQUE / ORIENTALE, / *ou* / DICTIONAIRE / UNIVER-SEL, / CONTENANT GENERALEMENT / Tout ce qui regarde la connoissance des Peuples / de l'Orient. / LEURS HISTOIRES ET TRADITIONS / VERITABLES OU FABULEUSES. / LEURS RELIGIONS, SECTES ET POLITIQUE. / Leurs Gouvernement, Loix, Coûtumes, Mœurs, Guerres, & les Révolutions de leurs Empires; / LEURS SCIENCES ET LEURS ARTS, / Leur Théologie, Mythologie, Magie, Physique, Morale, Médecine, Mathématiques, / Histoire naturelle, Chronologie, Géographie, Observations Astronomiques, / Grammaire, & Rhétorique. / LES VIES ET ACTIONS REMARQUABLES DE TOUS LEURS SAINTS, / Docteurs, Philosophes, Historiens, Poëtes, Capitaines, & de tous ceux qui sont rendus illustres / parmi eux, par leur Vertu, ou par leur Savoir. / DES JUGEMENTS CRITIQUES, ET DES EXTRAITS DE TOUS LEURS OUVRAGES. / De leurs Traitez, Traductions, Commentaires, Abregez, Recüeils de Fables, de Sentences, de Maximes, de Proverbes, / de Contes, de bons Mots, & de tous leurs livres écrits en Arabe, en Persan, ou en Turc, sur toutes sortes de / Sciences, d'Arts, & de Professions.

The preliminaries followed the conventions for scholarly works set by earlier generations: the volume opened with a short dedication to Louis XIV, written by d'Herbelot's brother; then came a long prefatory 'Discours' by Galland, which explained d'Herbelot's methods and defended the utility of Oriental studies,[11] followed by three Latin poems in praise of d'Herbelot. Then, before the main text, came a table listing some hundred and sixty 'Oriental authors and other works cited', identified only by the shortest form of their names. Then followed the main text, printed in double columns, followed by an index and errata list. Clearly, the content of the eight thousand or so entries could be analysed at great length: Henry Laurens, Dominique Torabi, Ahmad Gunny and Dominique Carnoy have done so by selecting certain themes, like d'Herbelot's treatment of Islam, or of Per-

with the text's rhetoric; this essay is concerned with the material conditions of the book's production (precisely what its rhetoric of scholarly authority has to suppress).

11. Antoine Galland, 'Discours pour servir de preface à la Bibliothèque Orientale', in d'Herbelot, *Bibliothèque orientale*, Paris, 1697, sigs a 1r–u 2r.

sia.[12] Here, however, rather than trying to assess d'Herbelot's handling of one particular theme, the aim will be to examine how he made use of his sources; how the book was shaped by the conventions of the erudite genre; and how the attempt to order the text alphabetically created problems.

What is striking about the dedication to Louis XIV is the degree to which the book is presented as the product of a single site of activity, in this case the royal 'public' library, the Bibliothèque du roi.[13] Dedications to high-ranking patrons often made the patron the true 'author' of the work, partly because without the patron's 'protection' the book might never have been written, and partly because the patron's name lends prestige and authority to the text.[14] However, as with any library or museum, the manuscripts in the Bibliothèque du roi were assembled in Paris by a long process of collecting, requiring networks of agents spread across many locations and several generations. In particular, the Oriental collection there had expanded rapidly under Colbert, who controlled Louis XIV's patronage of the arts and sciences from 1663, and who had sent expert collectors – one of them Galland – to the Levant to buy antiquities and books, for the Bibliothèque du roi and his own library.[15]

The best example of how d'Herbelot's work was the product of collecting networks is provided by his most important source. This was a text by the Ottoman scholar Katib Chelebi, author of several encyclopedic works of geography and history.[16] As well as

12. Laurens, *Aux sources de l'orientalisme*, pp. 37–47, 63–78; Dominique Torabi, 'La Perse de Barthélemy d'Herbelot', *Luqmān* (Tehran), vol. 8, 1992, pp. 43–58; Ahmad Gunny, *Images of Islam in Eighteenth-Century Writings*, London, 1996, pp. 45–54; Dominique Carnoy, *Représentations de l'Islam dans la France du XVIIe siècle: la ville des tentations*, Paris, 1998, pp. 300–10.

13. Dedicatory epistle 'Au Roy', in d'Herbelot, *Bibliothèque orientale* (1697), unmarked sig. 1r–v.

14. Roger Chartier, 'Patronage et dédicace', in his *Culture écrite et société: l'ordre des livres (XIVe–XVIIIe siècle)*, Paris, 1996, pp. 81–106, here pp. 95–6.

15. See Henri A. Omont, *Missions archéologiques françaises en Orient aux XVIIe et XVIIIe siècles*, Paris, 1902.

16. Mustafa ibn 'Abd Allah, known by the titles Hajji Khalifa (or Khalfa) and Katib Chelebi (AH 1017–67 / AD 1609–57). Most of what we know of him comes from his autobiographic conclusion to *The Balance of Truth* (*Mizan al-haqq*), trans. G. L. Lewis, London, 1957, pp. 7–14, 135–56. See Orhan Saik Gökyay, 'Katib Çelebi', in *The Encyclopaedia of Islam*, new edn, ed. H. A. R. Gibb et al., Leiden, 1954–, vol. 4, pp. 760–2; also Eleazar Birnbaum, 'The Questing Mind. Katib Chelebi, 1609–1657: A Chapter in Ottoman Intellectual History', in Emmet

being a 'polyhistor' of Islamic learning, Katib Chelebi was one of several Ottoman scholars interested in the new European science: he made several translations, including one of Mercator's *Atlas Minor*, with the help of Europeans who had converted to Islam.[17] As Galland noted in his preface to the *Bibliothèque orientale*, d'Herbelot's book owed an enormous amount to Katib Chelebi's bibliographic encyclopedia, the *Kashf al-zunūn 'an asāmī l-kutub wa-l-funūn* ('The Uncovering of Ideas: On the Titles of Books and the Names of the Sciences'), which listed over fourteen thousand works in Arabic, Persian and Turkish, arranged in alphabetical order of title.[18] What Galland knew at first hand – although this he does not mention in the preface – is that d'Herbelot only came across the *Kashf al-zunūn* because of the collecting missions to the Levant that he himself had been part of. Galland writes that d'Herbelot had access to two manuscripts of the *Kashf al-zunūn* in Paris. Both had been sent back from Istanbul by French ambassadors who had employed Galland as a collector.[19] In fact, Galland may have been the first Western European to become aware of the *Kashf al-zunūn* and to realize its importance. How he first discovered it is not certain, but it is seems likely that he was

Robbins and Stella Sandahl, eds, *Corolla Torontonensis: Studies in Honour of Ronald Morton Smith*, Toronto, 1994, pp. 133–58.

17. On Ottoman translations of European geographic texts, see Ekmeleddin Ihsanoğlu, ed., *Transfer of Modern Science and Technology to the Muslim World*, Istanbul, 1992, esp. pp. 31–6, 67–120, 371–83; Abdülhak Adnan-Adıvar, *La Science chez les Turcs ottomans*, Paris, 1939, pp. 102–20; Heidrun Wurm, *Der osmanische Historiker Hüseyn b. Ga'fer, genannt Hezarfenn, und die Istanbuler Gesellschaft in der zweiten Hälfte des 17. Jahrhunderts*, Freiburg-im-Breisgau, 1971, pp. 67–70.

18. On this text, see Eleazar Birnbaum, 'Katib Chelebi (1609–1657) and Alphabetization: A Methodological Investigation of the Autographs of his *Kashf al-Zunun* and *Sullam al-Wusūl*', in François Déroche and Francis Richard, eds, *Scribes et manuscrits du Moyen-Orient*, Paris, 1997, pp. 235–63. Cf. the entry 'Caschf Al Dhonún', in *Bibliothèque orientale* (1697), p. 261. On d'Herbelot's use of it, see Laurens, *Aux sources de l'orientalisme*, p. 50; Abdel–Halim, *Galland*, pp. 76–7, 162–5; and Galland, 'Discours pour servir de preface', sigs i 2v–o 1r. A French translation of the *Kashf al-zunūn*, made by François Pétis de La Croix *fils* in 1699–1705, was never published (Bibliothèque nationale de France, Paris [henceforth BnF], mss arabes 4462–4). The Arabic text with Latin translation was published only in the nineteenth century: Katib Chelebi, *Lexicon Bibliographicum et Encyclopædicum*, ed. Gustav Fluegel, 8 vols, Leipzig and London, 1835–58. The modern edition is: *Kesf el-zunūn*, ed. Şerefeddin Yaltkaya and Kilisli Rifat Bilge, 3 vols, Istanbul, 1941–45, reprinted Tehran, 1967.

19. Galland, 'Discours pour servir de preface', sig. o 1r. One copy had been sent by the marquis de Nointel to the Bibliothèque du roi in the 1670s, the other sent by Guilleragues to the Colbertine in 1682; see Omont, *Missions*, pp. 199–221; Abdel-Halim, *Galland*, pp. 29–50, 66–80.

lintroduced to it by a scholar in Istanbul called Hezarfenn.[20]
Galland's excitement at his discovery of the *Kashf al-zunūn* is
revealed in his correspondence. He wrote to his antiquarian
friend Jacob Spon that the bibliography contained some thirty
thousand titles – twice the actual amount – representing a library
of more than forty thousand volumes, and that he had made a
translation of a selection of some sixteen hundred titles, mainly
on history, to send back to Colbert with the full Arabic text.
Galland emphasizes that Istanbul is the best place to collect 'a
great mass of all these history books in very little time' ['un grand
amas de tous ces livres d'histoire en fort peu de temps'], adding
that the *Kashf al-zunūn* was a 'unique means for enriching the
royal library with a more or less complete corpus of Mahometan
history' ['il est certain que je donne l'unique moien pour enrichir
en moins de rien la Bibliotheque du Roy d'un corps assez complet
de l'histoire mahométane'].[21]

As this indicates, one of the reasons Galland was so excited by
the *Kashf al-zunūn* was that it could be used to facilitate the
collection of Oriental books. In a note prefacing his initial, select
translation, Galland makes this explicit: to avoid the collection of
books that are 'only good to look at', Katib Chelebi's bibliography
will help the minister to be 'well informed as to the number and
quality of these manuscripts', and to decide more easily what to
ask his agents to look for ['il [Colbert] pust estre bien informé
du nombre et de la qualité de ces manuscrits et prescrire ensuite
plus facilement ce que l'on en devoit choisir ou laisser']. He
depicts the Ottoman capital as a paradise for the manuscript-
hunter. Books from all over the empire could be found there
more easily than anywhere else ['la facilité de les trouver est plus
grande que dans aucun autre lieu']. Indeed, he thinks he could
collect more in one year in Istanbul than in 'ten or twenty' years
elsewhere. Galland describes how he could persuade the Turkish
booksellers to hunt down titles he was looking for, using their
own supply networks. He boasts that by this method, in less than
a month, he was able to find 'four or five' copies of the fifteenth-

---

20. This is argued in Wurm, *Der osmanische Historiker*, p. 86.
21. Galland to Jacob Spon, Istanbul, Oct. 1682, in Omont, *Missions*, pp. 218–19.
Galland's translations are at BnF, mss fr. 6130–1, fr. 14892 and lat. 11408.

century Persian historian Mirkhond, a text esteemed for its rarity in Europe.[22]

D'Herbelot only came across the text which became the most important source for the *Bibliothèque orientale* because of the collecting networks sponsored by Colbert, designed to bring books from the Levant to Paris. The same goes for the scores of other Oriental manuscripts in Paris libraries that d'Herbelot used (the set of some two hundred volumes given to him by Ferdinando II, grand duke of Tuscany, had likewise been collected by earlier agents of the Tuscan court). These networks owed their success not only to patronage from the 'centre', but also to the people they encountered at the 'periphery'; indeed the very notion of 'centre and periphery' seems inadequate, given that the Ottoman metropolis was the centre for book-trading networks stretching across the whole Ottoman Empire, and given that Istanbul intellectuals like Katib Chelebi, and his student Hezarfenn, used travellers from Europe to learn about and translate European scientific texts.[23] At first glance, d'Herbelot's book might appear to be the product of a relatively localized 'site' – his personal library, and the major Paris libraries. But to produce such a work in Paris was only possible because of the networks which fed those libraries – and it was only recently that the Paris Oriental collections had become large enough to make such a work possible. Like the baroque museum catalogues that were its contemporary, the *Bibliothèque orientale* was bound to de-emphasize its dependence on those supply networks, in order to glorify both its author and his patrons.[24]

For most of his later career, in the long years preparing the *Bibliothèque orientale* (c. 1670–95), d'Herbelot associated himself

22. Omont, *Missions*, pp. 216–18.

23. It should also be borne in mind, of course, that the economic, diplomatic and military power relations between the Ottoman Empire and European powers were in this period very different from those which would obtain from the late eighteenth century onwards.

24. For collecting networks, see Bruno Latour, 'Ces réseaux que la raison ignore: laboratoires, bibliothèques, collections', in Marc Baratin and Christian Jacob, eds, *Le Pouvoir des bibliothèques: la mémoire des livres en Occident*, Paris, 1996, pp. 23–46; for museums and patrons, see Paula Findlen, *Possessing Nature: Museums, Collecting and Scientific Culture in Early Modern Italy*, Berkeley, 1994, pp. 36–47, 380–92.

with the critical-historical scholars based at the Maurist (Benedictine) abbey of Saint-Germain-des-Prés, on the left bank in Paris. Galland was a similar kind of scholar, and frequented the same group; his correspondence has more discussion of classical coins and inscriptions than of Scheherazade's tales.[25] In keeping with these interests, the *Bibliothèque orientale* was designed as an instrument for the writing of history. By looking at the scholarly practices of the erudite community, we can understand a little better why the text took the form it did.

The seventeenth century saw the rise of a new historical erudition in France. Although the most prominent exponents of this were the Maurists of Saint-Germain, the concern for critical, source-based historical research was by no means limited to them. The erudite (or *docte*) approach was often defined in contrast to rhetorical (or *éloquent*) narrative history. The bulk of what the *Bibliothèque orientale* supplies is erudite material: series of facts designed to supplement the reading of other texts. Antiquarians, rather than producing synthetic narratives of ancient history, concentrated on amassing data which could be used as a commentary upon the already-existing narratives of the ancient historians. This is why they produced dictionaries, thesauri, annals, chronologies and genealogies – reference manuals to be read side-by-side with the ancient texts.[26] Although, in another sense, d'Herbelot's book is not strictly antiquarian – using only textual sources, he does not examine the material culture of the Orient – nevertheless it was written in the *docte* rather than the *éloquent* mode. Just as antiquarian manuals helped scholars read Livy or Tacitus, the *Bibliothèque orientale* invited its readers to use it as a supplement to other historical texts – for example, those histories of Genghis Khan and Tamerlane compiled and translated at about the same time by the Pétis de La Croix, and used later by Voltaire and Gibbon.[27]

---

25. See Abdel-Halim, *Galland*, pp. 51–65, 337–92; Marie Veillon, 'Antoine Galland, ou la vie d'un antiquaire dans la "République médallique"', in *Trésors Monétaires*, supp. 2: *Médailles et antiques*, vol. 1, 1989, pp. 31–48.

26. Arnaldo Momigliano, 'Ancient History and the Antiquarian', *Journal of the Warburg and Courtauld Institutes*, vol. 13, 1950, pp. 285–315. For *docte* vs. *éloquent*, see Orest Ranum, *Artisans of Glory: Writers and Historical Thought in Seventeenth-Century France*, Chapel Hill, NC, 1980.

27. François Pétis de La Croix (*père*), *Histoire du grand Genghizcan*, Paris, 1710; François Pétis de La Croix (*fils*), *Histoire de Timur-Bec*, 4 vols, Paris, 1722. On the

A characteristic of the erudite mode of history was the collection and definition of a body of trustworthy documents, which created a place for probable histories. Unlike modern libraries, which conserve a collection passed down from the past, early modern libraries had to be built up from scratch[28] – something captured by the French verb *dresser*, meaning both to assemble and to arrange, to collect and to organize, as in the title of Gabriel Naudé's *Advis pour dresser une bibliothèque* of 1627. Galland himself says as much in a text on numismatics: before one could begin analysis, one needed to amass a large enough corpus of medals and coins – and for this purpose, catalogues and inventories of various cabinets were an essential tool, allowing the constitution of a virtual *médaillier*. But in order to carry out comparative work, further tools were required. To this end, Galland himself compiled a *Dictionnaire historique et numismatique* based on the cabinet of Nicolas-Joseph Foucault, one of his patrons.[29]

An array of data was often described as a *corps d'histoire*.[30] Galland uses the expression *corps de l'histoire mahométane* to describe the utility of the *Kashf al-zunūn*.[31] Erudite reference works were instruments for anatomizing the 'body of history'. It is in keeping with the ideal of the *corps d'histoire* that d'Herbelot restricted the *Bibliothèque orientale*'s source-base to manuscripts in Arabic, Turkish and Persian, ignoring the accounts of modern European travellers. This decision – justified by the idea that each 'nation' knew its own history best[32] – would seem odd were it not

use of such texts, see Rolando Minuti, *Oriente barbarico e storiografia settecentesca: rappresentazioni della storia dei Tartari nella cultura francese del XVIII secolo*, Venice, 1994.

28. See Michel de Certeau, *L'écriture de l'histoire*, Paris, 1975, pp. 84–9.

29. Abdel-Halim, *Galland*, pp. 346–8. Galland's numismatic dictionary remained unpublished.

30. For example, a numismatic club hosted by the duc d'Aumont gave itself the task of collecting a complete series of medals of Roman emperors, in order to 'dresser ... un *corps d'histoire* romaine' (my emphasis): Krzysztof Pomian, *Collectionneurs, amateurs et curieux: Paris, Venise: XVIe–XVIIIe siècle*, Paris, 1987, p. 151, citing Ezechiel Spanheim.

31. Cited in Abdel-Halim, *Galland*, pp. 163–4: 'la lecture seule de ces titres est agréable, et elle peut suffire pour donner la plus belle idée que l'on ait jamais eue du corps de l'histoire d'une secte qui subsiste depuis si longtemps'. In the letter to Spon (note 21), he had spoken of 'un corps assez complet de l'histoire mahométane' in reference to Katib Chelebi's text.

32. Galland wrote ('Discours pour servir de preface', sig. a 1v) that d'Herbelot learned Arabic, Turkish and Persian because 'les Auteurs Arabes parlant mieux des affaires de leur Nation, que les Persans, & les Turcs; & ceux-ci des leurs

for the erudite model of history. D'Herbelot makes reference to his documents, frequently citing the number of the manuscript in the Bibliothèque du roi, a collection he had himself catalogued. Although these citations are not set off from the main text typographically, they function as d'Herbelot's footnotes. (This, we should note, seems at odds with Said's view that in the *Bibliothèque orientale* the Orient was 'circumscribed by a series of attitudes and judgments that sent the Western mind, not first to Oriental sources for correction and verification, but rather to other Orientalist works').[33]

Further features of d'Herbelot's working practices are equally typical of the erudite style. Take, for example, the fact that, while reading the large number of Oriental manuscripts making up his *corps d'histoire*, he began to compose first of all a *dictionary* of Arabic, Turkish and Persian. Like his friend Du Cange, author of a now-standard dictionary of mediaeval Latin, d'Herbelot filled a large chest with scraps of paper, each bearing one entry.[34] The dictionary was the first part of a family of projected reference tools. Galland describes how d'Herbelot then produced a kind of commonplace book: after compiling the dictionary, he made 'prodigious collections' of notes on the history, geography, theology, sciences and arts of 'all the nations of the Levant'. It then took him a long time to decide how to structure the work, and after much hesitation, he divided his work in two parts, one of which became the *Bibliothèque orientale*, the other a *Florilège ou Anthologie*, which is now lost.[35] Galland did manage to publish an Oriental commonplace book of his own, the collection of maxims and adages entitled *Les Paroles remarquables, les bons mots, et les maximes des Orientaux*, first published in 1694. Perhaps because of the fashion for 'maxims' literature in France at the time – and

---

propres, avec plus de connoissance que les Arabes, il n'y avoit pas d'autres voyes par où il pût arriver plus surement à la verité de leur Histoire'.

33. Said, *Orientalism*, p. 67. Admittedly, Said's point here is more applicable to the later editions, which he cites.

34. See Francis Richard, 'Le dictionnaire de d'Herbelot', in Frédéric Hitzel, ed., *Istanbul et les langues orientales*, Paris, 1997, pp. 79–88; for Du Cange see *Dictionnaire des lettres françaises: Le XVIIe siècle*, revised edn, ed. Patrick Dandrey, Paris 1996, art. 'Dictionnaire'.

35. Galland, 'Discours pour servir de preface', sig. a 1v: 'Enfin, après avoir longtemps balancé, il les separa en deux corps, à sçavoir en celui-ci, auquel il a donné le titre de Bibliothèque Orientale, & son intention estoit de faire paroistre l'autre sous celui de Florilege, ou d'Anthologie'.

perhaps because it was shorter – this enjoyed considerably more success than d'Herbelot's book, going through five editions by 1730 (including an English translation) before eventually re-appearing as part of the *Supplément* to the *Bibliothèque orientale* in 1780.[36]

So far we have seen what d'Herbelot held in common with the rest of the erudite community. However, the attempt to secure authenticity had particular repercussions because of the marginal position of Oriental scholarship within the Republic of Letters as a whole. According to one source, d'Herbelot's original plan, supported by Colbert, had been to print the book in Arabic at the Imprimerie royale.[37] This would have made his book more or less an abridged edition of Katib Chelebi's *Kashf al-zunūn*. But this initial design failed. In late seventeenth-century Paris, the ambition to print exotic languages in their original characters was frustrated by the lack of the necessary type and of workers with the relevant skills: d'Herbelot's project would have required large amounts of new Arabic type to be designed, cut and cast (not to mention composed). This would have been far too expensive, and the death of Colbert in 1683 probably put an end to the scheme. The story does suggest, however, that d'Herbelot's aim – again, in keeping with the erudite mode – was to *defer* translation, to facilitate future interpretation, even at the risk of losing large numbers of readers – and even if, in the end, such a goal was impossible to attain.

Within the broader context of humanist reading-instruments, two genres – both identified in the title of the book – are particularly important for understanding the *Bibliothèque orientale*: the *biblio-*

---

36. Galland, *Les Paroles remarquables, les bons mots, et les Maximes des Orientaux,* Paris, 1694, reprinted The Hague, 1694, Lyons, 1695; retitled *Orientaliana*, Paris, 1708, Amsterdam, 1730; English trans., London, 1695; German, Leipzig, 1787; included in the *Supplément* to d'Herbelot (1779–80); new edn with preface by Abdelwahab Meddeb, Paris, 1998.

37. Louis Cousin, 'Eloge de Monsieur Dherbelot', in *Bibliothèque orientale* (1697), sigs u 2v–3r: Cousin writes: 'D'abord il la composa en Arabe, & Monsieur Colbert avoit resolu qu'elle fût imprimée au Louvre, & qu'on fondît pour cet effet des caractères en cette Langue. Mais cette resolution n'ayant pas été exécutée, M. Dherbelot mit en François le même ouvrage.' I have found no other evidence for this scheme.

thèque and the *dictionnaire universel*. Both of these genres were growing in popularity at the end of the seventeenth century. *Bibliothèque* was a title used for what we would call bibliographies and library catalogues, but also for compilations and anthologies, often in periodical form, and often defined by a specific subject. Gabriel Naudé, in his *Advis pour dresser une bibliothèque*, explained the utility of such books. They performed for the collector a gainful reduction: rare and 'curious' books scattered across the libraries of the world could be brought before the reader's eyes without the need for costly expeditions, saving space on the library shelves as well as money.[38] Galland presented the *Bibliothèque orientale* in similar terms: 'since all the Oriental books, because of their excessive number, can not be found in one place', the *Bibliothèque orientale* allows the reader to 'acquire effortlessly, without leaving home, what one would otherwise have to go and find by travelling in the Orient'.[39] In other words, such reference tools re-structure information, so that what is lost in particularity, locality and material copiousness is gained in compatibility, standardization and comparability. Contemporary scholars were familiar with this as the tension between 'the exhaustive and the essential', or between the desire to have all knowledge assembled in a universal library and the desire to distil this down to its essence in a *bibliothèque choisie*.[40] As Galland put it, 'there could be no better title' for d'Herbelot's work than *Bibliothèque orientale*, 'because it *takes the place of* all the Oriental books written in Arabic, Persian and Turkish that [d'Herbelot] had read, in order to form an *abregé* of the whole history of the Levant'.[41]

In theory at least, the *bibliothèque* was a genre that presented

---

38. Cited in Chartier, 'Bibliothèques sans murs', in *Culture écrite et société*, pp. 107–31, here p. 110. Gabriel Naudé, *Advis pour dresser une bibliothèque*, facs. of 1644 edn, intro. by Claude Jolly, Paris, 1990, p. 57.

39. Galland, 'Discours pour servir de preface', sigs i 2r–v: 'comme tous les Livres Orientaux, à cause de leur nombre excessif, ne peuvent pas se rencontrer dans un même endroit . . . acquerir sans peine & sans sortir de chez soy, ce que l'on devroit aller chercher chez eux un voyageant'.

40. Latour, 'Ces réseaux', p. 26; Chartier, 'Bibliothèques sans murs', p. 113. See also Helmut Zedelmaier, *Bibliotheca universalis und Bibliotheca selecta: das Problem der Ordnung des gelehrten Wissens in der frühen Neuzeit*, Cologne, 1992.

41. My emphasis. Galland, 'Discours pour servir de preface', sig. a 1v: 'il ne pouvoit pas lui donner un titre plus convenable . . . puis qu'il tient lieu de tous les Livres Orientaux écrits en Arabe, en Persan, & en Turc qu'il a lûs, pour former un Abbregé de toute l'Histoire du Levant'.

the reader with an ideal collection, a utopian 'library without walls'. D'Herbelot's contribution to the genre, though, was even more utopian, since it represented an ideal library of an unfamiliar culture: a list of texts which ought to exist, regardless of whether actual copies – let alone translations – were available. Not all of the works d'Herbelot mentions are given references for the Bibliothèque du roi or the 'Bibliothèque du Grand Duc', because he is reporting the existence of texts in turn reported by Katib Chelebi.

By the later seventeenth century, the *bibliothèque* genre had been joined by other reading aids like the new learned journals and dictionaries.[42] The most important of the new dictionaries were those of Antoine Furetière and Pierre Bayle, both published by the Leers brothers, one of the largest publishing concerns in the Netherlands.[43] The new dictionaries of the 1690s were an expansion of what had previously been a scholarly genre to a broader, more 'polite', public. This gave traditional scholars cause to complain: Gilles Ménage is supposed to have quipped that 'dictionaries and lotteries, which we see multiplying from one day to another, are a sure sign of the ignorance and poverty of this age' ['les Dictionnaires, & les Lotteries qu'on voit multiplier de jour en jour sont pour le siècle une marque sûre d'ignorance & de gueuserie'].[44] The Oxford mathematician Edward Bernard remarked that Furetière's dictionary was 'fit for such as would rather be in an academy and dancing house than a university'.[45] Similar horror was expressed by traditional scholars towards the

42. Pierre Rétat, 'L'âge des dictionnaires', in Roger Chartier and Henri-Jean Martin, eds, *Histoire de l'édition française*, 2nd edn, Paris, 1990, vol. 2, pp. 232–41.

43. Antoine Furetière, *Dictionaire universel contenant généralement tous les mots françois tant vieux que moderne, & les termes de toutes les sciences et des arts*, preface by Pierre Bayle, 3 vols, The Hague and Rotterdam, 1690; Pierre Bayle, *Dictionaire historique et critique*, 4 vols, Rotterdam, 1697. Reinier Leers provided crucial financial backing for the printing of d'Herbelot's book, according to one contemporary: Bruno Neveu, *Érudition et religion aux XVIIe et XVIIIe siècles*, Paris, 1994, p. 57.

44. Antoine Galland, et al., eds, *Menagiana: ou les Bons mots et remarques critiques, historiques, morales et d'érudition, de Monsieur Menage, recueillies par ses amis*, 3rd edn, 4 vols, Paris, 1715, vol. 1, p. 137.

45. Bodleian Library, Oxford, ms Smith 47, p. 60, Edward Bernard to Thomas Smith, 1 Feb. 1689: 'I have seen the Dictionaire Universel of Furetiere but find nothing in it to commend him or the Society of Good Spirits: it is meant, and fit for such as would rather be in an Academy and Dancing house than an university and study of the letters and Arts.'

new journals, like Bayle's *Nouvelles de la République des lettres*.[46] The accusation was that such texts made life too easy for the reader. As will become clear, this could not have been claimed of d'Herbelot's book.

One result of the late seventeenth-century vogue for dictionaries was that the logical order of the traditional encyclopedia was gradually replaced by the alphabetical order used in the encyclopedias of the eighteenth century. The use of alphabetical order not only avoided any metaphysical claims for the structure of the work; it also invited the readers to lose themselves in – perhaps also to aestheticize – the baffling non-order. The change in arrangement probably reflected a changing sense of how such books should be used: whereas the 'significant order' of the Renaissance encyclopedia encouraged the reader to plough through the whole organon, alphabetic ordering encouraged *ad hoc* consultation. Although alphabetical order had been used in language dictionaries, indexes and *bibliothèques* from the sixteenth century, what was new in the later seventeenth was the trend to cast more general reference works into dictionary form.[47] However, at the time d'Herbelot's book appeared, the use of alphabetical order for anything other than language dictionaries was still sufficiently novel, at least for non-scholarly readers, for it to require comment and justification.

Within the *bibliothèque* genre, alphabetical order had been common since the mid-sixteenth century, but it was generally used within subject divisions. It was also familiar to Ottoman scholars. Crucially for d'Herbelot, Katib Chelebi's *Kashf al-zunūn* was organized as a single alphabetic series.[48] D'Herbelot followed Katib Chelebi in his use of a single alphabetic series, but in so doing was able to take advantage of the contemporary fashion for dictionaries; his book even bore the subtitle *dictionnaire universel*, the term used by Furetière to denote a dictionary of things rather

46. See Anne Goldgar, *Impolite Learning: Conduct and Community in the Republic of Letters, 1680–1750*, New Haven, 1995, pp. 54–5, citing Pierre-Daniel Huet.

47. Richard R. Yeo, *Encyclopaedic Visions: Scientific Dictionaries and Enlightenment Culture*, Cambridge, 2001; Neil Kenny, *The Palace of Secrets: Béroalde de Verville and Renaissance Conceptions of Knowledge*, Oxford, 1991, pp. 12–54, esp. pp. 33–4 and 40.

48. See Birnbaum, 'Katib Chelebi and Alphabetization'.

than words, or what today would be called an encyclopedic dictionary.[49]

The instruments produced by humanist scholars as reading-aids did not always work smoothly: the trouble with the dictionary format was the problem of continuity between the alphabetically ordered articles. Pierre Bayle, in his *Dictionnaire historique et critique*, drew attention to a mistake he had found in d'Herbelot, where two articles seemed to contradict each other. The problem Bayle identifies is that of the *récit incomplet*, the disjointed narrative, caused by the use of discrete articles. As he admits, this advice is important for all authors of dictionaries, himself included ('cet Avis est important à tous les Auteurs de Dictionaire, & il leur est très mal aisé de ne tomber pas dans cette faute. Je crains bien qu'elle ne me soit échappée plus d'une fois').[50]

Bayle's complaint brings us back to Gibbon's, that he 'could never digest' the *Bibliothèque orientale*. This unreadability was the result of the conflict between the ordering system and the desire to read sequentially (*lire de suite*). Once the *corps d'histoire* had been established, it should have been possible to trace narratives through it. The reader of the *Bibliothèque orientale* was expected to want to chase the lines of dynasties of Oriental kings through the book. Galland describes this in his preface in painstaking detail, as if to reassure readers.[51] The earliest reviews of the *Bibliothèque orientale* explain the alphabetic structure in similar fashion.[52]

However, the order in d'Herbelot's book frequently breaks down. Admittedly, standards of alphabetization were not high at the time: as with many of its contemporary dictionaries, the articles in the *Bibliothèque orientale* are often in the wrong place within each letter. But even the overall series was disrupted by

---

49. Jean-Charles Darmon, 'Furetière et l'universel', *Stanford French Review*, vol. 14, 1990, pp. 15–46. One contemporary refers to d'Herbelot's book as the 'Moreri Oriental': Louis Picques to Job Ludolf, 7 June 1695, in Louis Du Four de Longuerue, *Dissertationes*, ed. J. D. Winckler, Leipzig, 1750, p. 314.

50. Bayle, *Dictionnaire historique et critique*, 3rd edn, Amsterdam, 1720, vol. 3, pp. 1866–7, article 'Mahomet', note PP.

51. Galland, 'Discours pour servir de preface', sig. a 2r.

52. *Mercure Galant*, May 1697, pp. 130–9, at pp. 136–8; cf. *Histoire des Ouvrages des Sçavans*, July 1697, pp. 468–73, at p. 470; and *Journal des Sçavans*, 29 April 1697, pp. 159–61.

d'Herbelot's working methods. In the first edition, the main text runs from A to Z, missing out K, and is then followed by a 'supplement' in which entries are grouped under the 'letters' DH, KE, KH, KI and TH.[53] This seems explicable only as a leftover from the earlier arrangement of entries in the Arabic alphabet. As a result, one of the most important sections of the whole book – the long list, taken from Katib Chelebi, of titles that begin with the word *kitab* (book) – was relegated to the supplement (under KE, pages 962–81).

Perhaps the most important aspect of how d'Herbelot's book is organized has yet to be mentioned. Regardless of alphabetic order, what determines the success of a reference work is the choice of article headings. In d'Herbelot's book, articles are arranged under headwords that are 'Oriental' terms rather than their 'Western' equivalents. For many of d'Herbelot's entries – the names of people, places and works – this makes sense, since only a handful would have had recognized European spellings. But this is not just the inevitable question of how to Romanize Arabic, Turkish and Persian; it presents a deeper challenge to the European reader, because the exclusive use of 'Oriental' terms involves a refusal to classify by Western categories.

For example, rather than having an article on 'Islamic science' or 'philosophy' (the sort of heading we find, for example, in Diderot's *Encyclopédie*), d'Herbelot has articles headed 'Elm' (*'ilm*) and 'Filsafat' (*falsafa*).[54] To find what Islam teaches about Jesus, the reader needs to look under 'Issa ebn Miriam'. Likewise to read about China, the relevant heading is 'Sin'; for Mecca, it is 'Omm Alcora' (*Umm al-Qura*, 'the Mother of Cities'). The entry 'Cabil' (*Qābīl*) reveals what Islam teaches about Cain; 'Cadha & Cadr' refers to what d'Herbelot calls 'le Decret Divin et la Predestination' (*qadā'* and *qadar*); the article 'Engil' deals with Muslim attitudes to the gospels (*al-Injīl*). The entry 'Esma Allah' concerns the ninety-nine names of God; the Muslim con-

---

53. The main text runs pp. 1–940; then comes a 'Supplement: les lettres ou portions des lettres qui suivent, lesquelles ne doivent faire qu'un corps avec tout l'Ouvrage, seront mises au rang qu'elles doivent tenir', pp. 941–1032. There are no DH-words under D and no K-words at all in the main series.

54. On *'ilm*, see Franz Rosenthal, *Knowledge Triumphant: The Concept of Knowledge in Medieval Islam*, Leiden, 1970.

cept of faith or the spiritual sphere is described in the article 'Din'.[55]

No European work on Islamic culture before d'Herbelot had attempted to apply this principle so thoroughly. D'Herbelot's decision to organize his material in this way – which almost negates the decision to put the articles in alphabetical order – can be understood in the light of his debt to Katib Chelebi, and his reading of other Arabic, Turkish and Persian source texts. To a certain extent, the entry-headings in the *Bibliothèque orientale* give place to the concepts and categories of Islamic culture. But at the same time, they function as a rhetoric of exotic 'authenticity'; they create a distance between the European reader and the material, forcing the reader to trust the mediation of the Orientalist scholar.

What allows the non-specialist reader to access the *Bibliothèque orientale* is the presence of finding devices like the cross-references and, especially, the index. Galland explained in his preface how the index shifted the terms of the main text into those of European conventions ('nos Auteurs').[56] It was only in the index that the Western reader found subjects arranged according to a recognizable schema. Using the index, the reader could look up, say, 'Alep' (the French name for Aleppo) and find a reference to the article 'Halab'. Under 'Quietisme' the reference led to the long article 'Eschk Allah, L'Amour de Dieu'. The index was crucial in enabling the book to function as an instrument – but only within the limits set by its own capricious selection of headings.

What Gibbon calls the indigestibility of the *Bibliothèque orientale* was not simply a symptom of its being organized alphabetically. Not only were those readers desiring a sequential narrative frustrated by the alphabetical order; even those who were happy to consult the book occasionally would have struggled to find what they were looking for because of the non-translation of the headings. The index therefore takes on an extraordinary burden. If

---

55. For more examples see Carnoy, *Représentations de l'Islam*, pp. 306–7.
56. Galland, 'Discours pour servir de preface', sig. o 2v. The 'Table des noms propres et des matières' takes up pp. 1033–59 in the 1697 edition.

the main text of the *Bibliothèque orientale* had been organized like
its index, as a series of subject headings recognizable to the
Western reader, then we might agree with Said's point that the
alphabetical ordering acts as a kind of 'discursive confinement',
or that the book is a panoptic instrument. But it is not. Because
the main text (which vastly outweighs the index) is organized by
untranslated terms and proper nouns, the non-specialist reader
is less able to control the information presented. And since the
index is a far from efficient finding device, it becomes very
difficult to believe in a panoptic portrayal of the *Bibliothèque
orientale*; it seems fairer to suggest that the information in the
book is always one step beyond the reader, always likely to
escape.

The book's preliminaries create the impression of a totalizing
text, an encyclopedic universal history of an unknown world. Yet
for all this rhetoric, the *Bibliothèque orientale* was an unreliable
instrument. It was unable to impose meaning on the reader; it
was instead a place for readers to lose themselves. Its functioning
could be compared, not so much to Said's panoptic theatre, but
to the indecipherable encyclopedias imagined by Borges.[57]

---

57. This is to say that we still lack a model for baroque Orientalism. Said's book
is centred on the nineteenth and twentieth centuries, and has relatively little on
the early modern period.

12

Victor Segalen Abroad

John Sturrock

In the eighteenth century, it was left to Diderot to draw out the ruinous implications for the local population of Bougainville's pioneering landfall in Tahiti. In the account he wrote of his voyage, the great circumnavigator had not been slow to find in the inhabitants of the Oceanic islands he had visited opportune confirmation of Rousseauesque beliefs in the goodness of those who lived in what a native of Europe might choose to see as a state of nature, a state crying out to be contrasted, to the advantage of one and the detriment of the other, with the debased mores of Ancien Régime France. In his *Supplément au voyage de Bougainville*, Diderot went further, in arguing for the obvious superiority of the Tahitian way of life to the French, even if his reason for doing so seems to be to excite frustrated male readers by the prospect of a society in which a consensual sexual freedom – whose end, it's prudently, if disingenuously, stressed by his Tahitian spokesman, is always procreation – is held to be a rational and sovereign good. It was a good, however, which, once news of it caught on in Christian Europe, would surely come under threat from the future intrusions on Tahitian life of moralizing aliens, sailing out to the Pacific not just to trade and to expropriate, but also to convert: to tyrannize economically and pervert morally into the bargain.

The *Supplément* gives voice to a local elder, a man of the *longue durée*, who, refusing to share in the deluded islanders' weeping farewells on the shore to the departing Frenchmen, instead delivers a prophetic sermon:

Pleurez, malheureux Taïtiens! pleurez; mais que ce soit de l'arrivée,
et non du départ de ces hommes ambitieux et méchants: un jour,
vous les connaîtrez mieux. Un jour, ils reviendront, le morceau de
bois que vous voyez attaché à la ceinture de celui-ci, dans une main,
et le fer qui pend au côté de celui-là, dans l'autre, vous enchaîner,
vous égorger, ou vous assujettir à leurs extravagances et à leurs vices;
un jour vous servirez sous eux, aussi corrompus, aussi vils, aussi
malheureux qu'eux.

[Weep, luckless Tahitians, weep! But let it be at the coming, not at
the departure of these ambitious and wicked men; one day you will
know them better. One day they will return, the piece of wood you
see attached to this one's belt in one hand, and the blade which is
hanging at that one's side in the other, to enslave you, to butcher you
or make you subject to their extravagances and their vices; one day
you will serve under them, as corrupt, as vile, as unhappy as they!][1]

Bougainville may appear in the guise of an enlightened path-
finder to his own nation, but to the Tahitians, and to exceptional
critics of his own nation such as Diderot, he is to be looked on as
the first in what promises to be a line of self-righteous invaders,
bent on the subjection of a higher morality to a lower, unnatural
one. He is told to be gone: 'Nous suivons le pur instinct de la
nature; et tu as tenté d'effacer de nos âmes son caractère' ['We
follow the pure instinct of nature; and you have attempted to
erase its character from our souls']. None of your arrogant *mission
civilisatrice* here, if you please.

The 'pure instinct of nature' is something that has understand-
ably dropped out from the postcolonial discourse to which we've
grown attuned in recent years. The retrospective championship
of the rights of colonized populations by the descendants of the
colonizers no longer depends on hollow concepts such as that of
the prelapsarian innocence of primitive peoples. Not explicitly
that is, although, after exposure to the logothetes of postcoloni-
alism, one can easily come away with the impression that they are
so much more taken up with the sins of their forefathers than
with the welfare of their forefathers' victims that the culture and
prevailing morality of these last were, if not innocent, then
certainly more commendable than those of the colonizers. Such
is the eagerness to incriminate the agents of imperial expansion

1. Denis Diderot, *Œuvres*, Paris, 1953, p. 969.

that one can quickly lose sight of the possibility of deploring the consequences of colonialism without at the same time evaluating one's own culture against that perceived as having suffered. Colonialism may be seen rather as a peculiarly destructive form of a more general failure to respect Otherness; which is the argument of the anti-colonialist writer to whom I shall restrict my attention here.

The writer in question was Victor Segalen, someone whose work took longer than it should have done to emerge adequately into view, first in France and then outside. His books were published, if at all, only in obscure editions during his lifetime, and for quite some years after his death. It was only after the end of the Second World War, with, first, the nervous retreat from, and then the hurried dissolution of, European empires that this *fin-de-siècle* figure came into his own, recognized finally as having much that is of value to say to an age more sensitive than was his own to the preservation of the indigenous from the impact on it of migrant cultures made more aggressive by the new ease of travel and communication. It's good that Segalen's principal writings should now be available in popular editions, that they have begun to be translated, and that, as evidence that the setters of syllabuses also have caught the postcolonial tide, he has quite recently become a set author for the *agrégation*.

Segalen led a striking life as an itinerant devotee of Otherness, and died a striking death. Indeed, given that it invokes some of the principal themes of his work, the most profitable direction from which to come at his biography is the near end, not the far: from the suspiciously deliberate *mise-en-scène* of his death. It occurred in 1919, when he was only 41, and out of doors, in the forest of Huelgoat in the far west of Brittany. This was a legendary, Arthurian site, where the wicked daughter of King Gradlon did away with a whole relay team of dud candidates for her favours. It was visited and written about in the nineteenth century by Flaubert and by Hugo, and later by Segalen himself, in his first piece of real writing (its knightly associations fitting with his precocious taste, even as an adolescent, for the music of Wagner, and not least *Tristan*). He was found dead there two days after leaving for a day's walking from the hotel where he was staying; but the question was, and must remain, dead from what? He had a deep cut above the ankle, probably caused by a sharp root, and it's

imaginable that he had severed an artery and bled to death, the
blood having then been washed away by a storm. Except that
Segalen had spent twenty years as a qualified doctor and would
have been able if he'd wanted to put a tourniquet on the wound.
On the other hand, he had a recent history of fainting fits, he
might have passed out, and died from the cold or exhaustion.
There was no inquest and so no knowing medically how he came
to die.

Other people having looked for him in vain, his body was
found at once by his wife, lying in a spot where they had walked
together a few days earlier, and it was her wish that there should
be no investigation of his death. Rather than have it explained
impersonally away in the clinical language of a postmortem, she
preferred that it should remain open to whatever more private
interpretations might be put on it, fitting as those would be for a
man who had more than once quoted with approval the Taoist
saying that there is no such thing as a natural death. She was
helped by the fact that the forest setting wasn't as natural as it
might have been. Segalen had died with an edition of Shakespeare within reach of his hand, where certain passages in *Hamlet*
– we're not told which – had been underlined. Hamlet the
character – Mallarmé's 'seigneur latent qui ne peut devenir'
['latent lord who cannot become'] – had long attracted Segalen,
who may or may not have found something of that broodingly
estranged son in himself, as he fought to escape from the orbit of
an interfering mother, and was quick to find real-life Hamlets in
faraway courts, notably that of the Imperial family in Peking (as it
then was). The latent prince might also stand as a role model for
those whose lives have stalled, as had Segalen's, who at the time
of his death was on extended sick leave from the French Navy
suffering from what had been diagnosed as 'acute neurasthenia',
a depressive condition he'd known on and off all through his
adult life and which may have been brought on this final time by
his having fallen culpably in love with his wife's closest friend.
Injured leg or no, there's good reason to think that his was a
partly willed, not a simply accidental, death.

The forest of Huelgoat was no great distance from where
Segalen was born and raised, in the port of Brest, so the restless
seeker out of the distant and exotic had come back in the end to
a place familiar to him, as though accepting his defeat by the

spherical nature of what he disparagingly called the 'Great Ball' –
a flat Earth on which you could keep getting further away from
where you started might have suited him better. But then again,
travel a long way off, into the reality of what had first drawn you
as an Elsewhere, with all the allure of the imaginary, and the
forsaken reality of home can become an alluring Elsewhere in its
turn. In the notes he made over a number of years for an 'Essai
sur l'exotisme' that he never published,[2] Segalen observed that
the Félibrige poet Jules Boissière wrote his most beautiful Provençal poems when he was living in Hanoi, and that, more pointedly
still, the picture which Gauguin was working on at the time of his
death in the Marquesas Islands was of a Breton church under
snow. This wasn't, by Segalen's lights, the homesick act of an
unhappy man at the end of his tether, but a sovereign gesture of
the born traveller, the exote (his coining), caught up in the
'poised two-way play' ['ce double jeu balancé'] between the place
where you are and another place where you aren't, a dynamic to
and fro between perception and imagination that bestows on
those who cultivate it 'an inexhaustible, boundless diversity'.
Segalen's theory of the exotic draws its energy in fact from what
surviving structuralists will recognize and salute as an old Saussur-
ian friend, the 'play of difference'.

Segalen was an excitable rather than a measured thinker, more
a poet in his own eyes than a philosopher. Towards the end of
the 'Essai sur l'exotisme', he lays it down that the 'Fundamental
Law' in confronting the exotic is 'l'Intensité de la Sensation'. The
exotic, that's to say, is to be prized for the effects it produces on
the sensibility of the individual who experiences it, not for what it
may be in itself, a fundamental law that reveals well enough that
Segalen was himself a product of the age of Mallarmé. He raises
this aesthetic argument to its highest pitch, indeed, by arguing
that any object at all in the external world is at least potentially
'exotic' vis-à-vis a human subject, provided that the human subject
is capable of rising to an unnervingly severe challenge and de-
familiarizing the furniture of the world around him. This generalization of what has begun as a relatively restricted law would be
apt, you'd have thought, to induce an unproductive introversion
in the traveller rather than a sound curiosity towards his environ-

---

2. In Victor Segalen, *Œuvres complètes*, vol. 1, ed. Henri Bouillier, pp. 737ff.

ment – it would surely take a Roquentin to live up to it, and then only reluctantly, since, if that existentialist paragon's experience is thought to be valid, penetrating to the strangeness of the most ordinary of the world's contents is to be avoided.

Segalen's 'Essai' reads like something that a seeker after the exotic might have written before he had much serious experience of the exotic, but it must count in its way as an empirical work in so far as by the time he got down to it, Segalen had indeed travelled, and to good, thoughtful purpose. By a happy chance, once he had been commissioned as a naval doctor, his first posting, early in 1903, was to Tahiti, a byword for exoticism, less for Bougainville's visit and Diderot's polemical exploitation of it all those years before than for the spectacular emigration of Paul Gauguin, who had moved there on the proceeds of a sale of his canvases in 1891 and, after a return to France, had gone back to Oceania for a second, and final, time two years later. He died in the Marquesas Islands in 1903, soon after Segalen joined his ship in Tahiti. The coincidence was of lasting profit to Segalen.

He travelled to the Far East by way of New York. He disliked the city, as also other American cities he saw on his way across the continent, on the grounds that they contained little or no evidence of having a past. To lack a history was to lack a vital constituent of the exotic, in Segalen's theory of which the 'le recul dans le passé' ['the move back into the past'] was laid down as the temporal equivalent of 'le lointain dans l'espace' ['the distant in space'].[3] His nascent awareness of the indigenous as opposed to, or as overlaid by, the imposed was sharpened by the patent Eurocentrism of American urban life and the visible degradation and social exclusion of the pre-Columbian population. He responded favourably only to San Francisco, where he caught typhoid and was free to spend time convalescing. He took to the city chiefly because of its Chinatown, the opaque and hence compelling glamour of whose cultural life – he described the actors at the Chinese theatre as 'des fantoches de notre incompréhension et pantins de notre ignorance' ['puppets of our incomprehension and jumping-jacks of our ignorance'][4] – was just what the young doctor would have ordered for himself. By a

---

3. Ibid., p. 745.
4. Quoted from a letter in Gilles Manceron, *Segalen*, Paris, 1991, p. 143.

nice irony, the apprentice *exote* first had his mind turned in a sinological direction by an experience of Chinese life in its export version.

Once in Tahiti, Segalen was quickly persuaded, in line with what he had expected, that the island and others like it was in terrible decline, that the native people were 'des sauvages en voie de perversion civilisée' ['savages on the way to being perversely civilized'].[5] He began work almost at once on what was to be a novel dramatizing (all too thinly) the process and disastrous consequences of that perversion. In May 1903, Gauguin died and three months later, Segalen's ship arrived in the capital of the Marquesas to collect the painter's effects. Segalen went to the house he'd been living in, talked with some of the locals who had been his friends, and took his part without question against the French authorities who, first in Tahiti and then in the Marquesas, had hounded Gauguin as a 'defender of the savages'. At a subsequent auction, he bought several canvases, wood carvings, some notebooks and Gauguin's palette, twenty-four lots in all for 190 francs, or a little less than a month's pay.

This wasn't a piece of speculative connoisseurship: at the time he seems to have had little interest in the work as such; rather, he was declaring for Gauguin, the 'monstre' as he called him in an obituary piece ('Gauguin dans son dernier décor' ['Gauguin in his final setting']) that he published the following year in the *Mercure de France*, or alternatively an 'outlaw', a man of excess who had willed exile and contempt on himself by going from a relatively easy but hemmed-in existence in France to live autonomously but poor in the Pacific. As an artist he had, in Segalen's interpretation, done exactly as he should have done: he had recorded the encounter between a Westerner, culturally and intellectually of his time and place, and the exotic culture and outlook of the Polynesian inhabitants of the islands he lived on. He had taken the local forms, as displayed, for example, in the carvings of native craftsmen, and used them without – and this for Segalen is crucial – attempting to penetrate them, or understand them as it were from within. This was to show a true respect towards them. Neither as a man nor as an artist had he 'gone native', the phrase with which those like Gauguin who

---

5. Ibid., p. 150.

were seen as cultural apostates were mockingly written off in the age of colonialism; he had remained exactly what he had been, responding to the exotic with all the individuality he possessed. Segalen didn't of course believe that it was *feasible* for anyone to go native, however much they might fancy it, because diversity was diversity and not to be undone by any wilful process of assimilation. Nor should you want to undo it when the right thing above all was to secure its preservation. You could lodge with the diverse, run your eye and mind over it, make art or literature out of it, but there was to be no ultimate penetration or taking possession of it, which would have been a sinful ambition had it not first been illusory. Your due reward when you came up against diversity was 'la perception aigüe et immédiate d'une incompréhensibilité éternelle' ['the acute and immediate perception of an everlasting incomprehensibility'].[6] The experience of the Chinese theatre in San Francisco had been raised to the status of an axiom.

This is not for sure what the averagely hopeful traveller will be looking for: whatever promises to be everlastingly incomprehensible will be a turn-off, not an attraction. This is one of the moments, or one of the wordings, in his 'Essai' where the aesthetic ultra has got the upper hand over the traveller and taken up an extreme position that makes his theory seem absurd. Let's suppose, however, that in writing what he did Segalen had in mind only what we should look for in the initial shock of the exotic: that first sense of wholesale alienation for which the French have just the right word, *dépaysement.* We are back here with the Mallarméan requirement that, whatever the nature of the object, the subjective sensation be intense, and the sensation caused by an object that is going for ever to exceed our powers of comprehension is certainly that, coming close as it well might to panic.

One of the writers whom Segalen most admired early on, and subsequently got to know, was the later, Symbolist Huysmans, and especially his masterpiece, *À rebours,* that perverse demonstration of the impasse into which the cultivation of ever more refined sensations must lead. Rather than endure what he presumes will be the disillusionment of a first-hand encounter with the alien

---

6. 'Essai', p. 750.

townscape of London, Huysmans's hero, Des Esseintes, famously settles instead for the images of that city he already has in his head, derived from what he has read or heard. In contrast, and fastidious in his aesthetic views though he may have been, Segalen also possessed a robustness of temperament that led him to seek out the alien, not to play vicarious games with it. It's as well to keep in mind that this youthful Symbolist had also received the practical education of a doctor, even if he never for a moment countenanced looking for his literary models to the physiologically minded hard men of Naturalism.

He was very much of his time in the enthusiasm he felt for Wagner and for art forms directed at more senses than one. 'La synthèse en art me ravit' ['synthesis in art delights me'], he wrote in a letter to a friend in 1900, explaining at the same time that for him Verdi represented merely 'le démésuré des qualités italiennes' ['the immoderation of the Italian virtues'], and that he refused to 'vibrer à Chopin "doux rêveur"' ['vibrate to Chopin, "gentle dreamer"'].[7] And as forming a middle ground between the aesthetic and the physiological, he was especially welcoming of the notion of synaesthesia, or of correspondences between the senses, the notion of which Baudelaire had made much. Here, Segalen could simultaneously play the Symbolist poet and take issue with the medical establishment whose narrow-mindedness he had suffered from as a student. Medical orthodoxy looked on phenomena such as 'coloured hearing' as a freakish or a regressive malfunction; on the contrary, believed Segalen, they were evidence of a superior, because more fully evolved, adaptation to the external world. He was welcoming also of the newly assertive Freudianism of the turn of the century in France and the way in which it served to undermine the crude positivism of the Charcot generation in respect of the mind's workings – in what must have been a highly unusual naval medical school thesis he stressed the benefit that writers and other artists could derive from the exploration, or, better, exploitation, of their neuroses. Given its unorthodox subject matter, it's perhaps surprising that the thesis was accepted. Once it was, Segalen asked two of his influential literary connections, Huysmans and Rémy de Gourmont, to find him a Paris publisher, which they couldn't. Subsequently, as if to

7. Manceron, *Segalen*, p. 107.

establish his hybrid – or one might say synthetic – credentials as a
man both of letters and of medicine, he brought the thesis out in
two forms and under two different titles, one for professional and
the other for more popular attention. It received little or no
attention in either form.

When it came to his actual encounters with exotic places and
cultures, Segalen failed to live up to his own doctrine. Even
before he left France, to travel first to Polynesia and later to
China, he spent time reading up and informing himself on the
history and cultural condition of those places. This was bound to
mean that by the time he got there, their exoticism would be
diluted by the knowledge he had brought with him: their 'incomprehensibility' was relegated in his own case to the status of a
theoretical prop, to be invoked when cautioning other, less high-
minded travellers who were ready to believe they had penetrated
to the heart of this or that alien culture. In practice indeed, as
opposed to principle, Segalen struck a nice balance between what
he thought he did and knew he didn't understand as a traveller,
or between, in the terms which he favoured, the 'real' and the
'imaginary', the creative play between which once the *exote* is *in
situ* is simply a localized transposition of the original play between
the here and the there. The urge to court and to register the
strong effects that an exotic landscape and exotic manners have
on you when you are uncertain of how far and how justly you
understand them was to become the subject of what is far and
away the subtlest, most enjoyable and most popular thing Segalen
ever wrote, the novel *René Leys*.

His experience of China produced two works of fiction, his
much briefer experience of Polynesia just the one, *Les Immémoriaux* [The Ones without Memory], a novel that appeared four
years after his return to France and whose publication he had to
pay for himself, out of what he made by selling some of the items
he had bought at the sale of Gauguin's effects. It is close to
unreadable today, certainly if you attempt it as a work of fiction,
such is the unsparing fullness with which its author reports on
the rituals, customs, myths and beliefs of the Polynesians he'd
moved among during his time there. When it was reissued, many
years after its first publication, it was in a collection of ethnography, which is where it belongs. It's not ethnography of an
academic kind, but a work in which the author's presence is at

least implicit, looking forward to the new style of more subjective ethnographic writing that took hold in the last decades of the twentieth century, when the discipline finally acknowledged that it had depended for too long on the assumption that the ethnographer's own behaviour in the course of his fieldwork had no serious repercussions or distorting influences on that of the people he was studying.

In Polynesia, Segalen had a case to make, the same case that Gauguin and Robert Louis Stevenson had made before him, against the degradation of native life which had set in, first, with the coming of Christian missionaries to the islands early in the nineteenth century, and then with the onset of a colonial administration. The Polynesians had begun to die out, destroyed physically by European diseases they had no immunity against and spiritually by an imposed and repressive morality that led not to any improvement in their way of life but to deracination and, characteristically, apathy. They had been robbed of their collective memory, whence the title of *Les Immémoriaux*: the immemorial ones are those whose forgotten past ought urgently to be restored to them through the decontamination of their present. Their diversity should have been recognized as sacrosanct.

This was Segalen asking that the colonial clock be turned back, but without at the same time falling for any sentimental idea than Polynesian life may have been idyllic before the arrival of the Europeans. The diversity of the native populations was an absolute, nothing else mattered; the life the Polynesian islanders had led before the Europeans arrived could have been perfectly horrible, but no-one from outside had the right to try to 'improve' it. Segalen's cult of diversity, that is, is aesthetic to a disconcerting extreme of laissez-faire, the diverse seemingly requiring to be conserved more for the gratification of someone like himself who is capable of appreciating it than for any benefit that might come to the races who embodied it.

This troublingly dispassionate point of view – his reading of Nietzsche had done a lot to form it – makes Segalen an equivocal forerunner for postcolonialists. He was against colonialism, right enough, and the dispossession and exploitation that were entrenched by it, not out of any – demeaning, as he'd have argued – sense of fraternity with those who suffered but because the colonizers had committed the crime of working to erase cultural difference. He was a Lévi-Straussian *avant la lettre*, who saw the takeover of vulnerable cultures by strong, i.e. wealthier, ones as leading to a form of entropy, inasmuch as cultural differentiation was evidence of societal energy at work, and the contrary process, of cultural homogenization, could but be evidence of a leaking away of that same energy. Segalen's views overlapped up to a point with those of the *fin-de-siècle* degenerationists, of Max Nordau and his kind, who saw the mixing of cultures as a threat to the well-being of so-called Aryan peoples – not that Segalen, that I'm aware, ever expressed any belief in the inborn superiority of any one race over another. He saw the homogenization of what had hitherto survived as disparate cultures – the discontinuity between which could be held suggestively to echo that characterizing the elemental world of physics – as ushering in a 'Kingdom of the Tepid', a prospect that he regarded as 'worse than Nothing', a lukewarm End of History. Given which, he also had his piece to say naturally against the 'colonial school' of writing, which gained in strength in France over the opening years of the twentieth century and whose authors took colonial life as their subject matter only in the intention of assimilating it, of bringing it closer to home for easy consumption: the most successful novelist then writing that sort of thing, Pierre Loti, was dismissed by Segalen as a 'pimp of the exotic'.

Any *exote* of Segalen's generation worth his salt would hope eventually to set off for China, the most absorbingly different country of all, to find himself physically in the Orient instead of letting the Orient come to him, in the etiolated form of a taste for Chinoiserie. Segalen had long planned to get there and in 1909 he did, when he was sent to Peking by the Navy to learn the language and qualify as an interpreter. His entry to the country was through Shanghai, a city which had been Europeanized in no uncertain fashion by the 'concessions', or quarters granted to the imperial powers that had extensive commercial interests in China. The experience of Shanghai was as ambiguous as Segalen might have wished, the historical and the contemporary coming immediately into conflict. He visited the celebrated Jesuit observatory and was shown round by a Breton member of the order who reminded him of the Tahitian missionaries and to whom he reacted with predictable fury in a letter to his wife: 'Mais que ne lui tordrais-je le cou! Retrouver en pleine Chine les pires immondices de la rue

Bonaparte!' ['But how I would like to throttle him! To rediscover in China the worst filth from the rue Bonaparte!'].[8]

Peking proved to be the antidote to Shanghai that Segalen required, the European presence there being on a far lesser scale and more discreet. He lived there, or elsewhere in China, right up until the start of the First World War, with a single absence of a few months back in France. Not that even the Imperial city measured up in its present state to the supposed splendour of the Chinese past, but the dialectical relationship that this gave rise to, between the imagined place and the actual one, was for Segalen just the stimulus he needed. 'Mon premier mois de séjour à Pékin m'a montré une ville étrange,' Segalen wrote in a letter, 'au plan le plus grandiose et vraiment impérial, aux détails souvent délabrés et en loques' ['My first month's stay in Peking showed me a strange town, the most grandiose and truly imperial in its layout, frequently dilapidated and in tatters in its details'].[9] Hence the need for the indigenous arts and ancient monuments of the country to be called in to restore dignity to the present, in an act of restoration comparable with that which he had envisaged for a degraded Polynesia. He travelled widely and receptively outside the towns, becoming impressively well informed about the country's archaeology and artefacts and writing enough eventually to fill a thousand pages of the second volume of his collected works.

For all that, the constant theme in his writing remained the play between the two worlds, as defined in the book that forms a sort of *journal de route*, *Equipée* (first published long after it was written, in 1929): 'De même, par le mécanisme quotidien de la route, l'opposition sera flagrante entre ces deux mondes: celui que l'on pense et celui que l'on heurte, ce qu'on rêve et ce que l'on fait, entre ce qu'on désire et cela que l'on obtient' ['Similarly, through the everyday mechanism of the road, the opposition will be flagrant between these two worlds: that which one thinks and that which comes up against, what one dreams and what one does, between what one desires and that which one obtains'].[10] And so it is in *Equipée* itself, an abstract of Segalen's journeys

8. Ibid., p. 284.
9. Ibid., p. 288.
10. Victor Segalen, *Equipée*, Paris, 1983, p. 12.

across the Chinese landscape in the course of which – the traveller
as poet – he has to ask himself whether he is taking possession of
it by the movements he is making with his feet or those he is
making with his mind. So much is the opposition between the
two worlds the point with Segalen that he even declares that the
journey itself is a 'subterfuge' designed to dramatize it. As a *récit*,
Equipée is dramatic at one point only, in a description of a
dangerous descent of the rapids along a river where the traveller
himself takes charge of the raft. This might seem in context an
almost gross intrusion of the Real, but then the mind goes back
to the closing lines of a poem Segalen wrote quite soon after
arriving in China and included in a collection called *Stèles*, the
first edition of which appeared in Peking in 1912. The poem,
entitled 'Conseils au bon voyageur' [Advice to the Good Travel-
ler], ends: 'Ainsi, sans arrêt ni faux pas, sans licol et sans étable,
sans mérites ni peines, tu parviendras, mon ami, au marais des
joies immortelles, / Mais aux remous pleins d'ivresses du grand
fleuve Diversité' ['And so, with neither a pause nor a stumble,
with neither halter nor cowshed, with neither merit nor difficulties, you will come, my friend, to the marshland of immortal joys,
/ But to the rapturous eddyings of the great river Diversity'].[11] So
are the eddies which threaten the raft on its way down river in
Equipée real or are they metaphorical? Or a metaphor which
heightens the reality? There's no knowing and no need to know;
suffice it to say that rivers play a significant topographical role for
Segalen as fluid places where the real and imaginary are for once
brought into harmony.

The inwardness of *Equipée*, and the preciosity of *Stèles* (or the
heightened prose of *Peintures*, in which Segalen describes a
sequence of Chinese paintings, some real, some seemingly not),
give little hint that the man who wrote them might also turn while
he was in China to writing fiction, but he did: two novels, *Le Fils
du Ciel* (it seems never to have been translated into English) and
René Leys, the humour and directness of which last are at once a
surprise and a delight.

Neither novel has the form of a conventional narrative (of the
time), because Segalen had progressive views about what was
wrong with conventional narrative. For one thing it was imper-

---

11. Victor Segalen, *Stèles*, Paris, 1973, p. 103.

sonal, in the sense that the narrator, whether implicit or explicit, had little room to establish himself as an individual, which went against the grain with Segalen, who believed that a reality seen as if from nowhere in particular counted for nothing. And for a second thing, conventional narrative proceeded as if it were all-knowing, which was to eliminate the opposition between what is known and what is merely believed or imagined. Segalen's two narrators are personalized and they are beset by uncertainty; they are fulfilling the requirements he had laid down for the traveller in exotic places.

Both of Segalen's novels are grounded in the modern history of China, a country which was, during most of his time there, in turmoil, politically speaking. That turmoil, taken in conjunction with the very high degree of secrecy traditional in the local ruling circles, suited the novelist's purpose very well, opening the way as it did to the play of rumour, that source of information interme-diate between truth and fiction. In 1909, after three hundred years, the Manchu dynasty was near to its end. A year earlier, the Emperor Kuang-Hsu had died, perhaps put to death on the orders of his gruesome aunt, the Dowager Empress Tz'u Hsi, who had come to regret having once secured the succession for her then infant nephew, since he had grown up to be something of a political reformer. Finally, she had confined him to a bridgeless island within the Imperial precincts and resumed power herself as a self-appointed Regent, until she, too, died, at much the same time as Kuang. This was a situation Segalen found irresistibly mysterious, since hearsay far outweighed facts in whatever accounts were to be obtained of these Palace intrigues.

Segalen described *Le Fils du Ciel* as the 'libre roman' of Kuang-Hsu, as a book in which he meant to 'Prendre la Chine et la tordre à mon gré'. ['Take China and twist it as I liked'].[12] The unfortunate Son of Heaven is a man of two jarringly discordant worlds, one of them transcendent inasmuch as the Emperor is not an individual but the embodiment of an ancient, quasi-divine office, the other domestic and full of cruelty and pettiness – a discordance reproducing that of which Segelen had been instantly made aware on his arrival in the country, between its tremendous history and its fallen present. The novel is constructed in such a

---

12. Manceron, *Segalen*, p. 340.

way as to emphasize the division. It is purportedly compiled by an annalist, appointed by the Regent, to record Kuang's actions and words in his imprisonment, but the annalist's practised formality and the Emperor's emotions, obliquely expressed in the poetry he writes (just as Segalen let it be known his own were in the formal verses of *Stèles*), are necessarily in conflict. A conflict between, in Segalen's words, 'La solide, sèche, granitique Annale; et d'autre part toutes les passions, les espérances, les volontés *hamlétiques*, les efforts serrés, trahis . . . de mon seul personnage.' ['The solid, dry, granitic Annals; and on the other hand all the passions, the hopes, the *Hamlet-like* wishes, the compact efforts, betrayed . . . of my one character'] (Segalen's italics).[13]

As the Emperor of China, Kuang represented for Segalen a peculiar, Romantic ideal, of the political leader who was also a poet, a man of two worlds but on the grandest scale. Only in China did such an ideal stand to be realized, in 'l'admirable fiction de l'Empereur, Fils du Pur Souverain Ciel' ['the admirable fiction of the Emperor, Son of the Pure Sovereign Heaven']. Segalen felt an allegiance not to the Manchu dynasty as such but to the ancient Imperial institution, which was now on the way to being overthrown and whose loss he declared would leave behind a 'great void'. Segalen does not appear to have taken any great interest in politics for as long as he was living in France, but once transplanted into China he emerged as a thorough-going reactionary, a not uncommon position among self-conscious aesthetes of his kind, who find the *demos* in its coarseness undeserving of affection. They are in the unfortunate, unexotic position of lacking a history, unlike their rulers.

Although *Le Fils du Ciel* is in the main a serious book, it tends unexpectedly and agreeably to satire, or perhaps that should be irony, at those moments when foreigners come onto the scene. Foreign intrusions had of course played a central part politically in China in the nineteenth century, up until its end, when the Boxer Uprising broke out. This was in effect a nationalist protest against the growing influence of the imperialist powers that had gained trading concessions and extra-territorial rights in China. The armed action was secretly supported by the Dowager Empress, while her nephew Kuang believed that a peaceful mod-

---

13. Ibid.

ernization of the administrative system was what the country needed. The Uprising was put down by European troops, but the nationalist movement took heart from it and would have to wait only a few years before establishing itself in power. In *Le Fils du Ciel*, which opens some little time before the Uprising, the Dowager Empress is able to blame even natural disasters on the presence of so many foreigners in the country, while the modernizing Emperor, more conciliatory, gives an audience to the 'barbarians', or to the diplomats coming to present their credentials. Segalen, true to his philosophy, takes the side of the xenophobic elements against the aliens, and is pleased to make fun of the contemptuous and uncouth representatives of Europe.

In *René Leys*, the role of the outsider is recycled, to more broadly comic effect. Dropping the device of impersonation, the narrator now is a Frenchman by the name of Segalen, newly arrived in Peking and anxious to penetrate the secrets of the Forbidden City. He fears, however, that this is a hopeless ambition, that he'll never be able to get inside the walls or learn just what goes on there. All he can do is to walk or ride on horseback round the perimeter; the *Dedans* remains an unmapped and enticing blank (like the Imperial blank at the heart of the street plan of Tokyo with which Roland Barthes makes play in *L'Empire des signes*, an elegant report on a semiotician's fieldwork that might profitably be read in conjunction with *René Leys*).

Instead of having to imagine for himself what might be happening within, the fictional Segalen finds a surrogate, René Leys, a Belgian boy whose father runs a grocer's shop serving the foreign legations and who already, by the age of 17, has risen to be a teacher of political economy. René appears, by his own account, to come and go from the Forbidden City in absolute freedom, to be a high-up in the Imperial secret service, to have had an affair and even a child with the widow of the late Emperor Kuang. To every question put to him about life on the Inside, he has a full and colourful answer, involving rivalries, sexual shenanigans, assassination plots, concubines, the lot. And he himself comes particularly well out of the episodes he recounts.

The year, however, is 1911, the reigning Emperor is a small boy, and revolution is at hand. As René one day puts it, anxiously, to Segalen, 'there's this Sun-Yat-sen'. As indeed there is, and suddenly the Celestial Empire and the Manchus with it are finished. So, too, is René Leys, who is no longer of any use, either to the regime he has served so brilliantly or to the probing Segalen. He dies, poisoned it could be by his enemies or else by his own hand, leaving the way clear for a repressed reality to make its return following this brief but hyperactive reign of the imaginary.

The encounter with René Leys, the ever-resourceful fabulist, is a fitting punishment for someone like the fictional Segalen, who has gone against the real Segalen's austere principles and can't accept that the Forbidden City has to remain a mystery, its incomprehensibility secured. One might conclude therefore that the Belgian boy is nothing more than a comical plot device, employed in order to show how gimcrack the imagination can become when fed on a diet of clichéd excess – life in the Palace in René's version is assembled from the most naïve sources. The extraordinary thing is, however, that when he was in Peking, Segalen actually met and befriended a young Frenchman whose father ran the French postal service there and who spun him preposterous tales of Imperial goings-on of the very kind that René Leys is made to spin, even the one about having slept with the Dowager Empress. There's no knowing how far Segalen was taken in by this young man, although his excellent biographer, Gilles Manceron, suggests that he was by no means as sceptical as one would have hoped or expected.

That he should have found himself in China at the cardinal moment in its history when it went from being an empire to being a republic is ironic, for Segalen couldn't bear to see any institution so truly exotic give way to a form of government that had been imported from abroad. Sun Yat-sen, the prime carrier of this Western infection, he describes at different times as a 'crétin' and as 'un certain commis-voyageur en pacotille '89 et Droits de l'Homme' ['a certain commercial traveller in cheap '89 and Rights of Man junk'])[14] – a description that puts him into the wrong class of traveller altogether. The Chinese should have known better than to succumb, but then those of them whom Segalen had dealings with had by no means lived up to the elevated idea he had brought with him of their country and its Imperial past. 'A sentir vivement la Chine,' he wrote in the 'Essai',

_____

14. Victor Segalen, *René Leys*, Paris, 1971, p. 164.

'je n'ai jamais éprouvé le désir d'être Chinois' ['With a keen sense of China, I've never felt the desire to be Chinese']).[15] The Frenchman who, in *René Leys*, has felt that desire, to the extent of marrying a Chinese woman and being 'naturalized', is treated with the greatest contempt. And as with China, so, six years later, Segalen was to be found deploring the Revolution in Imperial Russia, as further proof that entropy was nigh, when the be-all and end-all of democracy, if that was the way things were headed, lay in the elimination of differences between one citizen and another. Hierarchical societies had a decisive edge when it came to the perpetuation of diversity.

Dying when he did, Segalen was spared the spectacle of a world in which travellers are no longer born but made, by the relentless and deceptive pimping of the exotic that yearly draws people out from their homelands by the million. Although, even this prospect had its inherent compensation if you knew where to locate it. In the 'Essai sur l'exotisme', he dares to look ahead to the age of '[Thomas] Cooks, les paquebots et les avions' ['Cooks, steamboats and aeroplanes'], and to reflect that there would still be a place in it for the *exote*, when, for a fanatic of difference such as Victor Segalen, the coming of the footloose, democratic, homogenized masses will serve inevitably to enhance the individuality of the elite class of the discerning.

---

15. 'Essai', p. 766.

13

Kafka and the Dialect of Minor Literature

Stanley Corngold

> In one's own language, however, were one only to say
> something as exactly and as uncompromisingly as possible,
> one might also hope through such relentless effort to
> become understandable as well.

Adorno[1]

The phrase in this title 'the dialect of minor literature' is meant to convey two things at once. It alludes, first of all, to the mistaken idea that Kafka wrote in a dialect called 'Prague German'; and, second, to the mistaken idea that in doing so, he intended to contribute to the construction of a 'minor literature' rebelliously aimed at a 'major' or master literature. I shall take up these two points separately.

The claim that Kafka wrote in dialect was recently advanced by Joachim Neugroschel in the introduction to his new translations of Kafka's stories: 'Kafka's oeuvre has now become a monument to Prague German, which, like so many dialects and regional variants of German, was liquidated along with the Fascist era.'[2]

---

1. Theodor Adorno, 'On the Question: "What Is German?"', trans. Thomas Y. Levin, *New German Critique*, 36, Fall 1985, p. 130. This is the crux. The point would be not to begin with the idiom but to think through the idiom.

2. Franz Kafka, *The Metamorphosis and Other Stories*, trans. Joachim Neugroschel, New York, 1993, p. xi.

For this argument to work, one has to ignore the most immediately transparent sense of the phrase 'Prague German' – the fearsome jargon spoken by Prague Czech-speaking butchers and scullion maids in conversation with their generally more affluent German-speaking customers and employers. In Kafka's case, therefore, the 'Prague German' he allegedly wrote has got to mean something else – it has to mean the German that Kafka spoke and therefore presumably wrote, because he did not write downward into dialect. This claim, however – even if there were some original minor language called 'Prague German' that Kafka spoke – is dubious, first, on general conceptual grounds: it relies on a dogmatic notion of style as a quasi-biological fact, *à la* early Barthes – as if Kafka, being a Prague German(-Jew), could not but speak the language of others and, furthermore, did indeed write in the language he spoke. But in truth the so-called 'Prague German' that Kafka allegedly spoke was only a faintly dialectical coloration of High German, audible as a regional sociolect but certainly not the distinctive language of a people. Max Brod, a trustworthy authority in such matters, reports that Kafka, along with almost all Germans in Prague, strove not to be recognized as speakers and especially as writers of 'Prague German' of whatever description: 'The German of the Prague German-speaker was distinctive only for its somewhat harsh accent; on the other hand, we were extremely careful not to let locally conditioned deviations get into the written language.'[3]

Meanwhile, Kafka's relation to the *literary* German of Prague authors is another matter – one of considerable interest, especially as it might be contrasted with the work, for example, of Rilke, Brod and Werfel. Kafka's reaction points chiefly to his discreet repugnance with regard to its perfumed literariness. Kafka had an entirely different idea of what he called, appreciatively, 'the most individual High German', which, as it happens, he distinguished precisely from 'dialect'. (He thought them both sources of liveliness as compared with the jejune middle ground of daily spoken German ['nothing but embers'].) But though he might have considered his own work a derivative of 'mauscheln'

---

3. Max Brod, *Streitbares Leben*, Munich, 1960, p. 219. Cited, along with other valuable materials, in Pavel Trost, 'Das später Prager Deutsch', *Acta Universitatis Carolinae – Philologica – Germanistica Pragensia*, vol. 2, 1962, p. 35.

– German spoken with a Yiddish flair, a 'fine . . ., organic compound of bookish German and pantomime' – he meant this
grimly pejorative word to describe his literary language in an only
ironic and elliptical way, as taken only in the broadest sense of
the phrase ('im weitesten Sinn genommen').[4] Kafka's relation to
Yiddish literature, a literature that he could read but not write, is
another story altogether – one now being studied by many
scholars.[5] In no plausible way, though, did Kafka consider his
work to have been written in dialect.

The phrase 'the dialect of minor literature' also alludes to
another sense of 'dialect' – a certain theory-dialect or discursive
type as it is found in Deleuze and Guattari's popular *Kafka: Toward
a Minor Literature*.[6] By claiming that Kafka wrote in the distinctive
dialect of turn-of-the-century Prague, they mean to provide him
with the linguistic vehicle of a so-called 'minor' literature and
hence with revolutionary authority. In their view, Kafka's literary
German figures as a kind of polemical ideolect aimed against
high German literature – the literary language of Greater
Germany (*Großdeutschland*). Kafka's work, they claim, is informed
by the pathos of political defiance, and this claim is implied
whenever it is said that Kafka meant to contribute to a so-called
'minor' literature. But this thesis is aberrant because what, after
all, is this subversive 'Prague German' that Kafka wrote? Deleuze
and Guattari offer no philological descriptors at all.

Despite its inaccuracy, Deleuze and Guattari's view of Kafka as
an author working within the constraints of a minor literature has
now located him exemplarily within a certain dialect – or, perhaps, pidgin – of critical theorizing. This is a political criticism

---

4. Franz Kafka, *Letters to Friends, Family, and Editors*, trans. Richard and Clara
Winston, New York, 1977, p. 288. This work will henceforth be referenced as L
plus page number. *Briefe 1902–1924*, ed. Max Brod, Frankfurt on Main, 1958,
pp. 336–7.
  5. Among many works bearing on this important subject are Giuliano Baioni,
Kafka: letteratura et ebraismo, Turin, 1984; Ritchie Robertson, *Kafka: Judaism, Politics,
and Literature*, New York, 1985; Jean Jofen, *The Jewish Mystic in Kafka*, New York,
1987; and Régine Robin, *Kafka*, Paris, 1989. For an overview of this material, see
Iris M. Bruce, *A Life of Metamorphosis: Franz Kafka and the Jewish Tradition*. disserta-
tion, University of Toronto, 1990.
  6. Gilles Deleuze and Félix Guattari, *Kafka: Pour une littérature mineure*, Paris,
1975. *Kafka – Toward a Minor Literature*, trans. Dana Polan, Minneapolis, 1986.
References to the latter work will henceforth be indicated in the text with DG and
the page number in parentheses.

empowering the literature of small nations, a literature said to be exemplary of strategies for exploding power at the underside. The thesis has found a home primarily in and around postcolonial studies, but it has also impacted on Kafka studies as well, since, according to Deleuze and Guattari, Kafka's work constructs 'linguistic Third World zones by which a language can escape' (DG 27). Deleuze and Guattari's eponymous figure of the 'anti-Oedipus' also belongs to this claim of the political efficacy of the literature of small nations – a claim in which Kafka turns out, somewhat surprisingly, to figure as the primal anti-Oedipus.

This reading of Kafka as a local revolutionary figures further in the larger event of self-reflection taking place in Central and Eastern Europe since the 1990s, where critics and writers have been displaying an acute awareness of the long suppressed factor of national identity. What was at first a backlash against Soviet communist domination is now a backlash against American-spurred 'globalization'. After decades of prohibition, East European writers are bent on defining their sense of national and ethnic specificity – as, for example, in Prague and Vilnius and Kiev; this is true, too, of cultural Croatians, Romanians, Estonians, in and outside their homeland. I am alluding here to the phenomenon that Professor Timothy Reiss has called 'falling back into the local'.[7]

In this context, the retranslation and reinterpretation of Kafka's own stories and novels have acquired a special significance. Consider, for example, the project of Kafka's Czech translators in the light of Václav Havel's allusions to Kafka as the inspiration for a necessary, an authenticating, anxiety-in-government. The ongoing Central and Eastern European use of Kafka aims chiefly to open a source of political and polemical impulses heightening the self-consciousness of peoples living on the margin of great powers. In all this, another sort of reading of Kafka is implicitly taking place. For when Central and Eastern European intellectuals address questions of ethnic or national identity, they are commenting willy-nilly on Kafka's now famous essay on the literature of small nations. This essay – a five-page diary entry

---

7. On the occasion of the Eastern Comparative Literature Conference held at New York University on 5 May 1990. The point is further pursued in his contribution to this volume.

written in 1911 – also occupies a central position in Deleuze and
Guattari's account of Kafka's own work as the project of someone
writing within the boundaries of a minor literature.[8] Both inside
and outside Central and Eastern European countries, it is used to
justify the claim of ethnic and linguistic difference *as such* to resist
hegemonic powers, institutions and discourses.

I said at the outset that I have little sympathy with much of the
use made of Kafka's work in the critical dialect of so-called
'minor' literature. But before saying what might be wrong about
such applications – this reaching out to and totalizing *a postmodern
literature and politics as such* from points allegedly made by Kafka
about minor literature – it will be important to get hold of Kafka's
views as he states them. This will not be easy, since this essay, too,
is a sort of prose poem written by Franz Kafka. I am concerned
chiefly with highlighting difficulties in the way of its most immediate political appropriation.

The diary entry composed on 25 December 1911 opens by

---

8. Deleuze and Guattari defend the idea of a so-called 'minor literature' (*littérature mineure*). This concept, which they apply to Kafka's work, appears on their
account to derive from Kafka's explicit analysis of just such a literature. There is
some usefulness to their idea; but its application to Kafka's work as a whole is
tendentious, and the claim that it derives from Kafka's own reflections on his
writing goals is unjustified. The concept of 'minor literature', especially as 'revolutionary literature' – Deleuze and Guattari write that 'there is nothing that is
major or revolutionary except the minor' (DG 26) – is essentially their invention.

Kafka's sources, for Deleuze and Guattari, consist of letters and diary entries
that Kafka wrote at widely different times. The earliest are three closely linked
diary entries on '*small* literatures' that Kafka began writing early on 25 December
1911 (the first entry has no heading, the second is headed 'Continuation', the
third, 'Character Sketch'). They are found in *The Diaries of Franz Kafka, 1910–1913*,
trans. Joseph Kresh, New York, 1948, p. 191. References to this text will henceforth
be indicated with DI plus page number. The German text is found in *Gesammelte
Werke*, 12 vols, ed. Hans-Gerd Koch, Frankfurt on Main, vol. 9, 1992, pp. 243–5,
249–50 and 253, to which I refer (I have made a number of small changes to the
translation). Further references to this text will be indicated with GW plus volume
number plus page number. In these entries Kafka does not stress, *à la* Deleuze
and Guattari, the distinction between 'major' and 'minor' in the strict sense. What
he does refer to is a 'literature whose development is not in actual fact unusually
broad in scope ['Litteratur . . . die sich in einer tatsächlich zwar nicht ungewöhn-
lichen Breite entwickelt'] (DI 192, GW 9:243–4); 'a small nation's memory' ['das
Gedächtnis einer kleinen Nation'] and 'the national consciousness of a small
people' ['das Nationalbewußtsein innerhalb eines kleinen Volkes'] (DI 193, GW
9:245). In the 'Continuation' the literature of small nations is implicitly opposed
to 'great literatures' ['große Litteraturen']; and the 'Character Sketch', too, speaks
of 'small literatures' ['kleine Litteraturen']. Something of the interdependence
and confrontational tension in the English terms major/minor, the effort of the
minor to usurp the major, is not present in Kafka's usage 'great/small'.

declaring that 'many of the benefits of literary activity . . . can be produced *even by* a literature whose development is not in actual fact *unusually broad in scope* . . .' (my emphasis). This, we can say, is a minor literature. What minor literature does Kafka actually have in mind? He gives the examples in 1911 of contemporary Yiddish literature in Warsaw – or as much as he knows about it from Löwy, one of the actors appearing in Yiddish plays in Prague that year – as well as 'contemporary Czech literature', as he has experienced it. I stress: typical minor literatures for Kafka are Yiddish and Czech – and certainly not, *pace* Deleuze and Guattari, the literature written in the German of Prague authors, through which Kafka intends to make a unique contribution to world literature as one whose very essence is literature (Kafka wrote: 'Not a bent for writing, my dearest Felice, not a bent, but my entire self.')[9]

The benefits of literary activity are significant even when that literature is minor. Kafka's essay begins with an engaging list of its advantages, put together anarchically, like the Chinese taxonomy of animals quoted from Borges by Foucault at the beginning of *The Order of Things*.[10] Literature, for Kafka, 'stirs minds [*bewegt die Geister*] and brings about the unity and solidarity [*das einheitliche Zusammenhalten*] of national consciousness, which, in social life, is often inactive and [whether active or not] is forever disintegrating there' (DI 191, GW 9:243). Literature could therefore never reflect or contain – it would more nearly constitute – a national consciousness always in the process of dissolving outside its frame. From this constitution arises 'the pride and support that the nation gains for itself in the face of a hostile environment' (DI 191, GW 9:243). Literary production could therefore be likened to 'keeping a diary by a nation – something entirely different from historiography', because this diary-keeping amounts to a 'detailed spiritualization [*detaillierte Vergeistichung (sic)*]' of the broad scope of public life.[11] (The orthographical

---

9. Franz Kafka, *Letters to Felice*, trans. James Stern and Elizabeth Duckworth, New York, 1973, p. 309.

10. Michel Foucault, *The Order of Things: An Archaeology of the Human Sciences*, a translation of *Les Mots et les choses*, New York, 1971.

11. Compare J. M. Coetzee, who defines 'history' as 'a society's collective self-interpretation of its own coming-into-being', against which 'the freedom of textuality, however meager and marginal that freedom may be,' might be asserted. J.

slip – the loss of the '*l*' from '*Vergeistlichung*' – is bemusing; it releases a *Stich*, the stab of a knife, the sting of an insect, the pang of a pain – the stroke of a pen; and just some eighteen months before, Kafka had begun keeping *his* diary in order to strengthen his hurt pride, as a blocked writer, in the 'face of a hostile environment'. The process of diary-keeping, however, is crucial, for by means of it 'dissatisfied elements are assimilated and immediately become useful, since it is only the slack tolerance [*Lässigkeit*] of them that can do harm' (DI 192, GW 9:243). This is literary idealism in the service of national unity, and at this moment Kafka does not sound very different from Dilthey writing in Germany around 1866.

The view, I might point out, is expressly opposed to that of another rigorous Gnostic writer, Herman Melville, who notes in *Billy Budd* of 'such events [as mutiny]': they 'cannot be ignored, but there is a considerate way of historically treating them. If a well-constituted individual refrains from blazoning aught amiss or calamitous in his family, a nation in the like circumstance may without reproach be equally discreet.'[12] Not so for Kafka, who will pay more than lip-service to this view a year later in writing about the metamorphosis of a Prague textile salesman into a giant dung beetle, which, as he himself noted, did blazon abroad things more than a little amiss in the family apartment.[13]

What is at stake in the domestic as well as the national sphere is the redemption of dissonance ('die Bindung unzufriedener Elemente'), occurring through 'a continual articulation of a people with respect to its experience'. In this development 'the incessant bustle of the literary magazines plays a key role'. Here

---

M. Coetzee, *Doubling the Point: Essays and Interviews*, ed. David Attwell, Cambridge, MA, 1992, p. 206.

12. Herman Melville, 'Billy Budd, Sailor (An Inside Narrative)', in *Billy Budd, Sailor & Other Stories*, ed. Harold Beaver, Harmondsworth, 1970, p. 333.

13. 'What do you say to the terrible things going on in our house?' Kafka is reported to have said to Professor Thieberger apropos of *The Metamorphosis* (Johannes Urzidil, *Da Geht Kafka*, Munich, 1965, p. 11). And then, allegedly, to Gustav Janouch: 'Is it perhaps delicate and discreet to talk about the bugs in one's own family?' (Gustav Janouch, *Conversations with Kafka*, New York, 1971, p. 32). But Kafka did also say to his sister, in dismissing her view that the apartment described in the linked novella *The Judgment* was the Kafka family's own, 'In that case, then, Father would have to be living in the toilet' (DI 280). Thus 'one man fights at Marathon, the other in the dining room'! (*Letters to Milena*, ed. Willi Haas, trans. Tania and James Stern, New York, 1953, p. 174).

Kafka's focus appears to be slipping onto the German-speaking Prague scene, with its literary journals and cafés, displaying the fact that the focus throughout this essay is undecidably binocular. Kafka is, after all, dealing with *literature* as such and also even and especially *the literature of small nations*. But we should be clear on this point: if Kafka shifts focus to the literary production of Prague authors writing in German, he does so because their work comes under the head of *literature*. The shift is not evidence that Kafka construes his own literary work in German as the literature *of a small nation* of Jewish Prague writers minded to revolt against writing in the German of Goethe and his acolytes (thus Deleuze and Guattari).

The list of literary benefits continues unexpectedly. Literature brings about a 'narrowing down of the attention of a nation upon itself [*auf ihren eigenen Kreis*] and the acceptance of what is foreign only in reflection [*in der Spiegelung*]'. Literature is, therefore, *as such* less a medium for preserving foreign differences than for producing unity, solidarity and the assimilation of the foreign within an intimate circle, mirror or hearth. This point will irritate, of course, any generally postmodern assimilation of this essay to a brief for literature's principled generosity to alien differences, negation of its own thing, break-up of the illusion of intimacy, and so forth.

Literature induces crucial changes in the subjective consciousness of family members: it marks 'the birth of a respect for persons active in literature' and brings about 'the transitory awakening in the younger generation of higher aspirations, which nevertheless leaves its permanent mark. Furthermore, it produces the acknowledgement of literary events as objects of political concern, the dignification of the antithesis between fathers and sons and the possibility of discussing this; the presentation of national faults in a manner that is especially painful, to be sure, but also liberating and deserving of forgiveness;[14] and the begin-

---

14. Compare Walter Benjamin on 'contemporary' Russian literature, circa 1927. 'The Russian literature of today fulfils, one might say, the physiological task of redeeming the political body [*Volkskörper*] from this excessive burden of themes, experiences and conjunctures (a monstrous process of excretion)' ['Die gegenwärtige russische Literatur erfüllt, man darf sagen die physiologische Aufgabe, den Volkskörper von dieser Überlast von Stoffen, von Erlebnissen, von Fügungen zu erlösen (ein ungeheuerer Auscheidungsprozeß)].' Walter Benjamin, 'Neue Dicht-

ning of a lively and therefore self-respecting book trade and the
eagerness for books.' Kafka now sounds as if he is telling the story
of his own literary education.

The above list mingles benefits from various spheres: nationalist ideology; aesthetic education; the economics of art, such as the
book trade; and generational struggles. Benefits accrue at different levels. One bonus – nothing less than a total unification of
national consciousness – mingles with a homelier one: a nicer
sort of quarrelling between father and son. Under the influence
of literature you will no longer find a father saying to his son,
around the dinner table, 'I'll tear you apart like a fish!' (thus
Hermann Kafka of Prague).[15] Perhaps.

This mixing of benefits at different levels could be explained
from the different impulses of the writer Kafka at work on this
extended diary entry. One could see him here jotting things down
rapidly for a future tract on literature and especially small literature – an essay that will be correctly worked out only when its
general programme has been confirmed or been adjusted by
Kafka's own literary production. (Deleuze and Guattari interpret
this jotting as if it had already been saturated with such a future
literary experience and hence as Kafka's official poetics, omitting
reflection on the time gap; it was written months before he had
even written *The Judgment*.) On the other hand, the disparities of
register in Kafka's list of literary benefits could point to the
spontaneity, swiftness and gaiety of its composition. The essay on
minor literature would then have been written by Kafka not as a
writer solemnly projecting in outline his future work but as one
gaily and slyly crafting a piece of his work as the writing of a
single night and day. The essay is (1) a Christmas caprice – it was
composed half on Christmas and half on Boxing Day; (2) a gift to
Löwy, the Yiddish actor, and to Mrs Tchissik, the Yiddish actress,
with whom Kafka had fallen in love the previous month (DI 139);
and (3) a celebration in advance of the joys of nativity of the
writer he was about to become. Nine months later, in the early
morning of 23 September 1912, Kafka would complete *The Judgment* – his breakthrough – in a single sitting.

ung in Russland', in *Gesammelte Schriften*, ed. Rolf Tiedemann and Hermann
Schweppenhäuser, Frankfurt on Main, 1972ff, vol. II (2), p. 761.

15. *Letter to his Father/Brief an den Vater*, trans. Ernst Kaiser and Eithne Wilkins,
New York, 1953, p. 35.

There is evidence of high spirits. The definition of a minor literature as one 'whose development is not in actual fact unusually broad in scope' is incomplete, for Kafka adds, 'but [whose development] *seems* to be [broad in scope] *because it lacks outstanding talents*' (my emphasis) (DI 192, GW 9:244). Stop and consider: Yiddish literature in Warsaw is, according to Kafka, an instance of a literature without major talents, one exemplarily not dominated by a single major talent, the struggle with which might conceivably define its whole future direction. In other words, Yiddish literature does not have its Goethe, does not live in the shadow of a single indomitable father talent (not even Mendele).

Of the mighty figure of Goethe, Kafka writes in his journal in the midst of composing this entry:

> Goethe probably retards the development of the German language by the force of his writing. Even though prose style has often travelled away from him in the interim, still, in the end, as at present, it returns to him with strengthened yearning and even adopts obsolete idioms found in Goethe but otherwise without any particular connection with him, in order to rejoice in the *completeness of its unlimited dependence.* (DI 197, GW 9:247, my emphasis)

Such a power, semi-divine, of the single instance is a crucial mark of the major literature. Quite otherwise minor literature – or . . .?

When I discussed this point with the Professor of Slavic Literatures at the University of Tel Aviv, he looked at me curiously. Modern Yiddish literature – i.e. Yiddish literature – was without its great precursor? Quite the contrary, he said. For whereas German writers had to contend (only) with Goethe, Yiddish writers had to contend with God: did Kafka mean to suggest that Goethe was a greater writer than God?

This perspective, I might note, would make God – leaving aside all questions of proportion – at least a writer; and sometimes Kafka indeed appears to think so, as when he writes, 'God doesn't want me to write – but I, I must' (L 10); and, indirectly, too, when he remarks that nothing can compare with the conclusion of Flaubert's *L'education sentimentale* except the conclusion of the Fifth Book of Moses, for both works record the failure of a man to arrive at his goal – Frédéric Moreau and Moses too, 'not because his life was too short but because it was a human life'

(DII 196, GW 11:190).[16] If my colleague's objection is true, it would be a mark of the irrefragable irony of Kafka's programme.

The benefits of literary work are mixed – and by no means easily assimilated in a contemporary climate favouring the fragmentation of integral personality, the radical entitlement of what's left, and the cultivation of difference. We say it is an altogether worthy enterprise *to understand difference*, however hard – an understanding not easily achieved, and certainly not by means of such intellectual labour-saving devices (following Walter Benjamin) as empathy (*Einfühlung*) or being in accord (*Einverständnis*), but rather through an obsessional immersion (*Versenkung*) in otherness with all holds barred. This being the case, what are we to make of minor literature's facility in reflecting what is different only in its own mirror? This point will make it impossible, I believe, to grant minor literature, according to Kafka, a subversive prestige vis-à-vis major literature.

We read on, stressing, again according to Kafka, the absence of a dominant talent in minor literature and, as a consequence, its compensatory strength or what he calls its 'liveliness' (*Lebhaftigkeit*). The word belongs importantly to his poetics.

> The liveliness of such a literature exceeds even that of one rich in talent, for, as it has no writer whose great gifts could silence at least the majority of cavillers, literary competition on the greatest scale has a real justification. A literature not broken into [*von keiner Begabung durchbrochen*, i.e. *ohne Durchbruch*, 'breakthrough'] by a great talent has, therefore, no gap through which the irrelevant or indifferent might force its way. (DI 192, GW 9:244)

It has no room for diatribe or aping.

Kafka's fine insight points up the negativity – the gap – that is the flip-side of every genius's breakthrough in a literary tradition, though it did not stop him nine months later from courting a breakthrough of his own. It creates an entrance for indifferent talents, whose task will be to dispute with and, equally, to imitate uselessly or complete speciously the work of that genius. Let us

---

16. There is, furthermore, the sense that Kafka as a writer rivals the author of the Old Testament when Kafka thinks of his characters (and indeed of himself) as prophets. See Malcolm Pasley, 'Kafkas Ruhm', *Neue Rundschau*, 98, Jahrgang 87, Heft 3, pp. 79–92.

agree that Kafka's essay is here at its least Bloomian and most anti-Oedipal and hence most Deleuzian and Guattarian.

The claim to attention of the specifically small literature now becomes more compelling. In it the independence of the individual writer – within national boundaries – is better preserved. The lack of irresistible national models keeps out writers without genuine talent – polemical types inspired by *ressentiment.* Equally, however, there appears to be a danger associated with writing within a minor literature that arises despite its democracy of talent (in minor literatures, remember, no writers are completely untalented and none are extravagantly talented). Kafka conjures the temptation of exotic influence (the 'exotic' and 'influence' are the same thing). This is the risk of being 'influenced by the indistinct qualities of the fashionable writers of the moment, or of introducing the works of foreign literatures, or of imitating the foreign literature that has already been introduced'. It appears to be less a temptation for writers in a major literature; 'this is plain', writes Kafka, 'in a literature rich in great talents, such as German . . . where the worst writers limit their imitation to what they find at home'. The difference between minor and major literature cannot yet be made to support a distinction of greater authenticity if this means resistance to influence.

The fact that some writers have little talent, whether in a minor or a major literature, does not affect the degree of their mimetic desire for the exotic of the moment – fashion – or the exotic from abroad. Even without extreme talents (including extremely weak talents), a minor literature suffers this influence, which has nothing to do with genius. Kafka does not say what the root of this susceptibility is: it is very likely an aspect of character – of an assimilationist bent. If this text were about Kafka, it could identify something like the temptation of 'Zionism' that was to interfere with his elaboration of 'a new secret doctrine, a Kabbalah' (DII 203).[17]

Kafka forces his way past this present difficulty of making a value distinction by turning to the past – to tradition:

---

17. 'All such writing [his writing] is an assault on the frontiers; if Zionism had not intervened, it might easily have developed into a new secret doctrine, a Kabbalah.'

The force ... of a literature poor in its component parts proves especially effective when it begins to create a literary history out of the records of its dead writers. These writers' undeniable influence, past and present, becomes so matter-of-fact that it can take the place of their writings. One speaks of the latter [their writings] and means the former [their influence], indeed, one even reads [their writings] and sees only [their influence]. But since that influence cannot be forgotten, and since the writings themselves do not act independently upon the memory, there is no forgetting and no remembering again. Literary history offers an unchangeable, dependable whole [*einen Block*] that is hardly affected by the taste of the day.

The literary history of small nations is a 'whole' because it exhibits no hysteresis between two histories: between the popular consciousness of a writer's work – a kind of sediment of the history of its reception – and an actual knowledge of it – the inner history of the work studied. Gerald Bruns wrote appositely: Words in literature 'echo or resonate with their historicality, that is, ... are expressive or reflective of their contexts'; even more, they 'situate you in their historicality in the sense of exposing you to it, placing you under its claims. ...'[18] Agreed, the manufacture of literary history in small nations does not follow a model guaranteeing good results either as history or as textual knowledge – and hence is not exemplary. Still the beautiful outcome, however illusory, is that literary history becomes the sacramental time of small nations. This view, too, will not be attractive to the postmodern interest in revising canons, and indeed it has its down-side for Kafka as well – congregational bias. Observe the fall:

A small nation's memory is not smaller than the memory of a large one and so can process [*verarbeiten*] the existing material more thoroughly. There are, to be sure, fewer experts in literary history employed, but literature is less a concern of literary history than of the people; and thus, if not purely, it is at least reliably preserved. For the claims that the national consciousness of a small people makes on the individual is such that everyone must always be prepared to know that part of the literature which comes down to him, to support it, to defend it – to defend it even if he does not know it and support it.

High spirits, gaiety, irony!

18. Gerald Bruns, *Heidegger's Estrangements*, New Haven, 1989, p. 15.

The old writings acquire a multiplicity of interpretations; despite the mediocre material, this goes on with an energy that is restrained only by the fear that one may too easily exhaust them [an ecological reverence hard to find in the postmodern scene], and by the reverence they are accorded by common consent. Everything is done very honestly, only within a bias that is never resolved ... and is broadcast for miles around when a skilful hand is lifted up. But in the end bias interferes not only with a broad view [*Ausblick*] but with a close insight [*Einblick*] as well. So that all these observations are cancelled out[!].

Finally,

since people [of small nations] lack a sense of context, their literary activities are out of context too. (They depreciate something in order to be able to look down upon it from above, or they praise it to the skies in order to have a place up there beside it. Wrong.) Even though something is often thought through calmly, one still does not reach the boundary where it connects up with similar things, one reaches soonest the boundary with politics, indeed, one even strives to see it before it is there, and often sees this limiting boundary everywhere. The narrowness of the field, the concern too for simplicity and uniformity, and, finally, the consideration that the inner independence of the literature makes the external connection with politics harmless, result in the dissemination of literature throughout a country on the basis of its clinging to political slogans [*sich an den politischen Schlagworten festhält*].

Festhalten (clinging) is also the word Kafka uses to describe in 1912 the relation of Gregor Samsa, the transmogrified salesman, to his fetish – the glass-encased woman in furs whom he once pinned up on his bedroom wall. The gesture suggests the most primitive attempt at covering up a loss of authority, of holding on to the rhetoric of lost identity.

In wanting to celebrate this aspect of minor literature – its ineluctably, instantaneously political character – Deleuze and Guattari are required to leave out these last sentences, for they damage their *valorization* of minor literature on radical grounds. These sentences say that *the literature of small nations disseminates itself by means of clinging to political slogans*. Kafka concludes:

There is [in minor literature] universal delight in the literary treatment of petty themes whose scope is not permitted to exceed the capacity of small enthusiasms and which are sustained by their polemical prospects and resources. Insults, given literary treatment, roll back and forth; in circles of writers with a great deal of temperament, they fairly fly. What in great literatures goes on down below, constituting a not indispensable cellar of the structure, here takes place in the full light of day, what is there a matter of passing interest for a few, here absorbs everyone not less than as a matter of life and death. (DI 194, GW 9:250)

I want to stress now Deleuze and Guattari's use – not reading – of this essay, their misprision of Kafka's already quite idiosyncratic and varied views on minor literature, and shall proceed by way of personal experience. Some time ago, in Philadelphia, I lectured to an audience on Kafka's aphorisms, analysing the shapes of their chiasmi and double helixes. The subject matter was formal, the question period, however, unexpectedly substantial. I was immediately asked, in the spirit of a small nation, for additional information about the character and personality of Kafka – for example, had he played basketball? I replied, no; although he was quite tall (six feet) and supple from exercise and, furthermore, in a remote sense, Czech, living in Prague, he was not a Croatian: it is Dalmatian Croatia that has produced excellent basketball players. This prompted an elderly woman, tired of those fumbling German translations, to ask, 'Well then, can you tell us what Kafka is like in the original Czech?'

This question could have been prompted by her reading of Deleuze and Guattari. Their appropriation of Kafka's essay begins: 'The problem of expression is staked out by Kafka not in an abstract and universal fashion but in relation to those literatures that are considered minor, for example the Jewish literature of Warsaw and Prague.' Note: 'the Jewish literature of Prague'. This is entirely Deleuze and Guattari's invention! In his own essay, of course, Kafka literally wrote 'Czech literature', something of which he was not a part. These critics continue: 'A minor literature doesn't come from a minor language' – but of course it does, for Kafka: it comes from Yiddish and from Czech – 'it is rather that which a minority constructs within a major language' (DG 16). This last point would have come as a great surprise to Kafka – that throughout his life he was at work constructing a Jewish Prague literature, meaning to do so by heightening the idiomatic disparities of Prague German. Deleuze and Guattari assert this thesis via a claim for the dignity of writing in a minor language. 'Using the path that Yiddish opens up to him' – Yiddish, according to Deleuze and Guattari, being 'intermixed with the German language in Czechoslovakia' (*sic*) (DG 20) – 'Kafka takes it in such a way as to convert it into a unique and solitary form of writing' (DG 25). But this idea, even apart from the absurd implication that the German Kafka spoke in the office and café was 'intermixed' with Yiddish, will not do, for it leaves out too baldly the elected influences of Goethe, Hegel and Nietzsche, not to mention Kafka's 'blood relations' Kleist, Grillparzer, Dostoevsky and Flaubert in developing the 'uniqueness and solitude' of his writing. And even if, in Deleuze and Guattari's sense, 'unique and solitary', Kafka's writing would have amounted to a minor literature of one. In the end Deleuze and Guattari substitute the powers of dialect for what in Kafka are more truly the powers of dialectic – and here point up the decline, in their hands, of Benjamin's concept of the dialectical image.

The theory of the dialectical image, a moment of explosive historical meaning, is spelled out in 'Sheaf [*Konvolut*] "N"' of the Arcades project (*Passagenwerk*), where Benjamin writes:

> It is not that what is past casts its light on what is present, or what is present its light on what is past; rather, image is that wherein what has been comes together [*zusammentritt*] in a flash with the now to form a constellation. In other words, image is dialectics at a standstill. For while the relation of the present to the past is purely temporal, the relation of what-has-been to the now is dialectical; not temporal in nature [*Verlauf*] but figural [*bildlich*] . . .[19]

This concept, nourished by Benjamin's understanding of Kafka, has been narrowed, especially under the impact of views on the national revolutions of the 1990s, into an idea of determinative dialect, into the idea of the gesture that resists a dominant political and linguistic power by means of dialect. An ideological image of the dialect undeservedly called 'historical' replaces the idea of the dialectical image. This idea is then turned back onto Kafka with the purpose of colouring him as a Yiddish-Czech political dissident – qualities that are then said to re-emerge in his work written in

19. Walter Benjamin, *The Arcades Project*, trans. Howard Eiland and Kevin Mc-Laughlin, Cambridge: Harvard University Press, 1999, p. 463; in German as 'Konvolut N: Erkenntnistheoretisches, Theorie des Fortschritts', in *Gesammelte Schriften*, ed. Rolf Tiedemann and Hermann Schweppenhäuser, vol. V (*Das Passagenwerk*), N3, 1. For an excellent discussion, see Michael Jennings, *Dialectical Images: Walter Benjamin's Theory of Literary Criticism*, Ithaca, NY, 1987.

German – and stripping him of the universality that an allegedly lazy tradition of criticism has ascribed to him.

Is the concrete universality of the dialectical image to be found in its local colour? I think not. What is truly dialectical in Kafka, as Benjamin suggests, is his *destruction* of metaphors and of the given image. Kafka's 'images' are not properly images – they are not positives. Rather, they are negatives: they are the fission products of the destruction (metamorphosis, deconstruction) of the imagery of standard metaphors. Kafka's explosion of the image suggests the force contained as a history of repressions in each such figurative nucleus. This is quite in line with Benjamin's own perspective, for Kafka's tropes are dialectical in the Benjaminian sense of continually liberating the repressed implications of dead metaphors. This procedure does not require dialect to be carried through.[20]

Deleuze and Guattari confuse an automatic potential in Prague German – as idiom or dialect – with Kafka's *own* German. Kafka wrote, 'As soon as a man comes along who has something primitive about him, so that he does not say: One must take the world as it is . . . but who says: However the world is, I shall stay with my original nature, which I am not about to change to suit what the world regards as good; the moment this word is pronounced, a metamorphosis takes place in the whole of existence' (L 203). (There is in Deleuze and Guattari no such category of 'original nature'.) It is important to note that the word stubbornly pronounced does not have to come from dialect (L 277).

Deleuze and Guattari enthusiastically politicize literature. But it is not so much that Kafka's work, being, allegedly, minor literature, permits of this appropriation as that Deleuze and Guattari are themselves writing in the *ideolect* of minor literature, politicizing wherever they go. This is a feature of life in a minor literature, but it is not true that Kafka's essay defends it.

Deleuze and Guattari deny, in Kafka's name, the subjective aspirations of individuals. Kafka says exactly the opposite: minor literature encourages 'the independence of the individual writer' (DI 192).

I conclude: on the strength of Kafka's views on minor litera-

---

20. See my *Franz Kafka: The Necessity of Form*, New York, 1988, esp. chapters 3 and 10.

ture, no argument can be made for the politicization of literature – for justifying its polemical use in heightening the
adversarial consciousness of being minor and marginal with
respect to a major language or literature. It is true that literature,
for Kafka, 'brings about the unity and solidarity of national consciousness', whence there arises 'the pride and support which
the nation gains for itself in the face of a hostile environment'
(DI 191, GW 9:243) But at what cost to its quality! 'There is [in
minor literature] universal delight in the literary treatment of
petty themes whose scope is not permitted to exceed the capacity
of small enthusiasms and which are sustained by their polemical
prospects and resources' (DI 194, GW 9:250). Kafka does not
teach you that a consciousness of ethnic or dialect-ical peculiarity
increases your chances of building escape routes, across a sense
of oppression, from a hegemonic literature, let alone exploding
its authority.

Reading Deleuze/Guattari on Kafka suggests that you can read
in order to formulate political slogans – that might be useful. Or
you can prefer to close-read texts. That could be politically
vacuous yet still produce a sense of power, in the way, say, that
reading Kafka or a critic like Benjamin reading Kafka gives you a
sense of power. But it is wrong to say that the closely read text
gives authority to political slogans.

Kafka's relation to the traditions of his literary community is
no different in principle from that of other German and European writers who turned for inspiration to non-European sources
(thus Goethe to Persian poetry, Schopenhauer to Sanskrit literature, Yeats and Brecht to No, Pound to Chinese ideograms). This
field covers Kafka's increasing sensitivity to the themes of Jewish
mysticism and the argumentative gestures of the Talmud, as these
come to him through Yiddish literature from the East, as well as
his attraction to Lao-tzu.

In general, his relation to his literary past is marked neither by
anxiety nor by querulousness – nor by excessive playfulness. He is,
first of all, prone to be awed by a consciousness of the specialness
of his gift. 'The tremendous world that I have in my head. But
how free myself and free it without being torn to pieces.'[21] He

---

21. 'And a thousand times rather be torn to pieces than retain it in me or bury
it. That, indeed, is why I am here, that is quite clear to me' (DI 288).

describes a persona of himself: 'All that he does seems to him, it is true, extraordinarily new, but also, because of the incredible spate of new things, extraordinarily amateurish' (GW 263–4). Kafka is eager to discover in other writers comparable passions; he searches not so much for mastery and guidance as something sharable in them, upon which his own nightmares can be reflected. He is strengthened by the consciousness that others have suffered even more than he for the same great cause. It is wonderful when another's strangeness can be less strange than he is to himself. The danger is not so much that other writers prove more massively truthful than he as that they might be trivial, bad or irrelevant – and he is once again condemned to selfhood. He is less bent on fighting off the supposed knowledge that the great hold on humanity of canonical writers excludes him – robs him of his right to 'settle' – than he is anxious to greet the spirit of other writers to whom he might raise a flag, like Robinson, considering them terra firma and in principle a harbour for his wandering bark. The claim of Deleuze and Guattari that Kafka is a deterritorializer of the territorializations of the cultural masters who oppress him flows from a contemporary paranoia insensitive to the finer shades of Kafka's literary schizophrenia, which is to say, to the 'monstrosity' he called literature.[22]

---

22. 'What *is* literature? Where does it come from? What use is it? What questionable things! Add to this questionableness the further questionableness of what you say, and what you get is a monstrosity' (DF 246).

14

'Rhythmical Knots':[1]
The World of English Poetry

Bruce Clunies Ross

> Everywhere in the world its syntax is being bent (not broken), its lexicon expanded with new, exciting entries, its semiotic range widened and deepened beyond the ken – and control – of its native speakers.
>
> Niyi Osundare[2]

In 1912, when artists of James Joyce's generation were turning 30 and Ezra Pound issued *Ripostes* with its appendix of five short lyrics comprising the complete poetical works of T. E. Hulme, the *Oxford Book of Victorian Verse* appeared for the first time. Its elusive introduction in the mandarin style of the Edwardians defined the Victorian age as the period from 1835 until the year of the book's publication. Its editor, Sir Arthur Quiller-Couch, did not attempt to characterize Victorian poetry but made a generous selection of 779 poems published between the limiting dates. He included dialect poems by William Barnes, translations from Sanskrit and

---

1. Adapted from Mallarmé, 'La Musique et les Lettres', lecture delivered at Oxford, 1 March 1894; discussed by Roberto Calasso in *Literature and the Gods*, New York: Vintage, 2002, pp. 123–41.

2. 'Yorùbá Thought: English Words: A Poet's Journey through the Tunnel of Two Tongues', in Stewart Brown, ed., *Kiss and Quarrel: Yorùbá/English Strategies of Mediation*, Birmingham: Birmingham University African Studies Series, no. 5, 2000, pp. 15–31.

Gaelic as well as poems with lines in Irish and Welsh and a mass of writing by English poets, some of them undeservedly forgotten. Scattered amongst these were poems by Emily Dickinson, Ralph Waldo Emerson, Bret Harte, Oliver Wendell Holmes, William Dean Howells, Henry Wadsworth Longfellow, James Russell Lowell, Edgar Allan Poe, Henry David Thoreau, Walt Whitman and John Greenleaf Whittier, without any indication that these were American poets who might consider they were part of a separate tradition. The anthology also included poems by the Australians Henry Kendell and Adam Lindsay Gordon, by the migrant Canadian Bliss Carman who worked in the United States, and by the Anglo-Australian Henry Kingsley. It was a great retrospective selection from more than seventy years of verse, but its closing pages included a metrically irregular song from *Chamber Music* (1907) by James Joyce and two intricately rhymed pieces by Ezra Pound, rich in the poetic diction he was about to denounce.

There is no suggestion in the *Oxford Book of Victorian Verse* that poetry in English might be differentiated according to national or regional criteria or confined to poems in a specific version of the English language. It represents English poetry coherently, though its limitations have become obvious and would have been apparent at the time to readers in the colonies and dominions. The American selection is restricted to work by important poets, whereas the selections by major English poets are supported by a mass of work by minor writers. The haphazard selection of poems by Australians and Canadians does not suggest an uninformed attempt to represent poetry in those dominions so much as an idea of English verse comparable to the images that appeared at the Diamond Jubilee of Queen Victoria surveying her soldiers in exotic uniforms. The inclusive range of the anthology reflects an imperial attitude to poetry in the colonized world.

The *Oxford Book of Victorian Verse* carried its integral idea of English poetry into the age of modernism and decolonization and was not replaced by a new and very different selection (edited by Christopher Ricks) until 1987. By that time American poetry was established as an independent tradition,[3] and verse in English was

---

3. English and American poetic traditions were carefully differentiated in two important mid-century anthologies: Donald Hall, Robert Pack and Louis Simpson, eds, *The New Poets of England and America*, New York: Meridian, 1957, and Al

being represented in specific regional and national anthologies which proliferated in the last quarter of the century.[4] As poetry in English spread around the world and diverged into separate traditions, the time for a comprehensive anthology seemed to have passed.

The publication in 1993 of an anthology of British and Irish verse, deliberately entitled *The New Poetry*,[5] after Al Alvarez's 1962 volume, invites a reconsideration of this issue. In the words of William Scammell, cited in the introduction, it reveals 'a flourishing contemporary poetic culture' which is also extremely diverse. This is not unprecedented; it is a reversion to a 'poetic culture' similiar to that which existed in England in the Middle Ages, as any anthology of fourteenth- or fifteenth-century verse would show. The difference is that it would have been unnecessary at that time to specify the location of English. The recent anthology demonstrates that contemporary poetry in Britain and Ireland is a multifarious art created in a language which exists as a cluster of variants, just as it was in the Middle Ages, but its range now extends beyond linguistic variations in Wales, Ireland, Scotland and England to include affiliations with the postcolonial world and the United States as well as interactions with non-European languages. Its diversity reflects the global spread of English, and its vitality is related to the fact that it is composed not in the centre of English poetry but in a globally devolved network where influences are dispersed. *The New Poetry* thus forms an instructive contrast to the *Oxford Book of Victorian Verse*. The Victorian anthology exemplifies an imperial conception of the English language

---

Alvarez, ed., *The New Poetry*, Harmondsworth: Penguin, 1962. All references to the *Oxford Book of Victorian Verse* are to the original 1912 selection.

4. For example, Wole Soyinka, ed., *Poems of Black Africa*, London: Secker & Warburg, 1975; R. Parthasarathy, ed., *Ten Twentieth-Century Indian Poets*, Delhi: Oxford University Press, 1976; Les Murray, ed., *The New Oxford Book of Australian Verse*, Melbourne: Oxford University Press, 1986; Miriama Evans, Harvey McQueen and Ian Wedde, eds, *Contemporary New Zealand Poetry / Nga Kupu Titohu o Aotearoa*, Auckland: Penguin, 1989; Dennis Lee, ed., *The New Canadian Poets*, Toronto: McClelland & Stewart, 1985; Paula Burnett, ed., *The Penguin Book of Caribbean Verse*, Harmondsworth: Penguin, 1986; Albert Wendt, ed., *Nuanua: Pacific Writing since 1980*, Auckland: Auckland University Press, 1995.

5. Michael Hulse, David Kennedy and David Morley, eds, *The New Poetry*, Newcastle upon Tyne: Bloodaxe Books, 1994. All references to *The New Poetry* hereafter are to this anthology. See also the critical companion to this anthology by David Kennedy, *New Relations: The Refashioning of British Poetry, 1980–94*, Bridgend: Seren (Poetry Wales Press), 1996.

and its poetry; the selections in the recent anthology assume that English is not a national but a world language, and reveal that contemporary poetry in Britain and Ireland is a fractal of English-language poetry altogether.

This compels a reconsideration of poetry in English as a coherent phenomenon, rather than as a tradition splitting into independent national and regional poetries. The fundamental problem with the latter approach is that poems and poetries have their existence in languages, not in nations, and English in its latest evolution as a world language is an extended range of variants comprising a single language. The limits of the range may be marked by creoles and pidgins which are difficult for the majority of speakers to comprehend, but within these limits there are few obstacles to comprehension across the range. The global currency of English is a good reason for supposing that it is not dislocating as Latin was. Major poetic compositions, such as the works of Whitman, explicitly imbued with ideas of nation, do not constitute counter-examples to the proposition that poems belong to languages, not to nations. Whitman's poetry, with all its rhythmic and idiomatic distinction, is part of English, as nineteenth-century readers and our Victorian anthologist acknowledged. The fact that poems may be inspired by ideas of nation no more requires the construction of national literary traditions than poems inspired by theosophy require the construction of a theosophical literary tradition.

The construction of national traditions within literature in the English language during the decades between the *Oxford Book of Victorian Verse* (1912) and *The New Poetry* (1993) counteracted the literary hierarchies imposed by empire and revealed the significance of works it relegated. It ceases to be useful, however, if it sequesters poems in national categories which are assumed, somehow, to account for them, and it neglects the creative influence of interactions across boundaries permeated by language. It also introduces distracting border disputes. A number of the poets whose work is included in *The New Poetry* are represented in other national and regional anthologies,[6] though they work in Britain or Ireland and in most cases have grown up there. The spread of the English language not only created distinct communities whose

---

6. For example, of Caribbean, Indian, Irish or Scottish verse.

histories (often relegated) shaped national and regional literatures, but also created an extended field defined by the migration
of ideas and literary practices and of speakers and writers using
idiomatic variants of the same language.

Postcolonial analyses of writing in English envisage this as a
centred field, at least in origin, and focus attention on interactions between centre and periphery. These approaches reveal how
conventions of literary representation and categories such as
'English literature'[7] can sustain imperial interests and how writers
from the periphery work against them, which is enlightening and
valuable, but they have limitations beyond the obvious one of
adequately defining 'centre' and 'periphery'. The main problem
is that the empire was not fully controlled from the centre. Its
growth was haphazard and not always consistent with imperial
ideology. This was particularly the case with language and the
arts, which nowhere evolved in accordance with the doctrines of
imperial education. For example, penal servitude in New South
Wales was not intended to 'plant in it those happy arts which
alone constitute the pre-eminence and dignity of other
countries'.[8] On the contrary, the idea was to remove degenerate
elements as far as possible from centres of polite civilization. Nor
were highland clearances, which drove Scots, including Gaelic
speakers, to the United States, Canada, Australia and New Zealand, motivated by imperial ideas. As a result of both, however,
language variants and the oral cultures associated with them
which were marginal or relegated in Britain became central when
they were transplanted in the empire.

The empire and the global network which succeeded it evolved
through movements in many directions impelled by a variety of
motives, some of which were contradictory. It was a sphere of
missionary activity, a dumping ground for criminals, a haven for
victims of poverty and persecution, and notoriously the scene of
African enslavement in America and the Caribbean. In the course
of empire, people from South Asia were re-settled in Africa and

---

7. Or even simply 'literature'; for a complex discussion of this issue see Tim
Reiss, *Against Autonomy*, Stanford, CA: Stanford University Press, 2002.

8. Watkin Tench, an officer in the first convict fleet, reflecting on its departure
from the last outpost of settlement, Cape Town, for a place completely unknown
to the voyagers (innocently called by Tench 'a remote and barbarous land'), in his
Narrative of the Expedition to Botany Bay, London, 1789.

the islands of the Caribbean and Pacific, while Pacific Islanders were press-ganged into labour in eastern Australia; the gospel was carried to Jamaica by Afro-American missionaries and to Micronesia by Polynesians. These and other tangential movements, crossing influences from the imperial centre, formed a complex web of interactions which determined the varied development of language and poetry in the extended English-speaking world. English was not transposed as a standard language, but in different variants. Its development in new settings was sometimes influenced by close association with other imperial languages, especially Spanish, Dutch and French,[9] and it was everywhere imposed on local languages which often left traces as they were obliterated.

These movements were not tangential to the people who experienced them. Whether forced or voluntary, they involved exile from centres (and often languages) somewhere else, which might be in Scotland, Ireland, Wales, India, West Africa or an island in the Pacific. They formed the basis for a polycentric devolution of the English-speaking domain, which became more apparent in the wake of British decolonization and recolonization by the United States. The accelerated global spread of English was no doubt influenced by American imperialism, but it does not explain the diverse development of the English language and its poetry in the second half of the twentieth century. This happened because the range of linguistic transpositions and interactions enlarged the poetic potential of the English language. According to Les Murray, writing of Australia, it gave poets 'the essentially poetic job' of 'recasting' their discursive inheritance in a new world of settlement[10] and in the process re-centring a variant of the language. Many of Murray's poems 'recasting' the European inheritance in the antipodes, including those on the seasons and months in Australia, could be cited to illustrate this process.[11] Similar impulses are at work in the poetry

---

9. In the Caribbean, for example. English supplanted Spanish and brief phase of French in Trinidad; English and a French patois are both current on the island of St Lucia.

10. Les Murray, *The Australian Year* (with photographs by Peter Solness), Sydney and London: Angus & Robertson, 1985, p. 5.

11. For example, 'The Grassfire Stanzas', in *The People's Otherworld*, Sydney: Angus & Robertson, 1983, or *The Idyll Wheel: Cycle of a Year at Bunyah, New South Wales, April 1986–April 1987*, Canberra: Officina Brindebella, 1989.

of Derek Walcott, Kamau Brathwaite and writers recasting the double inheritance of Africa and Europe in the Caribbean. Interactions with other languages in the extensive range of the English-speaking world which is polyglot have also been productive for poets in Africa, India and Oceania.[12] When all this is taken into account, there is enough to indicate that contemporary poetry in English is not centred anywhere in Britain or the United States of America. From the perspective of poetry, the English-speaking world is polycentric.

This holds even for poetry composed in Britain, as *The New Poetry* demonstrates, and also for the United States, where poetry currently exemplifies diverse regional and ethnic influences. Contemporary poetry in English, regardless of where it is composed, forms a reticulated system. Its nodes can be arranged in various ways, to conform to theories of national or postcolonial literature, and it can be represented on the map of world poetry, as W. N. Herbert pointedly observed in Scots:

> Vass tracts o land ur penntit reaid tae shaw
> Englan kens naethen aboot um. Ireland's
> bin shuftit tae London, whaur
> oafficis o thi Poetry Sock occupeh fehv
> squeer mile. Seamus Heany occupehs three
> o thon.
> . . .
> In this scenario Eh'm a bittern stoarm aft Ulm.[13]

The poem wittily illustrates how poetic maps can be deceptive. The ear is a safer guide into the tangle 'where nothing is diminished by perspective'.[14] Listen to this:

> In idle August while the sea soft,
> And leaves of brown islands stick to the rim
> Of this Caribbean, I blow out the light
> By the dreamless face of Maria Concepcion
> To ship as a seaman on the schooner *Flight.*

---

12. The term introduced by the leading writer of the Pacific, Albert Wendt, in 'The New Oceania', *Mana*, vol. I, no. 1, 1976, reprinted in G. Amirthanayagam, ed., *Writers in East–West Encounter: New Cultural Bearings*, London: Macmillan, 1982.

13. 'Mappamundi', *Forked Tongue*, Bloodaxe Books, 1994, anthologized in *The New Poetry*, p. 291.

14. Les Murray, 'Equanimity', in *Equanimities*, Copenhagen: Razorback Press, n.d., and *The People's Otherworld*, Sydney: Angus & Robertson, 1983.

These haunting rhythms, which open 'The Schooner *Flight*' from Derek Walcott's tenth book of poems,[15] recall a poem composed in the West Midlands of England six centuries before:

> In a somer seson whan soft was the sonne
> I shope me in shroudes as I a shepe were;
> In habite as an heremite unholy of workes
> Went wyde in this world wondres to here.[16]

The prologue to *Piers Plowman* (of which these are the opening lines) preserved the metres of alliterative verse through centuries when English prosody skipped on metrical feet of regularly alternating strong and weak accents. It continued to reverberate in the ears of later poets and readers, perhaps because its distinctive verbal music and comparatively smooth adagio movement set it apart from the emphatic consonantal chant of much alliterative poetry in Old and Middle English, and therefore sounded less archaic.

Walcott's poem is no doubt inspired by the Plowman's alliterative music, but after the allusive first line the echo is mainly rhythmical. There is a similar reflective movement sustained by alliteration, assonance, informal phonemic patterns and modulations (the placing of unvoiced 's'; the sequence '-st', '-ft', 'st-', for example) and rhyme (or pararhyme), but Walcott honours Langland by improvising a different music on the rhythm launched by the opening allusion. In *Piers Plowman* alliteration is metrical. In 'The Schooner *Flight*' it is musical; a component in the complex evolving acoustics of the poem which marks the accents informally. Alliterative verse in Middle English, particularly as it was used in *Piers Plowman*, was less systematic than in Old English with its inflected grammar, but Walcott takes this freedom much further. What follows from the allusive opening is a verse line of four accents with a varying number of unaccented syllables similar to alliterative verse, but without the regular patterns of alliteration across the cesura; 'with their big house, big car, big-time bohl-bohl' (1, line 31), is an exaggerated exception. The rhythms of 'The Schooner *Flight*' are frequently marked by irregular allitera-

---

15. *The Star-Apple Kingdom*, New York: Farrar Strauss Giroux, 1979.
16. William Langland, *Piers Plowman*, The Prologue and Passus I–VII of the B text as found in Bodleian MS, Laud 581, edited with notes and glossary by J. A. W. Bennett, Oxford: Clarendon Press, 1972.

tion, but other indications, such as assonance, as in 'stick to the rim', are used, and sometimes syntactical stress is sufficient to maintain a predominately accentual metre.[17] Its irregular movement is introduced through the adjacent stresses on the alliterating monosyllables of the first line ending. The consonants and vowels of 'séa sóft' (echoing Langland's 'seson') flow smoothly into each other and their duration may be extended at will until stopped by the dental 't'. This slurs and slows the rhythm, in a poetic equivalent of rubato, to produce an onomatopoetic suggestion of lapping waves.

However, the alliterating monosyllables at the end of the first line are not there simply for their music. They have a combinative function, for the omission of the copula in 'sea soft' cues a vernacular grammar and introduces the idiom of the sailor-poet Shabine, the persona of the poem. This is developed in the lines following those quoted above:

> Out in the yard turning grey in the dawn,
> I stood like a stone and nothing else move
> but the cold sea rippling like galvanize
> and the nail holes of stars in the sky roof,
> till a wind start to interfere with the trees.
> I pass me dry neighbour sweeping she yard
> as I went downhill, and I nearly said:
> 'Sweep soft, you witch, 'cause she don't sleep hard,'
> but the bitch look through me like I was dead.

Vernacular speech is composed here into verbal music. The passage is not an attempt to represent creole speech directly (except in the quoted line), as is the case in a few of Walcott's earlier poems.[18] Rather, elements of the creole, particularly its uninflected grammar and samples of its diction, are positioned through alliteration, assonance and rhyme to set up rhythms and sound patterns which open the range of local speech and carry Shabine's voice through the eleven sections of the poem. Its music is founded on accentual verse as it functioned in Middle English poetry, before the establishment of the prosodic system derived from French, Italian and classical sources which became

---

17. The short lyrical fourth section 'The *Flight*, Passing Blanchisseuse' is an exception.

18. For example, chapter VI of 'Tales of the Islands', in *In a Green Night*, 1962.

orthodox from about the middle of the sixteenth century. This orthodoxy obscured the dialectal variety of English verse as it had existed in the Middle Ages, and relegated non-standard dialects to popular, comic or characteristic verses. One effect of this was to deny a full poetic range to English as it developed in the Caribbean and other regions where the language was transported through colonization. Walcott's recovery of accentual metre in 'The Schooner *Flight*' (by no means the first) indicates that this metrical system, which derives from old Germanic sources, is embedded in the language, rather than imposed upon it, and, unlike the orthodox system, is available for English in all its variants.

Walcott's contemporary, Ted Hughes, might have given a slightly different account of this. In 'Myths, Metres, Rhythms',[19] an essay written in response to the criticism that some of his lines were 'unsayable', he develops an argument for the existence of two musical traditions in English verse: the orthodox system based on certain arrangements of stressed and unstressed syllables in metrical feet, whose names confusingly derive from classical prosody; and the old system which evolved in the Germanic languages, based on poetic lines of any number of syllables strung on four accents divided by a caesura.[20] His examples illustrate how the orthodox system matches the rhythms of conversation, whereas the old system preserves the connection between poetry and song or chant. He also points out that accentual-syllabic prosody based on poetic feet did not supplant the older accentual system, but relegated it, where it was kept alive in popular verses. At the end of the essay, Hughes deploys an allegory of the two systems coexisting in a contentious marriage, from which English poetry springs. From about the time of Edmund Spenser (1552?–99) until around the time of the *Oxford Book of Victorian Verse*, the orthodox system was dominant and sometimes treated as if it were exclusive, but the subdued presence of the older system can be felt in many poems and occasionally regained dominance, in Blake's prophetic books, Coleridge's *Christabel* and the 'sprung

---

19. In *Winter Pollen: Occasional Prose*, ed. William Scammell, London: Faber, 1994, pp. 310–72.
20. Lines of three accents occur in popular verse, for example the second and fourth lines of 'Baa baa black sheep'. They are metrically equivalent, though the second contains five syllables and the fourth only three.

rhythms' created by Gerard Manley Hopkins, for example. Used freely, as by Whitman, it founded verse in American English and, partly through the growth and influence of American poetry, became prominent again in the twentieth century.

In the same essay, Hughes argues that cadences formed according to the orthodox system were particularly adapted to what became the dominant accent of English and the practice of educated conversation and writing. This was a contingent development: the evidence of rhymes or recordings suggests that Wordsworth, Coleridge, Keats and Tennyson, for example, spoke with different regional accents, but their poems were 'dubbed' into the elocutionary realm of 'Received Pronunciations', as Tony Harrison's nicely spoken teacher explains in 'Them & [uz]: I':

> 4 words only of *mi 'art aches* and . . . 'Mine's broken,
> you barbarian, T.W.!' *He* was nicely spoken
> 'Can't have our glorious heritage done to death!'
>
> I played the Drunken Porter in *Macbeth.*
>
> 'Poetry's the speech of kings. You're one of those
> Shakespeare gives the comic bits to: prose!
> All poetry (even Cockney Keats?) you see
> 's been dubbed by [ʌs] into RP,
> Received Pronunciation, please believe [ʌs]
> Your speech is in the hands of the Receivers.'[21]

The diversification of English around the world did not follow the ideology of Received Pronunciation, though that may have been the privileged mode of speech. However, the triumph of English imperialism which initiated the process did coincide with the dominance of the orthodox system of poetic metre, and this is usually regarded as a constraint on the development of English poetry on a world-wide scale. According to this argument, distinctive regional and national modes of speech were unfitted for anything other than comic or trivial verse, unless they were neutralized and brought into line with what were assumed to be approved or correct accents, such as Received Pronunciation. Literary Australians, Canadians, Trinidadians, South Africans or

---

21. *From 'The School of Eloquence and Other Poems'*, London: Rex Collings, 1978. Quoted here from Tony Harrison, *Selected Poems*, 3rd edn, Harmondsworth: Penguin, 1987, p. 122.

Americans might, on this account, be expected to have in addition to their local accents a special one for composing and reading poetry. The recordings of T. S. Eliot suggest that this might have been the case; those of Ezra Pound decidedly do not.

Approaches along these lines conform to postcolonial theories of literature, but they do not allow for differences in the transmission and development of English in various parts of the world, and they fail to account adequately for the creativeness of its poets, from Whitman to Walcott and Les Murray. The richness and diversity of their work suggests another approach: that the transplantation of English around the world freed poetry from the constraints of the orthodox metrical system and opened up possibilities for new developments. In some cases, as the example of 'The Schooner *Flight*' illustrates, these were combined with the revival of poetic modes which had been dormant or marginalized.

The approach suggested here can be illustrated by reference to the work of Whitman. He may have imagined himself as the voice of America, but by the end of the nineteenth century he had become a poet of the world. His work, which broke completely with orthodox metrics and introduced a verbal music founded on American speech, made an impact on poets wherever English was spoken, and his influence transcended the boundaries of language and art. A number of late nineteenth- and early twentieth-century composers not only set his words but composed instrumental pieces inspired by his poetry.[22] The inclusion of selections of his work[23] and that of other poets now considered American in the *Oxford Book of Victorian Verse* indicates that, despite his example and declared aims, a separate American poetry had not been defined. At the time, Whitman's work was seen as innovative within a loosely coherent tradition rather than as diverging into a separate national one. His irregular cadences opened up the potential of poetry in English which his later seclusion in an American tradition obscures.

The development of English-language poetry in Australia illus-

---

22. For example, *Sea Drift* (1903–4) by Frederick Delius; a choral rhapsody by Samuel Coleridge-Taylor (date unknown); *Ode to Death* (1919) by Gustav Holst; several works by Percy Grainger; and John Alden Carpenter's *Symphonic Poem* (1933).

23. Among them 'Out of the Cradle Endless Rocking', blithely entitled 'The Brown Bird' by the editor.

trates this approach in another way. The title of first Australian poet was claimed by a judge of the Supreme Court in New South Wales, whose name actually was Barron Field, and his *First Fruits of Australian Poetry* (1819), consisting of two poems, confirms its serendipity. Barron Field later claimed that poetry was impossible in the antipodean environment,[24] but he overlooked the street ballads and popular verses transported with the convicts and adapted to life in the penal settlement. The authors or adapters of these ballads remain anonymous, except for one, who introduced himself in some of his poems. He is remembered as Frank the Poet, author of the ballad 'Moreton Bay', which uses the rhythms of an Irish folk-song once set by Beethoven, and of *A Convict's Tour to Hell*, a Dantesque satire of 228 lines in rhyming tetrametres.[25] The popular verse of the convicts gave rise to a lively written ballad tradition, which by the end of the nineteenth century was the prominent strand in Australian poetry. As a result of transportation, it escaped relegation by orthodox metrics and was available to influence developments in contemporary poetry. Les Murray refers to the presence in Australia of a double poetic tradition with what he calls 'formal' and 'vernacular' aspects.[26] Colonial and postcolonial approaches to literature focus attention on the formal aspects such as the concept of verse weakly introduced by Barron Field, but creative impulses in English poetry often flow from vernacular speech. Poetic developments in Australia can be compared to the impulses which inspired the *Lyrical Ballads* (1798) or the ideas about modern poetry advocated by Ezra Pound. The distinctive quality of Murray's own poetry derives from its combination of the vernacular with formality.

This is not to deny the spread throughout the English-speaking world of canonical ideas of literature and their association with imperialism, though the extensive evidence for this does not support a simple opposition between colonizers and the colonized. The complexity of the colonial position runs through all

---

24. *Geographical Memoirs in News South Wales*, London, 1825. I discussed Field's argument and its implication in 'Les Murray and the Poetry of Australia', in R. P. Draper, ed., *The Literature of Region and Nation*, London: Macmillian, 1989, pp. 209–12.

25. Probably the Irish convict Francis Macnamara, according to recent research. Les Murray included *A Convict's Tour to Hell* in his *New Oxford Book of Australian Verse*.

26. *The Australian Year*, pp. 5–6.

Derek Walcott's work and is the main topic of his essay 'What the Twilight Says': 'We knew the literature of empires, Greek, Roman, British, through their essential classics; and both the patois of the street and the language of the classroom hid the elation of discovery. If there was nothing, there was everything to be made.'[27] Walcott's island of St Lucia was bilingual and the language of the street was a French patois, but the point at issue is that everywhere English was spoken there were disjunctions between the vernacular and the 'literature of empires' and 'language of the classroom'. Since poetry (with marginal exceptions) is founded on speech, it was 'recast' (to use Les Murray's term) wherever these disjunctions occurred, with results which were akin to, though not the same as, creolization. As the quotation from Walcott's essay suggests, this was a potential inspiration, not surprisingly, as it is one of the recurrent processes through which English poetry has evolved from its beginnings in creolized Anglo-Saxon.

These issues are topically as well as formally embodied in 'The Schooner *Flight*' through the persona Shabine, 'a red nigger' with a 'sound colonial education' and 'Dutch, nigger and English in me'. He is a sailor who works around the Caribbean and a poet whose imagination encompasses its history and stories. The double vision alleged to be a symptom of a colonized mind turns out be a poetic gift; being colonial enables him 'to know the difference, / to know the pain of history words contain'. A preoccupation with words recurs throughout this voyaging poem and at one point its art is described in the 'common speech' of the sailor:

> When I write
> this poem, each phrase go be soaked in salt;
> I go draw and knot every line as tight
> as ropes in this rigging; in simple speech
> my common language go be the wind,
> my pages the sails of the schooner *Flight*.

This explicit suggestion that the poem is a new departure in its use of the vernacular was noticed in important essays acknowledging its achievement by two of Walcott's contemporaries: Seamus

---

27. *What the Twilight Says: Essays*, London: Faber, 1998, p. 4.

Heaney in 'The Murmur of Malvern' and Joseph Brodsky in 'The Sound of the Tide',[28] titles that reflect the haunting movement of 'The Schooner *Flight*'. Heaney calls the poem 'epoch-making', notably in its 'language woven out of dialect and literature', and, as the title of his essay suggests, he examines the connection with *Piers Plowman* and points out that Walcott's 'fidelity to West Indian speech leads him not away from but right into the genius of English'. Brodsky outlines an over-arching argument that civilizations and empires reach a point when they are no longer sustainable as centralized organizations. When the centre cannot hold, cultures and languages live on (if at all) through impulses from the outskirts. Walcott's poetic achievement illustrates this decentring process and Brodsky suggests that it would be as 'myopic' to call him 'a West Indian poet' as to 'call the Saviour a Galilean'. He is a 'great poet of the English language'.

The devolution Brodsky describes must result in polycentric organizations if it does not lead to annihilating fragmentation, but the implications are not spelt out. The process is envisaged through another metaphor: 'Contrary to popular belief, the outskirts are not where the world ends – they are precisely where it unravels. That affects a language no less than an eye.'

Another great poet of the English language, Kamau Brathwaite, also recognized 'The Schooner *Flight*' as Walcott's 'first major nation language effort' in *History of the Voice: The Development of Nation Language in Anglophone Caribbean Poetry*.[29] He takes a different line from Heaney and Brodsky and argues for a distinct Caribbean poetic language against what he regards as the inappropriateness of the imperial pentameter. His argument is compatible with the idea that English poetry has a double musical tradition and that it is devolving as Brodsky suggested, but it sequesters Walcott's poem in the Caribbean while acknowledging its connection with *Piers Plowman*.

The History of the Voice outlines a case which demonstrates that, although 'The Schooner *Flight*' was a new departure for Walcott, it was not unprecedented in Caribbean poetry. Brathwaite himself, among the many other poets discussed in his essay, was

---

28. Heaney, *The Government of the Tongue*, London: Faber, 1988, pp. 23–9; Brodsky, *Less Than One*, Harmondsworth, Penguin, 1987, pp. 164–75.

29. A lecture delivered at Harvard in 1978 and later published with a full, classified bibliography. London and Port of Spain: New Beacon Books, 1984.

composing freely rhythmic poetry drawing on oral and written traditions and the African musical heritage in the Caribbean. In fact, the 1970s were notable for developments in vernacular poetics in various parts of the anglophone world. According to a note in *History of the Voice*, 'The Schooner *Flight*' was first published in the *Trinidad and Tobago Review* in May 1978 and read by the author in Port of Spain the same year. Brathwaite's *Mother Poem* had been published in 1977; the first poems of Tony Harrison's sequence *From 'The School of Eloquence'* in 1978 and Les Murray's 'Buladelah-Taree Holiday Song Cycle' in 1975. Major essays by these and other poets engaged in similar developments were published in the same decade.[30]

In the poems by Walcott, Brathwaite, Harrison and Murray, a poetic language is created from the speech of the place in which it is centred: Trinidad and the Caribbean Sea, Barbados, Leeds, and the country between Bulahdelah[31] and Taree in northern New South Wales. 'The Buladelah-Taree Holiday Song Cycle' and 'The Schooner *Flight*' are comparably large poems with moving perspectives, and both go beyond the representation of speech to create poetic languages out of the sounds and cadences of their different vernaculars. Where Walcott does this in freely alliterated accentual verse, Murray uses very long lines derived from a translation of an Aboriginal poem from Arnhem Land.

> The people are eating dinner in that country north of Legge's
>   Lake;
> behind flywire and venetians, in the dimmed cool, town people
>   eat Lunch.
> Plying knives and forks with a peek-in sound, with a tuck-in sound
> they are thinking about relatives and inventory, they are talking
>   about customers and visitors.
> In the country of memorial iron, on the creek-facing hills there,
> they are thinking about bean plants, and rings of tank water, of
>   growing a pumpkin by Christmas;
> rolling a cigarette, they say thoughtfully Yes, and their companion
>   nods, considering.

---

30. Derek Walcott, 'What the Twilight Says', 1970; 'The Muse of History', 1974; Brathwaite, *History of the Voice*; Tony Harrison, 'The Inkwell of Dr. Agrippa', 1971; Les Murray, 'The Human-Hair Thread', 1977; Albert Wendt, 'The New Oceania', 1976.

31. The spelling on maps. Murray uses a variant.

Fresh sheets have been spread and tucked tight, childhood rooms
    have been seen to,
for this is the season of the holiday when the children return with
    their children

These long lines have a tautness completely different from
those of Whitman, for example, and this is the result of the
remarkable handling of the accents. Each line has four, five or six
fixed accents and some extra moveable or suspended accents. For
example, in the first line there are fixed accents on the first
syllable of 'péople', 'dínner' and 'cóuntry'; the accents on 'éating'
and 'nórth' can be applied or suspended and the two monsylla-
bles at the end of the line can take two accents or one can be
suspended, and the other placed on either word. The same
applies to the two monosyllables at the end of the second line.
The rhythms are flexible, but far from loose. Suspending some of
the accents smoothly accelerates the movement of the verse;
applying them introduces an ambling movement, and both are
appropriate. The compound rhythms are established through
syntax, syllabic juncture and phonetic patterns, as in Walcott's
poem, but Murray's musical effects rarely draw attention to themselves. The syntax, phrasing and diction are that of a yarning
voice making sense, but the phonological details are finely controlled. In addition to assonance and alliteration, Murray pays
attention to the closing sounds of words and syllables, as in
'dimmed cool' and 'tucked tight', to the distribution of phonemes, such as [k] and [g], to vocalic and consonantal combinations, as in 'bean plants, and rings of tank water', and to the
juxtaposition of monosyllabic and polysyllabic words.

The long lines, compound rhythms and understated musical
effects of the poem transform the drawl, falling cadences and
tendency to garrulousness of Australian speech into poetic
language, but this, remarkably, is achieved by modelling it on an
Aboriginal poem, or rather a translation by Ronald Berndt of the
Song Cycle of the Moon Bone of the Wonguri-Mandjigai people of
north-eastern Arnhem Land.[32] The translation inevitably rigidifies
the text of a song-poem which no doubt varies in performance.
Murray's *Song Cycle* follows the thirteen-part form of Berndt's

---

32. Murray included Berndt's translation in *The New Oxford Book of Australian Verse*.

translation and, like the Aboriginal cycle, maps a region and names its places. It also restores the sacredness of 'holiday' by suggesting parallels between holiday driving and the Aboriginal practice of revisiting spirit places in the land. The poem, in fact, is related to Murray's theory that the nature of Australia induces a convergence between the cultures of the people inhabiting it.[33]

The syntax of present participles in Murray's poem develops an aspect of the translation which presumably represents an inflection of the very different Aboriginal language, and its prominent use of rhythmic and acoustic repetitions is characteristic of song poetry. In an essay on his relation to Aboriginal Australia and the writing of the 'Buladelah-Taree Holiday Song Cycle', Murray reveals an understanding of Aboriginal poetics derived from the two great experts at the time.[34] Here, as elsewhere, he referred to Aboriginal song poetry as the 'senior' poetic tradition in Australia and the Wanguri-Mandjigai *Song Cycle of the Moon Bone* as the greatest poem composed in the country. Murray acknowledges that he was not the first Australian poet inspired by Aboriginal poetry, but the convergence of Aboriginal and European poetics in the idea of his *Song Cycle* and formation of its language is an innovation comparable with Walcott's use of creole.

Around the time of 'The Schooner *Flight*' and 'The Buladelah-Taree Holiday Song Cycle', similar developments were occurring in England. Poetic devolution had begun with the definition of Anglo-Irish, Scots and Anglo-Welsh poetry with results which were repeated whenever claims were staked for national poetic traditions in English. The work of a few writers could not be contained and many more were marginalized. Yeats kept his place as a major English poet and could not be secluded in an Irish tradition, though a recent book claims he was a postcolonial Irish poet.[35] Patrick Kavanagh, on the other hand, a major influence on Seamus Heaney, on the Anglo-Welsh poet R. S. Thomas, and, if not an influence, a forerunner of Les Murray, was sequestered

---

33. Outlined in his essay 'The Human-Hair Thread', *Meanjin* (Melbourne), vol. 36, no. 4, 1977. Reprinted in *Persistence in Folly*, Melbourne: Sirius Books, 1984, pp. 4–30 and *The Paperbark Tree*, Manchester: Carcanet, 1992, pp. 71–99.

34. T. G. H. Strehlow's monumental *Songs of Central Australia*, Sydney & Robertson, 1971, and Ronald Berndt's *Love Songs of Arnhem Land*, Melbourne: Nelson, 1976. The essay was 'The Human-Hair Thread'. See preceding footnote.

35. Jahan Ramazani, *The Hybrid Muse: Postcolonial Poetry in English*, Chicago: University of Chicago Press, 2001.

as an Irish poet, probably because of his success in forming a poetic language from English as spoken in Ireland. Similarly, the poetry of Hugh McDiarmid has been marginalized as Scottish, a tradition with strong claims because of its antiquity. In the fifteenth century, before the nationalization of literature, it produced in Dunbar and Henryson the major poets in the language they referred to as 'Inglis' and assumed they shared with their great predecessor Chaucer.[36]

The fate of Basil Bunting (1900–85), an associate of both McDiarmid and Ezra Pound, illustrates the distortions which result from splitting English poetry into national traditions. Bunting was Northumbrian; he could not be sidelined into a marginal national tradition, but his work, the major attempt by an English writer to introduce modernist poetics, was disregarded for most of his career. He was active as a poet from the publication of *Villon* in 1925, but was not recognized as a significant figure in English poetry until the publication of *Briggflats* in 1966. His poetry drew on the history and vernacular culture of Northumbria as well as wide-ranging learning, and put into practice an idea of poetry as verbal music. It was attentive not just to stress, but to gradations of vocalic and consonantal sounds, syllabic length, the closure as well as onset of words and syllables and the effect of their collisions. His versification is a complete departure from orthodox metrics, though it occasionally echoes alliterative verse. Bunting would have been aware that he was working in the tradition of the oldest surviving poem in English, 'Caedmon's Hymn', composed in Northumbria in the seventh century. The music of his verse is founded on Northumbrian speech,[37] but it is not restricted by a specific accent, as the opening of *Briggflats* illustrates:

> Brag, sweet tenor bull
> descant on Rawthey's madrigal
> each pebble its part
> for the fell's late spring.
> Dance tiptoe, bull,

---

36. Mr Robert Cummings of Glasgow University clarified my ideas on this point but the responsibility for the argument is mine.

37. This comes across strongly in the recordings of him reading his work issued by Bloodaxe Books.

> black against may.
> Ridiculous and lovely
> chase hurdling shadows
> morning into noon.
> May on the bull's hide
> and through the dale
> furrows fill with may,
> paving the slowworm's way.

The clash between orthodox metrics and the diversity of speech in English became a central theme in Tony Harrison's *From 'The School of Eloquence'*, an open sequence which he began publishing in 1978. It consists of poems in the sixteen-line form used by George Meredith in his verse novel *Modern Love* (1862) and sometimes confusingly called sonnets. Harrison's line is based on orthodox metrics, but its regularity is distorted through a scattering of phrases in languages other than English and the prominent intrusion of local speech, as it is refashioned into a poetic language founded on the vernacular of Leeds. He writes out of a sense that the English of Yorkshire, like that of Scotland and Northumbria, once sustained a poetic tradition.

The disruption of orthodox iambic pentameter in *From 'The School of Eloquence'* can be illustrated from the central lines (5–11) of 'On Not Being Milton', the first poem in the sequence after the sixteen-line Latin epigraph excerpted from Milton's 'Ad Patrem' (1637) and four lines reporting a colloquial exchange with his father.

> The stutter of the scold out of the branks
> of condescension, class and counter-class
> thickens with glottals to a lumpen mass
> of Ludding morphemes closing up their ranks.
> Each swung cast-iron Enoch of Leeds stress
> clangs a forged music on the frames of Art,
> the looms of owned language smashed apart.

The passage opens with a perfect alliterative half-line which sets up a four-stress accentual rhythm. It matches the diction: the ambiguous 'scold' derives from Old Norse 'skald', a court poet with limited scope to mock his master, and 'branks' is a dialect word for the metal headpiece used to muzzle and punish a 'scold'. There is then a brilliant modulation by enjambment into a smoothly alliterating iambic pentameter, again completely appropriate to its subject. The iambic rhythm is then violently reversed by a string of trochaic words: 'thíckens', 'glóttals', 'lúmpen', 'Lúdding', 'mórphemes', 'clósing'. This prepares a rhythmic climax in the following line: a regular ten syllables, but seven of them are accented: four in sequence at the beginning and two on the final 'Léeds stréss', with one in the middle on 'Énoch', the name of the sledge-hammer whose blows are imitated in the rhythm of the line. The climax subsides through lines which modulate from trochaic to iambic rhythms and the syncopation of adjacent accents on 'ówned lánguage', part of an allusion to a widely popular book on linguistics, Frederick Bodmer's *Loom of Language* (1944). The formulation of this line makes it clear that it is not language, but the idea that language can be owned, which is 'smashed apart'. Language is not a possession; it does not belong to a nation or a class, but it is 'loomed' from different strands which are unravelled to make the poem.

'On Not Being Milton' is dedicated to two Frelimo leaders who were themselves poets, and it was apparently written in Mozambique in 1971.[38] Harrison's challenge to the dominant tradition is heralded in the second line by an allusion to *Cahier d'un retour au pays natal* written in Paris by the Martinican poet Aimé Césaire in 1939. This was the founding manifesto of the movement known as 'negritude' (a term coined by Césaire) and subsequently a landmark in the formulation of postcolonial theories of literature. Harrison's allusion predates the development of these theories in the anglophone world, though not, of course, the writings which they aim to explain. He identifies the first poem in *From 'The School of Eloquence'* and perhaps the sixteen-line form used throughout the sequence as 'my *Cahier d'un retour au pays natal*, / my growing black enough to fit my boots', and firmly aligns his project with negritude and the postcolonial impulses in the poetry of the 1970s. This places *From 'The School of Eloquence'*, written from the perspective of Leeds, in the company of works such as Kamau Brathwaite's *Mother Poem*, written from the perspective of Barbados.

It can be assumed that *Mother Poem* was being composed

---

38. According to the fine essay on the poem by Rick Rylance in Neil Astley, ed., *Tony Harrison*, Newcastle upon Tyne: Bloodaxe Critical Anthologies, 1991.

around the same time as Tony Harrison was working on his
sequence, Les Murray on his *Song Cycle* and Derek Walcott on
'The Schooner *Flight*'. Two years after its publication in 1977,
Brathwaite gave a lecture at Harvard which remains the fullest
account of the way these poems were remodelling poetic
language.[39] His argument is confined to the Caribbean, but with
appropriate substitutions it can be transposed to other parts of
the anglophone world. For example, he makes the point that
education in the Caribbean disregarded its various languages,
including creoles, and promoted the 'language of the planter, the
language of the official, the language of the anglican preacher'
and the 'contours of the English heritage'. Writing of education,
he does not have to mention the language of the teacher, whose
voice we hear enforcing the same educational practices in the
lines already quoted from Tony Harrison's 'Them & [uz]'.

Brathwaite's account implicitly reveals the extraordinary vitality
of poetry in the Caribbean, which seems to be connected to the
complex linguistic interactions he describes in his lecture. It is
these, and not the imperially transposed English heritage, which
impel the creation of poetic language. The main thrust of his
argument is that orthodox metrics, which he usually refers to as
'iambic pentameter', is unfitted to the varieties of Caribbean
English and the whole nature of the place. As he famously puts it,
'[t]he hurricane does not roar in pentameters', and he cites a
number of poems to demonstrate the necessity of creating a
poetic language fitted to the hurricane and other forms of natural
violence: the volcano, earthquake, drought and fire. This raises
the general question: 'how do you get a rhythm which approxi-
mates the *natural* experience, the *environmental* experience?' The
concern of some Australian poets with 'environmental values'
intersects with this question and it is taken up in 'The Human-
Hair Thread', the essay contemporary with Brathwaite's lecture in
which Les Murray examines the convergence of his work with
Aboriginal poetry and explains the composition of the *Song Cycle*.
The compound rhythms of that poem are one approximation to
the 'environmental experience'.

Like Bunting, Brathwaite insists on the primacy of sound in
poetry – not that many poets, and certainly none of those dis-

---

39. Published as *History of the Voice*.

cussed here, would disagree. He draws attention to the continuum
between oral and written poetry in the Caribbean and the associated speech continuum running from deep creole to uninflected
English. *Mother Poem*, composed in what Brathwaite calls a 'pente-
costalism' of language, draws on a wide spectrum of this continuum. 'Angel / Engine', the opening poem of the fourth section
of the book, *Koumfort*, begins with three relatively uninflected
lines:[40]

> The yard around which the smoke circles
>   is bounded by kitchen latrine & the wall
>   of the house where her aunt die

but the poem moves increasingly into creole:

> but she fingers gone dead. an she isn't got eyes in she head

> then one two tree wutless men come up in hey
>   an impose a pregnant pun she
>   one tek. but de other two both foetus dead

and in the second part, syllables and phonemes become detached:

>   an it spinn
>   an it spinn
>   an it spinn
>
>   in rounn
>   -an it stagger-
>   in down
>
>   -to a gutter-
>   in shark
>   a de worl
>
>   *praaaze be to*
>   *praaaze be to*
>   *praaze be to* **gg**

Apart from a few traces of alliterative verse, *Mother Poem* breaks
with traditional metrics. Its predominantly short but unequal lines
resemble those of William Carlos Williams and the poets he
influenced, but Brathwaite's lines are not syntactically defined.
They are based on a syllabic music closer to the practice of Basil

---

40. Lineation and punctuation of quotations follows the version in Sycorax video
style in *Ancestors*, New York: New Directions, 2001.

Bunting, except that the syllables of Brathwaite's poetry derive
from the wide range of speech in the Caribbean and his rhythms
from Afro-Caribbean musical forms such as calypso:

> But e nevva maim what me mudda me name
> an e nevva nyam what me mane
>
> *back to back belly to belly*
> *uh doan give a damm*
> *uh dun dead aready*

In the 1970s, the work of Brathwaite, Walcott, Murray and
Harrison, along with that of Seamus Heaney, which carried
through a parallel development in vernacular poetics founded on
the speech of Northern Ireland, recovered the multifariousness
of English poetry which had been subdued for four centuries.
These poets subsequently produced the full-scale works which
define its range and condition in the early twenty-first century,[41]
and as their achievement and influence grew, poets of the next
generation extended the refashioning of poetic language, particularly by exploiting the interaction of English with other languages.

Most Indian and African poets are bilingual when they are not
polyglot, and those who write in English generally have another
language as their vernacular. In a multi-lingual situation such as
prevails in India, a poetic language may be a deliberate choice
from a range of possibilities, determined by a number of things,
including its poetic potential in relation to that of other
languages. Sujata Bhatt's 'Search For My Tongue',[42] written in
English and Gujarati, using the appropriate scripts for each
language and parenthetical English spellings of the Gujarati
words, is a long meditation on this dilemma.

> You ask me what I mean
> by saying I have lost my tongue.
> I ask you, what would you do
> if you had two tongues in your mouth,
> and lost the first one, the mother tongue,
> and could not really know the other,
> the foreign tongue.

41. For example, the three parts of *From 'The School of Eloquence'* published in
Harrison's *Selected Poems*; Walcott's *Omeros*, 1990; Murray's *Fredy Neptune*, 1998;
Heaney's translation of *Beowulf*, 2000 and Brathwaite's *Ancestors*.
42. *Point No Point*, Manchester: Carcanet, 1997, pp. 32–40.

> You could not use them both together
> even if you thought that way.

The poet Tabish Khair approaches this problem in a recent essay[43] by suggesting that in the complex multi-lingualism of India, English is a 'textual language' similar to Sanskrit and Persian. The implications seem to be that the resources of English poetry were transmitted to India not as speech (as in Australia and the Caribbean) but as a body of texts which were diffused by reading. It may follow from this that Indian English poems are created as texts for the reading eye. Sujata Bhatt's use of the Gujarati script is an example, but the parenthetical phonetic spellings in the poem indicate that it is not mute, as indeed no poem can be.

Having two tongues in the mouth may not be an obstacle. The Nigerian poet Niyi Osundare reveals in a recent essay[44] how he 'thinks out' a poem in Yorùbá and gives expression to it in English. The two languages and their poetic traditions are very different, as Osundare explains. 'English is a stress-timed language, Yorùbá is a syllable-timed one operating through a complex system of tones and glides. In this language, prosody mellows into melody. Sounding is meaning, meaning is sounding.' Syllabic rhythms are used in the poetry of Bunting and Brathwaite, but tones and glides cannot be managed in English. As Osundare points out, 'Yorùbá's phonological space remains the poet's most fertile, most challenging, and most indulgent terrain.' Thus, when he thinks in Yorùbá and composes poetry in English, he explores its phonological potential.

> A green desire, perfumed memories
> a leafy longing lure my wanderer feet
> to this forest of a thousand wonders.
> A green desire for this petalled umbrella
> of simple stars and compound suns.
> Suddenly, so soberly suddenly,
> the sky is tree-high
> and the horizon dips into an inky grove

---

43. 'Indian English Poetry: Problems of Language and Prosody'. Yet to be published. I am grateful to the author for allowing me to read it.
44. 'Yorùbá Thought: English Words', see footnote 2.

This phonological music is possible because, like Bunting, but through a process of translation rather than musical emulation, Osundare calculates the phonemic quality of every syllable. In fact, to read the poem effectively, it is necessary to 'bring out' its phonemic sequences without disturbing its syllabic and verbal order. Remarkably, given the intricate patterning of its phonemes, the English of the poem remains unforced. The way in which this refreshes the acoustical possibilities of English poetry is comparable to the impact of medieval Latin and Anglo-Norman on English verse at a time when poets were often bilingual.

The examples discussed here show how the vitality of English poetry is evident in its geographical dispersion, through interactive developments in different places rather than activities concentrated in a literary capital. The extended field of English is, in its nature, dynamic and continues to generate fresh poetic impulses. In recent decades there has been a notable emergence of English poetry from Oceania, a region with a large and complex array of languages. Poets writing in English as well as Polynesian languages are exploiting this variously. A recent anthology includes poems in pidgin, poems inspired by Polynesian verse, poems created through translation.[45] Its editor, the Samoan writer Albert Wendt, a pioneer of English literature in the South Pacific, has published part of a novel in verse[46] which uses a language studded with Polynesian expressions in a variety of verse forms. At the northern apex of the Polynesian triangle in Hawaii, English and Chinese poetics fuse in the poems of Carolyn Lei Lenilau, which do not imitate Chinese forms but emerge from the interaction between the varieties of English, Chinese and Polynesian spoken in her community. She called her first collection, pointedly, *Wode Shuofa (My Way of Speaking)*.[47]

A recent book on postcolonial poetry[48] begins from the assumption that 'the story of the globalization of English-language poetry remains largely untold', and wisely does not attempt to tell that entangled Shandean story. The loose ends traced here, however, suggest that perspectives established by postcolonial

---

45. Wendt, ed., *Nuanua*.
46. *The Adventures of Vela* in *Photographs*, Auckland: Auckland University Press, 1995.
47. Berkeley: Tooth of Time Books, 1988.
48. Ramazani, *The Hybrid Muse*.

studies of literature need to be supplemented to explain the global development of English poetry. The haphazard, uncentred aspects of colonization need to be taken into account, along with the positive residue of one-sided conflicts with other languages which left English dominant but changed. Postcolonial approaches have revealed insights about the politics of language but not about the latent aspects of language which appear through the study of poetry. The encounters with other poetries which were a delayed outcome of European imperialism suggest that poetry cannot be theoretically defined as a cultural 'construct', though it may have different functions in different cultures. It is an adjunct of language, of every language and its variant forms, and one of the ways by which languages survive. There is poetry wherever there is language.

The grim side of this is that, with the spread of empires, 'the age of unnoticed languages begins', as Les Murray put it in 'The Conquest'.[49] In some cases, indigenous languages were rapidly obliterated, as they were in the Caribbean along with the people who spoke them, but the normal process of extinction was often surprisingly slow, and in the course of colonization some oral languages acquired writing systems. Remarkably, enough survived of indigenous poetic traditions for them to influence contemporary poetry and ways of thinking about it. The Dyirbal song-poetry of north-eastern Australia, for example, was still surviving into the 1960s. It incorporated songs about such exotic events as erecting fences, making roads, getting drunk and hanging washing on the line, and went on elaborating love songs.[50] European imperialism may have been motivated by blind faith in the superiority of its civilization, partly instilled by regard for its literature, but colonization slowly revealed the evidence for its untenability. Its long-term outcome, evident in the development of English poetry, has been the useful discovery that European conceptions are not absolute.

Poetry in the English language did not develop in the world at large according to imperial principles. Indeed its development everywhere undermined them, as the epigraph by Niyi Osundare

---

49. In *Poems Against Economics*, Sydney: Angus & Robertson, 1972.
50. R. M. W. Dixon and Grace Koch, *Dyirbal Song Poetry*, St Lucia: University of Queensland Press, 1996.

at the head of this essay implies. Education may have had limited success in instilling canonical notions of English poetry, but the practice of the art was in its nature anti-imperial. The discussion here suggests that some of the approaches developed through studies of postcolonial literature can be reapplied to poets in the imperial homeland, such as Tony Harrison and Basil Bunting, and through their links with early states of the art back through the whole tradition of poetry in English to 'Caedmon's Hymn'. Seamus Heaney's recent version of *Beowulf*, which exploits associations and similarities between the Anglo-Saxon of the poem and the poetics he founded on the speech of Northern Ireland, is illuminating on this point. It might be necessary, and not altogether a bad thing, to dispose of the term 'postcolonial' while incorporating its doctrines into a comprehensive approach to the study of poetry. One of the things this would reveal is that imperial appropriations of language and literature do not form a basis on which to study or understand poetry.

The global development of English poetry as a literary exchange in which other languages and poetries are devalued while leaving traces indicates that an idea of literature – and of world literature – cannot be centred on European conceptions. It involves rethinking 'literature' as a field of linguistic as well as discursive interactions and exchanges. There appears to be no way of bounding a field of this kind or, consequently, of describing it comprehensively. It would, by default, be 'world literature', but it could only be investigated through entanglement along the lines suggested here, and this would involve a reversion to comparative literary and philological studies.

15

India in the Mirror of World Fiction

Francesca Orsini

What is Indian literature? The question is sharply posed in *The Picador Book of Modern Indian Literature*, a fine and, in many respects, polemical collection, whose explicit aim is to rebut prevailing Western expectations of what postcolonial Indian fiction ought to be.[1] Its editor, Amit Chaudhuri, argues that the critical and commercial reception accorded *Midnight's Children* has erected Rushdie's work as 'a gigantic edifice that all but obstructs the view of what lies behind'. This in turn has created a highly prescriptive set of assumptions. First: the new Indian novel must be written in English, the only language deemed capable of capturing modern subcontinental realities: Hindi, Tamil, Bengali, Urdu and the rest need not apply. Secondly, while eschewing realism, its tone and structure must be relentlessly mimetic: since India is a 'huge baggy monster', its fiction, too, must be vast and all-inclusive. Its voice must be 'robustly extroverted', clamorously polyphonic, rejecting any nuance or delicacy. Its subject matter must be fantastical, its narrative non-linear: 'Indian life is plural, garrulous, rambling, lacking a fixed centre, and the Indian novel must be the same.'

All this, as Chaudhuri points out, rides roughshod over ancient and modern traditions of miniaturism in the Subcontinent – the

I would like to thank Susan Daruvala for her perceptive comments and criticism on an earlier draft of this essay.

1. Amit Chaudhuri, ed., *The Picador Book of Modern Indian Literature*, London, 2001; henceforth, PBMIL.

use of ellipsis, rather than inclusion, as an aesthetic strategy. It ignores the crucial role of the novella and short story in Indian fiction – a genre Tagore introduced from France in the late nineteenth century, before it became established in England. Claims that the capacious, magical, non-linear novel could be seen as natural heir to the imaginary of the *Ramayana* and *Mahabharata* – 'at once contemporaneously postcolonial and anciently, inescapably Indian' – overlooked the stark contrast between the amorality of the Hindu epics and the impeccably liberal viewpoint of the postmodern best-seller: multicultural, anti-sexist, tolerant of difference, and so forth; while to celebrate Indian writing as merely 'overblown, fantastic, lush and non-linear' was surely to endorse the old colonialist chestnut that rational thought and discrimination were alien to Indian tradition.[2]

These arguments, first developed in a TLS essay, 'The Construction of the Indian Novel in English', together with a companion piece, 'Modernity and the Vernacular', form the twin-pillared introduction to Chaudhuri's anthology, which runs from the 1850s to the present day and includes translations from Bengali, Hindi, Urdu, Kannada, Malayalam, Tamil and Oriya, as well as writing in English.[3] The collection proposes both an historical narrative and a cultural contextualization for Indian literature – a sort of counter-manifesto to the assumptions of much postcolonial literary theory. Against conceptions of English-language writing as the natural medium of modernity, replacing a Babel of ancient tongues, Chaudhuri argues that Indian vernacular literatures are themselves modernity's offspring, directly linked to the emergence of a bourgeois-secular sensibility and the development of a new, educated Indian middle class. The nineteenth-century Bengal Renaissance is taken as the paradigm here, with the work of Michael Madhusudan Dutt as first fruit of the social and intellectual ferment that would create an eclectic, precocious modernism in Calcutta at a time when the culture of Victorian England was still 'provincial and inward-looking'.[4] A

---

2. PBMIL., pp. xxiv–xxvi.
3. These essays were first published under the titles 'Lure of the Hybrid', *Times Literary Supplement*, 3 September 1999, and 'Beyond the Language of the Raj', *Times Literary Supplement*, 8 August 1997.
4. PBMIL., p. 5.

restless cosmopolitan, Dutt seized on the horizons opened by the Western education at the 1840s Hindu College and, later, at Gray's Inn, before returning to re-engage with – and redefine – an indigenous cultural inheritance now fraught with interpretive tensions. 'I hate Rama and all his rabble,' Dutt could write; like his epic 1861 poem *Meghnada Badha Kabya*, which reworks an episode from the *Ramayana* – inverting the status of the Hindu protagonists in much the same way that Milton's troubled Satan dominates *Paradise Lost* – this is a statement less freely made, Chaudhuri suggests, in today's BJP-ruled India. Similarly, the work of Rabindranath Tagore and his successors, hailed in the West as an expression of ancient Eastern wisdom, is read here as that of a modernist sensibility, working out its relation to a fast-changing world. In differing ways – conditioned by local levels of develop- ment, education, commerce – Chaudhuri traces the same moment at work within the other Indian vernaculars.

Nuance, ellipsis and the exploration of realist boundaries predominate within the selection of contemporary writing, as might be expected. Naiyer Masud's 1996 Urdu story 'Sheesha Ghat' [Wharf of Glass] assembles all the elements from which magical realism would fashion a raucous extravaganza – *bazaari* clown, *dacoit*'s mistress – and creates instead a strange tableau of stillness and understanding, narrated with unfussed clarity by a boy who cannot speak. An extract from Krishna Sobti's Hindi novella of 1991 *Ai Larki* [Hey, girl] is all dialogue, notes on action set as stage directions: the conversation – mostly one-sided – of an old lady on her deathbed, talking to her daughter. The quiet domestic scene is the setting for wild flights of the night, flashes of anger and terror mixed with gentle chafing, women's memor- ies, sharp advice. Nirmal Verma's Hindi story 'Terminal' (1992), set within a strange symbolic landscape (almost Prague), displays a scrupulous sympathy for its lovers and the gulfs between them. Fine translations suggest a language of precision and sensitivity, without bluster or hullabaloo: writers silently stalking their prey.[5]

Their setting is enriched by an illuminating series of pieces –

---

5. As always, one wishes for more. Among Urdu writers, for example, Intizar Ahmad, Intizar Hussain and Khadija Mastur and, in Hindi, Nagarjun, Phanishwar- nath Renu, Rahi Masoom Reza, Srilal Shukla and Vinodkumar Shukla are unrepre- sented here.

essays, memoirs and letters as well as fiction – that provide some sense of modern India's discussion of its own cultural process: Tagore's 1892 account of the Shahzadpur postmaster – his model – reading 'The Postmaster' in the Bengali press; the newly orphaned literati in Bose's contestatory vision of a 'Tagore-less' Calcutta; Pankaj Mishra's depiction of the sullen mood of the Indian universities on the eve of the neoliberal transformation, mired in hopeless caste violence; Ashok Banker's deregulated Bombay. There are interesting discussions of literary multilingualism – with poets proposed as the most creative Indian theorists – and of traditional forms. In a memorable reading of a Tamil love lyric – a sulky concubine's complaint about her lover and his wife – framed within its interior and exterior landscapes, A. K. Ramanujan explores the basis of Sanskrit aesthetics: 'what is contained mirrors the container'. Chaudhuri's argument here is that it is impossible to be interested in a canon without some idea of a community or a nation's history and, even more important, some conception of how it sees itself.[6]

There are omissions from this collection, of course, and some of them are important. This is an India innocent of the trauma of Partition or communal violence; one that has never known war with its neighbours, a communist movement or an industrial working class. Small-town and village life predominate over the teeming city. High-caste experience, though questioned, is preponderant. Nevertheless, this is a rich and stimulating collection, striking proof of the sheer literary excellence within what Chaudhuri calls the 'multiple traditions' of Indian writing.

How then are we to make sense of Rushdie's famous remark that he could find scarcely a single vernacular text worthy of inclusion in his own compendium of Indian literature?[7] How are we to account for such startling disparities in Indian writers'

---

6. Here again he takes issue with a postcolonial literary theory whose emphasis on ontological difference and disregard for class is just as guilty of 'consigning India to a historical vacuum' as the classic colonial notion that history only happens in the West, PBMIL, p. xviii.

7. *Vintage Book of Indian Writing 1947–97*, ed. Salman Rushdie and Elizabeth West, London, 1997, p. x. Rushdie declared that 'Indo-Anglian' work was quite simply 'stronger and more important'. For reactions, see 'Modernity and the Vernacular'; Pankaj Mishra, 'Midnight's Grandchildren', *Prospect*, April 1997; Radhakrishnan Nayar, 'Tryst with Westerny', *Times Higher Education Supplement*, 27 June 1997.

fortunes, if not on the basis of apparent literary worth? What is
the relationship between regional, vernacular literatures such as
these and 'world literature', if one can speak of such a thing?
What governs the access of writers – or, as here, entire traditions
– to the world stage? Two recent accounts, by Franco Moretti and
Pascale Casanova,[8] have remapped the realm of world literature,
proposing radically new – and divergent – approaches. Both tip
their hats to Goethe; but for both – in stark contrast to his
egalitarian *Weltliteratur* ideal – the inequalities of global literary
practice over the past two hundred years are almost as glaring as
those of the economic sphere. For Moretti, taking an analogy
from world-systems theory, world literature is '*one*, and *unequal*',
structured by periphery and core. For Casanova, drawing on Paul
Valéry and, above all, Bourdieu, it is governed by national accu-
mulations of cultural capital, the most powerful cities then governing access to literary recognition on a world scale. For both it
is a zone of conflict, a 'struggle for symbolic hegemony' (Moretti)
or a 'perpetual contest for legitimacy' (Casanova). Both employ
market metaphors: debt, importation, direct and indirect loans,
in Moretti; capital accumulation and literary 'value' in Casanova.
For both, initially, the dominant centres are England and France.[9]

Moretti's conjectures are structured around the evolution of
forms: under what conditions was the novel, for example, first
imported to Brazil, Japan, Russia, Italy, Africa, China – India?
Hypothesized here is an inherently unstable compromise between
West European patterns, local realities and – the unpredictable
element – local narrator; with the surprising twist that it is this
later, peripheral version of the novel that will turn out to be the
rule in world literature, while the Anglo-French original is really
the exception. One objection to this 'law of evolution' would be
the absence in the scheme of a 'local audience', the readers – a
crucial factor for Benedict Anderson, on whose work Moretti (as
Casanova) partly draws, and for vernacular writers (think of
Tagore and the postmaster).

A further problem is that, at first sight, Moretti's novel-based
theses would seem to have little application to the Subcontinent,

---

8. See Franco Moretti, 'Conjectures on World Literature', this volume; Pascale
Casanova, *La République mondiale des lettres*, Paris, 1999; see also Christopher
Prendergast's 'The World Republic of Letters', this volume.

9. 'Conjectures', pp. 149, 158; *République mondiale des lettres*, pp. 24, 28.

where the major nineteenth- and twentieth-century forms were
poetry, drama and the short story, whose evolution may show
quite different patterns of change.[10] Yet Moretti's 'compromise'
takes various forms: 'At times' – alluding to Meenakshi Mukherjee, in *Realism and Reality*, on the problems of the encounter
between Western form and Indian social reality – 'especially in
the second half of the nineteenth century, and in Asia, it tended
to be very unstable.' Local reality '*was* different in the various
places, just as Western influence was also very uneven'.[11] Rubbed
against Indian literary practice, Moretti's conjectures may yield
interesting negative results: could it be that English influence on
the nineteenth-century Indian middle classes was much weaker
than the colonialists supposed? Chaudhuri certainly seems to
suggest as much when he points to the peripherality – indeed,
near invisibility – of the white occupiers in Bengal Renaissance
literature; the colonial experience is represented rather in tan-
gible local signs: the post office; street names.[12]

   Casanova's model of competing literatures and unequal
national languages, in which the literary guardians of the dominant Western cities determine access, recognition and diffusion
at a world level, would seem to have more immediate affinities
with Indian writers' plight. In her account, the foundational
moment for the development of a national literature lies in the
'valorization' of its vernacular, in the face of cultural domination
by another language. Skipping over sixteenth-century Bible translations, Casanova takes Joachim du Bellay's 1549 *Deffence et Illustration de la langue françoyse* against the 'empire of Latin' as the
starting point – the beginning of the 'literarization' of the French
language, and its accumulation of literary capital.[13] In the 1790s,
Herder's bid for an emergent German literature against the
universal language of French, and then – a revolutionary gesture
– his extension of the same principle to all other peoples of

---

10. Although poetry haunts the Picador collection, it is scarcely represented in
its contents. For a companion volume see *The Oxford Anthology of Modern Indian
Poetry*, ed. Vinay Dharwadker and A. K. Ramanujan, New Delhi, 1994. Another
good anthology, although without the valuable prefaces to each writer that
Chaudhuri provides, is *The Penguin New Writing in India*, ed. Aditya Behl and David
Nicholls, New Delhi, 1992.

11. 'Conjectures', pp. 156, 158.

12. PBMIL, p. xix.

13. *République mondiale des lettres*, p. 70.

Europe, whose genius could find expression only in their native tongue, supplied the charter for national literatures in any dominated language. The Indian experience is largely absent from Casanova's exploration of the vernacular literatures that followed – Irish, Czech, Tunisian, Brazilian, Cuban, Nigerian, Québecois and Kikuyu, among others – but the resonance of such an account with the Bengal Renaissance, for example, needs to be qualified. While there was certainly a new Herderian feeling towards the language – 'What a vast field does our country now present for literary enterprise!' wrote Dutt in 1860 – there was also a highly complex relationship to centuries of earlier literature.[14]

The hierarchy of Casanova's world republic of letters is dictated by the chronology of national literatures' first emergence. Those of Paris or London, with a long tradition of vernacular valorization and a large stock of inherited literary capital, supported by substantial publishing industries and large national, and international, readerships – buttressed, in turn, by histories of colonial power – predominate over more recent arrivals. For the past two centuries, it is argued, only publication in French or English could bestow international recognition – consecration is Casanova's term – on writers from peripheral cultures, with mediators such as Valéry Larbaud or Paul Valéry having the power to usher writers through the gates of translation into the realm of literary universality, and to set the 'Greenwich Mean Time' of world taste. (In the case of India, recent gatekeepers have often been Indian writers in English: Rushdie, Chaudhuri, and so on.) The act of consecration is an ambiguous one, with both positive and negative consequences:

> The great consecrators reduce foreign literary works to their own categories of perception, constituted as universal norms, and overlook the entire context – historical, cultural, political and above all literary – that would allow a non-reductive understanding of them. Thus do the literary powers exact an *octroi* tax on the right to universal circulation.[15]

Casanova makes plain her own critical stance towards existing literary power relations, hoping that her book will become a 'weapon of use to all marginal (peripheral, unendowed, domi-

---

14. Letter to Raj Narain, 15 May 1860. PBMIL., p. 9.
15. *République mondiale des lettres*, pp. 127, 214, 479.

nated) writers' and 'an instrument of struggle against the self-
assurance and arrogance, the impositions and dictates of a
metropolitan criticism oblivious to the realities of unequal access
to the universe of literature'. Nevertheless, if individual writers
can break through these barriers, her model seems to permanently preclude whole literatures from doing the same. Where
does this leave the immsensely rich and sophisticated traditions
of China and Japan? Casanova's insistence on the stark inequalities between 'great' and 'small' languages may blind her to some
of the subjective subtleties available to multilingual writers.
Implicit in her view – explicit in Moretti's – is the traditional
assumption of a 'source' language, or culture – invariably carrying
an aura of authenticity – and a 'target' one, seen as in some way
imitative. In place of this, Lydia Liu much more usefully proposed
the concept of 'guest' and 'host' languages, to focus attention on
the translingual practice through which the hosts may appropriate
concepts and forms.[16] The question then becomes not whether
'individualism', for example, means something different in modern Indian (or, here, Chinese) culture, but how Chinese or Indian
writers might translate and deploy the concept to make locally
significant points. In this way, what is untraditional is not necessarily seen as Western, or as un-Indian or un-Chinese. Cultural
influence becomes a study of appropriation, rather than of centres and peripheries – an approach which finds clear echoes in
Chaudhuri's volume. Thus A. K. Mehrotra suggests that, for
multilingual writers, the other language will always act as a
'torsional force': 'Nabokov's position is analogous to ours.'

The world-literary force-field Casanova depicts is a dynamic
one, subject to alteration by its practitioners' choice of strategy –
assimilation, rebellion or a revolutionary storming of the metropolis. Nevertheless, competing national literatures remain the key
units. Christopher Prendergast has already suggested that there
may be 'variables other than nation and relations other than
competition': Wordsworth is only one example of a writer whose
main preoccupations – class, gender, region – seem more expressive of conflicts internal to, or unbounded by, the nation state.[17]
Modern Indian writing poses a further challenge to the unitary

---

16. *Translingual Practices*, Berkeley, 1995.
17. 'The World Republic of Letters', p. 12.

agon through the exceptional complexity of its national field. Language is the most apparent faultline; but linguistic differentiation also delineates a series of competing, sometimes overlapping distinctions of region, culture and class, each with its own sphere of literary production, and with multiple sets of artistic mediators – at least three in any given location – who may assign different meanings and values to works. Table A is a representation of production, transmission and recognition within this fractured and multilayered field.

Literary production in English is triply privileged within this field, drawing on the language's American-based global ascendancy, on the subcontinental legacy of British colonialism and, relatedly, on Indian class divisions: this is the preferred language of the urban middle classes – in the case of the elite, sometimes the only language. Despite official emphasis on Sanskritized Hindi, in practice the ruling BJP has shown no signs of abandoning English as status symbol and lingua franca of the global market. Within the literary sphere – confirming Casanova's configuration – English is the language in which most Indians would read Dostoevsky, Maupassant or Mann. English alone commands international access to Western publishing houses, journals and prizes.

But if – to use Casanova's terms – the flow of literary exchange, as of economic capital, is heavily weighted in favour of English, the case of cultural and symbolic capital is slightly different. Within state institutions, indigenous languages are preferred and Hindi in particular – spoken by only about three-fifths of the population; its literature read by far fewer – plays a special role as official language of the Indian Union. State institutions – especially the national academy of letters, Sahitya Akademi, crucial in channelling and distributing cultural capital – pursue a vision of a 'federal republic of letters' in which all Indian languages receive equal representation, with Hindi *primus inter pares*. The global role of English is ignored in this view: it is just another Indian language. Hindi literary institutions are possibly the most vociferous in their hostility to the hegemony of English: the federal republic resents forms of recognition that supersede its own.[18]

---

18. Chaudhuri wryly registers the antagonism when he comments that, while Rushdie's remark on the clear superiority of English-language writing was 'interesting, if somewhat mystifying', the sanctimonious outrage of the Indian middle-class

TABLE A: *Institutions of regional, national and world literature in India*

	Regional/Vernacular languages	English language within India	International
Publishers	Publish Indian writers in Indian languages; some cross-translations from other Indian languages; some translations of world writers	Indian branches of international publishers (Penguin India, Heinemann, Longman): publish English-language Indian writers; some translations of Indian writers. Indian English-language publishers (Katha, Seagull, Kali, Stree): publish good translations from Indian languages	Multinational publishers (HarperCollins, Picador, Penguin): publish a small number of English-language Indian writers; virtually no vernacular authors
Education: schools and universities	Two-tier system with English/Indian language; regional-language schools teach Indian literature, but hardly any English language or literature	English-medium: all teaching is done in English; token presence of regional language and literature. Eng. Lit. departments at the vanguard of introducing Anglo-Indian and, recently, Indian literature in translation.	English-language South Asian writers now part of the multicultural curriculum; Indian writers in English taught in Eng. Lit. departments as 'Commonwealth' or postcolonial literature; recently also some Indian literature in translation
Journals	Hindi journals discuss Hindi books and translations into Hindi, and cultural and political affairs (regional public sphere); rarely if ever discuss English-language Indian writing; bestow local, regional and supra-regional recognition	*India Today, Outlook, Frontline, Biblio* and *Indian Review of Books.* Discuss global culture, world literature and Indian writers in English; rarely discuss literary books in Indian languages (*The Hindu* is an exception); bestow national recognition	NYRB, TLS, etc.: discuss only English-language Indian writers and books published by international publishers; bestow international recognition and seal of 'world literature'
Literary associations/ Prizes	Regional members of Sahitya Academi. Hindi associations defend Hindi as the national language and are reluctant to accept English as an 'Indian language'. English-language Indian writers largely excluded from this sphere. Prizes give regional recognition	Sahitya Akademi: organizes pan-Indian seminars; privileges Hindi as national language (e.g. sponsors translations), but has both a Hindi and an English journal; English is accepted as one of India's languages. Gives prizes for every Indian language, bestowing national recognition	PEN International: 130 national and diasporic conventions, awards national and international prizes. English-language prizes: Booker, Pulitzer, Commonwealth. French-language: Goncourt, Medicis. Nobel: gives genuinely international recognition

Hindi literary publishing is heavily subsidized, with government-sponsored seminars, library funding, state prizes and national translation programmes – by far the greatest being from regional languages into Hindi. State libraries and university curricula ensure sufficient turnover, despite low levels of literacy and readership: a novel will break even if it sells 500 copies a year; at 5,000 it is a best-seller. It is not to denigrate the best of Hindi writing to point out that, as the official language, its literature has been systematically privileged over other, longer traditions: Bengali, Tamil, Urdu, to name but three. We should also register a contemporary degeneration in inter-lingual practice: whereas writers like Tagore, Bankimchandra and Saratchandra were widely read in other Indian languages, including Urdu, translations nowadays are unlikely to go beyond Hindi and English. Chaudhuri's argument that it was the widespread teaching of good English, even in remote country districts, during the colonial period which – far from rendering the regional vernaculars obsolete – helped Indian-language literatures to flourish may be of relevance here. He points out that many of the most interesting and creative vernacular writers have been students or teachers of English literature as well. By contrast, the increasing appeal of English-medium education in independent India, which is seen even by lower middle-class families as a necessary instrument to ensure their children's future, has entailed a systematic devaluation of the vernaculars and their literatures.[19]

There are other signs of a lack of linguistic awareness and cultural sensitivity between Indian traditions, mirroring that of the West towards India as a whole. Thus reviewers of translated books may not have read the original, and can make no comment on the translation. The Sahitya Akademi's official English-language journal tends to accept *prima facie* the value assigned by original regional critics, in line with its policy of pan-Indian federalism: the transition between language fields is presented as

---

response was a great deal less so: rarely had they been heard to extol the virtues of regional writing at such length. PBMIL, p. xxxiii.

19. While there has been a strong expansion of the Indian vernacular press over the last two decades, based on the greater penetration of newspapers in the rural and small-town hinterland and rising working-class purchasing, the results in literary terms remain to be seen. See Robin Jeffrey, *India's Newspaper Revolution*, London, 2000.

unproblematic. This is the reverse of Rushdie's refusal to venture
beyond the limits of English-language fiction; instead, the equiva-
lence of other systems of taste and meaning is taken for granted.
There is little mutual recognition or dialogue between cultural
agents in English and in other Indian languages: the audiences
are separate, messages are targeted and distinct. In sum: if the
laws of cultural capital governing Casanova's literary world may
be stretched to cover the case of Indian writing in English, it is
hard to see how the complex social and political relations between
vernacular traditions can be reduced to purely competitive terms.

In one brief chapter, 'From Literary Internationalism to Commercial Globalization?', Casanova admits the possibility that the
long reign of world literature's capital cities may be under threat.
While Paris retains its consecrational powers – and can claim to
have bestowed the crucial first rites of recognition-through-trans-
lation on 2000's Nobel laureate Gao Xingjian – we may be
entering a transition phase towards a more polycentric sphere
with new capitals in Barcelona, Frankfurt and New York. Within
this space, she discerns the emergence of an increasingly powerful
commercial pole, imposing itself as the new guardian of world-
literary legitimation and threatening not just the marketing and
distributional strategies of publishing houses but also the choice
of books. Casanova devotes no more than a couple of pages to
current transformations: concentration of ownership and production, homogenization, elimination of small, innovative houses;
mergers and acquisitions with the 'communications industry', and
the resulting expectation of profit rates to match those of press,
film and cable TV – 12 to 15 per cent, rather than publishers'
traditional 4 per cent; the systematic privileging of short-term
profitability driving the hunt for world-fiction best-sellers.

This is the limit of Casanova's horizon and, untypically, she
mentions only a few, rather weak examples of authors – Umberto
Eco, David Lodge – and genres: travel writing, or 'neo-colonial
novels with all the tried and tested recipes of exoticism, like
Vikram Seth'.[20] But this, in a sense, is Chaudhuri's starting point.
The filters that determine what a world-fiction best-seller will be
effectively exclude Indian vernacular literatures: like Rushdie and
West, publishing conglomerates chasing the next 'big' Indian

---

20. *République mondiale des lettres*, pp. 234–6.

novel will select only English-language works. The phrase 'translated from' has started to acquire negative connotations: difficult,
obsolete, non-global. Nor is it sufficient simply to be a gifted
Indian English-language writer with a notable body of work: only
a first novel will attract serious media attention and pre-publica-
tion deals from publishers searching for the next *God of Small
Things*.[21] Besides, mature practitioners may be writing for the
wrong audience – a subcontinental one – rather than, as in *A
Suitable Boy*, painstakingly explaining to the foreigners what
Indian trains and mud-thatched huts look like. In this sense, a
conception of global culture such as Arjun Appadurai's, that sees
local, national and regional spaces as dissolved within planetary
flows of media and migration, is inadequate to describe the
transformation of the literary sphere. The global does not incorporate the regional literatures of India. It cold-shoulders them.[22]

   This is not to say that best-selling Indian novels in English are
devoid of literary interest. The global cultural market now sub-
verts Bourdieu's description of the field as an 'economic world
reversed', in which commercial success is a bar to symbolic
recognition: the new equation, prizes + sales = international
success, breaks down his neat division between the sub-fields of
'restricted production' – high art – and 'large-scale production' –
low-brow.[23] But as Chaudhuri argues, the West's 'discovery' of
Indian fiction since *Midnight's Children* has served to obscure
rather than to illuminate some of the most interesting aspects of
subcontinental literature. He traces one theme in particular,
which he links to the fundamentally ambivalent attitude of the
middle classes towards their rural, feudal antecedents: a consistent
tension, from Dutt onwards, between the impulse of rejection and
that of recovery – disowning the constituting, indigenous world
and then rehabilitating it, through the secular act of creative
expression, which understands the indigenous as being in some
way essential.[24] There are a multitude of different approaches to
this contradiction here, from the psychological crisis of the educated Marxist narrator confronted with the disastrous life of his
unevolved schoolfriend (in U. R. Anantha Murthy's Kannada-

---

21. Personal communication by Arvind Krishna Mehrotra, August 2000.
22. Arjun Appadurai, *Modernity at Large*, Minneapolis, 1995.
23. Pierre Bourdieu, *The Field of Cultural Production*, Cambridge, 1993.
24. PBMIL, p. 485.

language short story), or the halting and dislocated assertions of
Raja Rao's protagonist, as his marriage to a French woman
crumbles –

> I was born a Brahmin – that is, devoted to Truth and all that.
>   'Brahmin is he who knows Brahman', etc. etc. . . . .[25]

– to Mishra's recognition, through Flaubert, of the 'grimy underside' of middle-class society, 'the same shoddiness and lack of
principle' in Benares as in Paris. The interesting exception is
Rushdie's work. Excerpted here is the well-known passage from
Midnight's Children in which the narrator, Saleem Sinai, hiding in
the dirty-laundry chest to eavesdrop on his mother's phone call
to her lover, accidentally sniffs a pyjama cord up his enormous
and permanently runny nose, upon which all the voices of midnight's children are switched on in his head. 'Oddly', Chaudhuri
notes, there is no impulse towards disowning here, or of that
'deep-rooted conflict, or tension, or ambivalence': Rushdie's fiction 'promiscuously, embraces everything'.[26]

I would say that it is their settings and sensibilities that most
clearly differentiate the best Hindi and Urdu writing, at least,
from the sensuous exoticism of world-fiction blockbusters. As in
classic nineteenth-century French fiction, the themes here are of
lower-middle-class life: small-town tedium, frustrated youth, cou-
ples incapable of communicating with each other, the impossible
gulfs between aspiration and reality. Works such as Phanishwar-
nath Renu's *The Soiled Border* or Srilal Shukla's *Raag Darbari*
explore the fiercely competitive world of rural corruption, where
it is vital to know the rules to survive, and words are more likely
to dissemble meaning than convey it.[27] The opening scene of
Raag Darbari – mosquitoes, trucks and dusty tea-stalls on a state
highway – comes like a slap in the face. But this is an India that
the West does not like to think about for too long: disturbingly
competitive, immediate, challenging; a modern mass society with

---

25. *The Serpent and the Rope*, from PBMIL, p. 398.

26. Included in the extract is Rushdie's reference to 'Valmiki, the author of the
Ramayana', dictating his masterpiece to elephant-headed Ganesh, to which Chaudhuri adds the deadpan footnote: 'One of the many deliberate errors strewn
through the novel': it was the *Mahabharata* that was dictated to Ganesh, by Vyasa.
PBMIL, pp. 485–6.

27. Renu, *Soiled Border* (1954), English trans. New Delhi, 1991; Shukla, *Raag
Darbari* (1968), English trans. New Delhi, 1992.

laws of its own. By contrast, as Chaudhuri suggests, in the florid, sensuous, inclusive, multicultural world of the post-Rushdie, post-colonial novel, the West can settle down to contemplate, not India, but its latest reinterpretation of itself.

Notes on Contributors

Christopher Prendergast is currently a Fellow at King's College, Cambridge. His most recent books are *The Triangle of Representation* (Columbia University Press, 2000) and *Eugene Sue's 'Les Mysteres de Paris': For the People By The People?* (Legenda Publications, 2003).

Stefan Hoesel-Uhlig is a Research Fellow at King's College, Cambridge. He is completing a study of the modern concept of literature.

Peter Madsen is Professor of Comparative Literature, University of Copenhagen. He recently edited a 2-volume edition in Danish translation of selected essays by Walter Benjamin, and was also co-editor (with Richard Plunz) of *The Urban Lifeworld* (Routledge, 2002).

Emily Apter is Professor of French and Comparative Literature at New York University. She is completing a book titled *The Translation Zone: Language Wars and Literary Politics*.

Timothy J. Reiss is Professor of Comparative Literature at New York University. His most recent books are *Against Autonomy: Global Dialectics of Cultural Exchange* (Stanford University Press, 2003) and *Mirages of the Selfe: Patterns of Personhood in Ancient and Early Modern Europe* (Stanford University Press, 2003).

Franco Moretti teaches literature at Stanford University. He was general editor of the 5-volume collective history of the novel published in Italy by Einaudi (*Il romanzo*, 2001–3).

Stephen Heath is a Fellow at Jesus College, Cambridge.

Simon Goldhill is Professor of Greek at the University of Cambridge. His most recent publications are *Who Needs Greek?* (Cambridge University Press, 2002) and *Being Greek Under Rome* (Cambridge University Press, 2002).

Benedict Anderson teaches International Studies at Cornell University. His most recent book is *The Spectre of Comparisons* (Verso, 1998).

Elisa Sampson Vera Tudela lectures at King's College, University of London. She is writing a book on Ricardo Palma.

Nicholas Dew is a British Academy Post-Doctoral Fellow in the history faculty at the University of Cambridge. His book, *Oriental Learning and Louis XIV's France*, is due to be published by Oxford University Press.

John Sturrock is Consulting Editor at the *London Review of Books*. His *Word from Paris* is also published by Verso.

Stanley Corngold is Professor of German and Comparative Literature at Princeton University. He last published *Complex Pleasure: Forms of Feeling in German Literature* (Stanford University Press, 1998). Princeton University Press will bring out his *Lambent Traces: Franz Kafka* in spring 2004.

Bruce Clunies Ross lectured until recently at the English Institute, University of Copenhagen, where he taught courses in the literatures of the English-speaking world. His principal publications are on Australian literature, music and cultural history.

Francesca Orsini teaches Hindi language and literature at the University of Cambridge. Her book, *The Hindi Public Sphere: Language and Literature in the Age of Nationalism*, was published by Oxford University Press, New Delhi, 2002.

Acknowledgements

Christopher Prendergast's 'The World Republic of Letters' first appeared (as 'Negotiating World Literature') in *New Left Review*, second series, 8 (March/April 2001).

Emily Apter's 'Global *Translatio*: The 'Invention' of Comparative Literature, Istanbul, 1933' first appeared in *Critical Inquiry*, vol. 29, no. 2, Winter 2003.

Timothy J. Reiss's 'Mapping Identities: Literature, Nationalism, Colonialism' first appeared in *American Literary History*, vol. 4, no. 4, 1992.

Franco Moretti's 'Conjectures on World Literature' first appeared in *New Left Review*, second series, 1 (January/February, 2000).

Stephen Heath's 'The Politics of Genre' first appeared in Mary Ann Caws, Patricia Laurence and Sarah Bird Wright, eds, *Issues in World Literature*, New York: HarperCollins, 1994, published as an accompaniment to Mary Ann Caws and Christopher Prendergast, eds, *The HarperCollins World Reader*, New York: HarperCollins, 1993.

Simon Goldhill's 'Literary History without Literature' first appeared in *Substance* (special issue: 'Literary History', ed. Eric Mechoulan and Christopher Prendergast), vol. XXVIII, no. 1, 1999.

Benedict Anderson's 'The Rooster's Egg: Pioneering World Folklore in the Philippines' first appeared in *New Left Review*, second series, 2 (March/April 2000).

John Sturrock's 'Victor Segalen Abroad' first appeared in *The London Review of Books*, March 22, 2001.

Stanley Corngold's 'Kafka and the Dialect of Minor Literatures' first appeared in *College Literature*, special issue: 'Critical Theory in Post-Communist Cultures', 21, no. 1, February 1994.

Francesca Orsini's 'India in the Mirror of World Fiction' first appeared in *New Left Review*, second series, 13 (January/February 2002).

Permission to reprint these texts is gratefully acknowledged. All of them, bar Benedict Anderson's, have been revised, either slightly or substantially, for publication here.

*

Excerpts from W.N. Herbert, *Forked Tongue* (1994) and Basil Bunting, *Complete Poems* (2000) are reproduced here by kind permission of Bloodaxe Books.

Excerpts from Kamau Braithwaite, *Ancestors*, copyright © 1977, 1982, 1987, 2001 by Kamau Braithwaite are reprinted here by permission of New Directions Publishing Corp.

Excerpts from Sujata Bhatt, *Point no Point* and Les Murray, *New Selected Poems* are reproduced here by kind permission of Carcanet Press.

Excerpts from Tony Harrison, *Selected Poems* (Penguin, 1987) are reproduced here by kind permission of Gordon Dickerson.

Excerpts from Niyi Osundare, *Forest Echoes* are reprinted here by permission of Harcourt Education.

Excerpts from 'The Schooner Flight' from *Collected Poems 1948–1984* by Derek Walcott, copyright © 1986 by Derek Walcott are reprinted by permission of Farrar, Straus and Giroux, LLC.

Index